THE MAD MANCHURIAN

from the Internment Camps of Tokyo to the Hardwood Courts of the NBA

TOM MESCHERY

coffeetownpress

KENMORE, WA

coffeetownpress

A Coffeetown Press book published by Epicenter Press

Epicenter Press
6524 NE 181st St.
Suite 2
Kenmore, WA 98028

For more information go to:
www.Camelpress.com
www.Coffeetownpress.com
www.Epicenterpress.com

Author's website: TomMeschery.com

Cover image used with permission from The Athletic
Design by Rudy Ramos

The Mad Manchurian
2025 © Tom Meschery

ISBN: 9781684920938 (hardcover)
ISBN: 9781684920914 (softcover)
ISBN: 9781684921522 (ebook)

LOC: 2022946237

To my beloved sister, Ann, nee Militsa Mescheriakova who saved my teddy bear, and to my dearest Melanie my wife these past 15 glorious years. How can a man go wrong with two strong women supporting him.

Acknowledgments

To Melitsa Ann Mescherikova, my sister, to whom I dedicate this memoir, I thank you and love you. Grace, dear granddaughter, thank you for helping your Auntie Ann get her photos together and sent to us. Thank you John Montone for contributing an awesome subtitle, *From the internment camps of Japan to the hardwood courts of the NBA* and so much that made the intro work. To my friends whom I had to rely upon for many of my lost memories, I am truly grateful for your help remindng me of some parts of my life I'd forgotten, even those that were not so pleasant. You are too many to list individually, but you are in my heart. Thanks to my children Janai, Megan and Matthew for input and comments about their dad, and for growing up as I grew up and becoming the best people a pop could ever hope for. Jennifer McCord, Associate Publisher and editor supreme, my thanks for all Your work. To Jason Quik, for your sensitive article in The Athletic, Melanie and I thank you for getting us as we truly are. Thanks also to The Athletic for permission to republish Jason's article in the postscript. And to the the NBA and the Golden State Warriors, my heart's-home and to the Dubs' Raymond Ridder, candidate for the Warriors' rafters and his outstanding assistant, Christina Pederson, Director of Corporate Communications for their support, thank you. Thanks also to Jon Jackson for the four-corner tablecloth. Sometimes, it's the little things, right? Jim, thanks for your kind words and sorry about your arm. Last but never least to my my wife and my muse, Melanie Marchant Meschery, more than my thanks, my undying respect and love.

"I am from there. I am from here. I am not there and I am not here. I have two names, which meet and part, and I have two languages. I forget which of them I dream in."
Mahmoud Darwich

Memoirs are the back stairs to history
George Meredith

INTRODUCTION

In 1946, I stepped off the ship that carried me, my mother and sister from Japan where we had been held in an internment camp during the Second World War. We stepped directly into the American Dream that presupposes that with hard work, a person can accomplish anything. True or not, it is this promise that binds immigrants of all generations together. It is easy to see now with the advantage of hindsight, that the mindset of being an immigrant has affected most of the important decisions of my life.

For me, that life became one of reinvention, a uniquely American phenomenon. Always an immigrant, but one of many stripes: high school and college All-American basketball player, a ten year NBA veteran, coach, traveler, teacher, poet, and novelist. Every juncture required self discovery and change. Along the way (call it a journey if you will) I have experienced many of life's lessons. These lessons have included the study of classic literature, museums of art and, of course, poetry. It seemed to me that in many instances poetry served the truth better than prose.

By the example of my life, I will hopefully dispel some stereotypes, such as athletes are dumb jocks and poetry is for sissies. By my enduring friendship with people of color – like San Francisco high school basketball legend Fred LaCour and the iconic basketball giant, Wilt Chamberlain – I hope the reader will find comfort that the scourge of systemic racism does not infect all white men.

You will learn from The Mad Manchurian (that's me, a nickname gained on the hardwood courts of the NBA because of my birthplace, Manchuria) of my family's Russian history, whose lineage includes 20th century luminaries, such as Leo Tolstoy, a cousin on my mother's maternal side and other Russian historical figures such as Nikolai Alexandrovich Lvov, architect and ethnographer on her father's side of the family. The family history includes eye-witness accounts of the Bolshevik Revolution of 1917 (excerpts from letters and diaries) that brought the Communists into power. My father fought with the White Russian Army against the Red Russian Army (Bolsheviks). My grandfather Nikolai Lvov was desperately entangled in the intrigues of the Revolution. This person, Grandpa Lvov, was an important part of the search for my identity.

I lived a life of metamorphosis, arriving in America the descendent of Russian nobility and virulently anti-communist (These days, anti Putin) and slowly moved left of center and later farther to the left as I am now a Bernie guy. My take is that concentrated wealth in the hands of a small percentage of a country's population, which brought down the nobility in Russia, is an increasing threat to American democracy.

I lived the dream of most red-blooded males of America. I played a sport – and got paid to do it – at the highest level. I describe what it was like to play for the Warriors (both Philadelphia and Golden State) and Seattle Sonics. There are lots of Mad Manchurian stories.

I lived a life of second chances, none greater than my second marriage at age 70 to my beloved Melanie, my lover, my friend, my traveling companion, my art instructor, my long-suffering editor and my basketball buddy, the last not being exactly the term of endearment to which she would have aspired. Without Melanie's patient optimism, my life as a cancer patient (I was diagnosed with Multiple Myeloma in 2006) would have been far more difficult. Science has much to do with my remission, but I attribute the length of my remission finally to the love of Melanie Marchant and all the attributes of her love: kindness, sense of humor, support, practicality, and her passion for life.

As many of my high school students said to me, over my 26 years of teaching, "Mr. Meschery, you have lived such an interesting life, you should write a memoir." Dear students, here it is. I hope it will live up to your standards.

MANCHURIA TO SAN FRANCISCO
1938 - 1946

CHAPTER 1
HARBIN, MANCHURIA
1938 - 1941

I am two years old, sitting under a table, hidden by a tablecloth, four triangles hanging down. Four sets of knees. – two draped with skirts, two clothed in trousers. The grown-ups are talking, oblivious of me, the white triangles within easy reach of my hands. I grab the end of one of the triangles and pull. What follows are screams, curses, crashing dishes and silverware. I do not remember getting a spanking.

I did not remember a spanking because this childhood memory did not belong to me, even though I owned it and relished its childhood audacity for most of my life. That is until the fall of 2016, when my wife, Melanie and I visited my older sister, Militsa, in New York City. We were discussing our childhood. When I finished recounting my first memory, my sister shook her head. "That wasn't you," she said, "that was me under the table. I remember Dad spanking me."

What do you say to a sister who'd just robbed you of your first memory?

My second memory – which has now become my first memory - takes place in December of 1941 in Yokohama, a port city in Japan:

I am kneeling looking over the back of an armchair through an open window into a harbor filled with white seagulls and gray ships. The room is sparsely furnished. Over my head, an electric cord is hanging down from the ceiling, its naked light bulb swaying gently. I am crying because I am sure that we have arrived in the United States of America where my father is waiting for us. But my father is not here.

Shortly after I was born on October 26, my father, Nikolai Mescheriakov, acquired a single visa and left Harbin, Manchuria (an independent country and later part of China) for the United States to find a job and a home for his family. He promised he would send for us, which he did, but too late. America's war with Japan had begun.

I was three years old, too young to know that our family of three was under house arrest as were many others living in Harbin. The Japanese placed us aboard a ship along with a great number of noncombatant civilians of Allied countries to take us to Japan. This was not long after the Japanese bombed Pearl Harbor. I believed the ship was taking us to the United States where my father would be waiting. At that time, all I knew was I wanted my father.

My mother's recollection of me is that I was a sickly child. By the time I arrived in Japan, according to her, I had survived numerous diseases: diphtheria, whooping cough, yellow fever, smallpox and tuberculosis. Such afflictions, to my mother's astonishment, did not keep me from growing to my adult height of 6'6" and muscular weight of 220 pounds. Nor did it keep me from becoming strong enough and skillful enough to become a professional basketball player and play 10 years in the National Basketball Association, the first ethnic Russian and immigrant to do so.

CHAPTER 2
TOKYO, JAPAN
1941 - 1945

The Second World War would have to end before I would see my father again. My mother, Maria Mescheriakova, my sister, Militsa, and I lived out those four years in Tokyo in a Japanese internment camp. Most of what I can recall of the early days in the camp are a child's shadowy memories not to be entirely trusted because it is difficult to separate my own early memories from those told to me by my mother and sister.

Our camp building stands out because it was home, so to speak. It was a two-story rectangular structure, a one time Catholic school, surrounded by a cement wall. Along the interior of the wall were cherry trees that in spring were clothed in white blossoms. Of this memory I am confident. I am also confident that there were green caterpillars, and later the surprise of butterflies, so astonishing that I remember standing and watching for hours, and my sister trying to tug me away to join her in some game, which required a little brother. Even today, almost eight decades later, I remain fascinated by butterflies. As an adult, I learned that those cherry trees of delicate white blossoms (probably of the variety called Yoshino) have a short life span, 60 to 100 years, and to the Japanese represent the brief transience of life. In the midst of war, what could have been more symbolic? I brought the memory of cherry blossoms and butterflies to America to comfort my dreams. I brought different memoires of the war with me to America that were not comforting and haunted my dreams. To this day, an occasional war dream will startle me awake.

The internment camp housed women and children only. We were told that the men with us in the relocation camp in Yokohama were taken to their own camp. My mother always included those men - priests, religious brothers, and missionaries - in her nightly prayers. There were no bars on our camp windows, no locks on the doors. All of us; nuns, missionaries, school teachers, my mother, my sister and I, (we were the only children) lived on the second floor. Metal framed beds with mattresses stood against the two long interior walls facing each other. One side with windows opened to the east and the rising sun. They looked out over the courtyard with its cherry trees and the boundary wall beyond which we were not allowed to go. As my mother recalled, no one felt intimidated or imprisoned. Blankets were hung between beds for privacy. Our three beds made up one family unit. Above her bed my mother hung her family icon of the Virgin of Iversk. The Holy Virgin would protect us, my mother promised. Mothers always keep promises, so I was never frightened. Just beyond the wall within walking distance was a Catholic Church. The bells of its bell tower never rang, and I never saw anyone entering the church until eventually the nuns in our group were allowed to pray there on Sundays. The camp and details as I've described them did not come into focus until I was five years old with a greater capacity to store memory.

I am climbing up into one of the cherry trees so I can reach the blossoms that seem to me more beautiful the higher I climb. One moment I am clinging safely to a branch, and the next moment tumbling out.

I was four years old. I broke my right collar bone. I was taken to a hospital where my collar bone was set and a metal plate installed.

In my hospital bed I turn my knees into twin Mount Fujiyamas for my jade frog and ivory elephant to climb. They descend from the peaks to engage imaginary enemies. Frog and elephant never lose a battle.

Of the approximately 60 people interned with us, only a few are part of my memory. Miss Mauk and Miss Kramer, American Methodist missionaries, taught my sister and me English. Miss Mauk's home was in Kansas. She showed us on a map where Kansas was in the United States, kind of in the middle and told us stories about cowboys and Indians that left me imagining those wide open plains and buffalo, she described so vividly. She showed us Kansas was a long way from San Francisco where our father was waiting for us when the war ended. Miss Baggs and Miss Kilburn were missionaries from England. I remember Miss Baggs being pretty, although I can't recall her face. My sister claims that I announced to the camp at dinner one night that when I grew up, I would marry Miss Baggs. I do not remember which language I spoke, Russian probably, but I was already learning French and English. Miss Kilburn spent much of her afternoons, except during winter, tending a rose bush that miraculously grew out of the gravel next to one of the entrances to our building. I enjoyed watching her prune the branches in the fall and tend to the blossoms in the spring. That this seemed important has to do either with my curiosity or the boredom of camp life. Miss Kilburn rarely spoke to me, but one day told me that if the devil did not exist, God would have had to invent him. I asked my mother what this meant. Mother explained that Betty Kilburn had lost her faith and was an atheist. This needed clarification. An Atheist was a person who didn't believe in God. Was I five years old at the time? I knew we were not Atheists because my mother always prayed and made my sister and me say our prayers every night, kneeling beside our bunks. I prayed looking up at the family's icon of the Mother of God that my mother claimed was miraculous. I think that we survived the war could be considered a miracle.

Mostly, I prayed that I would see my father soon. My mother had a photograph of him. He was seated, wearing a uniform of an officer in the White Russian army, epaulets on his shoulders. There was a belt stretched down at an angle across his chest that held a scabbard, the hilt of a sword visible. A fur hat sat on his head. His eyebrows were black and his eyes were dark. My mother said he was very handsome and that women stopped on the street to look at him when he passed by.

My sisters' favorite missionary was Lumpy. Miss Lumpkin was one of my favorite's as well. She played with us and was full of good humor, although I can no longer remember what she looked like. My sister describes Lumpy as short, on the stout side, with tight brown curly hair. She was always smiling and telling us funny stories. My sister told me that Lumpy did not stay with us in the camp for the entire four years, something I hadn't recalled. Two years into our internment, the Swiss Government, which was neutral in the war, negotiated an exchange of prisoners with the United States. Miss Lumpkin was one of those chosen to leave our camp.

Our meals were fish and rice, with some cabbage and radishes. I remember once complaining, half in French and half in English, much to the delight of my language teachers, the American missionaries, and Belgian nuns, "Fish, fish, toujour fish, *pauvre* Tommy."

I'm reminded as I write this that on occasion when trying to get my wife's sympathy, I have resorted to that childish voice: "Vacuuming,

vacuuming, *pauvre* Tommy." In Japan, the menu never changed, neither has my household chore.

One of our young camp guards brought me tangerines. Once, he took me by the hand and led me into the basement under the stairs. There, he gave me a tangerine, then unzipped my pants and fondled me. I must not have thought there was anything to be alarmed about because I never told my mother or anyone else. In my years as a high school teacher if I'd heard about something like this happening to a child, I would have reported the abuse to the police, and urged the parents to seek counseling for the child. Whether or not I suffered psychological problems later in life because of this incident, I don't know. I suspect not because I have never felt any shame over it, and I have experienced enough shame in my life to know what that feels like. After the war ended, my mother sent parcels of food and other essentials via the Red Cross to his family and to Mr. Ogawa, our camp superintendent every year. Mr. Ogawa (Ogawa-san, the san in Japanese is an honorific) was always neatly dressed in a dark suit and never without a tie. He was particularly polite to our mother because, as she explained, the Japanese honored motherhood and children.

Sister Xenobia was a tall and heavy set nun and always jolly. For some reason, which I attributed to our miraculous icon, Sister Xenobia never failed to have candy to give us. She would dig into the chasm of her habit and out would come her hands with a candy wrapped in colorful paper for each of us. Another nun, Sister Saint Frances and our mother became close friends. Both loved to discuss religion. My sister reminded me of the three Belgian nuns of the order of Notre Dame de Namur. A letter of introduction written by one of the nuns helped my sister gain entrance to the Notre Dame School in San Francisco, even though we were not Catholic. One of the Belgian nuns, Sister Marie-something-perhaps Celeste, who taught us French, called me Ma Cherie, an endearment that I would be called again later in my life by another teacher.

With no other children in the camp, my sister and I were left to entertain ourselves.Considering I grew up to become a professional basketball player, I don't believe I showed any early signs of athleticism. Was I a jumper, a leaper, a runner? Did I throw rocks at targets? Not to my recollection. My games were mostly of the fantasy variety. I found myself a lot under my bunk with frog and elephant for company, looking up at the metal coils that held the mattress. I moved my tiny animals carefully up along the spirals that my imagination had transformed into castles and towers and stairs leading to battlements. Beyond the battlements were the approaching armies of my enemy. I named frog and elephant's enemy Armageddon. a word I heard often used by the missionaries. Armageddon was a long, unfamiliar, and strange sounding word that I thought was fun to say aloud, pronouncing each syllable separately. I named the raucous crows that visited our cherry trees Armageddons. I christened the spiders I occasionally found in my blankets, Armageddons. When the clouds formed over our camp, dark with rain, I would point and say, "Look, Armageddons."

I liked words. I would say a word and suddenly a picture appeared in front of my eyes.

In French I liked the word *mechant*, which means naughty. "Tu est tres mechant," (You are very naughty) Sister Xenobia would say while she reached into her robe and pulled out a candy. Since Russian was my native language, there were plenty of Russian words that appealed to my senses: Dourak, which means fool; Kochka, cat. I liked the verb to scream, Kreechats. "Neelzya kreecheets," "No need to scream," my mother would scold me. I don't remember screaming a lot, but I guess I must have. Douraki, (foolish ones) mother would say sometimes if my sister and I were being silly.

• • •

Given that words made an impression on me as a child, I do not find it unusual that I grew up to write poetry and fiction, and that I'm even now attempting to write a memoir, trying to find the right words to describe our internment camp. The right words to describe my life.

• • •

Someone had painted a large red cross in the middle of the roof of our camp building so that the American airplanes that flew over dropping Red Cross packages could see where to aim. As I remember those drops, mostly the parachutes carrying the packages landed outside the walls of our grounds. Once, one landed right on top of the cross. I was eager to see what was inside. There were letters. None from our father. There were winter clothes. Underwear for women. No underpants for little boys. Chocolates, salty crackers, chewing gum, cigarettes. The cigarette packages had pictures of camels on them. There were cans of vegetables and canned meats. The meat was either corned beef or Spam. Mrs. Mauk creamed the corned beef, and we ate it over rice. It was a relief from our daily diet of fish. Mrs. Mauk fried the Spam, and we ate it with - you guessed it - rice. I am shocked today that as much rice as I ate in the camp, that I still enjoy rice. I do not feel the same way about Spam. In the camp, it tasted slimy. To this day, I still consider Spam slimy. (I will leave its consumption to the Hawaiians who, only God knows why, find the meat irresistible.) I am sure in the camp I never refused to eat Spam, but once the war ended, never again. I do not have the same aversion to canned corned beef. My wife, Melanie, loves Spam. It is one of the few foods we disagree on.

About a year after we arrived in the internment camp, Tokyo suffered its first bombing. Our building was too far away from the center of the city to be affected. Or so we thought. Of course, I knew nothing of this at the time. History places that first bombing raid, the Doolittle Raid, in April of 1942, which would have still been three years old and my sister barely six. After that singular air raid we often practiced going down to our basement bomb shelter. Mother would take my hand and lead me down the stairs. My sister, Militsa - stubborn then, stubborn still - refused to hold hands. We were told to be very quiet because the enemy in the sky could detect our voices and steer their airplanes in our direction. It is part of my memory that my sister whispered to me that this was not the truth. *Dear sister, you are still the truth teller.* We sat on the cement floor, our backs against the wall, clutching our knees, blankets tucked around us. It was cold. Thinking of those early nights practicing for the American bombers, it is my memory that everybody prayed as though we were in immediate danger. Our mother told us not to worry, our Icon would take care of us. For my mother, it was never God, always the Holy Mother Mary. My mother was large, what today would be called "full-figured" and had a commanding voice. To me, she was as good as God.

It should not have surprised me that there was a lot of praying going on in our camp, since the majority of the women were nuns or missionaries. God was the primary topic of conversation. It seemed to me our mother was an expert because she was always in discussions with someone about the All Mighty. I don't recall exactly when I started thinking about God, but when I did, I counted three deities: God, Dieu and Bog. American, French, and Russian. I knew that was silly, that all three were the same

God, but I liked to pretend they were different. I made pictures of the different Gods in my head. Bog was the biggest and had the longest beard and the most hair. His beard and hair were black. God was the tall God, his beard and hair, not as long as Bog's, and white. Dieu had wings, so maybe Dieu was really an angel and not a deity. God lived in Kansas. Bog lived in Russia, but I decided He could also live in San Francisco. My mother had a postcard of the Eiffel Tower; it seemed like it was a good home for Dieu. I imagined Dieu flapping his wings taking off from the tip of the Tower.

My sister recalls that I was always imagining.

• • •

I am 82 years old and nothing has changed. Waiting for me in our office is my computer. I can open it to this memoir. Or I can open it to a collection of poems that I am close to finishing. The poems in this collection are all about sports. I have completed two chapters of a mystery novel. I'm a retired teacher. I am a writer. I live in Sacramento with my wife, Melanie, who paints Icons. Outside the window on most mornings I am greeted by two crows. I have named them both Armageddon.

• • •

I liked talking about God (Bog in Russian) with my mother. She told me that I might become a priest like her brother Nathaniel, a priest then, later to become a bishop. She showed me his photograph. His beard looked the way I imagined Bog's beard - long and black. God's beard was white. In the photograph, Uncle Nathaniel was dressed entirely in a black robe. Yes, Bog, without a doubt.

My sister and I were sort of trilingual, speaking a mixture of French, English and Russian, often getting the languages mixed up. Mother spoke Russian to us, but in the last year of the war only English, since she said that's what we would have to speak in America. Although my sister and I were encouraged to speak English, it is my recollection that I dreamt in Russian. I'm not certain how long it took after we arrived in America before I began to dream in English. By third grade partially. By the fourth grade my dreams were completely in English.

By the beginning of 1945, Tokyo was being bombed. Our air raid drills were no longer drills. In the spring of 1945, for two nights we lived in our basement because the sky was full of American bombers.

CHAPTER 3

NIGHT OF THE BLACK SNOW

On those nights with the bombers flying overhead, my sister and I with our mother and all the residents of our internment camp sat on the floor of our basement bomb-shelter:

*It is pitch-black. Sounds like thunder reaching us. My sister and I are crawling away from our mother and climbing onto the interior ledge below a narrow window. Pulling back the blackout curtain enough to peek through, we watch searchlights, like bright ribbons crisscrossing the night sky, seeking and finding bombers. We can make out planes in the distant heights and puffs of artillery fire bursting in the sky around them. The artillery sounds like the rattle of drums. **Fires** illuminate the city. Our building shakes.*

I remember thinking how close the airplanes seemed to be to our camp building as they passed over. What I didn't know then was this was a strategic calculation by the U.S. Air Force command to have its bombers fly low to better avoid antiaircraft fire.

On the 9th and 10th of March 1945, the United States Air Force conducted devastating firebombing attacks on Tokyo. More than 100,000 Japanese civilians were killed and over a million left homeless. The Japanese called the two nights of the firebombing of Tokyo, *Night of the Black Snow*.

Snuggled into that corner ledge, Militsa and I watched bomber after bomber dropping fire over Tokyo. We watched until our mother dragged us away. At night, it seemed as if the world was ablaze. In the morning, shrouds of smoke covered the city. I could not see the rice fields beyond the wall for the gray veil. We were allowed upstairs only briefly the next day. And that night the bombers came again with the same ferocious effect. Militsa and I escaped our mother and climbed back on our ledge and pulled back the blackout curtain. I saw a parachute floating to the ground, or did I? It could have been smoke, but I had parachutes on my mind. Once, a young guard made me a parachute out of a handkerchief. He tied four short lengths of string to the corners of the handkerchief and a rock to the end of the strings. He tossed the rock from the roof of our building, and I watched it float down. My sister and I tried to count the planes, but there were too many. Mrs. Mauk had told us that she had a brother and a cousin in the American Air Force. Her prayers were that they would not be the pilots of the bombers flying over us. I'm sure I was frightened, but I don't remember crying. At one point I recall feeling angry with the planes for causing such destruction. I liked our Japanese guards and the Japanese women who occasionally brought us fish. According to our mother, after one night of bombing, many of our Japanese - *ours* because we'd come to think of them as friends and protectors - had lost families.

My sister and I were fascinated by what we saw: white explosions and yellow beams of artillery lights and planes on fire, twisting down out of the sparkling sky.

• • •

In the first two or three years in America, not a month went by without at least one dream of war. Sometimes it was only a fragment of the violence, more like a torn scrap of a photograph that left me with only a sense of the whole picture, but enough to frighten me awake.

• • •

The church next door to our building caught fire, then spread to our building. We were ordered to evacuate. Of that evacuation my sister and I have different memories. In my version Militsa had forgotten her teddy bear, Mishka, on the second floor where we slept. As we were being escorted out of the building, she broke free of our mother's hand and raced back into the burning building, returning out of the smoke clutching the bear in her hands. It must have been during one of our adult conversations that Militsa (she had started using her middle name, Ann, after she left high school) set me straight: "First of all," Ann explained, "Mishka was your teddy bear. Originally, he was mine, but I was so delighted to have a baby brother when you were born that I gave him to you as a present. You had brought Mishka down into the bomb shelter. When we were evacuated, you forgot him, and I ran back into the basement to get him for you. There was no fire in the basement, no smoke." I prefer my more dramatic version of Mishka's rescue, but I have included her version because in both cases my sister is the hero and having an older sister as a hero is important to me.

Our mother carried me on her back as our group walked through the destruction of Tokyo looking for any standing building that had room for us. We were forced to sleep outdoors on the ground surrounded by rubble.

I'm awake. My mother and sister are still asleep. So are the nuns and missionaries and our guards. I turn around to investigate the gray morning. There is a tiny hand, a child's hand no bigger than mine, sticking out of the blocks of concrete next to me. The fingers are pointing to the sky. I roll over and lay quietly next to my mother so as not to wake her. I am not crying.

While our group spent many days roaming the streets of Tokyo, I don't recall seeing dead bodies, although there must have been some. Our guards remained with us and suffered the same privations. It was March. A few cherry trees were in bloom, but there would not be a blossoming this year because most of the trees in Tokyo had burned. In 1981, as I was writing my first collection of poetry, I remembered the fire-bombing followed by a cherry tree on fire and wrote of a *cherry tree blooming twice*.

Finally, a place was found for our group of internees in the attic of a hospital. There was no food for days except some kind of boiled greens. I remember being very hungry and thinking a lot about food. *Pauvre Tommy*. What I wouldn't have given for the fish that I had previously scorned. Our time in the hospital extended into summer. Outside, it was hot, hotter still in the attic where we slept. There was a lot of conversation among the guards that a big bomb had dropped on the city of Hiroshima and soon after another big bomb on the city of Nagasaki. All the nuns and missionaries agreed the second bomb was inhumane and immoral, except Miss. Kilburn who had grumbled about God inventing the devil. Soon after that - I don't recall how many days or weeks - Mr. Ogawa-san entered the attic, still impeccably dressed. With tears in his eyes, he bowed deeply from the waist. Straightening, he stated in broken English that the Emperor had called upon Japan to surrender. He hurried out of the room as if he was, according to our mother, embarrassed by his words. We all went outside into the bleak rubble of the city. After the firebombing of Tokyo, our hospital was one of the few buildings left standing. As far as I can remember, no one expressed any joy over the war's end. The Japanese Emperor Hirohito's surrender over the radio was called, *"Gyokuon-hoso"*

The Jewel-Voice Broadcast. Our internment camp guards, like most of the people of Japan, had never heard their Emperor's voice before.

I was two months from my seventh birthday when the War in the Pacific came to an official end on August 14, 1945. I hoped that in October by my birthday I'd be in the arms of my father.

From the Japanese surrender to the time our military transport ship cruised under the Golden Gate Bridge, my memory is spotty. I only slightly recall a camp in the Philippines. My sister says we also spent time on the Island of Okinawa. On our voyage to the United States I couldn't tell you if our ship encountered any storms or if we sailed on tranquil seas. There must have been plenty aboard a military ship to attract the imagination of a six-year-old, but I have no recollection of games played or parts of the ship explored, which in retrospect I find strange given my active imagination. My mother, sister and I were given military fatigues to wear. We wore armbands on which the letters DP were printed. I was told that the letters stood for Displaced Person. I remember my mother looking at those armbands with disgust.

I must have been awed by the sight of the Golden Gate Bridge, and ahead the skyline of San Francisco, and certainly I was wondering about this new country that we would live in. But my thoughts were mostly about seeing my father. Back then I only had the vaguest memory of my father. The picture of him in mind was the one in my mother's photograph of him as a young man, dressed in his military uniform.

The following is the last stanza in a poem I wrote in my mother's voice for my first book of poetry. The photograph my mother is talking about in the poem was on the front page of the San Francisco *Call Bulletin*.

from the poem,

> Remember this photograph: these clothes
> the army gave us, called fatigues, that never fit,
> no matter how I tucked and sewed. The letters D.P.
> stenciled on our sleeves, they made us wear
> seemed so shameful. Tom, I didn't need to be reminded.
> I knew the minute I left Russia when I was nineteen,
> no matter where I lived, I'd always be displaced.
> At last in San Francisco, walking down the gangplank
> into crowds waving family names above their heads,

a voice kept yelling over a loudspeaker: citizens to the left,
stateless to the right. A band was playing something cheerful.
You pointed to the wrong father. I to the wrong husband.

Mescheyr, Tom. From the poem "Small Embrace." *Nothing You
Lose Can Be Replaced*. Black Rock Press; Rain Shadow Edition,
1999. University of Nevada, Reno, Reno, NV

There was a lot of confusion before our father found us in the crowd,
and we were embracing. He did not look like the person in my mother's
photograph of him. But as he lifted my sister and me into his arms, he was
as strong and as big as he had been in my imagination.

Recently when I spoke to my sister Ann about our internment camp,
she again edited my memory. According to her, there never was a red cross
painted on the roof of our internment camp building. She had no idea
where I came up with that. *How could I have been so certain?* According to
Ann, it was after the atomic bombs on Hiroshima and Nagasaki had been
dropped and the war was over that Mr. Ogawa informed us that we should
sew a huge American flag and place it on the roof of the hospital that had
given us refuge.

"Didn't I remember?" she asked, "all the internees cutting and sewing
from whatever red, white and blue scraps of cloth that could be found?"
Ann described it, in retrospect, like it was a quilting scene out of a western
movie. Finally, the flag was completed and stretched out on the roof. Soon
the boxes with red crosses on them floated out of the sky. One *did* hit the
roof of the hospital. I had at least been correct about that.

"You were so young," Ann said. (She was only two years older.) "Do
you remember the burned bodies in the hospital?"

I did not.

"There were not enough rooms and the bodies lay on cots in the
hospital hall," Ann said. "Mother must have put her hands over your eyes."

I can only imagine what sights my mother saved me from, and I am
filled with gratitude.

• • •

It was during the time I was rewriting and editing my memoir that
the horrors we were part of in Tokyo at the end of the war of which my

sister had spoken, resulted in my experiencing nightmares. They were of a different sort from the persistent nightmare of the child's hand that I had lived with on and off all my life. These nightmares were nonspecific and strongly sensual, the kind that are indescribable but terrifying. I began to suffer bouts of anxiety that kept me awake at night and often remained with me during the day. The source of the nightmares were self-evident. But I asked myself, why were they now, seven decades later, haunting me?

That question was answered by my general practitioner, Doctor David Lehman. I had gone to him in the hope that he would prescribe a medication to help me through my anxiety. Doctor Lehman is a slender seventy year old snazzy dresser with a snappy intelligence, the kind of doctor who listens carefully to his patients. I explained what I was going through. After I'd finished, he said and I am paraphrasing: *Tom, you were a little boy in the middle of a world war, bombs dropping all over the place, you witnessed terrible things. You're writing your memoir means revisiting those times during the war. Now, you're suffering from anxiety. What a surprise!*

He was right. It should have occurred to me that my mother didn't have enough hands to shield me from all the horrors of the war. I ought to have anticipated the possibility that dredging up my memories of those years would have an effect on me. I left the doctor's office, if not feeling entirely better, at least feeling I didn't need medication. As it turned out, some months later, after I finished the final draft *The Mad Manchurian* and sent it off to an agent, the nightmares ended. Later, when I returned to the memoir, working on a rewrite, the nightmares came back. And so it went, nightmares and anxiety while I worked on the memoir, no nightmares, no anxiety when I wasn't. It was difficult to deal with, but understandable.

SAN FRANCISCO
1946 - 1957

CHAPTER 4
IMMIGRANTS

It is impossible for me to listen to Donald Trump's depiction of the immigrants from Mexico and Central America as criminals, drug dealers, rapists, and animals, and not be furious.

If our generation of post Second World War Russian immigrants had been dropped off in Mexico, we'd have had to enter the U.S.A at the various border crossings where "the huddled masses" are trying to cross today. How would Trump have vilified us?

In 1946, my mother, sister and I were labeled DPs. Those letters standing for Displaced Persons made me feel unhappy. Today, I would describe it as being embarrassed. It was not the meaning so much, which I sort of understood after my mother explained. It was the labeling that we were some kind of *other* that bothered me. I don't remember thinking this all out fully at the age of seven, but the embarrassment remained with me and remains with me to this day. Later, I don't recall how old I was. Someone made the mistake and called us *misplaced* persons. That sounded like we were lost toys. We were also called refugees.

In 1945, even the United States allowed displaced persons from Europe and Asia into the county, with few questions asked. Was our country a kinder, more accepting nation back then? History seems to indicate it was. At least there *was* an effort by the government to help people displaced by war - war brides and spouses, for example. Later, there was the Refugees Act of 1956 that allowed people fleeing the terror of Communism to immigrate to the United States. There is no such act today to allow people fleeing the terror of Central American gangs and systemic government violence to enter our country.

Where has our kindness gone?

When we arrived in San Francisco, there was already a well-established Russian community, many of them having arrived via the same Manchurian route. Of the earlier aristocratic immigration, those who escaped Russia prior to the Bolshevik takeover, departed to European cities, Paris mostly. From Europe, many found their way to New York. The later Russians fleeing the Communist regime that included aristocrats and general citizenry traveled via the Siberian Express across Siberia to Manchuria, eventually ending up in either Australia or in San Francisco.

Our first home in America was with our sponsors, Aunt Maroucia and her husband, Gene Bilkevich, on their farm located north of San Francisco in the tiny town of Fallon. We were required by law - or so I believed at the time - to live with our sponsors for six months before we could settle into our own home with our father.

• • •

Today, when I think of our immigration, I realize how lucky our family was to have Aunt Maroucia as a sponsor. She was also our father's sponsor. In December 1941, shortly before Pearl Harbor, our mother had already received our immigration visas. By July of 1941 the United States severely restricted visa applications. And not long after the end of the war, the rising fear of Communism, the second Red Scare, drove the U.S. government to further restrict Russian immigration, which on the East Coast impacted Russian Jews the most.

• • •

In 1946, Fallon was a town in name only. It consisted of one building, the area postal office that included a small grocery store, which was within walking distance of our aunt's house. The post office has long been closed.. The closest real town was and still is Tomales. The population of Tomales then was less than 100, mostly dairy farmers.

Aunt Maroucia did not work on the farm, but she ran the post office in Fallon. Her husband, Gene Belkevich, ran the dairy farm. Our Aunt Marousia was not technically our aunt but a distant relation to our mother's side of the family. I remember Aunt Maroucia always fashionably dressed for work, makeup perfect, hair stylishly arranged. Her husband, on the other hand, was not exactly dirty but unkempt. I don't remember him ever smiling or liking me or my sister. Later when I was older, my mother said of him that he wasn't very smart. Aunt Maroucia's maiden name was Kropotkin descendants of the Rurik dynasty, which had preceded the Romanov dynasty on the throne of Russia. In theory, it made her a Princess.

Aunt Maroucia was by no means a snob. She rejected outright a plan put forth by a friend, Countess Ilyin, to have all the names of the noble Russian families living in San Francisco inscribed in the Blue Book. This book contained San Francisco's most prominent families. Believing our aunt's name and stature as a princess would convince other Russians to follow suit, Countess Ilyin approached her first. When Aunt Maroucia heard that only noble names would be inscribed, she refused to participate. Her husband was a Russian-American dairy farmer, definitely not nobility.

• • •

"I'd rather shovel cow shit as a Bilkevich than be in their Blue Book," she'd told her friend, the Countess, who never forgave her. My aunt had always been a free thinker. My mother told me that when Aunt Maroucia was a young Princess in Russia, she married against her parents' wishes and followed her husband to Egypt where he joined a group of followers of Allister Crowley, the English occultist and self-proclaimed prophet. Aunt Maroucia's son was born there. She took the baby, left her husband in Egypt and returned to Russia. After the Revolution, she fled Russia to Harbin, Manchuria, like my mother and her family and countless other anti-Bolshevik Russians.

• • •

I was curious why my intelligent, stately well-born aunt had married her unkempt, commoner husband. When I asked the question, my mother replied, "To get to America." Even back then, with little experience in matters of the heart, marrying someone to get into a country seemed like a desperate way to go about it. Still, I wonder if the women waiting to cross the Mexican border into our country today wouldn't gladly marry someone sight unseen, rather than risk their children's lives trekking across a waterless wilderness or having their children stolen from them the way the Trump administration has done.

• • •

Aunt Marousia's 92-year-old father also lived on the dairy farm. He was tall and bone-thin, the veins of his hands visible under his rice-paper skin. He smoked Lucky Strike cigarettes endlessly, his beard and fingernails stained yellow. In my sister's memory his fingernails were long and curved, claw-like. In my memory his beard and mustache were tobacco yellow. Grandpa spoke only Russian, when he spoke at all. Each morning after a breakfast of porridge, he'd go to the front of the house and rake leaves. If there were no leaves, he'd sweep. He raked and swept with a smoking cigarette dangling from the corner of his mouth. If our aunt was a Princess I asked my mother, wouldn't Aunt Marousia's father be a King? No, my mother explained that kings in Russia were called Tsars and the Rurik Royal Dynasty to which Grandpa and his daughter, our Aunt Marousia were members of the Krapotin family had been replaced by the Romanov Dynastic family. Prince was about as high up the mountain of nobility a Kropotkin could climb. My sister told me that once she'd learned that Grandpa was a Prince, she'd begun to notice certain princely features about him. He walked very nobly while he raked. He often held his head high and stared into the air, a kind of noble stance. Between puffs on his endless cigarettes, I thought. He died in a princely fashion, calling for his best underclothing, his best suit, his best shirts and cravat. He asked that his shoes be polished to a high gloss. All this he took into his bedroom. My aunt Marousia thought he wanted her to drive him to church, as it was Sunday. An hour later, worried that she'd not heard from him, she went into the bedroom and found him lying in bed, fully clothed with both hands folded across his chest. He was dead.

My mother's maternal family, the Tolstoys and on her father's side, the Lvovs, were nobles, part of the aristocracy of the Russian Empire. Like our Aunt Marousia, my mother had also married a commoner, our father, whose family came from ordinary soldiers and railroad engineers. I had to grow up to make sense of these class distinctions. And then I had to make some decisions about what they meant to me.

As the farm was located not far from the Pacific Ocean and most mornings it was shrouded in coastal fog. The two-lane road that passed the farmhouse and post office was lined on one side by eucalyptus trees and rolling green pastures. If you continued driving west on the road, you'd arrive at the Pacific Ocean. The farm and surrounding fields were lovely and peaceful, in the air the scent of alfalfa and eucalyptus. For me Dillon Beach, where we occasionally visited, was the place to be, watching the ocean waves slide onto the sand or crash onto rocks and cliffs. My mother told me if I could fly all the way across the ocean I would be in Japan where we had spent the last five years of our lives. I imagined this flight, my arms turning to wings.

• • •

I was told by my sister how our father found out we were alive: a photographer for the San Francisco *Call Bulletin* traveling with the army in the Philippines, took a photograph of my sister and me dressed in army fatigues too big for us with large black letters D.P. on our sleeves. In the photograph we are standing on either side of one of the Sisters of Notre Dame de Namur. The photographer interviewed our mother. When he returned to the U.S., he contacted our father. According to my sister, he said, "Mr. Mescherikov, I've located your missing family."

• • •

I wonder what went through our father's mind when he heard the news that we were alive. Relief? Certainly surprise, but was he glad?

I never asked **him**. I'm reasonably sure he was happy to have his children safe with him. I'm also sure he was not as delighted to see his wife. I was in high school when he told me that he wished he was a Muslim, so he could have more than one wife. I don't remember feeling particularly shocked. It had been years since they'd slept in the same room.

It was during one of our adult conversations that my sister told me the true reason why we had to live six months in Fallon before moving into San Francisco with our father. It was not very flattering to our father. While we were in the internment camp, hearing no word from us and thinking we were dead, my father began a relationship with a Russian woman he'd met. How they met, Ann didn't know. According to my sister, the six months we spent at the farm was the time our father required to end his affair and find a new apartment where we could live together as a family. "You know, our father was very handsome," my sister said, as if this exonerated his infidelity. In the case of my father's indiscretion, I wish my sister had not corrected my early memories.

CHAPTER 5

NOTHING YOU LOSE CAN BE REPLACED

I asked my mother once why she had married my father. I was in high school by then and curious because for years the silence between my parents was palpable. Her response was that "He was kind to animals." The following two lines are part of a longer poem I wrote. It would have been spoken in my mother's voice about their relationship. It says a lot about how war - in their case, the Bolshevik Revolution - forced men and women into marriages they would not otherwise have chosen.

> We married quickly, out of mutual kindness.
> For most of us, all that was left of passion was survival.

Meschery, Tom. From the poem, "Small Embrace" *Nothing You Lose Can Be Replaced;* Black Rock Press, Rain Shadow Edition, 1999. University of Nevada, Reno. Reno, NV

Although the poem is four pages long, it is not nearly long enough to explain the strange and sad circumstances that led my mother and father to marry.

Prior to the Revolution of 1917, my mother was a debutante in Russia. She attended balls which were also attended by officer cadets from Saint Petersburg's Pavlovskoe Military Academy. Two of the cadets that came to the same balls that my mother attended were my father and his younger brother, Orest. My mother fell in love with Orest. Their courtship was brief as the Revolution caused my mother's father, Grandfather Lvov, to send his wife and children away from the violence in Saint Petersburg and Moscow on to Krotkovo, in the eastern province of Samara, where their family country estate was located and they would be safe.

My mother and Orest never saw each other again.

It is often difficult to tell the difference between myth and legend in the history of my family. This account of my father and his acceptance into the military academy straddles the fence between the two: according to the family, (This part of it is fact) my father was expelled from the cadet school he and his brother Orest were enrolled in in the province of Samara, not far from my mother's family estate. There is no mention of why he was expelled. His mother (our grandmother Mescherikova) had in her possession a decree from Tsar Ivan the Terrible (1533-1584) honoring the Ataman Matvey Mescheriak, a leader in the Don Cossack Army of Yermack Timofeyevich that conquered Siberia. This was proof of their family lineage, with which she hoped to impress Tsar Nicholas II and have her son reinstated. (There is no evidence of this document's existence.) According to the story, that is family lore (or myth) the Tsar was indeed impressed and readmitted our father to the cadet academy. He successfully completed his training and moved on to the Pavlovskoe Military Academy in Saint Petersburg, where He graduated as an officer at the end of the First World War and the beginning of civil unrest in Russia.

The following story also includes both myth and legend. When the Bolsheviks (The Reds) came into power in October 1917, a group of young hothead officers recently graduated from the military academy in Saint Petersburg, among them our father, Nikolai Mescheriakov, were arrested and thrown into prison. The reason for their arrest is unclear, but obviously they did something that angered the Bolsheviks. They were scheduled to be executed the next morning. However, it would appear almost as though *God's hand diverted the execution of Nikolai.* (This last statement is from my sister's account of the incident). The wife of the Commissar, impressed by our father's good looks, took the jail keys from under her husband's pillow. She opened the jail, called our father out and brought him a horse. He rode from Saint Petersburg until he reached the regions that were held by the White Russian troops in Siberia, the anti-Bolsheviks. There he joined the White Army on the Western Front while the remainder of his classmates were shot the next day.

• • •

The photograph I have of him in his officer's uniform bears out his dark good looks: strong jaw, sensual lips, black, penetrating eyes. A young Anthony Quinn, my sister claims. My children know these family stories. I would like to be the fly on the wall a couple of generations from now and listen to how these stories of my parents have evolved. I hope the key under the pillow is unchanged. I hope that the officer's wife has been turned into a beautiful model. All families have stories, but not all families understand the importance of details.

• • •

My father continued the fight against the Bolsheviks until the Red Army destroyed all resistance. With the rest of the fleeing soldiers, my father rode his horse Sharik, *little ball* the five hundred miles east through Siberia to the Manchurian border. (fact) For the last hundred miles of the journey, Sharik carried my father and a wounded fellow soldier. (Legend) Soon after crossing into Manchuria, Little Ball died of exhaustion. The wounded soldier, Sergei, whom my father saved, made his way to the United States where he settled in San Francisco, only a few blocks from the flat we lived in. (Fact)

Much of the following has been verified. While my father was fighting in Siberia, my mother's family was in Manchuria, living in the northern city of Harbin. Along with thousands of other White Russians, they had made their escape by train across Siberia. My uncle Nikolai had been wounded, captured, and was convalescing in a Communist hospital. My grandfather had escaped to Paris. Life in Harbin was not easy for the White Russian refugees. Many of them were from the aristocracy and had no job skills. Here again is a portion of the poem *A Small Embrace* written in my mother's voice:

> Poor nobility how we suffered, untrained
> for anything. It wasn't long before I saw
> countesses leaving for brothels in Shanghai.

Meschery, Tom. From the poem, "Small Embrace," *Nothing We Lose Can Be Replaced.*Black Rock Press; Rain Shadow Edition, 1999. University of Nevada, Reno, NV

• • •

George Meredith, the 19th century poet, wrote that memoirs were the back stairs of history. In my mother's version of our family history the back stairs led to many doors, each of them concealing a different family story. As a boy, I opened many of those doors where my mother would be waiting for me. Tomishka, let me tell you about your Uncle Vanya. Tomishka, have I ever told you about the soldiers who leaped from the church tower into the snowbank? I continued opening those doors into my teens, until finally I became too engrossed in basketball to listen anymore. It was at that point that I began writing my own narrative. But the doors to our family's past remained unlocked, and I found that I could not avoid going through them.

• • •

Because my mother spoke four languages fluently, one of which was English, she found a job as a secretary and translator with the American Consulate in Harbin. She was 20 years old, tall, buxom, blonde, grayish-blue eyed Slavic beauty. The photographs I have of her at that time resemble my eldest daughter, Janai, when she was about the same age. Meanwhile, my future father had moved from Harbin to Shanghai where he'd found work as a bodyguard for a Chinese millionaire. My parents might never have met at all except for my mother's youngest brother, Vanya. He was working in Shanghai as a translator for the Chinese government and knew my father, Nikolai. Vanya was aware that his sister had once been in love with Nikolai's younger brother, Orest and brought the two together. The way I heard the story from my sister, my mother would not have married except for the dogged insistence of her little brother, Vanya. He ordered her down from Harbin and introduced them to each other with these words for his sister: "This is your future husband." It was more of a command than a suggestion, but it served the same purpose for my father, who was very shy. My father returned with his future bride to Harbin where they continued to see each other and finally married - *out of mutual kindness.* Not romantic. In chaotic times, men and women married for many reasons other than love.

My parents' Orthodox Religion forbid divorce, but I've often wondered if they'd been able to, would my sister and I have been better off if they'd divorced. Would my own three children have been better off, if Joanne, my former wife of thirty-nine years, and I had had the courage to divorce much earlier in our marriage when we knew we were not right for each other? Would we have avoided our painful extended conclusion? My guess is that my children, all of them grown with their own families, and hopefully secure in their own marriages, have from time to time wondered too.

It is not unlikely that there are a great number of adult children, their parents deceased, at family reunions, sitting around the kitchen table, over cups of coffee or glasses of wine, discussing their parents - all the joy, but also all the pain. This backdoor to family history opens and closes with every generation and opens again, I suspect, to embellishments of their own memories of their parents. It's what makes family history so compelling.

CHAPTER 6
3114 CLAY STREET

In the summer of 1946, Aunt Maroucia drove us across the Golden Gate Bridge to San Francisco to the apartment building on Clay Street that our father had rented. Our family would live in that apartment between Baker and Lyon Streets for the next decade. As we crossed the bridge, I looked out of the car window and saw Angel Island where until 1940 all immigration into San Francisco had been processed. Beyond Angel Island I saw the prison island of Alcatraz in the middle of the bay and beyond it the white skyline of buildings perched on the hillsides, the highest of the hills was topped by a white tower. Aunt Maroucia told us this was Coit Tower.

• • •

In the fall of 1962 as a 23-year-old NBA basketball player for the San Francisco Warriors, I rented my first apartment just below Coit Tower. I would walk a few blocks up the hill and look out over the bay and imagine the ship bringing us to America. If I closed my eyes, I could see my sister and me dressed in army fatigues, looking up wide-eyed at the Golden Gate Bridge above us as we passed underneath.

• • •

Our family's first apartment in San Francisco was on the second floor. We walked up a flight of stairs and entered a long hall. To the left was the bedroom my sister and I shared, the master bedroom straight ahead, kitchen and living room to the right of the master bedroom. There was no dining room. We ate at the kitchen table. Between the kitchen and the living room was a walk-through pantry. There, on a counter stood a metal contraption that looked like the letter A. I was told it was a bread toaster. You opened the two sides of the A from the top, placed two slices of Wonder Bread inside, closed the sides and waited for one side to toast, then you turned the bread over and repeated the process. I remember years of coming home from elementary school and toasting half a loaf of Wonder Bread, buttering the toast, and taking the plate piled high along with a glass of milk to sit in front of the radio. I would pull over an easy chair, close the curtains, switch on the radio to my favorite afternoon shows: *The Lone Ranger, The Green Hornet, The Shadow, BullDog Drummond*. I would sit with the plate on my lap, glass of milk on the floor, and eat and drink while *The Shadow*, Lamont Cranston, cackled his invisible presence before striking down the villains. These radio shows taught me English faster than the teachers at school.

It might have been the first day we walked into the apartment or a week later that I discovered that my mother and father's mattress rested on a frame of metal coils like the ones that buttressed our mattresses in the internment camp in Japan. Thus began the new adventures of frog and elephant as they maneuvered in and around the bedsprings defeating enemies, discovering exotic lands, meeting my newly purchased friends, the blue and red uniformed lead soldiers. Most of the day, my teddy bear, Mishka, leaned against my bedroom pillows, waiting for me to hug him to my chest while I slept. I felt safe in America. I didn't know at the time that my feeling of safety would not last.

On the opposite side of the street from our apartment building was a library surrounded by lawn and bushes that provided numerous hiding places for a boy. I spent many weekends either in the children's section of the library or outside playing imaginary games on the library grounds. I was too young yet to assume the roles of radio heroes like the *Lone Ranger* and *Green Hornet*, but old enough to understand the universal conflict between good guys and bad guys. Good vs evil and the forces of light vs dark. I grew out of those Manichaean beliefs and lived most of my life believing that there was always some good in humans. In my old age, having lived through the Trump presidency and his Russian ally Putin, I have decided that as a child playing on the Clay Street library grounds, I decided my original belief about good and evil was the correct one.

• • •

My parents had enrolled me in the second grade in Saint Dominic's Elementary School, a 10- block walk from our apartment. They enrolled Ann in Notre Dame School for Girls. For her, that meant a bus ride with one transfer across town to the school in the Mission District every morning and back home every afternoon.

I hated Saint Dominic's. My English was weak. I spoke with an accent. I made no friends. The nuns who taught at the school were not the kind nuns I remembered from the internment camp. They were stern. They all carried rulers that they wielded like swords. Those rulers found their way to my knuckles no matter how hard I tried not to be noticed. Although deeply faded by age, my knuckles still carry those scars.

But you are the Mad Manchurian, right. Those scars are from fights.

Wrong. The real story:

Saint Dominic's Elementary School, second grad. I'm holding my palm down on the desktop. My eyes are closed, and I am gritting my teeth. I am being punished for saying the Hail Mary in French: Je vous salue, Maiie, plaine de grace; le Seigmei est avec vous. . . I will not be corrected. This is how I was taught by the nuns in the internment camp to say it, I explain. I'm told that I am committing the sin of willfulness. I get one last chance. I shake my head. The ruler descends, but I do not cry. The ruler descends again.

The scars are now faint, and I still say the Catholic prayer to the Virgin Mary better in French than in English.

Those punishments, of which there were many, brought back memories of Miss. Kilburn in Tokyo telling me about God inventing the Devil. After a year at the mercy of Saint Dominic's Sisters of the Immaculate Heart of Mary, in my mind, they were what Miss Kilburn was referring to.

While other children remained behind on the playground after school to play, I bolted for home. Sometimes, if I'd had a particularly bad day, I ran all the way. At home I'd head to the library, or grabbing frog, elephant, and tin soldiers, slide under my parent's bed. If I wasn't playing with them, I was reading books, colorful with big letters and new words. It was with great relief, at the end of the school year, that the principal of Saint Dominic's told my parents that the school was too crowded, and they could only allow Catholics to attend. Because we were Russian Orthodox, Eastern Rite, I would have to leave. I'm reasonably certain my mother would not have taken this slight lightly. If I am any judge of my mother's personality, I suspect she might have let the Catholics know that her Orthodox Christianity was the first Christian church, and it was the Pope in Rome who caused the schism. Do I know this happened? No, but oh, to have witnessed the stunned faces of the nuns as my large 5'11" mother bombarded them with doctrinal differences: Nicene Creed, clerical celibacy and the Eucharist. I have carried this fantasy in my mind all my life, and it has pleased me to know the end.

I don't remember my sister complaining about her school, but that doesn't surprise me. In my memory, Ann was never a complainer or a whiner. She was already the force she would be as an adult, the high school graduate who climbed her way up the corporate ladder to be President of Campbell Soup Media, Inc., someone to admire, the sister who saved Mishka from the flames that consumed our internment camp building.

For the third grade I would be enrolled in Grant Elementary School, the public school on Pacific Avenue, up three blocks from Clay Street. Pacific Avenue was the center of the wealthiest neighborhood in San Francisco called The Pacific Heights. Mansion after mansion lined the avenue on either side of our school. The mansions started in the west at Lyon Street and continued east all the way to Gough Street. There were mansions to the north on Broadway, Vallejo, and Green streets. Clay Street was the dividing line between school districts. If our apartment building had been one block south on Sacramento Street, I would have attended a different elementary school that serviced a poorer neighborhood. Instead, for six years I walked two blocks to Jackson Street, then climbed the last block, up one of the steepest hills in San Francisco, to the rich kids' school on Pacific Avenue. There is no doubt in my mind walking up that ascent daily developed the muscles in my legs, which served me well for ten years in the NBA, and still serve me, but not as well, even with the help of a cane. If I walked down from the school a block to Broderick Street, I could stand on the corner and face north and see the San Francisco Bay, often filled with little dots of white sails and gigantic ships and the water blue and glistening.

I made my first American friend at Grant, Howard Buckle, the shortest kid in our class. He had a sweet and freckled face with curly red hair, that Raphael could have used as a model for his famous cherubs. For me, an immigrant Russian, not a native speaker and clumsy in the ways of America, Howard Buckle was essential. I was no longer alone. I did not make friends with my third-grade teacher, who did not wield a ruler, but wasn't without physical resources, especially during our arithmetic lessons. I'm certain that my dislike of anything to do with numbers today is the result of her violent teaching style. She would line her students facing the chalkboard to do our arithmetic. 4+4=8; 7-3=4 and so on, but my numbers looked more like: 4+4=9 or 7-3=5. Such mathematical mistakes brought my teacher's hand to the back of my head, propelling my forehead against the chalkboard. She made miscreant students sit in the corner with our backs to the class. We miscreants did not have to wear a dunce hat, although dunce hats were still modus operandi in many schools during this time in history - often referred to as the Silent Generation. Students didn't complain back then, neither did their parents.

• • •

I'm tall for a third grader. Kickball teams are chosen. I'm at home plate, waiting for the ball to be rolled to me. My shoe connects with the ball and the ball sails into the air over the outfielder's head. I run all around the bases. I'm told I made a home run. Future recesses, I become the first kid picked for teams. I kick lots of home runs.

Was this an *aha* moment? No doubt, but not of a Road-to-Damascus variety. It was felt rather than thought. My body was sending signals to my brain: *this is easy; this is fun; this feels good, this is acceptance.* I was too young at the time to consider what I was being accepted into. Had I been older with a little more experience the answer to that question might have been my class, or my school or into another kind of club whose motto might have been The Best. However from then on, I knew whenever the class leaders were choosing sides, I would be chosen first.

Many years later, my NBA career behind me, and teaching high school, my own childhood experience helped me understand the importance teenagers placed on being accepted by their peers. Only the form of initiation changed from my school days, a test that was more mental than physical. I watched with a sinking heart the extent to which some of the students debased themselves in order to be included. My female students suffered the most, but not exclusively. I found myself counseling several boys as well as girls. It does not take much imagination to see how exclusion is the first step on the path to bullying. And I daresay, how bullying becomes a habit that is carried into adulthood. And if you have spent any time in a classroom, no matter what grade level, you know how bullying inevitably leads to tragedy.

• • •

My fourth grade at Grant Elementary qualified as a miracle. No more getting my head slammed into the chalkboard, no more sitting in the corner, I was now in Mrs. Squataquatsa's class. Mrs. Squataquatsa, whose name took me a long time to learn to pronounce, was tall and wide with big bosoms. She called me *ma cheri*, turning my Russian surname into French. The first time she called me *her darling*, I wanted to jump into her arms and snuggle. Considering I was already a pretty big kid, this might have presented her with a problem. I had found a teacher who loved me. The terror of the previous years of teacher-persecution diminished. My math skills did not improve, but I thought who needed math anyway? When your teacher praises the way you read and the stories you make up are read in front of the class, and your drawings of frogs and elephants are displayed on the wall, the division and multiplication of numbers are left to other less talented students.

Is it any wonder, given the effusive enthusiasm of my fourth-grade teacher for my reading and stories and drawings that as I moved through grades, I chose the path of the humanities over mathematics and the sciences? In large part I have never progressed beyond my disdain for mathematics. As an adult, this manifests itself in my belief that all occupations are unworthy whose sole purpose is the accumulation of wealth. As for science, you will find me glued to the radio every Friday tuned in to the public channel listening to *Science Friday*.

• • •

In the fourth grade, instead of making up illnesses so that I could stay home from school, I was up early, eating Wheaties, *The Breakfast of Champions*, and out the door and heading for the heights of Pacific Avenue and Mrs. Squataqautsa's embrace. The fourth grade helped me shed immigrant shyness. I had a friend and a teacher who appreciated me. I kicked balls farther than any of the boys in school. When it came time to draw posters for school activities, my teacher chose me, which meant I could kneel in the hall in front of a long piece of butcher paper spread out on the floor next to Renee Klein, the school's best artist and the prettiest girl in our class. We crayoned lots of horses, cattle and on a wide-open range if I remember correctly. To become fully confident would take me some years more, but I was headed in that direction.

Much later in life after I had begun teaching high school, it was state policy to mainstream foreign students (English Language Learners) into regular classrooms. I watched how hard they struggled and how little attention over all they were provided. I remember thinking of my elementary school years, and especially about Mrs. Squataqautsa. What that dear woman did for me I could not have done if I'd been left by myself to compete for an even playing field with my fellow classmates. I didn't recognize it at the time, but the confidence she helped me attain leveled the playing field in the classroom for me. There are classes today all over our country filled with immigrant children and not enough teachers like Mrs. Squataquatsa.

• • •

I cannot say with any certainty that when I became a teacher later in life, I was any more successful teaching second language learners than my colleagues. I did, however, let the kids know that I, like them, came to the United States with little English, and would have been considered a Second Language learner.

• • •

In the fourth grade Richard Price became my friend, which gave me a total of two friends. Richard was Jewish as were many of the students at Grant. Richard lived a few blocks down from Grant School across from Alta Plaza Park in a beautiful home. Richard and I shared a love of cowboy heroes. We did not honor any one cowboy, but paid allegiance to the pantheon: Gene Autry, the singing cowboy; Roy Rogers and his wife Dale; *The Lone Ranger and Tonto; and Red Ryder* and *Little Beaver*. I was always the Native American, which today I consider ironic since *The Lone Ranger*, being a white man, was the immigrant. Richard owned all the cowboy essentials from clothing to weaponry. And doubles of everything, in all of their cowboy hero manifestations. Usually, I was not only the faithful partner, I was also the villain and it never occurred to me that Richard made me wear the black hat on purpose. Noblesse oblige, I suspect. I was certainly the least privileged in our relationship. As I recall, it didn't matter to me, but maybe it did, and I just didn't understand. We practiced drawing our cap pistols and became really fast at it.

What I didn't know back in those days of cowboys and Indians and quick-draw artistry was that Richard would continue his love of cowboys, learning to play the guitar and sing and yodel as though the range of purple sage and longhorns was his home. And perhaps it was the home he was most comfortable in, a narrative about himself he'd constructed and one he preferred to live in. By the time I was long past my prime as a basketball player, Richard was hitting his stride as a cowboy singer, recording albums under the name of Rich Price, the "Singing Sierran." I tip my yesteryear cowboy hat to Richard. It is totally cool. Perhaps in our late seventies Richard and I should strap on our Lone Ranger holsters and cap pistols and head for Alta-Plaza Park to see who can draw the fastest. I suspect Rich would still beat me. But at our age, I bet we would draw a crowd.

• • •

The area along Clement Street between 1st and 11th Avenue was filled with Russian stores and restaurants. Today, the area would have been called Little Russia. On the corner of 11th and Clement was a bakery called Harbin, named for the city in Manchuria where I was born and the owner and our family had lived after escaping the Bolsheviks. Its cakes and pastries were unrivaled. The majority of the shops along Clement Street these days are mostly owned by Asians, with the exception perhaps of Green Apple Books, one of the greatest bookstores in the Bay area.

The Russians have moved farther west to the higher avenues called the Outer Richmond, closer to the great Orthodox Cathedral of The Holy Virgin that was built in 1965.

When we first arrived in San Francisco, we went to the big Russian Cathedral on Fulton Street at Fillmore where we attended one afternoon a week after school for Russian language lessons. "So we wouldn't forget," our mother told us. Did she mean forget the language or our Russian heritage? It was a question I didn't ask myself at the time, too young and too obstinate to care.

The church was beautiful in that Orthodox way of icons and burning candles, shadows and incense, and ancient women dressed in black on their knees bending their heads to the floor and coming up making long, exaggerated signs of the cross. Mysterious, beautiful, and scary. All the priests looked like the photographs our mother showed us of her younger brother, Uncle Nathaniel, dressed in long black robes, with long full beards, wearing black caps. The class was not for me. I was determined to distance myself from anything Russian. Already the newspapers were publishing articles about the threat of Soviet Communism. People in the 50s didn't differentiate between Communists and Russians. I may have been young, but I must have sensed where this was headed. I saw myself as an American – a cowboy in my fantasies. *I might have acknowledged that there were Cossacks in Russia, but there sure as heck were no riders of the Purple Sage.* There was, of course, the family legend that my father's family, the Mescheriakovs, were the descendants of Matvey Mescheriak, an Ataman (leader) in the Don Cossack army who conquered most of Siberia in 1581. I was happy to acknowledge this legend as truth, but for a boy determined to be an American, a legendary Cossack, despite some reasonable anecdotal evidence to its legitimacy, did not possess the same cache as the myth of *The Lone Ranger*.

The day I told my mother I would no longer attend Russian school; I remember it followed an afternoon watching the movie *Broken Arrow* with my friend Howard Buckle. I argued with my mother for my freedom in sentences with long pauses like my new western movie hero, Jimmy Stewart. I remember my mother smiling at my pantomime. She finally relented, with these words: "Russian will always be in your blood." I thought she meant Russia, the country, but found out many years later to my astonishment that she was talking about the language.

Ann was not as determined as I was to leave the language behind. For another two years, my sister continued to take Russian lessons at the church's after-school program before she too gave them up.

My fifth-grade teacher selected Renee Klein and me to draw our class posters. We would start work kneeling in the hall at either end of a long piece of butcher paper and wind up a couple of days later almost touching. I could have touched Renee, but I didn't. Cowboys are shy. In the fifth grade I began reading the *Tales of King Arthur and the Knights of the Round Table.* This was almost as good as John Wayne and Montgomery Clift meeting in the middle of a dusty Cowtown ready to shoot it out. I saw myself at various times as Lancelot or his son, the saintly Knight, Sir Galahad. I was fluent in English by this time, but it was a difficult book to read with many words I didn't recognize. If I didn't know what a word was exactly, I could figure it out. I studied the words the way I studied the accents of my cowboy heroes and later my Private Eye heroes. I practiced speaking English as I heard it spoken in movies and around me at school and in stores. By the fifth grade I felt the Russian language slipping away like a ship sailing out of sight over the horizon.

My parents had just received their naturalization papers making them citizens, but I could not be a citizen until I was 13. Then, I could make my own choice. In the fifth grade, it didn't cross my mind that without legal status I was in jeopardy of being tossed out of the country, the way the DACA young people are endangered today.

We were poor. How poor? Not so poor that we went hungry or were not properly clothed. But poor enough that one holiday season I sneaked out of the apartment at night and stole a small Christmas tree from the nearest lot. I carried it home, worrying all the way that I'd be stopped by a policeman and arrested. But in the morning with the tree standing in our living room, I was a proud criminal.

If we were poor at Christmas, we were rich in tradition at Easter. For Russians Orthodox Easter hardly ever falls on the same Sunday as the traditional Christian Easter. The reason for this is that the Orthodox Church determines Easter Sunday by the old Julian calendar and not the Gregorian calendar that came into use in 1582. Considering the sumptuous meal that accompanied the end of the Holy Week, even an American cowboy-in-training such as myself became Russian for that day. My memory of that time is filled with preparations leading up to Easter. My mother would be in the kitchen baking Kulitch, a sweet bread filled with raisins and currents. From the Harbin bakery, we would have already bought our pasha, a desert of thick cream shaped into a pyramid. In the refrigerator there would be salmon and stuffed cabbages. For weeks we saved little scraps of cloth, hiding our treasures so that each of us could win the competition creating the most imaginative decoration for our eggs. The Friday before Easter we would all gather around the table and proceed to create these masterpieces of design. It was a simple process of soaking our scraps of fabric in water and placing them on the eggs, then wrapping the eggs in a piece of white cloth, which we secured with string before boiling the eggs. The results were often dazzling. Colorfast materials have ruined the fun for the later generations, although my oldest daughter, Janai, who's the most invested in our Russian heritage, the keeper of the Lvov and Tolstoy family stories, has managed to find cloth that still runs. On Saturday night, dressed in our finery, we went to midnight services. (Christmas and Easter were the only days my father attended church.) We would arrive a little before midnight when the church would still be draped in black. Candles were lit and then at midnight the procession began. All the tapestry banners and icons were carried by the altar boys and elders of the church, the rest followed with the incense containers and behind them came the choir and the whole congregation carrying lit candles and singing "Christos Voskresi!" "The Lord has Risen!" The parade circled the church three times singing and, while this was going on the church doors were locked and inside, all the black was converted to white. After the final circle, the bishop would rap on the door three times repeating, "Christos Vskresi!" From within a voice would reply "He is risen!" Then, the door was thrown open and everyone went back inside to conclude the Easter service. After the service, at home our Easter feast was waiting for us. In the center of the table were our colorful eggs and all kinds of Russian delicacies.

• • •

Eventually to make ends meet, our mother took a job as a secretary for Hartford Insurance Company because my father couldn't support us on his earnings making false teeth. My father had earned a degree in dentistry in Manchuria before he left to come to America. Because he never learned English well enough, he couldn't practice dentistry here or work for large dental tech companies that required a knowledge of English. He started his own business making and repairing false teeth that mostly served the Russian immigrant community. I'm pretty certain that he was working under the radar without a business license.

Language Barrier

Father, when you speak English,
it's like a man losing his breath,
your hands always trying to make sure.
Clenched fist means anger
Thumb up approval.
 In confusion, your fingers
 groping in the space between us.
Some signs I never learn.

When your English fails,
you return to Russian,
but I turn away.
Foreigners, we live together
with no common language.

from the poem, *Nothing You Lose Can Be Replaced;* Black Rock
Press; Rain Shadow Edition; University of Nevada, Reno, Reno,
NV 1999

When I wrote this poem, I was not thinking beyond my own experience, but I suspect that many new immigrant children today are facing the same language-shame toward their parents that I felt for my father, especially since President Trump and his minions call their parents terrorists and rapists in the same way Senator McCarthy called all Russians Communists and traitors.

CHAPTER 7
JOE MCCARTHY & THE RED SCARE

I don't remember who called me a Commie for the first time. It happened on the elementary school playground. I remember hearing other kids laughing. I knew the slur was directed at me. Who else was there whose name had been changed from Mescheriakov to Meschery? Students who'd been in the third grade with me would remember me in short pants and with a heavy foreign accent. Prior to this, there had been no reason for me to pay attention to politics. What did I care if there was some government group called the House Un-American ActivitiesCommittee (HUAC)? My mother and father hated the Communists. I hated the Communists. So did all the people in the Russian community in San Francisco, except, perhaps, the Russians who attended the services of the little Orthodox Church on California Street that my mother referred to as the Bolshevik Church. The House Un-American Activities Committee was setting the stage for the years called the Red Scare. For the American public, the Red Scare began September 23rd, 1949, when President Truman revealed that the Soviets had detonated their first atom bomb. America was no longer the sole atomic power in the world. It was front page news, and my mother was shocked. I don't remember paying a lot of attention, until I began to hear the slurs Pinko and Commie directed at me. I would have been eleven years old and working on being an American. I was anxiously waiting for the day I could raise my hand and become a legal American. I was perfecting my John Wayne walk, my Humphry Bogart accent. I remember telling myself I was not a Communist; I was a White Russian, an anti-Communist.

• • •

The thought today that I believed John Wayne was representative of America makes me wince.

• • •

In February of 1950 the Korean War began. In June of that year Senator Joe McCarthy announced that 205 Communists had infiltrated the U.S. State Department. I understood the word war but worried only to the same extent as my classmates did, which was about war in the abstract. I knew this war in Korea could not affect me. I had no idea at the time how much McCarthy's speech to the Senate and his subsequent actions would trouble my young life. Later, having lived through The Red Scare, it would never have occurred to me that in my old age I would have to live again during such political evil.

From 1950 on, I increasingly heard the words *Commie* and *Pinko*. I noticed that Richard didn't invite me to play cowboys as often as he had before, but it could be that I was becoming less interested in cowboy games and began to think of Richard as a little weird with his cap guns, holsters, his guitar, and cowboy songs. Not that I had lost interest completely in cowboy heroes. I remember very much enjoying the movie *Red River* with John Wayne and Montgomery Clift. But by the seventh grade I'd moved on from John Wayne toHumphry Bogart and Robert Mitchum, the tough-guy actors of gangster and detective movies. Decades later I taught these movies called *Film Noirs*, known for their dark shadows and anti-heroes, to a night class at our Truckee community college.

Richard distancing himself hurt my feelings.

There was so much hate in the newspapers and on the radio that I became worried that our family would be singled out as Communists. When I spoke of this to my mother, she reminded me that the Red Russians, the Communists, were the ones that had executed so many of our relatives. She assured me that White Russians would not be persecuted. I didn't feel reassured about our safety when every newspaper headline was about the on-going national search to root out Russian spies.

In 1951 Julius and Ethel Rosenberg were arrested and convicted of being Communist spies. It began a lonely period in my life. After school, I hurried home. On weekends, I remember hours spent behind Bates School, a block from our apartment, alone, batting a tennis ball against the cement wall in the school'ssmall playground. Forehand, backhand, forehand, aiming for just above the chalk line I had drawn to approximate the height of the net. I would return home feeling better. For the rest of my life, physical activity would remain a way to deal with unhappiness, depression, and anxiety. The word endorphin was not yet a part of the national vocabulary.

I am walking with my mother. We are shopping. She is wearing a babushka tied around her head. Her coat is one bought at the Salvation Army and looks like it. She wears no stockings. She is carrying a bag made of string that is derisively called a Polish suitcase. We start out together, but as we walk, I find myself drifting back so maybe passersby will not associate me with her.

Afterwards, I remember feeling deeply ashamed. How could I have been embarrassed by the woman who carried me on her back through the bombed-out rubble of Tokyo, who held me safe in her arms so that I could sleep? From that day on, I hated Joe McCarthy and bigots and tyrants like him that had caused me to behave like an ungrateful coward. These days, recalling that experience fuels my enmity towards Donald Trump, who has brought back the divisiveness and hatefulness of the McCarthy years that tormented me as a youngster.

• • •

Later in my life, during one of many conversations with my sister, I asked her, "Ann, how did you handle it when the kids called you Commie or a Red?" By that time Ann was an executive with a New York advertising firm. Her answer said everything about her personality. "If they were too stupid to know the difference between White Russians and Red Russians, I had no time for them. I let whatever they said about me motivate me to be better than them."

• • •

I wish I could have possessed my sister's strength of personality. Instead, I felt aggrieved. I yearned for revenge, not later, but in real time. I began drawing crude pictures of Senator McCarthy with Devil's horns, his name printed over his head in case my drawing was unrecognizable. I would wait in bed until midnight, then creep out of the house. I'd drop the satanic pictures at the front doors of homes and apartments all through our neighborhood and run like hell, terrified that if caught I'd be hauled in front of the House Un-American Activities Committee and deported.

Where to, I could not imagine. I arrived in America labeled a Displaced Person. America was the only country I knew.

• • •

It has crossed my mind that I could duplicate my childhood protest during these insane years of the Trump presidency by drawing pictures of a horned Trump. But how would I distribute them door to door at my age now out of shape with arthritic knees?

It is a night in 2020, an 82 years old man is limping from door to door leaning on his trekking poles to keep his old body steady, aching, but happy to do his part to save the country he loves from another demagogue. In the morning, people will awaken and find ugly renderings of Trump's face along with their newspaper.

All it takes is a little imagination.

• • •

The following might have happened in the fifth or sixth grade. I'm unsure. Anti-Communist sentiments were already rife in the country, that I do know. What happened frightened me sufficiently that for months I did not sleep well.

My mother takes my hand and leads me to the couch. We sit together. She places her arm around me. She tells me that her youngest brother Vanya (Johnny in English) has contacted her from the Soviet Union. I do not ask how, and she doesn't tell me. It would be a secret between us. She places her finger to her lips, then to mine, her fingers trembling. "You must not speak of this to anyone." She goes on to explain that Vanya is working secretly to overthrow the Communist regime. He is helping their father, Vladimir Nikolaevich Lvov, my grandpa, who had been a Senator in the Duma and Ober Procurator of the Holy Synod (minister in charge of the Russian Orthodox Church) before the revolution. Vanya is not dead as she had been led to believe. They have called her to join them, and she will be leaving for Russia. I am terrified. When was she leaving? I asked. She tells me early in the morning. "When you wake up, I'll be gone." She makes me promise to be a good boy and take care of my father and sister. It is all I can do not to cry. Tough boys don't cry. Isn't that what all American boys are taught?

I remember holding on to my mother tightly as I did in Japan, in the rubble of bombed out Tokyo, trying to be brave. Today, I can't speculate why I didn't rush out of the room immediately and tell my father. Perhaps my mother's words, "You will be the man of the family," kept me in my place and silent. I didn't want to be the 'man of the family.' That night I stayed awake listening for the door to open and close, and my mother to disappear from my life. As I lay awake, I remember wondering why my grandfather would take my mother away from me. What possible role could my mother play in some underground anti-Communist movement? Would she be a spy? She couldn't live in the Soviet Union using her own name. She would be in danger. In America, the Bolsheviks couldn't get us. I was confused. At some point, I fell asleep. In the morning, I found my mother in the kitchen cooking. She'd packed our school lunches. She never said another word to me about what had transpired. I didn't bring it up.

It never entered my mind to question my mother. (I'm not sure I ever questioned her.) I took it for granted that something had changed, and she was no longer needed. For this I was grateful. As stressful and frightening as that experience was for me, it served a purpose.

From then on during those fear-fraught McCarthy years when I was provoked by my schoolmates about being a "Red," I whipped my grandfather's name out of my holster like a quick-draw-artist: *Yeah, well, my grandpa is fighting the Commies right now, you know.* Which of course, they didn't know or believe and continued to harass me, even those who acknowledged I was the best kickball player in the school. After the Red Scare ended and my youthful hero worship of American radio and film idols became a thing of the past, my grandfather Vladimir Lvov remained my hero.

• • •

Much later in life, after I told my sister about this incident, I remember Ann using the word eccentric to describe our mother. Today, I would say our mother's eccentricity deserves a couple of footnotes. 1) There is a possibility that for a certain period of time her father may actually have been working within the Soviet Union to overthrow the Communist government. 2) My grandfather's clandestine activities in the Soviet Union, even in the face of future conflicting evidence, will never be fully ascertained. 3) In the Fifties, my grandfather would no longer have been alive.

• • •

The stories of my grandfather Lvov and my uncle, Vanya remained a central part of the narrative of my childhood and my early teens and to a lesser extent into my adulthood. My mother never stopped referring to some kind of anti-Communist espionage going on in the Soviet Union that she attributed to her father and her brother, Vanya. *Do you see that, Tomishka, the man in the photograph just behind Malenkov, that's your uncle Vanya.* My mother was pointing to the front page of the *Examiner* to a photograph of a man, his features fuzzy, standing behind the ruling members of the Soviet Politburo observing a May Day Parade. Until her death, she continued to express her belief - long after her father could possibly have been alive - that her brother, Vanya, was continuing the struggle against the Bolsheviks. And I, already an adult, married with children, on some level, continued to believe. I traveled to Russia in the summer of 2007 in hopes of learning about my family and of course my Uncle and Grandfather, especially my grandfather.

My mother described her father as being 6'8" and one of the tallest men in Russia. It was from him that I got my height, she claimed. By the start of the eighth grade, I was already sprouting toward six feet, starting my ascent to 6'6" the height I was in the NBA. Had I known back then the career my height would take me, I might have wished my grandfather would have provided me with an additional couple of inches. At 6'8" I might have been a perennial NBA All Star.

My mother showed me a photograph of Grandfather Lvov. He was bald, with piercing dark eyes below bushy eyebrows. His beard was neatly trimmed in a fashion that resembled the beard of Czar Nikolas ll and other Romanovs. I asked my mother for more information about my grandfather. By then, I was determined to understand as much as I could about this larger-than-life figure in our lives. She told me that as a young man her father had wanted to join a monastery, but the bishop in charge, Father Barnabas, had not allowed him to be a monk, and instead arranged a marriage for him with my grandmother, Maria Tolstova. According to my mother, the Tolstoys were a noble family, but *not, heaven forbid,* as noble as The Lvovs. The hierarchical status of the paternal side of her family often prefaced my mother's stories about the Lvovs. Not that she didn't believe the Tolstoys were worthy of recognition, but she was quick to point out that Peter the Great had made the Tolstoy ancestor a Count for capturing the Tsarevich Alexie Petrovich, the Tsar's son and bringing him back to be murdered by his father. In the eyes of the Lvovs, this was the same as murdering the boy and unworthy of nobility. My mother was unquestionably Daddy's girl. Her father was a Saint, she'd said more than once. As the Ober-Procurator of the Holy Synod (the government's Minister of Religion), she claimed her father had saved the Russian Orthodox Church from losing its authority within the post-Tsarist government. It had something to do about convincing the religious leader of the church, Metropolit (Arch Bishop) Makarov to resign in favor of another bishop more acceptable to the more democratic government. She didn't seem to know much more than that, except for a brief entry from her mother's diary in which her mother had written complaining bitterly about rumors being spread that the Ober-Procurator had accomplished this task by the use of a pistol pointed at the old Archbishop's head. This had been instantly and vehemently denied by the entire Lvov clan. It was their belief that it must have been the Tolstoys that started the rumors. As a youngster, I remember listening to my mother and thinking if her father was a Saint in her eyes, it was fine with me. He was a hero in mine too, my protector against the slings and arrows of McCarthyism.

While I was growing up my mother often referred to the patriarch of the Lvovs, the famous architect and ethnographer, Nikolai Alexandrovich Lvov. I was not aware how those stories about Tsars, royalty, counts, and nobles were influencing my personality. Most likely, they were the start of my life-long inclination toward daydreaming, as well as my love of imagery, fiction and all things that had to do with the imagination.

• • •

On September 17 of 1951 at the age of twelve I held up my right hand and swore allegiance to the United States of America, but I would have to wait a year until I was thirteen before receiving the certificate, which is dated August 18, 1952. It remains in a metal box under my desk. Recently, I took it out and studied my absurdly young face, that silly haircut and tropical print shirt I'm wearing. I ask myself why I was worried about not being American enough. I could have passed for a California surfer or a New York City Street hoodlum.

I have looked at my naturalization certificate often while writing this memoir. It makes me wonder why at the time I didn't take a greater interest in my adopted country. I was certainly old enough. And there were reasons enough. I had signed my name, professing my loyalty to America, even while America was painting all Russian immigrants with the broad brush of disloyalty. I wish I could say this offense motivated me to search beyond the basics of reading the Bill of Rights for the essence of the America that I was embracing. I could have talked to teachers and read more history of America. I didn't. I allowed my idea of America to be the America of popular culture, heroism, and individualism. It occurs to me that at that age, I would have bought in completely with the later political theory of American Exceptionalism. Why I didn't take the time to study the history of my adopted country might have had something to do with what happened next in my life.

• • •

I was starting the seventh grade, the tallest boy in our school, which attracted the attention of Arthur "Cappy" Lavin, our after-school playground director and one-time starting guard for the University of San Francisco Dons basketball team. He must have seen some potential for basketball in me. He taught me the basics. After a couple of weeks of instruction, Cappy pronounced me a natural, and praised me for my athletic instincts. From that day on, you couldn't get me off the basketball court. It was the beginning of my obsession with the game.

• • •

It has also occurred to me that my motivation for playing basketball was similar to what had motivated generations of young black men to take up sports. They saw basketball *as a way out* of poverty. I saw basketball *as a way in*to America.

• • •

A way into America did not mean for me a way into the upper strata of San Francisco society. Most students at Grant Elementary School, residents of Pacific Heights, belonged to families at the top of the city's pecking order. The scions of these wealthy families were introduced into society at a cotillion ball. But first, they needed to learn the social graces and how to dance. In elementary school there was Mr. Kitchens' Dance Class. Mandatory even if, like me, not one of the "rich kids." We lined up in the recreation room, boys on one side, girls on the other. I was too shy to ask petite, beautiful Renee Klein to dance. Another student, Chris Cole, with whom I'd become friends, didn't have a problem with shyness. He was graceful. I was awkward. I watched with envy as they waltzed. I'm not sure if Renee was aware that she was the love object of most of the boys in elementary school. Mr. Kitchens dance class prepared us for the next level of dances called *La Jeunesse*, which means young people in French.

• • •

I was halfway through the first draft of the memoir when I was reminded of these torturous dancing lessons. One of my Grant School classmates decided to start a Class of '52 thread. It came as a surprise and a bit of a shock. We were all in our late 70s. *Why on earth?* The following email dredged up memories that were not very pleasant of years in which I was a self-conscious grade-schooler hoping desperately to be accepted.

From Susie:
Does "Clair de Lune" give anyone a wave of dancing school nausea?

Reply from Jane:
La Jeunesse was the natural progression (starting, I think in eighth grade), to large evening dances in swanky attire. I still have a picture of myself in pink taffeta with a full net skirt.

Reply from Renee:

Because these dances were a preamble for debutants, for an invitation to Informals, girls needed recommendations from parents of "proper" boys if they were to attend.

• • •

Uninvited to Frolics because I was not considered a "proper boy," I remember being offended. I complained to my mother about not being "proper." She reminded me that I was a descendant of Russian nobles. That helped. Besides, I told myself, playing basketball did not give me any time to go to silly dance classes. I decided that I would become a "proper" basketball player. From that time on, I do not remember many days I did not have a basketball in my hands. And not to overstate my growing obsession with the sport, but to clarify, there were many times as a boy that I went to sleep with my basketball. It was, according to my wife, a natural evolution of a boy going to bed with his teddy bear.

In bedrooms all across the United States there are boys asleep clutching their basketballs, footballs, baseball gloves – count on it. Those same boys are watching Kobe Bryant's Academy Award winning animated short film: Dear Basketball and saying, that's me, too, Kobe.

I whisper, "Add my name to theirs."

• • •

The McCarthy Period with its anti-Communist paranoia began to engulf the nation. Unfortunately, being "a natural" athlete didn't help my self-image much. Guys would joke around, and I hesitated joining in afraid I'd say something that would arouse suspicions. This was surely not the case, but I had a vivid imagination, fueled by newspaper articles and radio broadcasts. When it came to basketball, I had no trouble joining in. As inexperienced as I was, my game spoke for me. During those times, basketball became an ointment I could rub on the bruises of my uncertainties and anxieties. That held true for the rest of my life. Whenever I was deeply troubled or feeling depressed, or anxious, I would head for a gym, or any place I could work out physically. It didn't have to be basketball. *Work up a good sweat, feel the rush of endorphins.*

• • •

In the seventh grade, I made a new friend who played basketball. His name was Magnase Nagase, a Japanese American. On weekends it was Magnase and me at the playground up the street from my house on the basketball court where we first met. The apartment in which Maganse's family lived was in another school district, so I didn't see much of him during the week, but most weekends we were together on the basketball court. He was swift and could get around me easily at first. But as the year passed, and my skills improved, our competition on the court became less one-sided.

When we played one-on-one, Magnase was always Notre Dame, and I was always Army. Why I chose Army, the military academy never known as a basketball powerhouse, I don't recall. Perhaps because my father praised the virtues of military life.

Magnase invited me to lunch at his home. I met his mother and father, two older brothers and his cute little sister, who I learned many years later had a crush on me. If I'd been older, I might have recognized it and reciprocated. She grew up to be gorgeous. I was served udon, Japanese noodle soup and vegetables. Rice was served. The older brothers carried the conversation; the parents barely spoke. They were surprised that I knew how to use chopsticks. The main course was fish. *Fish, fish, toujour fish, pauvre Tommy.* I didn't say it, but it did cross my mind. By the end of dinner, I learned that their family had spent the Second World War in an internment camp in Ohio. They explained that the entire Japanese population on the West Coast had been taken by the United States Army from their homes and placed in camps. The Japanese families lost everything, homes, and businesses. I was surprised that Americans would do what the Japanese did to my family and the nuns and missionaries that were interned with us in Tokyo. I wanted to ask them if they ever felt displaced. But I was embarrassed to bring up a subject that I was trying to figure out for myself. When the Japanese were finally allowed to return to their homes, they had few resources to start over again. Mr. and Mrs. Nagase opened a small neighborhood grocery store. I thought it was cool that Magnase and I shared sort of the same history. I didn't mention the fire-bombing of Tokyo and the child's hand that still appeared in my dreams, and they didn't mention Tule Lake or Manzanar or the dreadful conditions in their camp in Ohio.

Now that I had basketball, my anxiety over the Red Scare diminished but did not entirely disappear. There was a recurring dream: *My grandfather is standing in front of a wall. He is offered a scarf to tie around his eyes. He refuses. He looks firmly, unflinching, as the executioner yells "Fire!"* I had long ago stopped dreaming in Russian, but I remember the last word "Fire!" was in Russian, my first language.

It is curious and perhaps symptomatic of delving deeply into memory that since I started writing about my life, parts of my dreams are dreamt in Russian. When that happens, I wake up feeling pleased with myself as if I'd just made a 30-foot jumper or written a poem.

CHAPTER 8
THE STATUE OF LIBERTY

Toward the end of the eighth grade, Cappy Lavin, our elementary school playground director, started a one-on-one basketball tournament. One by one I eliminated my opponents. The championship was played between me and the only African American student in our school, James Edwards. I won. Cappy handed me a small gold trophy. "Champion, 1952" was engraved on the base. The trophy was no bigger than my hand, but the figure holding the gold ball over its head seemed to me to be as tall as the Statue of Liberty. Walking home with Chris Cole, a fellow Grant student, Chris asked to see the trophy. When I handed it to him, it slipped from his grasp and broke into pieces on the sidewalk. I clenched my fist but didn't slug him. I picked up the pieces and put them in my pocket. I kept them wrapped in a handkerchief in my dresser drawer. I told myself I would throw them away after I won my next trophy. I won many more trophies in my career as a basketball player, but I never threw the pieces of the Statue of Liberty away. But I did finally lose them, perhaps in one of many moves from home to home and state to state. How did I know in the 8th grade I would win more trophies? I felt it in my body. I had already experienced this physical sensation before. I call it instinct or intuition. It was like a tutorial that I came to trust and never failed to follow its instructions my entire life - sometimes to my detriment.

You did what? You mean without thinking it through, you just made a decision?

Such is the voice that could have been anyone in my life: my mother, college professor, a coach, one of my teaching colleagues. It would *not* be the voice of my wife, Melanie, who would understand completely, often acknowledging that she rarely thought through a decision logically.

In 1952 with half of my eighth grade completed and summer beginning, my basketball skills rapidly improving, I stopped playing with Magnase at our local playground. Instead, I began going to Julius Kahn playground in the Presidio Military Base where many of the best high school and college hoopsters played three-on-three in the afternoon. I would stand on the sidelines watching their games. Often, if a player was tired, or if one of a trio didn't show up, I was allowed to fill in. In the 8th grade I was 5' 10" and reasonably muscular for my age, which meant I would not be an embarrassment when the rough stuff happened. I had developed an accurate jump shot. I was not fast, but I was quick. It was a description of my reaction time that would follow me throughout the rest of my career in the NBA. *Yeah, Meschery's not fast, but he'll surprise you.* In addition, even back in those playground days, I was a determined kid, which also remained part of my personality profile on the court and off.

Melanie calls this stubbornness.

Mel is right. Stubborn is a far more accurate description of my jut jawed pugnacious personality than determined. During those years growing up, I needed a lot of that stubbornness. I had something to prove–that I belonged on the court, that I belonged in America. That I belonged.

But there was more than just belonging. It was on the court of Julius Kahn playground (In my memory it has always been JK, not Julius Kahn.) that I first became aware of how much I loved the game of basketball. Not sports - basketball, that round pebbly sphere that soon became as much a part of my hands as my fingers. That after the games ended late in the afternoon, the sky already darkening, I would dribble all fifteen city blocks home from JK - left hand, right hand, from time to time stopping and tossing the ball back-spinning ahead of me and watching as it hit the cement and spin miraculously back into my waiting hands.

Those days remind me of Kobe Bryant's short Academy Award film, *Dear Basketball.* I watched that movie and felt all his emotions for basketball as though they were mine. I suspect most of us who took the sport of basketball from childhood to the highest tiers of the NBA have had a *Dear Basketball* moment. It pleases me to think so. And wouldn't Kobe be pleased?

• • •

Early in elementary school before basketball entered my life as a friend or as a life preserver - I already knew what to do for loneliness, unhappiness, and depression. You run, kick, hit, throw and let your body fix what ails you. Over the years, I have had no reason to change my mind and have often given this advice to people in my life who've suffered from depression.

At Grant Elementary, the sport was kickball and meant belonging, the foreign kid no longer feeling so foreign being chosen first on the team during recess. *The team?* I had yet to appreciate what that term fully meant. On my elementary school playground, all I understood was that being chosen first gave me status. Now I realize that in those early formative years it need not have been a sport. It could have been having a good singing voice, or solving math problems, or being the class clown. It just happened that I was already tall for my age and physically coordinated. By the 7th grade when Magnase Nagase and I played together, our chosen sport had become basketball. The togetherness was about friendship. It was on those cracked asphalt courts of JK, surrounded by chain link fences, with wooden backboards and chain nets that I first became addicted to hoops, but I prefer the word love. Those memories of *hooping* - the term players today use to refer to playing basketball - come back to me often, once as a poem:

CHAIN

The ball rose into the air and fell
dead center. Someone yelled, "Chain!"

We called him Chain. He never missed
"Chain!," someone yelled.
The ball was in mid flight

Chain link net, two links missing.
Charlie was a poet.
He said she had a hole in her skirt.

Meschery, Tom. "Chain," *Clear Path*. Random Lane Press, 2022.
Sacramento, CA

• • •

And it was on the Julius Kahn basketball courts that I began to hear the name, Ben Neff. It was spoken with reverence and with some good humor and, perhaps, with a little fear. I was an outsider and not privy to the jokes and banter of the older guys. What I overheard was about the coach of Lowell High School who'd won most of the city's prep championships. Those who'd played for him spoke about how mean he was and in the same breath how much they'd learned from him. In January of 1953, I would be enrolling at Lowell High because we lived in the district. I was thrilled and nervous.

I can't recall how many hours I spent practicing on the court at Julius Kahn playground. If there had been lights on the court, I would have been there past my dinner time and conceivably until midnight. I know that often I'd arrive early in the afternoon so I could practice by myself. Then, I would be both the player and play-by-play broadcaster. *Meschery dribbles off the screen, looking to drive; Meschery spins into his patented jump-shot; Meschery takes the game winning shot, nothing but net.* I remember that during one of my individual performances, two tennis players from the tennis courts next door stopped to watch. As I finished my play-by-play, they clapped. I thought I was doing the play-by-play in my head, but I must have been speaking out loud. Melanie points out that it appears to her from the time I was a child I was always making up some kind of narrative. She sights my early days in the internment camp when I'd created three different images of the All Mighty. She is right. For as long as I can remember, in order to go to sleep at night, I have to make up stories, usually about adventures. It's like bedtime stories I'm reading to myself.

By the time I graduated from Grant Elementary School, I qualified as a gym-rat. That term was not in vogue back then. Later, when I heard it, well, there it was, who I had become, a young man so fixated on basketball that for years I could think of nothing else. So much of my life from then on was measured by the parameters of the game of basketball that remained with me well into adulthood and, as I've come to realize, kept me from fully knowing who I was.

CHAPTER 9
OH, MESCHERY, YOU LITTLE
SONAVABITCH!

When I enrolled in the ninth grade in Lowell High School in January of 1953, I was 5' 11". During the summer of my freshman year, I grew an improbable seven inches. All the joints in my body ached. If I could have observed myself outside my body, I might have looked like some kind of vine sprouting - that skinny. A worried doctor prescribed bed rest and a diet of steaks and milk with lots of cream. I'm reasonably certain this would not be something my present general practitioner or any 21st century doctor would prescribe for a growing boy. From June through August, most of the time, I lay in bed reading novels my mother brought me from the library: James Fenimore Cooper's *Last of the Mohicans, Tales of King Arthur, Ivanhoe*. Compared to these adventurers and knights, Natty Bumpus and Lancelot, the radio heroes of my childhood seemed puny and unimaginative. There were TVs in many homes already, but we didn't have one to tempt me away from Galahad and the search for the Holy Grail. I read and slept and read and grew. One afternoon, having finished the last of my adventure novels, out of desperation I began reading one of my sister's books, *Little Women*. The main characters were four young women, so I was not expecting much, hoping for at least some vigorous male suitors. As it turned out I found myself enjoying reading about the Marsh family, a mother and four daughters, coping with life without a father away fighting in the Civil War. *The boys, suitors, and friends, turned out to be far less interesting than the girls. Was it the absent father theme?* I especially liked the second oldest sister, Jo, who was funny, willful, energetic, and smart. I forgot to send my mother to the library for more adventures and continued reading. By the end of summer, I had devoured *Little Women* and the sequels: *Little Men* and *Jo's Boys*. Back in school, I might have talked about my summer reading to my friends, but I doubt I would have mentioned Louisa May Alcott's trilogy in case they thought the books too feminine and would have made fun of me. It was the Fifties, and we were a generation of young hyper-privileged males, perhaps the last of a breed, as the 60's and women's liberation was fast approaching.

It pleases me to think that Tom Meschery, *The Mad Manchurian*, might be one of the few men of his generation who read all three books in the *Little Women* series. This is not meant to convey the idea that as a young man I possessed a raised consciousness. Far from it. Beginning with the Sixties as women embraced feminism, I was as befuddled as the rest of my generation of white males.

• • •

We are well into the 21st century, and it's safe to say that old white men are still befuddled. This time, I fear, combined with an even greater resentment. I say this sadly because before real equity between the sexes happens, my generation of white males, which includes me and a lot of my friends, must pass into the hereafter. I emailed this to one of my friends and he emailed me: *What did Nathan Hale say? I have one life to give for my country*. I questioned whether this was a tiny bit hyperbolic.

• • •

While I was confined to bed growing like a vine, the Korean War came to an end with an armistice. I returned to high school in the fall of 1953, 6'6" tall. I would grow less than an inch more.

Lowell was not yet the academic magnet school it is today, but it was considered the best college prep high school in Northern California. That meant nothing to me. I was not interested in academics. When I closed my eyes, all I could see was a basketball court. Many years later, already playing in the NBA, in 1969, my first year as a Seattle Super Sonic, I remember being interviewed by Frank Deford of *Sports Illustrated* and telling him that the first time I stepped onto a basketball court, it was like coming home. I had not yet written my first book of poetry, but you can see that my mind was headed in that direction. I suppose I was thinking of the comfort and security of home. My own home, tense with my mother and father's dysfunctional marriage, was not the model for my thoughts. I suspect I was really thinking about a fantasy homeland.

• • •

Lowell High teams were called the Indians. Our mascot was a cartoonish looking feathered Indian with a bulbous nose. No one at that time saw any problem with that mascot.

Lowell High's gymnasium consisted of four rectangular brick walls surrounding the court with very little room to walk outside the playing floor itself. On either end of the court, the basketball backboards extended out only a couple of feet from the wall, so that after a layup, momentum would often drive a player crashing into brick. The gym smelled of sweat, foot-funk, and leather.

I was in heaven.

Which brings me to the omnipotent ruler of that gymnasium, Coach Benjamin Neff. He was diminutive and wiry, and by the time I arrived well into his Fifties, with graying hair. He looked more like a college professor or a drug store clerk than a basketball coach. Nothing could have been further from the truth. Coach Neff on the basketball court was a fearsome tyrant. If Ben Neff were coaching today, he'd be fired before the ink on his contract dried and probably slapped with numerous discrimination lawsuits. Race, gender, culture, religion, nationality meant nothing to our fire-breathing coach. I'm certain such considerations meant nothing to most sports coaches of that time. If our generation was called the silent one, it might have something to do with not speaking out in the face of blatant racism, misogyny, and religious bigotry that riddled the 1950's

When it came to expletives, Coach Ben Neff took name-calling to another level. Curses sprung from Coach Neff's mouth like vines; all of us on the team at one time or another were entangled in them. He called our one black player a Mao Mao, our Chinese player, one of his favorite targets, a C_ _ nk. Neff would make fun of our chubby forward, calling him a fat moron and ridicule our tall skinny center. You little turd, he'd yell at him. Which was laughable since Coach Neff was no taller than 5'4". Neff did not leave me unscathed. "Oh, Meschery, you little sonavabitch!" he'd yell at me. The first time I thought, what did he call me? The second time, I just hung my head. By the end of my senior year,

I told a friend that *sonav*abitch had become my middle name. But that was better than if Neff had called me a Rouski or a Commie, although I wouldn't have put it past him. Even though McCarthyism was over, Communism was still the enemy to most Americans. I was just as happy not to have my teammates know about my Russian background. So I accepted sonavabitch as an equal opportunity pejorative.

Decades later, I see Ben, his jaw set, his brow furrowed, eyes on fire, striding toward me, and me hoping he wouldn't lunge. I see him bending in front of me, his finger making an imaginary X on the court in front of my feet, looking up, his eyes squinting and screaming, "You little sonavabitch, stand right there," pointing to the X spot on the court, "Catch the ball and shoot, that's all you're good for." Then striding back to his chair centered at midcourt, grinning, he'd yell, "Okay, start the goddamn play again and let's get it right for once." To this day, I have no idea why Ben didn't intimidate or frighten me. I'd like to believe it was because I recognized something else in Coach Neff that mitigated his slurs and rages that so often at the end of practices wound up with him putting his arm around one of his targets, black, white, Asian, it didn't matter, and praising him and calling him 'son'. At our Lowell High School 50 year reunion, I spoke with our only black player and our only Chinese player and was surprised how much they admired Ben Neff, speaking of him in fatherly terms.

In 1953, the word condescension was not a part of my vocabulary. Was Ben being condescending? I don't think so. Coach Neff believed he was in equal parts the fearful God of the Old Testament, and the loving God of the New. We were playing in his heavenly court, and by God the Father, we'd better play the game the way he wanted us to play it – perfectly.

And I did. And I learned. And every year I learned more. Back then, my willingness to overlook Ben's temper tantrums must have had to do with my burning desire to be the kind of athlete that qualified me to be an All-American. For me, this was not an athletic award. It was acceptance and citizenship.

And then there were Ben's famous pennies. During games, he would call time outs, dig into his pocket and withdraw five coins and kneel on the floor. We would kneel around him and watch our coach move the pennies to demonstrate a set play he wanted us to run when we returned to the court. His fingers moved swiftly, and it was often difficult to follow which penny was you. This became easier the longer you played for Ben.

Usually, the play worked. Coach Ben Neff was a basketball genius. When Ben retired, his ex-players presented him with a bronze plaque with an engraved court and five shiny pennies on it, each at their respective positions. When Ben passed, Lowell High School dedicated their new gymnasium to him. Ben, not any of his players, many of whom went on to play in college and professionaly, was rightly the symbol of Lowell High winning basketball. I and a bunch of his players attended the ceremony. We told stories about Ben, many that had to do with the names he called us. I remember thinking they sounded like terms of endearment.

I have told Ben Neff stories at get-togethers of old jocks, and we've had a good chuckle. Once I told a Neff story to a group of younger coaches, and they looked horrified.

There is no doubt we all suffered humiliation. And I cannot think of a better example of male tribalism in this country when I was growing up than team sports.

Was I aware how wrong my high school coach was? It certainly invites the question, doesn't it? There's no telling how many good young players Neff frightened away. What would another of my wife's grandson's, John-Clark, say reading about the antics of my high school coach? *Dude, what's up with that?* I do not have an answer for him. In high school, had I been guilty of neglecting my teammates of color? I was a white male, at the top of the pecking order, with certain inalienable rights, the kind of unquestioned privilege certain factions of far-right wing conservatives are trying their best to reestablish. It pleases me to believe that they will never succeed. All you have to do is observe the young people of today; they pay no attention to color; they date whom they please. Interracial couples can be found in every state of the union. Melanie says that as a portrait painter such blending is a visual relief.

• • •

It wasn't until after Doctor Jack Scott, a sociologist and political activist, published *Athletic Revolution* in 1971 that athletes began to challenge the authority of coaches. It took a while to gain traction, but after that publication, coaches began to stop verbally abusing their players, (slowly and not without pushback) until today such verbal abuse is cause for dismissal in high schools and colleges. And unthinkable in the pros where most of the athletes are men and women of color.

As great a coach as Ben Neff was, while I was at Lowell High School, we never won the City Championship. That honor belonged to Saint Ignatius High's young Mexican American coach, Rene Herrerias, and his star player, Fred LaCour. Fred was a six-five, wiry, quick, all-purpose guard who could shoot from distance, penetrate the paint, pass with precision, and lead the offense, in other words, the target of my enormous jealousy and admiration. He moved with economy and grace and always in complete control of his body, which earned him the nickname, "The Cat." Intense high school rivals on the basketball court, off the court, Fred and I became close friends. Together, we played pickup ball at various gyms and outdoor courts around the city. On weekends we drove across the Golden Gate Bridge to Marin Town and Country Club to play more basketball. On Saturday nights we remained after the games ended to attend the club's outdoor dances. *Electric lights, jukebox music: Red Sails in the Sunset, Sinatra doing it his way. Ah, Fred, remember our dates standing on the tops of our shoes and holding on to our necks while we shuffled around the dance floor? And where were our hands, so indelicately placed?* Fred and I double-dated. Fred's girlfriend was Diane Moceri. Her Italian family was not delighted with her choice of a boyfriend, who was biracial - African American on his father's side, Creole on his mother's. In the Fifties, it was rare to see inter-racial couples. It remains clear in my mind that I never had any negative thoughts of Fred and Diane being a couple. That was the case for all of the guys that hung out with Fred.

At the end of his senior year, Fred was selected to travel to Louisville, Kentucky to play in an All-American North/South High School tournament. The Game in Lexington, Kentucky, was the first such event that showcased high school basketball players nationally, which recognizes the top high school player in the nation each year. Fred played for the North. The North won, and Fred LaCour was voted MVP. Not until NBA Hall of Famer Jason Kidd played for St. Joseph's High School, in Alameda , CA in 1991, has there been a better high school basketball player in the Bay Area.

• • •

I have never understood with any clarity why Fred and I became friends given that we were fierce rivals throughout high school. What was it about Fred's and my relationship that brought us together? It's a bit of a head-shaker, even today. It couldn't have been simply respect for each other's game. I remember someone once suggesting that it had to do with me needing a brother. Maybe, but back then I was perfectly happy, as I recall, being the only son, which among old fashioned Russian families allowed privileges not accorded to girls. And I loved my sister. It is more likely that Fred and I recognized each other as outsiders - Fred being of mixed race and me being an immigrant. It amounted to the nearly same thing.

• • •

At the end of my sophomore year, on December 2, 1954, the United States Senate censured Senator Joseph McCarthy. I remember cheering. I was not celebrating for Tom Meschery but for Tomislav Nikolaievich Mescheriakov. I was whooping it up for my father and his struggle to learn a language not his own and all of the disappointments and shame that came his way because of his awkward use of English. I was celebrating less for my mother and sister who didn't need my celebration, both of them too strong-willed to allow a low-brow like McCarthy to interfere with their self-image. Perhaps, without realizing it, I was celebrating for the United States of America that had finally had enough courage to disavow McCarthy's tyranny.

McCarthy was gone, but not the fear of Communism and the threat of atomic annihilation. In neighborhoods throughout America fallout shelters were being built in backyards or constructed in basements, and Hydrogen bombs were being tested in the Nevada deserts. There was even a plan to build a city entirely underground called Atomville. I remember *Duck and Cover*, a movie shown in American schools demonstrating what to do in the event of an atomic attack: *duck under our desks and cover our heads with our arms. My memory of grade school* is that we never practiced duck and cover. Instead, we were taken en masse to the recreation room. For what reason I cannot now imagine unless it was to have us group-incinerated had an atom bomb actually fallen on our neighborhood. I do not remember thinking this, but does a child have to remember? Let's say it was a visual memory of Japan in 1945, the stunned looks on the faces of our Japanese guards, doctors and nurses working in the Tokyo hospital where we were being held, at the news of the atomic bombs destroying the entire cities of Hiroshima and Nagasaki. I didn't need to be a grown up to understand their grief.

About this time in high school, there was a photograph in the newspaper that was so strange I have never forgotten it: A Miss Atomic Pageant was crowned. The photograph showed a curvaceous young woman in a white one-piece bathing suit with a mushroom crown atop her head, surrounded by army servicemen. Just to be sure my memory had not failed me; I looked the photograph up on the internet and found it as bizarre in the 21st century as I remembered it as a kid. It brought back the memory of Japan and the atomic destruction of Hiroshima and Nagasaki, and the description of the explosion as told to us by one of the nuns who'd overheard it from the guards talking fearfully among themselves. There were only shadow outlines of people left on the walls of buildings left standing.

• • •

Some people today, mostly conservative whites, point to the decade of the Fifties as an example of more tranquil times before the turbulent Sixties. I have never believed that. For Russian immigrants the Fifties were fraught with anxiety. I am reasonably certain that my basic personality traits – good and bad, conscious and unconscious – were formed by the years I spent in an internment camp in Japan and in San Francisco living through the Fifties and McCarthyism. As part of the Fifties, a decade I find easy to disparage, I acknowledge my discovery of basketball and its continued influence on me. I'd have had a much more difficult time growing up without the sense of direction basketball provided me.

• • •

In my senior year of high school, I was named to the High School All-American Basketball First Team, and traveled to New York City in 1957 to join the other four selectees on the Steve Allen Show. Among my memorabilia is a photograph of that occasion: High School All Americans seated, standing behind us the College All Americans. I was seated directly in front of Wilt Chamberlain. Four years later he and I would be playing on the same NBA team.

When I stepped on to the basketball court of Saint Mary's College in September of 1957 as a highly recruited freshman, I knew more about the game of basketball than the rest of the players on the freshman team and, I dare say, the varsity team as well. It was due to Coach Neff's knowledge of the game and his ferocious insistence I play up to my potential that I turned out to be one prepared *little sonavabitch.*

CHAPTER 10
OLYMPIC CLUB

I was a mid-year high school graduate, which meant that between January of 1961 when I graduated and August there would be eight months before I began college in the fall. The day after I received my high school diploma, Carl Minetti, the basketball coach of the Olympic Club, asked me to join his team that was part of a Bay Area Amateur Athletic Union league. It made a lot of sense for me to use the time to compete and work on my skills. Besides, the club was a big deal, and I felt honored. Cappy Lavin of USF, the playground director who first taught me to play basketball, was on the team. So was my friend, Fred LaCour. I signed on for the remainder of their season, which included the National AAU tournament in Denver, Colorado. By then, I was getting a number of athletic scholarship offers from schools in California. By the time I finished playing in the AAU Tournament, I was being recruited by university basketball programs from every region of the country.

The Olympic Club is the oldest athletic club in the United States, founded in 1860. It is still housed in an elegant three-story building located on Post Street just west of Union Square in downtown San Francisco. In 1957 - the year I entered the building for my first practice - women were not allowed to be members and would not be until after a discrimination lawsuit was filed against the club in 1990. There were dining rooms, meeting rooms, banquet halls and guest rooms, handball, and squash courts and two full sized basketball courts. Its pub, where I was introduced to a cool post-practice drink called a shandy, a mixture of beer and lemonade, was all leather and mahogany. This was real manly stuff, and I was impressed. But in my memory, it will always be the showers, the stalls made of marble, the shower heads a tall man could fit beneath with a foot to spare, the water pressure like a good rainstorm. And the towels, long and plentiful and *oh so soft*. As a high school graduate, I was not without some experience of wealth, not that our family ever had any, but the Olympic Club opened my eyes to a degree of wealth I had not imagined. In our country today, we hear a lot about privilege. Those who are and those who're not. There are no longer money-managers, but wealth-managers.

In 1957, I left my first club practice with my membership card in my pocket, feeling that I was a privileged part of San Francisco society. This was not, I suspect, unlike the way young men or women felt having been accepted into university fraternities and sororities. Unlike university fraternities, however, there was no initiation I had to go through to be a member of the Olympic Club. Because of my proficiency at basketball, my fees were waived, and I was already white and male. Had she been alive, my Aunt Maroucia, the Princess, would have been disgusted with my gaucherie.

The term tribe postulates that human beings have evolved to live in a tribal society as opposed to a mass society. What I was not aware of back then as I left the Olympic Club, nor could I have been aware, being an impressionable and inexperienced teenager, was that America was better defined as tribal rather than a political or historical entity. From a very early age, my generation of Americans were offered a smorgasbord of tribes they could belong to-- from Boy and Girl Scouts, all manner of high school and college teams from sports to debate societies, cheerleaders, fraternities, sororities, political parties, Lions Clubs, Rotary, Moose, and Masons, Daughters of the Revolution, and Knights of Columbus as well as the evil tribes of racial exclusion such as the Aryan Nation, KKK, and the tribes that are called gangbangers whose initiation practices often called for murder. The land we call The United States of America was originally tribal. The whites that invaded the land and systematically decimated the indigenous people replaced those native tribes with tribes of their own. I was already a member of Coach Ben Neff's Lowell High School Basketball Tribe. God knows Coach Neff's initiation had been severe, and now I was a member of an exclusive Whites Only athletic club. It is probably coincidence, but I prefer to think of it as symbolic that the Olympic Club sits next to the building that houses the ultra-exclusive males only Bohemian Club, whose rituals during their 17-day July Bohemian Grove camp meeting have been described as weird, disgusting and occult.

• • •

It didn't take me long to become a starter on the Olympic Club basketball team. I was a high school kid mixing it up with the big boys, not only holding his own, but often outplaying his older and more experienced teammates. It was not because I was precocious, only determined and fearless. If I didn't know, I certainly sensed that I was not an exceptional physical athlete. I was marginal in speed, hops, and strength. I was however possessed with determination and a willingness to out work anyone. In high school at 6'6" I was a center. For the Olympic Club I played the forward position. Just plain forward, no designation existed back then such as power forward or stretch-three. Having a *handle* in todays' game means how creatively you dribble the basketball. It was my job on offense to both score and rebound.

College scouts began coming to games to watch me. The Olympic Club and the United States Air Force All-Star team made it to the 1957 AAU Finals. The Air Force team beat us. I scored 18 points, two less than Cappy. I remember thinking how cool that was.

I am back in San Francisco riding on the municipal bus from my home across town to Lawton gym to play pick-up games. At a stop, a man and his son climb aboard. The boy keeps turning around in his seat and staring at me. Three or four blocks go by. The boy stands up and approaches me. He holds out a piece of paper and a pen. Would I sign it for him? It would be my first autograph.

For the first time that I can recall I felt pleased with the attention. It was not just being recognized as a good athlete; it was more like being recognized as Meschery-the- Somebody-Special.

A week later, a tall, handsome gentleman with black hair silvering at the temples, wearing a custom tailored black double-breasted suit arrived at our home and introduced himself to my parents as John Henning. He was the president of the AFL/CIO union on the West Coast. Henning was arguably the most powerful man in the State of California and an alumnus of Saint Mary's College, an all-male Catholic College located about twenty miles east of Oakland in the town of Moraga. As the president of the Alumni Association, he had come to offer me a full tuition room and board scholarship. I knew little about Saint Mary's College. He brought brochures, and he offered to take me on a tour. He claimed they were going to have a great group of basketball players enrolling in the fall. He was the first recruiter to actually come to our home. Henning explained that Saint Mary's College was run by the Christian Brothers. I did not immediately realize why that was important, but my mother did. I remember her words to Jack Henning, that took him, as well as me, by surprise. "Our family is so grateful to the Christian Brothers."

Then I remembered: 1941, Yokohama, Japan, a small boy leaning against the back of an armchair crying for his father. A man in a black robe lifting that boy into his arms and consoling him. For weeks other black robed men entertaining him. Not priests - Christian Brothers.

I believe my mother fell in love with John Henning. It was obvious from the way she treated him with such deference. Her behavior was a reverse-spin-move from her normal belief that men sought after her, even though she was long past her prime and had gained weight, which seems to happen to Russians as they age. I've seen photographs of my mother when she was young. Maria Lvova was a beauty. Even into her late fifties, my mother had a perfect complexion, and a regal bearing, befitting her view of herself as a Russian noble woman. My mother saw this face in the mirror, which fed her idea that men fell instantly in love with her. The butcher down the street was smitten. As was a certain saintly Orthodox Bishop. Her doctor was head-over-heels. As was the postman.

On a Saturday morning, Mr. John Henning drove me to Saint Mary's College located in Moraga Valley, east of Oakland, for a campus visit. The campus was tucked into a valley surrounded by hills, that day spring green. The architecture of the buildings were in the style known as Spanish Mission, shimmering white with red tile roofs as was the chapel at the center of the campus with its white bell tower. Our tour guide pointed to the tower and said those were the Bells of Saint Mary's, and Jack Henning began singing the school anthem:

The bells of Saint Mary's, I hear they are calling,
the young loves, the true loves that come from the hills,
and now my beloved. . .

Startled, I didn't know what to make of this dignified alum, target of my mother's fantasies, breaking into song. An impressive Irish tenor if I remember correctly. Our tour guide was as startled as I was. Mr. Henning did not elaborate on his enthusiasm.

• • •

When I think back on that afternoon and Mr. Henning breaking spontaneously into song, I remember it as being touching, but sort of silly. I realize that he was passing on a lesson to me that spontaneity and silliness did not belong exclusively to youth. It was a lesson that helped me be a better high school teacher. It was fun to see my students delighted when their 6'6" 220 pound teacher went into some off-the-wall rendition of a Shakespeare soliloquy or burst into tears while reciting a poem, or leap onto his desk to illustrate the height of the Brobdingnagians in Johnathoan Swift's *Gulliver's Travels*. If I passed on Mr. Hennings lesson to them, it would be a victory for spontaneity and silliness. And they could pass it on. It would be like a chain letter.

• • •

Our Saint Mary's tour continued. We examined dorms and the library that was too tiny for a college, not much bigger than my high school library. I recall thinking that the interiors were sort of shabby, like they could use a good cleaning or a new paint job. The countryside surrounding the college was fields of walnut groves and hillsides of grass and manzanita. This was country living and I was thrilled to be away from the big city. But I was not yet ready to commit.

There were many other college athletic scholarship possibilities to consider. Some of the offers were against NCAA rules. It would be a lie if I said I was not aware of that. I listened to the wink and nod stories told me by alum recruiters, sometimes by past players. It was the way things were done, they all assured me. A car when I needed one; cash from time to time; promises of future high paying jobs. In one instance, from a school in Louisiana, I was offered a monthly check, a house, and a scholarship for my girlfriend. (I did not have a steady girlfriend at the time, but I immediately considered looking for one.) Inducements were part of the corporate way of life in America as it was explained to me by one recruiter from a MId-West University. This was a completely new America for me, and I was unsure how I felt about it. Our family was poor, and I was tempted. I can only imagine now as I reflect on that time, how such inducements enticed players whose financial state was far more dire than mine. I may be wrong, but I don't believe such "inducements" by colleges have changed much over the years. Finally, I was saved from temptation because in the end my choice of college had been made for me by my mother, a long time ago, in our first internment camp in Yokohama, Japan.

SAINT MARY'S COLLEGE
September 1957 – June 1961

CHAPTER 11
HOOPS, LIFE MAGAZINE & THE CLASSICS

My father never attended a single basketball game that I played in high school or college. In his mind college was all well and good, but a career in the military was a noble way to live a life, and that's what he wanted for me. Being an officer had been his goal in Czarist Russia. He would have attained it, had the Bolshevik Revolution not happened. Because I never inquired, I don't know what my father's career goals in the military were: Colonel? General? Having lost the life he'd set his heart on, my father seemed perpetually sad. My sister might have experienced a happier father, I did not.

• • •

In high school, I'd been a C student, and probably would have been an F student had it not been for Coach Ben Neff's subtle advice, "Stay eligible, you little sonavabitch!"

Saint Mary's College changed my view of education. It began with the *Iliad*. I'm not kidding. Our World Classics professor introduced Homer to us in such a way that I felt as if he was the blind bard himself come to enlighten our classroom. He read those long, startlingly beautiful dactylic hexameter lines so convincingly that I saw myself back in the summer of 1953 lying in bed feeling my bones grow and loving the adventure novels about bigger-than-life heroes. Later in my life, I tried writing a poem in dactylic hexameter. It was a frustrating and humbling experience.

That day's recitation of the *Iliad* was perhaps the first time I began to think that anything could compete with basketball for my attention. I should amend that to read *feel* rather than *think*. Yes, some part of me felt the possibility.

My roommate for four years of college was John Shirley, who'd made the freshman basketball team as a walk-on. This, despite the fact he had one leg shorter than the other, which made his on-court moves look a little like a snake sidewinding across the sand. He already had the rep of being a wild man; energetic, abrasive, annoying, funny, smart, and entertaining. He could recite from memory the entire *Saint Crispin's Day* speech from Shakespeare's *Henry V* in which King Henry exhorts his army before the Battle of Agincourt. John had also memorized the poem, *The Highway Man*. His recitations were especially eloquent after a few beers. I helped John get through his French class, and he helped me get through freshman algebra.

In my freshman year, professional basketball seemed too difficult a goal for me to achieve. My future beyond college was, as I saw it, a career in the United States Foreign Service. I'd be working for America while I'd be traveling and living in exotic countries and doing exciting work, having adventures, maybe even covert stuff, which my mother had done on occasion while working for the American Consulate in Harbin, acting as a courier between Harbin and Beijing. When my mother had spoken of these "missions" it had always been in a low, serious voice: I was never in real danger, she'd whisper to me. And I, her wide-eyed son, in grade school and impressionable, was left thinking about what the word, "real" really meant.

With the Foreign Service in mind, I declared French as my major, although the decision was not required until the end of the sophomore year. I could have chosen a more complimentary major, such as political science, but I already spoke some French, and I have to admit to looking for an easier route through college that would not interfere with basketball, keeping in mind my grade point average and staying eligible for basketball.

• • •

John Henning had been right. Saint Mary's had recruited a terrific freshman basketball team. In fact, in practice games we beat the varsity, a group of excellent juniors. At the end of the first semester, our team was unbeaten. Much of that success, I modestly attribute to my play. But in the pursuit of modesty, I give a nod to our high flying and lightning quick point guard Joe Gardere and a very savvy coach, Bob Hagler. By the end of the season, we were still unbeaten and set a Saint Mary's College freshman team and West Coast Athletic Conference freshman team record. In today's collegiate game, there are no longer freshman teams. And the amount of time a superior basketball player spends in college these days is "One and Done."

My summer basketball schedule was four hours of practice in the morning, four hours in the afternoon, and two hours in the evening. I'd return home sticky with sweat, sometimes bruised with floor burns from sliding after loose balls. "Crazy fucker," I heard an opposing player say one time after I'd slid across the floor, into the gym wall and leaping to my feet clapping my hands as if applauding myself. *Early days for the Mad Manchurian?* I was basketball crazy. We say we're crazy in love, don't we?

• • •

I've learned a lot about writing a memoir, having to do with dredging up painful memories. But there are also surprises of the good sort. Thinking about that summer's rigorous practice schedule, I flashed on how much I enjoyed those pick-up games on the playground courts and gyms where we set the rules and disciplined ourselves and were at our spontaneous best. One might consider basketball played in that way as an example of pure democracy. I'm sure I didn't recognize this at the time, but when I meet with players of my generation these days, and we start talking about playgrounds, their faces turn dreamily nostalgic.

• • •

During the off-season in college, on weekends and in the summers, I played in the same local gyms as I had in high school. On weekends, Fred LaCour and I or another of my hoop buddies were driving across the Golden Gate Bridge to Fairfax, a small town north of San Francisco to the Marin Town and Country Club's outdoor courts. Fred and I were still the best of pals and practiced together. I learned a lot watching Fred. The University of San Francisco had placed Fred on academic probation for the fall semester and his future college playing days were in question. I remember, not without some shame, that, perhaps, I wouldn't have to compete with Fred to be the best college player in Northern California, that I could be number one for a change.

The Saint Mary's Gaels won the 1958-59 West Coast Athletic Conference Championship and went to the NCAA Regionals – The Elite Eight -- where we competed against the University of California Bears for the right to play in the Final Four. We might have won had our teams traded coaches. Pete Newell coaching us and Jim Weaver coaching the Bears. On the desk where I write today is a two-inch square block of white marble with a gold Saint Mary's College insignia on it and below it on a blue background in gold lettering; '59 SMC GAELS NCAA ELITE 8. Occasionally, I pick it up and weigh it in my hand. It has a nice heft to it. A reminder that once I was young and one hell of a basketball player. I do not consider this ego, but Mental Health Management.

Our Gael 1959 team might have had a better chance to reach the Final Four had we not lost our point guard, Joe Gardere, to academic failure or, more precisely, academic neglect. I can still hear the dialogue: *Joe, can I borrow your history book? Yeah, man, if you can find it under all the dust.* We really missed Joe, not only for his basketball skill but for the humor and playfulness that he brought to an otherwise sober group of young Catholic men. Joe played with joy. It is a theme promoted by the present Golden State Warriors coach Steve Kerr. Kerr, who is himself full of joy, would have loved Joe. And visa-versa.

• • •

Carved on the desk of my room in the sophomore dorm at the start of the fall semester was a quote by the father of the atomic bomb, Dr. Robert Openhiemer: *No man should escape our universities without knowing how little he knows.* Given how near I was as a child to the devastation his creation caused, I could have taken his words as a bad omen. I just thought it silly and scratched it out. In my senior year, I'd remember the truthfulness of those words.

Sophomore year is the year of the intellectuals when students acquire just enough philosophy and theology to make them excruciatingly boring. Guys tried writing poetry. Somewhere in my memory, I hear Robert Hass, a fellow student and later in life the Poet Laureate of the United States, in one of the dorm rooms reciting a poem. I started reading poetry. Being a sophomore intellectual, I decided that the French poets were the ones who best fit our exalted status. I was particularly impressed with the French symbolists, Baudelaire and 19-year-old Arthur Rimbaud. In one of my least favorite but dramatic memories, I am hanging out of my dorm window, drunk, reciting Rimbaud's *Bateau Ivre*, (The Drunken Boat) to a crowd of student onlookers below, who were, I suspect, less impressed with the poem than my ability to hang on and not fall to my death.

Today my bookshelves are filled with poetry collections, and I spend many mornings in my retirement at the computer composing poems. But in college, poetry was only one of a variety of intellectual pursuits that competed with basketball and drinking beer. For a while intellectual pursuit won. I gave up beer, until I decided I could multitask. Today I have given up beer entirely as it requires too many trips to the bathroom. I have found no comparable substitute for a cold glass of pale ale. It appears that I never gave up my love of basketball, no matter how many years have passed and my many attempts at alternative mind-sets.

• • •

The North Beach and the Beat Generation was one of the topics of our sophomore intellectual conversations, and often a place to visit and gawk at the strange and exotic denizens of this increasingly popular subculture. Its music drew us in, and we were soon humming the music. There were blues guitarists like Josh White, and a guy named Miles Davis blowing his horn. These were names my roommate John spoke of with awe. At first, I didn't have a clue. I'd been listening to Elvis, Johnny Mathis and the Kingston Trio. I'd heard about the Beat Poets like Jack Kerouac and Allen Ginsberg. I knew about Ginsberg. His book of poems, *Howl,* highly critical of the United States, was still enraging most of the population of the country including me. Even as a sophomore intellectual, I don't think I'd be wrong to say that most immigrants of my generation saw patriotism for our adopted country as a requirement of continued citizenship.

The clubs in the North Beach didn't look too carefully at fake drivers' licenses. My roommate John and I were particularly interested in the Beats' avant-garde ideas on sexual liberation. We decided to see for ourselves if there was any truth to it. Our plan was simple. We headed for the library, looked up ancient poets, Greek or Roman, it didn't matter, as long as they were not likely to be recognized. Each of us wrote down a stanza or two on scraps of paper. That night, we dressed in our best imitation of Beatnik attire, black everything. I wore a red bandana around my head and earrings for some contrast. I must have thought that beatniks and pirates were somehow related. We drove to Vesuvio's, a tavern across the alley from Lawrence Ferlinghetti's City Lights Bookstore on Columbus Avenue. There were bound to be Beatnik chicks hanging out there. We would impress them with the few stanzas we'd scribbled that would, we would tell them modestly, become an important cycle of anti-establishment poems we were working on. We'd throw around names John picked out for us, like Gary Snyder and Gregory Corso (whoever the hell they were) and with a little luck, we'd get laid.

It didn't turn out the way we'd planned. What did Mark Twain say about fools and tricksters eventually being found out? Spurned by the chicks who recognized fakers, we drove to John's palatial home in Pacific Heights, three blocks away from my elementary school, where Brownie Magee and Sonny Terry, a pair of African American blues singers were jamming following their performance in a Berkeley night club. John's mother, Dolores, was a 50-year-old beauty who, as a young woman, had been a Hollywood stand-in for Dorothy Lamour. She was also a devotee of folk music and opened her home and checkbook to musicians and singers. There was a life-size nude painting of Dolores hanging on the dining room wall. It did not seem to embarrass John. Nor did it seem to embarrass John's father, who was one of San Francisco's most successful attorneys and a bit eccentric. Every few years he'd buy a new Rolls-Royce and, to the astonishment and dismay of the Rolls-Royce Company, immediately have it painted fire-engine red. A couple of visits to my roomie's home, and I had all the evidence I needed to explain John's wild nature.

The rest of the night, 'till dawn we sat around the living room listening to Brownie and Sonny play the guitar and the harmonica and sing their souls out, – and watched a fifth of Jack Daniels disappear. Brownie was lame and Sonny was blind. The lame leading the blind, they'd joke. Their music was raw, the lyrics painful. I'd never heard anything quite like it. I couldn't fit Fats Domino or Little Richard into these soul wrenching songs. The Kingston Trio folk songs were being played all over the radio. Fun and sometimes sad, but in no way comparable. That night at John's, I remember thinking that I was listening to a sadness that I wondered if white people could ever understand.

If I had been older, perhaps 10 years older, but certainly by the time I was forty and more traveled, I'd have recognized that these blues were the equivalent to the Fados and Flamencos of Spain. And the same sentiments of yearning, loss, pain, departures, and unrequited love,

being expressed in similar songs of West Africa, had been sung by Cossacks and gypsies sitting around fires on the Steppes of Russia and today and yesteryears at Native Americans' sings.

Brownie and Sunny sang and played and when they finished, we drank, and they talked about their lives growing up in the South and their music and joked around with us. I suspect they must have thought it funny and perhaps a little curious having two white boys and an adoring white mom as their audience. As a basketball player, I was used to being around black men, my teammates and my opponents, but I had only one black friend, Fred LaCour, and he didn't consider himself black, so my cultural knowledge of African Americans was, at the time, nil.

One might argue that my first understanding about the black culture of America must have been through playing basketball with black players. But I believe, now, as I reflect, it was those songs of Brownie and Sonny's that were my baby steps toward the beginnings of understanding and appreciation of black culture, augmented by the historical truths I learned later in my life during my coaching trips to West Africa.

• • •

As I recall, in college my roommate's all night blues sessions with Brownie and Sonny (There were three, perhaps four of them) began sometime in the spring of 1958. In June of that year, we would be officially juniors. On the 29th of that month the Ku Klux Klan bombed the Bethel Baptist Church in Birmingham, Alabama. As horrific as the destruction and deaths were, I can't remember a single person, classmate or teammate, talking about it. That I didn't think beyond my own personal circle of friends says a lot about how I isolated myself. There were undoubtedly students at Saint Mary's College who were ready to join the Freedom Riders. They just weren't playing ball and downing beers.

• • •

Decades later, if I turn on the television, the screen is full of *Black Lives Matter* protestors, whites and blacks and all other races marching together. As an image, it looks to me like finally our country will rid itself of the plague of racism that was so prevalent in the Fifties.

• • •

For the next two years in college, I never missed a Brownie and Sonny concert and after-hours session at John's home. It was better than a classroom. I consider it one of my many backdoors of personal history.

In my junior year in religious studies our class was introduced to the *Summa Theologica* of Saint Thomas Aquinas. It's odd to remember that Aquinas' logic attracted me at the same time that I was becoming a fan of the blues, a form of music that depended mostly on spontaneity rather than logic. Coming from a home ruled by a deeply religious mother, who had in turn been ruled by a deeply religious mother, theology was a constant topic of conversation in our family. One of my favorite family anecdotes had to do with Leo Tolstoy, cousin to my maternal grandmother. Leo had arrived at Krotkovo, my great grandmother's family estate, to pay a courtesy visit. My grandmother's parents sent the famous novelist of *War and Peace* packing because Cousin Leo was an avowed atheist. Regarding the question of the existence of God, my mother's answer was always faith. There was not a mountain or a skeptical son that faith couldn't move.

After the first lecture on Aquinas' Five Proofs of Gods' Existence, I remember thinking, *okay, now this makes sense. Not just faith, but actual proof.* Wasn't I named Thomas, after Christ's disciple who needed proof of the resurrection? I imagined God Himself talking to me. *Yeah, it's me, stupid, listen up.* As a result, I began to use the chapel for more than a quiet place before games to calm my mind. I began attending mass. I even went to confession and took communion, although I was not a Catholic. Russian Orthodoxy and Catholicism being so closely related, I didn't think that God, *or Bog, or Dieu* would mind. When late night dormitory discussions turned to the existence of God, I hit the detractors with Saint Aquinas. My roomie wasn't going for my new conversion. He pointed out certain profligate parties as proof of my hypocrisy. I responded that that was what confession was all about, once referencing an old Russian Orthodox aphorism, attributed to a Siberian sect that went like this: *Sin, sin, it will be easier on your soul.* I said it in Russian first to impress my listeners before translating. The idea was, I explained, that the more sins you accumulate, the greater the act of forgiveness. I remember lots of hoots and snide comments about sexual acts and drunken vomiting.

I'm glad to say that Saint Thomas' influence did not last long. Melanie disagrees. She tells me I am always looking for causes and effects. There are no *Whys*, she claims.

• • •

In the last few months as I'm editing and reediting this memoir, I have begun to hear sports referred to as a religion - the religion of sports. It astonishes me that someone has brought out this hackneyed cliché that probably originated somewhere in the Midwest or the South after witnessing the season of filled football stadiums. It astonishes me even more that religion and sports are being linked to spirituality and mystery. The term religion cannot and never will be able to escape its connotations of wars, misogyny, bigotry, exclusivity, dogmatism and persecution. Sports does not need this dubious connection to religion. It has its own mysteries, all of which grew out of the body's original need for physical excellence, not original sin.

Back when I was in college, I was not so profoundly opposed to religions, organized, or disorganized. I was my mother's son. I prayed to Bog. I believed in a God. Dieu still had wings.

• • •

In October of 1999, long retired from the NBA, the five proofs of Saint Thomas Aquinas came back. I received a call from Al Attles, my teammate from the Warriors, telling me of the sudden death of Wilt Chamberlain. I wrote an elegy memory of my fallen teammate.

MOURNING WILT

"The game's not over until the fat lady sings."

Dick Motta

This morning, I wake up thinking big:
time to crack a dozen eggs, fry all the bacon.
I think I'll never shave, let my beard grow
as long as an epic, dust off those books
with thick spines: Gibbon's Rise and Fall,
War and Peace, The Summa Theologica.
I'll spend the day with Aquinas's five proofs
for God's existence: The Uncaused Cause,
or was it The Divine Plan that toppled Wilt?
It might help reading about the Prime Mover,
but I doubt it. Words are never enough.

Let the day end as it began with a red sun,
and let there be a blonde soprano
with big bosoms belting out her last aria.

Meschery, Tom. "Mourning Wilt," *Some Men,* Black Rock
Press, Rain Shadow Edition, 2012. University of Nevada,
Reno. Reno, NV

Wilt died of a heart attack at the age of 63, and I remembered after hearing about it saying something stupid, like that's not possible because in my mind and in the minds of most of us who played with him, The Dipper was indestructible. To call him a giant would do Wilt a disservice as the term conjures images of mythological creatures or biblical Goliaths that in no way do justice to Wilt Chamberlain's marvelous physique, handsome features and intelligence.

For several nights after his death I dreamt of Wilt fallen face down, spread-eagled on his huge circular bed, its bedcover made from the muzzles of wolves, and the stars from beyond the skylight drifting into the room, covering his immense body that not even death could diminish.

• • •

In March of 1960 after the end of my junior basketball season, I joined the Olympic Club as I had done the previous two years to play in the National AAU Tournament in Denver, Colorado. This year it was a prequel to the 1960 summer Olympic Games trials that would be played following the AAU tournament. The Olympic Club did well but lost in the playoffs. The AAU League's Peoria Cats won the tournament. Winning qualified the Peoria team to participate in the Olympic Selection Tournament in April along with other teams such as that years' NCAA champs, the Ohio Buckeyes, a NCAA All Star Team led by the Big O, Oscar Robertson, and Jerry West, and a NAIA All Star Team. For the tournament, the Peoria team was allowed to select two players from the losing AAU teams. Peoria chose me and a talented and feisty point guard Carol Williams from the Seattle AAU team, the Buchanan Bakers. I had replaced the usual starters at forward for the Cats and played at a very high level. In that last championship game against the NCAA All Stars, I played my best, scoring in double figures, rebounding, and defending. I was determined to be selected to play in the Olympics that would be held in Rome. The Peoria Cats wound up playing in the finals against the NCAA All Star Team. The All-Stars won.

For the entire selection tournament, I played superbly. If the ball came anywhere near me on a rebound, it was mine. I scored over guys taller than me and drove to the basket past guys faster than me. I was in *The Zone* before the term was coined. I left the court certain that my performance would be enough to make the Olympic team. I looked forward to playing against the Soviets and giving them some White Russian elbows.

After the tournament, I remember feeling I was a lock to be picked for the Olympic team, especially since the coach of the Olympic team was Pete Newell of the California Bears against whom I'd played as a Saint Mary's Gael. Pete had seen me play since I was in high school. Coach Newell did not select me. I was stunned. Newell did, however, select the center from his own Cal team, Darrall Imhoff, who'd had a very ordinary tournament playing for the NCAA All-Stars. Darrall was a center. I was a forward. Maybe Pete felt he needed height. Against whom, I remember wondering. International basketball was in its infancy. The U.S.A. team could have played without a center and won the gold easily. I don't remember ever being jealous of another basketball player in my life. I was satisfied with the player I was. But after I read that Darrall was going to the Olympics, I was jealous of him. I decided I would not like Darrall Imhoff for the rest of my life. And for many years I held onto that childish grudge. Once in an NBA game against the Los Angeles Lakers team that Darrall was playing for at the time, I got in a fight with him. He was not ready for The Mad Manchurian's fury and ran into the stands to get away from me. I chased after him. Whether I was swinging a chair, or not, I'll leave to someone else's memory. I've listened to people who were at that game describe it to me as comical. In retrospect, I find the scene today pathetic and not worthy of him or me. Darrall was a nice guy. I might have seriously hurt him. Such acts of violence of which I was often regrettably a part during my NBA career was a kind of madness that gave credence to my nickname. From what part of me did it originate? It never occurred to me during my ten years in the NBA that I must do something about my bouts of anger. I never thought it strange that those fits of anger only happened on the court, as if the court was a boxing ring and each time I stepped through the ropes, I was given a license to fight.

• • •

In March of 1959, twenty-two of the smallest students in Saint Mary's College crammed into a telephone booth and set a record that placed the Gaels in the Guinness Book of World Records. At 6'6" and 215 pounds, I had not been recruited, but I cheered for my team, which included several of my classmates. The photograph became a classic image of Americana and is part of Life Magazine's 100 greatest pictures.

• • •

Our Gaels 58-59 basketball team remains the winningest team in Saint Mary's College basketball history. My jersey #31 was the first retired and hangs in the basketball arena rafters along with two retired Gael players, worthy youngsters of the 21st century - Patty Mills and Matthew Delavadova. I concede the 21st century to them. The 20th belongs to me.

Saint Mary's College continues to be part of my life, although I regret, I'm not the donor they expect of an alumnus. I suspect it has to do with their misguided notion of the fortunes of retired NBA players of my generation, which is laughable compared to what the players of today's NBA make.

When I played in the Sixties, there were not many NBA players who did not have off-season second jobs to make ends meet. One off season, I tried selling life insurance. I lasted one week. I tried selling cars. I might have lasted a month before I quit. As for today's NBA multimillion dollar contracts, here's how I used to deal with my envy. Once a month, I would enter a closet, close the door, burrow into its farthest corner behind coats and jackets and scream. It is called primal scream therapy, which has its origin in ancient Chinese medicine. It calls for people to *Shake like a noisy tree*. For years it worked for me. I'd step out of the closet like Lazarus, free of jealousy. Thankfully, I have gotten over the need to primal scream. But, occasionally I daydream *if only. . .* And I imagine me signing one of those delicious multi-million first-round NBA contracts and joining the ranks of the Nouveau Riche, a term my aristocratic mother would apply scornfully to all those of newly acquired wealth whom she considered ostentatious and lacking in taste.

• • •

Since 2001 with the hiring of Coach Randy Bennett, the Saint Mary's College Gaels have become consistent WCC conference winners and twice champions. My wife and I attend some of the basketball games. I would consider my memoir a failure if I didn't include one particular game Melanie and I went to. I offer it with trepidation as part of the game's color-commentary.

In a game against Santa Clara University, Saint Mary's principal rival, Melanie and I were seated courtside next to president of the college, Brother Ron Gallagher. Melanie was sitting next to Brother Ron. The game was close and the action fierce. At a crucial moment at the end of the game, a Gael player threw an errant pass that resulted in an opponent's basket. Melanie rose out of her seat and yelled, "*shitfuckepiss*"

I didn't.

Yes, you did.

Brother Ron looked at Mel at first sternly, then after a pause to absorb the full meaning of her epithet, smiled broadly.

Saint Mary's won.

CHAPTER 12
A SOVIET UNION PRISON
WAITING FOR ME

At the end of my senior season in college, I was selected to the United Press Collegiate All-American First Team and Look Magazine's All-American First Team. A few weeks later I was also selected to the Amateur Athletic Union's First Team All-American, which brought with it a team tour of the Soviet Union in the summer to play games against the Soviet Olympic Team. I was excited. This would not make up for being snubbed for the Olympic Games, and it was restorative.

That I was personally excited to visit Russia was a revelation. I had done everything in my power to leave my Russian heritage where I thought heritages belonged - in family albums. I might not have known it, but this was the start, however slight, of an interest in my Russian roots. I drove home to tell my parents. Specifically, I imagined visiting the home which my grandfather, Vladimir Lvov, owned in Saint Petersburg, and occupied when the Russian Senate, the Duma, was in session. If there would be free time available, I thought of the possibility of finding out more about him. He was not as significant a figure in my life as he had been during the McCarthy years. I remembered feeling grateful to Grandfather Lvov for being my personal support system whenever I had been bullied as a youngster. I regarded him as a heroic Anti-Communist, albeit a mysterious presence. Could I unravel some of his mystery?

"Nyet, nyet," my mother scolded, shaking her head. "Ty sumasshedshiy. (No, no, you are insane.) "If you go to the Soviet Union, the Communists will arrest you and put you in prison."

Could I have anticipated my mother's reaction?

She was in tears. "You are the grandson of Vladimir Lvov," she lamented. "The Ober Procurator of the Holy Synod. The Communists will never allow you to leave. You will be lost to me."

I remember wondering why being the government's Minister of the Orthodox Church was so important. I didn't ask her, and it wouldn't have mattered. I knew that whatever arguments I presented to my mother would not move her. When she began speaking about her brother, Vanya, I knew what was coming. *Vanya is still alive, as you well know, working to overthrow the Bolsheviks. They will torture you to find him.* Now I was back in my bed as a ten-year old waiting for the door to our apartment to close and my mother to disappear forever.

It sounded so ridiculous. I was a naturalized citizen. I would be traveling with an American basketball team. There were international laws. But my mother would not be persuaded. I knew when I was beaten. If I traveled to the Soviet Union, I would leave my mother frantically worrying about me. The next day, I called the AAU office and told them I was unable to go. I gave some lame excuse. Where was my father during this time? Sitting in his easy chair reading a western novel, or perhaps listening to opera on the radio. Russia was lost to him.

• • •

It would be five decades later, in 2007, at the age of 68, that I finally traveled to Russia - no longer the Soviet Union. I was not clapped into prison. Russia was struggling to be a capitalist democracy. I visited with my friend Dmitri, a retired Russian professional basketball player in Saint Petersburg. I took a Russian language course and met my two cousins, Nikolai and Lev for the first time.

• • •

In March of 1961, I returned to Saint Mary's from the March 1961 AAU Tournament in Denver in time to fail a couple of my senior exams, after which, with a shrug at my devolving academic standing. I took off to Kansas City, Missouri to play in the East-West All-Star Game.

On Monday, March 27, the day I flew to Kansas City, the NBA held its college draft. I was selected by the Philadelphia Warriors in the first round, the seventh pick overall in the NBA. In my mind that meant the seventh-best player in the country. It was pointed out to me by a sportswriter that this was no small affirmation of my basketball skills. Of all the college players playing on a Division One level, a number that exceeded 1,500 players, I was the seventh best. I remember days walking around campus feeling sort of numb wondering how this all came to be. It had little to do with a lack of confidence. By the time I left high school, I knew I was a gifted basketball player. What I didn't understand was how gifted I was. The scouts who knew the game knew me better than I knew myself.

Wilt Chamberlain played for the Philadelphia Warriors. I would be one of his teammates. I telephoned my parents. *"Ya znal cemyou Cheberlena v Kutae,"* my mother said. I told her Wilt was probably not related to the Chamberlain family she knew in China. Clearly my mother did not know Wilt was an African American. My father didn't come to the phone. I called my friends. I tried acting cool, like someone 7th best would act, like I'd never been in doubt.

• • •

These days the NBA Draft is a major event televised from Barclays Center, Brooklyn, full of glamor, fan appreciation, family and college coaches gathering. Lots of attention given to the best dressed draft pick. I am amazed and fascinated by the production and hype, and a little bit envious. When I tell Melanie, she says she feels sorry for the players having to dress up and be paraded in front of cameras and made spectacles for television ratings. On the other hand, she says she likes the glittery outfits the guys wear. I bought Melanie a present for her birthday, a sign that read: *I was ready to take on the world, but I got distracted by something glittery.*

• • •

In Kansas City in the afternoon while my roommate and I were preparing for the night's college All Star game, there was a knock on my hotel room door. I opened it and faced a short, plump elderly man, unshaven and balding, wearing a shabby gray suit with gray vest. He had large bags under his eyes. He reminded me of an overfed basset hound. He pointed to my roommate, who must have been at least two feet taller than he was and ordered him out of the room. My roommate, whose name I don't recall, surprisingly stood up, perhaps sensing authority, and did what he was told, leaving me alone with Mr. Bad Manners.

"I'm Eddie Gottlieb of the Philadelphia Warriors," The man , Eddie Gottlieb said, and without pausing to see my reaction, asked "How much do you want?" It sounded more like a dare than a question. I thought Mr. Eddie Gottlieb was crazy.

"How much do I want? For what?" I asked. "To play for my team, the Warriors. We drafted you number one," he said as if I didn't already know. Hell, now I *was* nervous and asked if he had identification. Eddie produced his business card. It had stains on it. There were matching stains on the lapels of his suit. I was not impressed.

"How much money do you want?" he repeated after I had carefully studied the card. At this point I was no longer nervous but in a state of panic. In 1961, college basketball players did not have agents like they have today.

I have no recollection why I said "$13,000.00 and a two-year no-cut contract." Where I'd heard of no-cut contracts I also have no idea.

"I'll give you $12,000 and a $2,000 dollar bonus and two years no cut." Eddie stuck out his hand. I shook it. What else could I have done? He reached into his briefcase and pulled out the contract printed for the exact amount we had agreed upon. I signed. We shook hands again. Eddie walked out. Not too long ago, I related this account of my signing to my wife's grandson, John-Clark, a knowledgeable fan of all things to do with the modern NBA game. His response was, "No way, Dude!"

In 2019, I would have signed an NBA rookie contract for $3,184,700 dollars per year for two years. While my 1961 contract seems miniscule by comparison, I was reminded by my friend Dell that my $12,000 dollars in terms of today's purchasing power would be equivalent to $104,314 dollars. This made me feel a little better, but then he pointed out that an undrafted rookie in the NBA today that made the team and never played a minute of a regular season game earns $898,310 dollars per year. I almost headed to the closet.

• • •

I stood looking at the hotel door closing behind the owner of the Warriors, and felt like a rich man. I could not wait to tell my family, my father most of all.

That night after the All-Star Game, York Larese, a guard on the East Team from the University of North Carolina and I drove across the river to

Kansas for beers because Missouri was a dry state on Sundays. A couple of beers into our conversation, York told me not to miss the morning's sport page. When I asked him why, he said something really big was about to happen, sounding mysterious.

True to his word, the morning paper revealed the mystery: a national college basketball point-shaving scandal. In the next few days, the names of players accused of point-shaving appeared in the newspapers. Connie Hawkins from Iowa, I'd heard of. I'd read about Roger Brown of Dayton University. They were both said to be the best players in college. Doug Moe of North Carolina was named. I was sorry to see Tony Jackson, from St. John's University, because he had been on the All-American High School Team with me.

I wondered if West Coast players would be implicated, which reminded me of a curious visit I'd had from Tom Cleary, a teammate from our freshman squad, who had dropped out of Saint Mary's in his sophomore year. He'd driven up from his home in Fresno to see a game. After the game, Tom and I went out for beers. In the course of our conversation, he began talking about how it was too bad players in college didn't get paid for playing and stayed on that theme until I began to get nervous, wondering where he was headed. Yeah, I was sympathetic, I told him, but what could we do, and steered us back to basketball talk. I didn't know much about point shaving, but instinct saved me from talking about anything illegal that might have followed.

During the summer before I left for Philadelphia, the local newspapers announced that the scandal that had hitherto been confined to the East Coast and Midwest had reached the West Coast. I recalled games against some of the players mentioned that were implicated. A couple of games in which I'd been outstanding - outscoring and outrebounding my opponents big time. I wondered if those players had been dumping. Had they just allowed me to humiliate them on the court? How much money had they earned for taking the ass-kicking I gave them? There would not have been enough money in the world to entice me to be outplayed so embarrassingly.

When I told my roommate, John, he said, "But maybe if you were black and came from a really poor family." John was right, of course, but at the time, my social consciousness was barely elevated beyond self-interest.

I was attempting to salvage my senior grade-point average, and I might have succeeded if I hadn't been selected to tour with a College All-Star Team for several games against the Harlem Globetrotters. How could I turn down an opportunity to play against Meadow Lark Lemon, the Clown Prince of Basketball, to see how good the Globetrotters were, *really were*, to be on the court and experience their sleight-of-hand. The Globbies in their red, white and blue striped uniforms were the American carnivals of my boyhood. No way could I pass that up. I signed a contract. I was no longer an amateur athlete.

The check I received for one game was more than my father made in six months.

We played in the Cow Palace on April 4th in front of 10,000 fans, many of whom were children. From time to time, I looked into the stands and saw myself, the wide-eyed boy from elementary school, years away from realizing the game he was watching would be the game that when he grew up would support him and his family. The Globetrotters may have been scripted to clown, but they were damn good basketball players. We beat them 76 to 69.

I returned to college from the tour and studied hard - to no avail. I managed to pull off a C average. If I was upset by my grades, I don't recall. My life was too filled up with hoop success and accolades and thoughts of further glories in the NBA. I was not overly concerned about anything else going on in the world around me. While I shot hoops non-stop, not just a gym rat, but a gym hermit, Harper Lee was winning the Pulitzer Prize for *To Kill a Mocking Brid*, Alan Shepard left the earth in Freedom 7 to become America's first man in space, and a bus carrying the first Freedom Riders was bombed and burned in Alabama. It's kind of frightening how self-absorbed and single-minded I was as I think of my life back then.

I graduated. I have a photograph in my cap and gown, standing between my mother and father, my sister next to him. My father is wearing a corduroy sports coat. He did not own a suit. Earning a degree s was a minor accomplishment to me compared to being drafted by the NBA.

In the NBA I would once again be playing against my high school friend and opponent, Fred LaCour, who'd left the University of San Francisco the year before and been drafted by the St. Louis Hawks. I would also be Wilt Chamberlain's teammate.

Many years later, I learned that Saint Mary's College had been considering nominating me for a Rhodes scholarship. In retrospect, I wish I had been told. It might have motivated me to study harder and avoid the academic disaster, which summed up my senior year's scholarly performance.

CHAPTER 13
CADETS

Nikolai Vassiliavich Mescheriakov, my father, reached out to me in a meaningful way only once. It took place in October of 1961, one week before I was to leave home to fly to Philadelphia to begin my rookie season in the NBA. He took me to meet a friend. "A close friend from Russia," he'd informed me. We walked down our street three blocks to his friend's flat. My father had never spoken of having a friend, let alone one from Russia. Other than the first couple of years after our arrival in the United States, when my father would occasionally meet some white Russian army buddies in the Russian Center for drinks, I don't remember my father ever leaving our apartment other than to go to work. Home from work, he would join us for dinner, then sit in his armchair reading Western novels all evening. It is my one indelible impression of him in the armchair, a Zane Gray novel in his hand, his finger moving under the sentences, his mouth silently forming the words. At the time, it never occurred to me what a struggle that was for him. This poem about him appears in my recent collection called *Time Out*.

WESTERNS

My father sat in his armchair reading
Zane Gray, Luke Short, Louis L'Amour
his finger tracing words across the page.
Sometimes he'd stop at a word, shift his huge
body, and sigh, as if his cowboy had come
to a swollen river and needed to decide

where the best place would be to ford.
For my father, the English language
was full of rapids and strange currents
coursing through a hard landscape.
He spoke to me mostly in Russian.
He was an officer in the White Russian
Army, fought a losing war in Siberia
against the Bolsheviks. Wounded,
he escaped to China. My father
never fully understood what happened
to his life that started out in a uniform
and ended up in a bathrobe, jobless,
reading about cattle drives and sheriffs,
and riders of the purple sage.
His plan for me was to join the army.
He could never understand why I chose
to play professional basketball, a career
he believed lacked dignity and offered
no chance to die for one's country.

Meschery, Tom. "Westerns," *Clear Path*, Random Lane Press, 2022.
Sacramento. CA

That afternoon in October, my father was dressed in his corduroy sport coat with leather elbows that he wore like a uniform when he left daily for work. Considering my strained relationship with my father, at every stage of my life I have always owned a corduroy sports coat. There is one in my closet as I write this. I find it a puzzling connection to him.

We arrived at a flat. A man, whom my father introduced as Sergei, admitted us into his apartment. It was dark and smelled of tobacco. I do not remember Sergei's patronymic or his family name. He was short and slightly bent, with thinning gray hair, but thick eyebrows that gave him sort of a Groucho Marx look. He welcomed me in Russian. I replied in Russian. I could handle that. When my eyes adjusted to the gloom, I saw the walls of the living room were decorated with photographs. I toured the room inspecting the photographs, all of Russian army officers posing for the camera in groups and individually. There were lots of hat-waving and sword-waving, officers on horseback, and soldiers standing in front of artillery, and soldiers, stripped to the waist, wrestling soldiers, drinking soldiers. By the time I'd circled the room, I knew this was not a home, but a personal gallery of the Russian Revolutionary War. My father explained to me these were the men who made up his regiment in the White Russian Army of Admiral Kolchak. I remember that my father, who normally spoke his hesitant English to me at home, was speaking Russian. And I remember to my surprise that I understood every single word he said. He pointed out comrades alive and dead. He pointed to a photograph of his younger brother Orest. There was no mistaking they were brothers. I remembered my mother telling me that she'd met Orest when cadets from the military academy came to a dance given by a neighboring count. She'd admitted to having a crush on him. And that Orest had shown a great interest in her. I wondered if my father knew. There was a photograph of my father holding the reins of his horse, Sharik, (little ball) that he'd ridden across most of Siberia with the retreating White Russian army.

Above the fireplace was a large photograph of Tsar Nicholas II and the Tsarina. Above the photograph were crossed flags, one of Imperial Russia, and the other of the cavalry regiment my father and Sergei served in. Sergei opened closets filled with army uniforms, sabers, pistols, a saddle, boots, spurs, and an assortment of strange gear for which I had no name that he dragged out for me to inspect. I felt I was inside a Russian history book.

The three of us drank black tea poured from a silver samovar. I think I had expected vodka. Sergei served us cookies. We ate while he smoked – a lot. The old soldier didn't speak English well. But it didn't matter. I could understand enough. Speaking was a different matter. My Russian was rudimentary, but I managed with a little help from sign language, to be understood. I learned that he and my father renewed their friendship while we were in the Japanese concentration camp in Tokyo. They were part of a group of White Russian officers that called themselves *The Cadets*, young men who'd been taken out of the Military Academy at the beginning of the Revolution, made officers, and sent out to fight. The San Francisco Cadets met regularly at the Russian Community Center on Sutter Street to drink vodka and swap stories of their days fighting the Bolsheviks. Many of them, I learned, had hidden their weapons after escaping into Manchuria. From time to time, perhaps, after enough vodka and anger, they retrieved their rifles and sneaked back across the Manchurian border into Siberia and shot Bolsheviks. In a poem I wrote later in my life in the voice of my mother, I described it this way:

> Some nights our young men, bored and full of vodka,
> slipped back into Siberia to fight the Reds,
> as if dying was the only job they could find.

Meschery, Tom. From the poem, "Small Embrace," *Nothing We Lose Can Be Replaced*. Black Rock Press, Rain Shadow Edition, 1999. University of Nevada, Reno. Reno, NV

Sergei told me about the time the Cadets heard that Alexander Kerensky was lecturing at Stanford University's Hoover Center. It was 1955 or 1956, the best he could recall. Kerensky, who'd been the Socialist President of Russia following the removal of the Tsar from power, was, in their eyes, as much a Bolshevik as Lenin, and a traitor to the Tsar. Sergei, my father and two other Cadets plotted to assassinate Kerensky. According to Sergei – all the while my father, nodding in agreement - they fortified themselves with vodka, then set off for Stanford. On the drive down the peninsula, they pulled over to sleep off the booze, and woke up to the stupidity of their plan. Luckily, no cop stopped them and found the pistols and rifles in the trunk of the car.

It was a good story. Did I believe it? I am not sure. It's how family legends begin with a mixture of truths and half truths. I have no doubt that had they managed to locate Alexander Kerensky they would have executed him. It has always been my belief that my father, a taciturn man, lived with a lifetime of repressed anger because of his lost military career caused by the Bolshevik Revolution. It is reasonable to believe that the same anger lived in all the Cadets. While my father lived the color red was not allowed in the house. My sister says that is not true, but it remains firmly in my memory. As this is not a childhood memory, which of us is right? I have read about how memory can distort accuracy. It is one of the mistaken assumptions of a person writing a memoir that he or she will be able to know and write the truth.

A few days later I boarded my flight for Philadelphia, looking forward to starting my career as a professional basketball player. I had no idea that 10 months later, in the summer of 1962, my father would be dead, a victim of leukemia. Thinking back, I feel a profound sadness that I didn't understand what my father was doing taking me to visit his friend. He was saying goodbye to me and showing me who he had been.

WARRIORS
1961 - 1967

"Not only is there more to life than basketball,
there is a lot more to basketball than basketball."
Phil Jackson

CHAPTER 14
ROOK

Eddie Gottlieb, the owner and general manager of the Warriors met me at the Philadelphia airport. I had not seen him since the afternoon in Kansas City when we negotiated my contract. I was not wrong earlier describing him as having the face of a basset hound. Later in my career, I thought of Eddie as a beloved basset hound. Eddie was barely able to see above the steering wheel, yet he drove us west out of the City of Brotherly Love through Amish farmland to the city of Hershey, Pennsylvania, the site of our training camp. Along the drive, we passed some horses and buggies that prompted Eddie to explain the Amish, a Christian sect that eschewed most modern conveniences. I saw some weird names for towns: Intercourse, Mount Joy, and Paradise. I asked Eddie. He said there were also towns in Lancaster County called Blue Balls and Climax. I wasn't sure he wasn't putting me on, so I decided not to ask him about the origin of the names. He might have anticipated my thoughts because after a minute or so, Eddie said, "Amish," as if that explained it. Eddie ended the drive to Hershey with this advice: *Never buy anything retail, always buy holsil (wholesale)*. As I came to know Eddie over the years, this advice was nothing less than a way of life for him. As I discovered, it was also a way of life for the NBA players of my era. There was a furrier, Milt Goldberg, whose *holsil* prices drew most of the married players of my era to his door. Are today's NBA players, being paid so much better than we were, not as interested in *holsil* prices?

Finding myself on the same team with Wilt Chamberlain made me extremely nervous. In high school when I'd met him on the Steve Allan Show I was too tongue tied to say more than *hi, how are you. I sure like the way you play*. He must have thought I was some kind of West coast weirdo. To know Wilt is to stand next to him and realize how massive he is. Goliath is a name that often comes up. The depictions in paintings and Bibles of the Canaanite Giant are always uncomplimentary, always some brutish thug. And David, of course, is always depicted as this ordinary sized handsome human with a sling. I digress, but it is unfair that Wilt was saddled with that monster image while Bill Russell, Wilt's legendary opponent from the Celtics, was portrayed as David.

Back in training camp. My nervousness over Wilt ended during an early practice scrimmage. Coach Frank McGuire divided our team into reds and blues. Wilt was on the blue team with this year's starters. Being a rookie, I was on the reds with two other rookies and two second-year players. Our red team was not doing very well. Meschery, the rookie, was not doing very well. I couldn't seem to defend Paul Arizinn. He kept making his jump shot over me. It didn't surprise me that the ball kept going to Wilt.. Close to the basket, he was unstoppable. Occasionally I had to switch and guard Wilt, an impossible task. He moved me through the air with a shift of his hip and I floated away like I was weightless. On my second day of practice, I felt as if I should give Eddie back his contract, pack my bags, get on a plane and go home. Join the army. Make my father happy. I felt thoroughly intimidated. One more bucket and the scrimmage was over, and we could shower and go have lunch. Guy Rodgers, our point guard, passed the ball to Wilt. I was sagging off my man and saw Wilt move into position to do his favorite finger-roll shot. I took two steps and leaped. I was in the air. I had never been this high. Wilt wheeled into position. He rose to shoot, but I was there before him. I blocked the shot at the rim. I returned to earth. As we sprinted down the court, Wilt slapped me on the butt. I thought, maybe I should wait to join the army.

I consider that stratospheric leap of mine, the highest I ever jumped in my 10-years in the NBA, as one of a number of miracles I've experienced in my life. As my mother would say, "Miracles are all around us," as if she were talking about the air we breathe. I could argue that Wilt Chamberlain was a basketball miracle, and a superbly conditioned athlete who looked very much like an Egyptian pharaoh.

From that moment on, the rest of the training camp was not at all intimidating. I did not question how one simple basketball move could have accomplished this for me. I remembered an acronym from my high school days on the court, KISS. It stood for *Keep It Simple Stupid*. It sounded like something my cantankerous high school coach would have come up with. Keeping it simple by relying on the basics not only got me through a competitive training camp but left me on the last day with the absolute understanding that I was a professional basketball player. Or, as my high school coach would have reminded me, I was one talented *sonavabitch*.

The image of that one blocked shot lives in a golden frame in my memory.

• • •

After two weeks of training camp, the team returned to Philadelphia. Another rookie, Frank Radovich, a 6'11' center from the University of Indiana, and I decided we would room together to cut costs. We found a two bedroom apartment in a quiet residential neighborhood, close to a Jewish delicatessen. Philly was my introduction to the NBA, the deli was my introduction to Jewish food. Borscht served cold; I had never heard of such a thing. It sounded unappetizing and sort of heretical. But with my first spoonful, I became a convert. It is my memory that during my time in Philadelphia for home games my pregame meal was taken in the deli, a bowl of cold borscht, a couple of pastrami on rye sandwiches, and a giant pickle selected from a barrel in the center of the store. Sometimes, instead of borscht, I began with matzo-ball soup.

Many of today's NBA players, especially the stars, have personal dieticians who'd be horrified to learn what were considered pre game meals in the NBA Sixties. Wilt Chamberlain, for example, relied on a diet of hot dogs. My roommate from the state of Indiana, Frank Radovich, ate a gigantic T-bone steak and two baked potatoes for his pregame meals. Being from the heartland, I think he believed my choice of food was un-American. As much as I had invested in being an American with a capital A, it must never have occurred to me that food had anything to do with patriotism.

My first NBA game was in Johnson City, Tennessee at the start of a 13-game exhibition tour through the Midwest. All the games were played against the Saint Louis Hawks. We traveled together flying from one small town to another in the same airplane. Wilt was granted the seat in the back with the most leg room, but probably not without a lot of grumbling from the guys who were 6'10".

Flying into Dodge City, Iowa, we encountered a storm. We managed to land but slid through a fence at the end of the runway into a corn field. I stepped off the plane wondering if the Army as a career choice would have been less dangerous. As a rookie, I was coming off the bench, but our Coach, Frank McGuire, was giving me lots of minutes. That exhibition tour provided me with a sample of how rugged the pro game was. In my first game against the Hawks, I drove to the basket. Clyde Lovellette, the Hawks, 6'11" center, knocked me to the floor. To my surprise, he helped me up and asked me if I was okay, had he hurt me. Very sportsmanlike, I thought. The next time I drove he knocked me down again, and again helped up, followed by his solicitous concern for my well-being. Hmm? I thought. This behavior went on for a couple of knockdowns. After the third time I questioned his sincerity. After the fourth time, I leaped from the floor and threw a punch, which he deftly blocked. This should be recorded in NBA legend-lore as The Mad Manchurian's first punch. I remember returning to Philadelphia thinking that playing in the NBA was not quite as interesting as I had previously thought. After Lovellette retired, he was elected Sheriff of Terre Haute, Indiana, a job that was a good fit for him given his inclination to solicitous knockdowns.

One of the lesser, lasting impressions of that road trip was how many of the players smoked. Two of our players, Ed Conlin and Joe Graboski smoked. Coach would start his pre-game talk and they'd light up. I found it coincidental that the time it took to smoke their cigarettes and the end of the coach's talk seemed to coincide.

I don't remember the first game that started our regular NBA season. I know it was a home game in Philly at the Convention Center, a drafty old barn of an arena with locker rooms no bigger than my college ones. It was early days, but the romantic notion of the NBA was losing its charm. It occurred to me to go on the internet to find out what the name of the team was and what my stats were for that game but I decided against it. There are simply too many games in an NBA season to remember that specific one. My memory of my ten years playing in the NBA has more to do with highlights, both on the court and off, like trailers for films. I recall after I'd retired from the NBA, a fan letter arrived with my rookie card in it. He wanted the card signed. He told me he was at the game where I scored 36 points against the Saint Louis Hawks Hall of Fame forward Bob Petit. I had no recollection of ever scoring that many points in a game, let alone against Petit. As an example of my selective memory, I do remember with great fondness hitting Petit with an elbow (the reason for the elbow will be revealed later in the memoir). These days I would be called for a flagrant foul and be ejected from the game. And fined. In my day, such a blow would be considered incidental contact. Maybe a common foul and two free-throws - if the ref was paying attention. I signed the card and added a brief thank you note in the envelope.

We were only a few weeks into the season, and I became one of the five Warriors' starters. Tom Gola and Guy Rodgers started at guards; Paul Arizin and I at the forwards and Wilt-the-Stilt at center. I had taken it for granted that eventually I would be a starter. I had never come off the bench in high school or college. As it turned out, I would never come off the bench as a pro, which is a matter of legitimate pride or legitimate advanced ego. As the season progressed, it was clear that next to the previous year's championship team, the Boston Celtics, the Philadelphia Warriors were the second-best team in the NBA. We aspired to be first. Our coach Frank McGuire announced to the press that we would win the Eastern Conference. Coach McGuire also predicted that Wilt Chamberlain would score 100 points in a game this season. The prediction made the headlines. I couldn't imagine such a feat. Nobody could.

Early in my rookie season I heard this dubious adage: *He who gets the first punch in, has the first punch in.* The logic is indisputable. The results, however, are not. Over my ten-year NBA career this "first-strike" approach led to several altercations with players, which resulted in my often leading the league in technical fouls.

• • •

In my rookie season, I was not yet certain that professional basketball was something I wanted to do long term. I was contemplating a career in the United States Foreign Service. I figured I'd play for a few years, prove to myself I belonged with the best basketball players in the world, retire and become a diplomat.

In my dream, *Philadelphia fans are mourning my sudden departure. I'm the talk of radio and TV and on the front of the sports page. The owner of the team offers me more than Wilt Chamberlain to return. I shake my head. Nothing will make me give up my dream of honorably serving my country.*

In the spring of 1962, by the end of my rookie year, all thoughts of serving my country as an officer in the diplomatic service evaporated. I was hooked on the pro game. And there was so much bait to hook me: New York City, Boston, Los Angeles - all the cities and sights, admiring fans, the restaurants, the stores willing to discount for a chance to talk to an NBA player. To rub shoulders as they say. After a game at Madison Square Garden, I would stroll into Jack Dempsey's on Broadway, sit at the bar, and order a beer. I was an NBA pro. I was noticed. I imagined the best women in the restaurant eyeing me. I'd finish my drink, leave a couple of bucks tip. I would join a couple of my teammates and cab to West 44 Street to Mama Leone's for Italian where the waiters were also NBA fans. *Mr. Tom, or Mr. Bill, or Mr. George, they'd say, your table is ready.* And afterwards, the three of us, and possibly a fourth teammate would join us. We'd head to *Willy Peps, a night club,* for beers and talk hoops. In Los Angeles, there was the Brown Derby. In Boston, the swanky exclusive French restaurant, Locke-Ober. That it did not allow women didn't bother me at the time. It may have been the start of the Sixties, but it was still a male dominant society, and I was a big-dog-male. And maybe in my post game memories as I made my way from one NBA city to another, there were women eager to meet a great professional basketball player. Or so I dreamed and continued to dream even if the dazzling damzels never materialized. It didn't take long, I'm happy to say, for those high-life dreams to fade, replaced by the realization that the game was what mattered and not the frills. That's when I became a real pro. It's what all young NBA draft choices today must come to understand, especially since so many are being drafted into the league barely out of high school. The glamor of the NBA life can often get in the way of what truly matters.

At eighty, the NBA still has me hooked. Ask my wife where she can find me most evenings during the NBA season. She will tell you that I'll be watching NBA games on television. And occasionally, when the spirit moves me, cursing the referees in Russian.

CHAPTER 15
FRED'S STORY

It was December of my rookie season. I began reading in the sports section's NBA box scores that my friend Fred LaCour was starting to get minutes for the Saint Louis Hawks. His scoring and assists were up. I was excited for him that his luck was changing. Fred was scoring in double digits. For the next two weeks, while my season with the Warriors progressed and my point production grew, so did Fred's. The Hawks were in the Western Conference, the Warriors in the East. I began to imagine an NBA Championship between our two teams. Lowell High and St. Ignatius High deja vu. This time I was planning to come out the winner.

And then, sometime after the first of the year, came the morning sports page and a box score of a Saint Louis game: Fred LaCour – DNP, which stands for *Did Not Play*. Players pronounced them *D'nips*. The next day's box score, another *d'nip* next to Fred's name. Was he injured? I called him at his apartment in Saint Louis. No answer. And no answer the next night. Followed by two more DNPs and a continuous silence. The Warriors went on a five-day road trip, ending in Saint Louis. I asked about Fred and was told he had left the team. I had a bad feeling about what happened to Fred. I tried calling him in San Francisco, but never received a call back. I tried to get through to Fred for the rest of the season with no luck. In the meantime I was in the middle of my rookie year and most of my time was taken up with earning my starting role.

What I heard after the season ended and I had a chance to talk to some people I knew in Saint Louis was that the Hawks Big Guns were not pleased with Fred who, as a point guard in control of the ball, had been taking "touches" away from them. But I was suspicious that the problem had to do with Missouri in 1961 having a reputation for racial discrimination and Fred, of mixed race, dating white women. I recalled Fred telling me excitedly before Christmas that he was flying his Italian girlfriend, into Saint Louis for a visit. It seemed too coincidental that Fred had been cut from the team soon after that visit. Over the years, I've talked to other players that played with the Hawks at that time. The white guys said, not true, the blacks said no doubt. As recently as a year ago, I spoke to a Hawk ex-player, not an African American, and he shrugged, as if to say, what did I expect; it was Missouri. I was reminded of the end of the movie *Chinatown*, the cop saying, "Forget it Jake; it's Chinatown."

Fred's contract was not guaranteed, so there was nothing he could do but leave. I believe Fred "The Cat" LaCour would have had a long and successful career in the NBA, but he was never given the opportunity. This would not happen in the NBA today, as our league under the leadership of David Stern and Adam Silver, has become the steadfast defender of equal rights for all races, religious beliefs, and gender equality. Today, the NBA includes many players in interracial marriages and the sons and daughters (in the WNBA) the children of interracial marriages.

From that time on during that season whenever we played the Saint Louis Hawks, I went into the game thinking of my friend and how despicably the Saint Louis team had treated him. Consequently, I threw more elbows and set harder screens than I would have normally, reserving my sharpest elbows for the Hawks' Big Three white guys. It may have been about "touches" which was the preferred basketball interpretation for Fred's ouster, but I'm convinced the reality was racism.

With the Hawks Big Three in mind, I think back with great affection to Wilt Chamberlain, Guy Rodgers, and Al Attles, three veteran black guys of the Philadelphia Warriors and how supportive they were of the white rookie, Tom Meschery.

If I could speak to my friend, Fred LaCour, today about racism, what would I say? We have elected a racist President and some police are still shooting black men and women for no apparent reason. White nationalism is on the rise. He would not be happy, but maybe not surprised. But I do believe he would have sat back, popped open a beer and toasted Commisioner Adam Silver's stand against the racism of Donald Sterling, the LA Clippers' owner.

I would also thank Fred because it was the anger I felt about the way he was treated that started me thinking seriously about racism in America. Slowly, and painfully, I began to study the real America, not the idealistic one that as a young super patriotic naturalized citizen I was conditioned to believe could do no wrong.

CHAPTER 16
THE 100 POINT GAME

In sport's history, the second of March 1962 will always be remembered as the date Wilt Chamberlain scored 100 points in a single game. It was an extraordinary feat, and I was part of it, although in context, my teammates and I were merely footnotes at the bottom of that epic chapter of Wilt's career.

On the morning of that history-making game, our team traveled from Philadelphia to the city of Hershey, PA, about an hours' drive west to play against the New York Knicks. As we arrived and got off the bus, I remembered from training camp the chocolate fumes from the Hershey factory. Wilt had been complaining he'd not slept at all the night before. Our hotel rooms were not ready. I headed to the restaurant to get something to eat. Wilt and other players went to the arcade and played pinball and other games to pass the time. In his autobiography, Wilt claims he shot 100% of the targets on the arcade shooting range. When it comes to hyperbole, Wilt Chamberlain and Mark Twain have a lot in common. Recalling that day, Wilt insists his flawless target shooting was predictive of the upcoming record setting game against the Knicks. It is even more astounding because back then there was no basket that counted for three points.

By the end of the third quarter, Wilt had 69 points. The outcome of the game was already decided. It was clear to everybody in the arena that Wilt could reach 100 points in the fourth quarter. By this time all the fans were standing and cheering each of Wilt's baskets. And in the background, Dave Zinkoff, "The Zink," our team announcer and statistician, was heralding each of Wilt's baskets like a medieval town crier: Dipppaaaa, 87; Dipppa-dunks, 89. When Wilt scored 91, I saw Richie Guerin, point guard, and team captain of the Knicks, excoriating his teammates to stop that "fucking

Chamberlain." Earlier the Knicks, knowing Wilt was a notoriously bad free-throw shooter, had begun fouling him. But Wilt couldn't miss. I've often used Wilt's sudden accuracy at the free-throw line as proof that miracles exist. Realizing the futility of fouling Wilt, Richie Guerin began yelling, "Foul the other guys, Goddamn it, foul the other guys!" The Knicks began fouling. It was a scene out of a Keystone Cops movie; some of us being chased off the court trying to avoid getting fouled. Wilt yelled, "Throw me the ball from out of bounds. I'll get it." And he did. Wilt scored 31 points in the fourth quarter. I watched Wilt's historic 100th point from the bench, hardly believing my eyes. Certainly not thinking that my name and my piddly 16 points would become part of sports history. In the locker room after the game, Wilt sat quietly talking to a local newspaper man. No Philadelphia or New York City reporters or radio broadcasters had traveled to the game in Hershey. The silence was really eerie. I remember thinking we were all a part of a silent film, mouths moving, but no voices. The Zink had written "100 Points" in ballpointpen on a sheet of white paper. Zink took a photograph of Wilt holding the number up in front of his chest. Coach Frank McGuire was hovering around his star, like a protective parent, tugging on his cufflinks looking for someone whom he could remind that he'd predicted this performance before the season began. The locker room silence might have been in my head, but I don't believe so. Uniforms off, showers taken, street clothes on, one brief look at the empty court as we walked out to the bus and the long ride home. On the ride back to Philly, no one hardly spoke. It was as if the momentous achievement we'd been part of finally registered and thinking about it was better than talking about it. I remember feeling pleased that Darrall Imhoff was the Knicks center that Wilt had dropped 100 points on. *A little college revenge – take that Darrall!* It also occurred to me how ironic that the greatest single performance in sports history had gone virtually unnoticed.

My first collection of poetry *Nothing You Lose Can Be Replaced* included a poem about Wilt's 100-point performance:

WILT

A rookie in '61, I watched
Wilt score a century in one game
in Hershey, PA, with the aroma

of chocolate floating through the arena
and Zink's voice also in the air
Dipper, Dipper, dunk, announcing
each new point, like a medieval
town crier. That night all of us
passed the ball to Wilt the full length
of the court, straight and high into the dark
around the rafters, and every time
the dipper sky'ed, he caught the ball
and scored. After the game,
there was Coach McGuire, reminding
the lone reporter from the local newspaper
he'd predicted before the season started,
Wilt would hit 100 points. But mostly
what I remember about that game is this:
coach tugging at his gold cufflinks
then pointing at the Dipper as if he'd just
discovered a new constellation, and, later,
on the bus passing through dark Amish
countryside, on the road, a farmer
driving a horse and buggy, hurrying home
in the all too brief light of his lantern.

Meschery, Tom. "Wilt," *Nothing We Lose Can Be Replaced.* Black Rock Press, Rain Shadow Edition, 1999. University of Nevada, Reno. Reno, NV

CHAPTER 17
NOT MY FINEST HOURS

Not long after racism cost my friend Fred LaCour his chance at the NBA, I came face to face with racism in my own life, and it turned out to be not my finest hour. I have spoken of this before to a writer and what happened has been recorded in his biography of Wilt. I would have been just as happy consigning this memory to oblivion, but I can't. Because this part of my story is not about me, but about understanding the true character of the much-maligned Wilt Chamberlain. Here's what happened: The Philadelphia Warriors were returning from the West Coast where we'd defeated the Los Angeles Lakers. On the flight, I had been chatting up one of the stewardesses. She was a total knockout, and my imagination was running in the direction of something erotic. The crew had a layover in Philly, and she agreed to go out with me. After we landed, Wilt approached me in the terminal. He told me that the stewardess he talked into a date was a friend of my date. He suggested we double date at Small's Paradise, a nightclub in Harlem, as his guests. I agreed. No hesitation. Double date with the legendary Wilt Chamberlain. It was a no brainer. Harlem, the famous night club *Small's Paradise*, why not? The team had a day off from practice. We set the time. I promised to pick up the girls at their hotel and meet Wilt at the club. He said he'd be waiting outside to escort us in. I do not recall thinking there was anything unusual about what I was about to do.

A couple of my white teammates had overheard Wilt and me talking. As we were waiting for our bags in the airport, they began giving me crap about pimping white girls for Wilt. One of them was my high school hero. What should have been a great time with Wilt, beers, dancing, suddenly seemed like a terrible mistake. It bothered me that my white teammates might think I was acting as a procurer for the Dipper. At the apartment, I went to my room and lay down to think about that. Finally, and to this day to my shame, I telephoned Wilt. I lied that I was sick and couldn't make it. He said he understood. *Another time maybe.* His voice revealed nothing. If this was the end of it, perhaps I would have eventually forgotten that I had acted in such a cowardly way. But I decided that I'd date my stewardess anyway. I called her, and she agreed. I drove to the hotel and walked into the lobby. Wilt was walking toward the elevators. I made a U turn and scurried out, but I knew he had seen me. I slept little that night, tossing and turning. I felt sick to my stomach as if I'd eaten something tainted. And maybe I had–a kind of poison called racism–that I had allowed to happen because I was too weak to stand up for my beliefs.

I stayed up all night worrying about our next practice. I told myself I couldn't face Wilt. I'd have to quit the team. I'd make an excuse to our owner, Eddie Gottlieb. *Medical emergency at home. I hated basketball, my girlfriend was pregnant. My father had convinced me to join the Army.* The drive to practice, usually a 15-minute drive, seemed like it took hours. A couple of times I turned around and headed in the opposite direction before I decided there was nothing II could do but suck it up and take what was coming to me.

In the locker room Wilt didn't say a word to me. I changed into my workout gear. Ed Conlin was having his pre-workout smoke. Coach McGuire had left for the court. I waited until everyone was out before leaving the locker room. As I walked toward the court, Wilt was standing off to the side. He waved me over. He didn't mince words. He pointed to his skin and to mine, touching his forearm and mine with his finger. "Black and white," he said. "We're teammates. If you want me to be a friend, I'll be a friend, but you have to make some choices." That was it. Not another word. It was silence as deep as a canyon. There is no doubt in my mind that had I acted this way with Bill Russell, I would have been toast. But this was the Dipper, a totally different person. When I think back on that moment, I am confident that there was no anger in Wilt's voice, only disappointment. His disappointment was my shame.

Choices. Wilt was right. *Some friend I was.*

Memoirs are fallible because memory is untrustworthy. It may be true, but I trust the memory of that moment with Wilt. It shamed me to my core, and I vowed that I would never be influenced by others to act against my beliefs again. That Wilt and I did become friends and remained friends until his death astonishes me. I should not have been surprised; Wilt Chamberlain did not possess a single racist bone in his seven-foot body.

I am going on 80, and I hope I've lived up to Wilt's gentle admonishment.

• • •

One of the principal themes of my life's story is that I never got over being an immigrant. This may be true of all immigrants. By this I mean we [immigrants] never stop trying to fit in, trying not to make waves, trying to be good citizens. The need to conform becomes a part of our personality. I may be speaking for an earlier generation of immigrants and not the present ones, (I hope that is true.) but I'd be willing to argue that this is not the case. I'm reasonably sure that this strong desire to conform exists in all immigrants. It is how I lived a great deal of my life. It may be a reason why I chose the foolish path of conformity when I lied to Wilt. It is possible the Dipper, being a black man, understood that he too was the descendant of displaced persons, the difference being the Africans' displacement turned into slavery. While we displaced Russians were allowed to integrate into society, it took the slaves a Civil War and decades of civil disobedience to achieve something akin to integration. Wilt's empathy was way ahead of his time. Damn lucky for me.

CHAPTER 18
ARMY

The Philadelphia Warriors lost to the Boston Celtics by two points in game seven of the 1962 NBA Eastern Conference Championship. Had we won, there was no doubt we would have defeated the L.A. Lakers, champs in the West. The Lakers had never beaten us in the regular season. I don't remember what I did after the loss. Presumably I downed a few beers in the bar below the Boston Garden. Maybe I replayed the game in my mind - that last second shot by Sam Jones. So many years later, I can still see those last seconds unfold:

Boston Garden, we're tied, a green wave of fans standing. Celts have the ball at their end of the court, time out. I'm a rook. In the huddle. I'm waiting for instructions. Tom Gola asks Coach McGuire to put him in to guard Sam Jones instead of Paul Arizin. Tom doesn't say it, but we all know, Paul sucks on defense. Coach refuses. The Boston Garden goes silent. Ref puts the ball in play on the sideline. I'm guarding Heinsohn hard. Damned if I'll let him get the ball. Celtics' inbound the ball. The pass goes to Russell at the top of the key. Russell catches it and in one motion fires a slant pass to Sam at top of the key. Sam dribbles to his right, reverses and rises up for his shot. Wilt vaults into the air in a vain attempt to block the shot. As I watch the ball backspin into the net, I know it is a deuce.

How many beers did I drink that night? I was too mad to get drunk. My rookie season was over. The following week, rather than risk getting drafted, I signed up for the Army Reserve.

• • •

In the spring of 1962 newspapers were talking about Asian countries falling like dominos to Communist regimes. Six months sounded a lot better to me than two years. While the military meant everything to my father, the army was only a memory of John Wayne cavalry or Second World War propaganda movies. I was due to report to Fort Knox, Kentucky for my basic training.

• • •

It occurs to me these days that when my father spoke of the military life as being noble, he might have forgotten the plight of the average Russian foot soldier of his day, the ones the officers sent over the trenches in the First World War, some without rifles, to face the German machine guns. This was the kind of soldier I would be trained to be, not an officer.

• • •

A couple of weeks in boot camp, a young Amish farmer in my barracks, unable to get a religious deferment, committed suicide. How he found a round of ammunition and an M-14 rifle that was not under lock and key was a mystery that was never solved. From then on, basic training seemed pointless to me. As I cleaned toilets, crawled under barbed wire, shot on the rifle range, and oriented at night without a compass, I kept seeing the Amish boy's face, the one who'd cried because he couldn't square his bunk.

A quarter better bounce on that fucking blanket, trooper!

I would have liked to have met that sergeant in civvies in an alley. I know that countless recruits through the history of armies have turned this wish into a cliché, but I remember making plans, going so far as to find out at which bar this particular sergeant drank on the weekends.

It is not a memory that is vivid anymore. While memories do not need to be visual, the visual ones usually sustain their emotional power.

I remember wondering what my father had found so attractive about army life.

Two months later, 10 pounds lighter and depressed, I gladly left Fort Knox, Kentucky and headed for specialist school at Fort Campbell, South Carolina. I had requested Truck Drivers School, figuring it was better than having to march carrying a heavy backpack and crawling in mud. At Fort Campbell I was told that the Philadelphia Warriors had been sold to a group of San Francisco business men. I would be returning to my hometown, my second year in the NBA, would be as a San Francisco Warrior.

But first came learning to drive a military truck:

I am sitting in the cab of my M-35 Series, 2 ½-ton cargo truck. I have driven my truck to the edge of a ravine. There is a line of us, the wheels of our trucks inches from the edge. We are waiting for the signal from our instructor to release our handbrakes, shift into low gear and move over the edge and down the slope, which seems to me the most insanely death-defying thing to do. The drop looks like the Grand Canyon. There are no seatbelts or anything to keep me from flying through the windshield. We have been warned not to touch our brakes on the descent, or our trucks will slide sideways and flip over. We could be injured or killed. I am terrified. I say a prayer. The signal, a long siren, sounds, and I follow instructions. Three drivers do not and I can see their trucks flipping. I make it to the bottom, low gear, no breaking, all the way. Talk about clutch.

"Is that a pun?" Melanie asks.

"Unintentional," I say. My wife is not a great fan of puns. I go back to my writing. It's the Cuban Missile Crisis. It's also October 26, my birthday.

I am watching television in the barracks recreation room about a possible war with the Soviet Union over Soviet missiles in Cuba aimed at America. It is the 11th day of the crisis and tensions on the base are high. Rumors are flying that we are going to be driving troops and equipment down the coast to Florida where the military is gathering forces for an invasion of Cuba. There have already been convoys heading south. All my fellow enlisted soldiers are excited. Let's get it on, they're yelling, HooWah! According to the radio and television, it's a standoff between the Russian premier, Nikita Khrushchev and President Kennedy. President Kennedy has ordered a blockade so no Soviet ships can reach Cuba. Some guy says to me that it's like playing chicken. As an example he cites the Movie Rebel Without a Cause: Two cars heading for a cliff and the first person who bails is chicken. I don't tell him that's stupid because in the movie the James Dean character leaps first . He's the chicken and lives and the other guy goes off the cliff and dies. During the first three or four days of the crises, my thoughts were what if I have to stay in the army and miss my second NBA season. It occurs to me if that happened my father would be thrilled. But as the crisis deepens and television, radio and newspapers warn the country of the real threat of a nuclear Third World War, I begin to see things beyond my future in the NBA. I owe this country. It has been a while since I thought about what I went through as a youngster and teen trying so hard to be worthy of citizenship. Time passes slowly from day eleven to day thirteen. The war never happens as the Russian Premier Khrushchev, at the last minute agrees to withdraw the missiles.

That I felt so patriotic surprised me. I was no longer a kid influenced by John Wayne charging up Mount Suribachi in the movie, *Iwo Jima*, or Gregory Peck leading his B29s over Germany in *Twelve O'Clock High*. I felt I had put McCarthyism and the phony Red Scare behind me, or at least out of my conscious mind. It had been a long time since I'd thought about being an immigrant and a naturalized American citizen. I was just a citizen. Considering there was an NBA season waiting for me, I must have been relieved that there would be no war, but I recall a lot of the soldiers at the base looking downright glum about it. War in the abstract for them might have sounded like paths to glory. By the time I was six years old, I'd already lived through a world war. And even this far from those years in Japan, I dreamt about it.

For those of us in our seventies and eighties, it is not uncommon to ask each other where we were during those huge events in the uncommon chronology of our lives: The Second World War; Korean War, Vietnam, First Man on the Moon, the assassinations of President Kennedy, the assassination of Martin Luther King Jr. and Robert Kennedy, Berlin Wall and the end of Communism, the turn of a century. And these days the COVID epidemic that the world has not experienced since the Black Plague. Has there ever been a generation that has lived through so many major historical events and crisis?

I asked my wife, Melanie where she was during the Cuban Missile Crises. Working in a sock factory in Oklahoma City was her reply. *I was 18 years old and would run to my car during breaks and listen to the news. I remember thinking I didn't want to die.* I asked my friend Larry where he was. He was a student at the University of California, Berkeley. He was at a basketball game, Cal vs Penn State. He named a player for Cal, Craig Morton who made his debut in that game and played so well that it "lifted the spirits after such a depressive week."

Arthur Sclessinger said it was the most dangerous moment in human history.

Which has proven untrue. In 1983 on September 2nd, the nuclear early warning radar of the Soviet Union reported the launch of one intercontinental ballistic missile and four more missles behind it from a base in the United States. The world was one decision away from all-out nuke war. The 1983 Nobel Peace Prize should have gone to Stanislav Petrov, an officer in the Soviet Defense Forces on duty at the Soviet command center who did not call for an immediate retaliatory missle response, which he was under orders to do but, suspecting it was a false alarm, waited for confirmation. The risk to his country of waiting was great, but it paid off as it was reported that the misstle launch was a false alarm.

At that time in 1983 I was in Philadelphia launching a new career as the assistant commissioner of the Continental Basketball Association, a professional basketball minor league. Soviet nukes would have wiped out the east coast of the United States. I'm tempted to say it would have saved me from an embarrassing year in which I proved to be a miserable administrator. Unlike the Cuban Missile Crisis, I don't believe many people could recall where they were on that near disastrous September day.

• • •

On the heels of the Cuban Missile Crisis came my father's death:

I am lying in my bunk asleep. Suddenly a light flashes me awake. I am staring into my sergeant's flashlight. I hear, "Get to the Red Cross. Your father's dying." I am on an airplane flying to San Francisco. I have spoken to my sister. Our father is in the hospital. Advanced leukemia, the doctors say. They are unsure exactly how long he has to live, but it is not long. I am numb, but I am not sad. I do not understand why I'm not sad. I could have worn civvies, but I decided I wanted my father to see me in a military uniform. I make it to the hospital in time to say goodbye, but my father is too sedated to recognize me. My leave ends. My father clings to life. I fly back to Fort Campbell.

A week later, I was back in an airplane, flying home for my father's funeral. At the funeral, my mother told me my father called for a priest to say last rites. I remember thinking that the Orthodox rites the priest performed meant my father died a Russian and not an American, no matter what his naturalization papers said. I said a prayer that my father returned in spirit to the country of his birth, where he had briefly been a happy man as a young army officer before the Revolution that changed everything for him. And that he arrived young and handsome again, wearing the uniform of the White Russian Army and his beloved Czar. And I prayed that his brother Orest was there to greet him.

Many years later, my sister told me something about that time my father was in the hospital. I can barely think about what she told me without feeling enormously sad. My sister explained that the woman whom my father had lived with in Shanghai had come to the hospital to say goodbye to him. I'd asked if she was the one with whom he lived while we were in the internment camp. No, my sister replied. "This woman might have been the love of his life."

According to Ann, our mother stood in front of the hospital room door with her arms crossed over her chest and would not allow the woman to enter my father's room. My mother's obstinacy made no sense to me. I had always thought of my mother as a compassionate woman.

My poor father – *the love of his life.* I thought of Melanie. What if I was dying and someone kept her from saying goodbye to me. For the first time in my life, I remembered being angry with my mother.

After my father's funeral, I telephoned my friend Fred LaCour. After his abrupt departure from the St. Louis Hawks, he'd finished out the basketball season with the Oakland Oaks, a team in the American Basketball League, the NBA's short-lived rival league. I told him I'd pick him up. We drove in my new Chevy to an outdoor basketball court. We did not talk about the NBA. We begin playing one-on-one half-court, winner keeps the ball – to 21 points, the game known in the Bay Area as Hunch. We played for hours, one game after another. We played beyond exhaustion, pounding and bloodying each other. The sun was going down before we staggered off the court. I have no idea who won. At some point we must have stopped counting.

IMMIGRANT

After his funeral my good friend, Fred
and I wore ourselves out on the outdoor
court playing one-on-one against each other
as if our lives depended on it. As if
whoever lost would have to join
my old man in his grave. All afternoon,
it went that way, shot after shot after shot
until, sun setting, neither one of us won
and we sat down, bloody and sweaty,
our backs pressed against the link.
His father had died recently too.
Five years later so would he, from cancer

that on that day he couldn't have known
was already growing inside of him.
It's how men cope we told each other
at the tavern, although we didn't,
words being unnecessary between us.
He left. One beer later so did I,
to the funeral meal where my sister
and my mother were waiting.

Meschery, Tom. "Immigrant," *Clear Path,* Random Lane Press, 2022.
Sacramento, C

When I think back on the years I watched my father sitting in his easy
chair reading his western novels, his finger tracing words across the pages,
struggling with the vocabulary and the American idiom, I am reminded
of myself as a boy reaching for my cap pistol, dreaming of Roy Rogers and
The Lone Ranger, both of us searching for an identity.

• • •

Back in Fort Campbell, I had been recruited to play for our base
basketball team in a military tournament, reluctantly, I might add, because
I was due to be discharged soon and did not want to risk injury. So, given
that lives are lived at the mercy of Irony, injury is exactly what happened.

*I'm driving in for a layup in a game against a team from an army base in
New Jersey, in the air, extending my arm and ball upward for an easy deuce,
I feel my legs being knocked out from under me, I'm falling backwards. I
place my arms behind me to break my fall. I land hard. When I try to push
up to stand, I know something is wrong with my left wrist. The soldier who
knocked my legs out from under me is asking if I am all right.*

I was not. If my wrist wasn't hurting so badly, I would have punched him.
I was taken to the infirmary where an X-ray showed my wrist was broken.

The San Francisco Warriors had already started training camp and my
wrist was broken.

Thirteen years later, retired from playing in the NBA and coaching
the ABA Carolina Cougars, I found out the name of the soldier who had
undercut me in that game on the army base. The Cougars were playing the
New York Nets in New York City. The poet, Mark Strand, and I went to

a tavern after the game. Mark told me that a friend, a fellow poet named Stephan Dunn, had related the story of what happened to him in an army game. Dunn thought it was curious that after leaping to my feet, I'd yelled, "mortal sin, mortal sin!" such a Catholic term. I have no recollection of my sudden conversion to Catholicism. Dunn had tried to write a poem about it and failed. It was a failure of religious conviction, I told Mark. By then, I was no longer imagining a solid right cross. Dunn was a well-known American poet, and I liked his poems.

A few weeks later, Mark sent me a couple of poems written by Dunn. I wrote back to Mark that Dunn was a terrific poet but a dirty basketball player. In 2016, Melanie and I met with Stephan Dunn after a reading he'd given at the Sacramento Poetry Center. We talked. He swore he was not the player on his team who undercut me. By that time, I was far more invested in poetry than basketball, so I absolved Dunn of the responsibility of nearly ruining my NBA career. We were eating at *The Firebird*, a Russian Restaurant. We clicked vodka glasses to finalize the absolution.

• • •

In November of 1962, I mustered out of the army, having risen no higher than Private Second Class, definitely a military bench-player, and a disappointment to my father. I suspected he had been hoping that the time I spent in the army would bring me to my senses, and I'd exchange my Warrior uniform for an army one. The suspicion remained a suspicion. He was gone by the time I returned to San Francisco.

Shedding the drudgery of military life, I was excited to get back to basketball. The team was now the San Francisco Warriors. I renewed old friendships. I rented an apartment on Greenwich Street close to Coit Tower. The season itself was a catastrophe. We set an NBA record for losses. There is not one thing that I can think of that makes constant losing instructive. Sports prepares you for sports, not for life. Is there any possibility that losing a game, even a championship can prepare you for the losses men and women experience in their ongoing daily lives: loss of job, loss of a loved one, loss of faith? So, we can dispense with the cliché.

Of that losing NBA season, I remember our coach Bob Ferrick after our last road-trip walking through airport passenger halls, hunched over, a picture of dejection, his camel hair overcoat dragging on the floor, mumbling, "Nothing is easy, nothing is easy."

At the time, I did not consider Coach Ferrick's words as a lesson in life. But upon reflection from the vantage point of hindsight, there's a hell of a lot of truth in it.

Not everything was horrible. I made the All-Star Team for the West. Against the East, I scored two points. It would be my first and last All-Star Team. At the time I believed it was the first of many All-Star teams I'd be on.

It was in this first season in San Francisco that I remember being labeled The Mad Manchurian. A sports magazine published a story about me, and my unusual background entitled *The Mad Manchurian*. Manchuria because of my birthplace and mad, I suppose, to explain the intensity with which I played. The writer was not wrong, but his attempt was a career away from the statistic that revealed that over my career in the NBA I had committed 2,641 personal fouls.

At the end of the season, my two-year rookie contract expired, and I was a free agent. I was no longer thinking of applying to the Foreign Service. All my friends were encouraging me to ask our general manager Eddie Gottlieb for a big raise. I do not recall if the possibility of increased riches influenced me to forego my diplomatic career for more years playing hoops. Maybe. But mostly, it was how much I loved playing the game of basketball. My friends reminded me that I had been selected to the All-Star team. I succumbed to the entreaties of friends who convinced me to ask for a significant raise. I entered Eddie Gottlieb's office on the 7th floor of the Sansome Building in downtown San Francisco, as Dylan Thomas once wrote, "cocky as a bullfrog." Always to the point, Eddie asked outright what I wanted. I told him forty-thousand dollars. Eddie stood up from his desk, walked to the window, and opened it. He leaned out of the window, perhaps measuring the distance to the sidewalk, then turned to me. "Before I pay you that kind of money," he said, "I'll jump." In my memory the image of little Eddie ready to fling himself to his death still makes me laugh. I signed for the exact amount of money Eddie had already written on the contract, remembering that this was precisely the way it happened two years earlier in Kansas City. Eddie gave me a raise but not nearly forty grand.

Most NBA fans today would be surprised to know that the average player's salary in 1963 was $8,000. A starter might be paid as high as $20,000. Bill Russell and Wilt Chamberlain were unique at $50,000. There was no minimum wage, no medical benefits beyond on court injuries and no pension. For the first six seasons of my career, I taped my ankles myself. I became good at it and a few times I taped my teammate's ankles.

CHAPTER 19
THE ARRIVAL OF COACH ALEX HANNUM

The 1963-64 preseason training camp was held at the University of California, Santa Cruz under the leadership of our newly hired coach, Alex Hannum. Alex came from six years coaching the Syracuse Nationals with a reputation for being ex-marine tough. He'd played for several teams in the NBA, a 6'9" power forward who was considered by all his teams as their enforcer. Tough was an understatement. I cannot remember how many physically punishing drills Hannum put us through during those mornings and afternoons in Santa Cruz. I was surprised our super star Wilt went along with this nightmarish regimen. But as we humans cursed and sweated, nary a glimmer of perspiration appeared on Wilt's gigantic body. With us that season was Kenny Sears, a twelve-year veteran of the NBA we'd acquired the year before from the New York Knicks. As I write this, I can see Kenny sitting on the floor after the third day of practice, muttering to himself, 'I don't need this shit. I'm retiring.' Two days later, he left camp. There was a tavern he owned waiting for a 6'10' bartender who didn't need any shit anymore.

I can still see our 6'10" first-round draft choice from the previous year, Wayne Hightower out of the University of Kansas, following a particularly insane morning practice at lunch - his face dropping into his bowl of minestrone. The picture is much funnier in retrospect. The legend or the myth – your choice – is that Wilt Chamberlain saved him from drowning.

Another memory from that training camp that remains one of my favorites is of Wilt Chamberlain after practice walking out of the gymnasium toward a waiting Kim Novak, standing by her Rolls Royce. And where was I at that moment? Along with the rest of my teammates, still wet from the shower, naked except for towels, crowding around the window in the locker room jockeying for a better view.

• • •

The 1963 Warriors was a far superior team than the one the year before that set an NBA record for losses. Our resurgence was due primarily to our new coach and the play of our 6'11" first round draft choice Nate Thurmond out of Bowling Green University. Nate played in the front court with Wilt and me. By November our record marked us as contenders for the Western Conference championship. Such sudden turnarounds in sports are rare. I was excited. Nate Thurmond – not yet Nate, The Great – was tremendously skilled. In today's NBA lexicon Nate would be described as "a beast."

On the 19th of November we returned from the East Coast to San Francisco and played the Saint Louis Hawks and won. Any win felt good, but a win over Bob Petit and his Hawks doubled the pleasure and doubled the fun for me.

Two days later in Dallas, Texas, President John F Kennedy was assassinated. Like most people in the United States, I was horrified. President Kennedy was young and handsome and energetic. It had been only a year ago while I was in the Army waiting for war that he'd faced off against the Soviets and won the blinking contest. At his inauguration, President Kennedy had asked America to consider not what the country could do for them, but what they could do for their country. I was very much a patriot and found Kennedy's idealism compelling. He had started the Peace Corps. I did not know it at the time, but I would soon meet many Peace Corps volunteers in Africa. But that would not be until after my season was over.

• • •

It is Sunday the 24th of November 1963, I am sitting in my teammate Gary's apartment watching the caisson carrying President Kennedy's casket from the White House to the U.S. Capital. It does not seem possible to me that a President of the United States could have been assassinated. Things like that only happen in unstable Third World countries. I am watching the television, but in my mind I'm listening to my mother in tears lamenting the execution of the entire Russian royal family in a cellar in Ekaterinburg.

As the Kennedy cortege reaches its destination in front of the steps leading to the capital, Gary's friend and lawyer, visiting from Gary's hometown of Houston, states, "I deeply grieve that the president of the United States has been assassinated and not removed from office by due process of law." I stand up and leave the apartment.

Had I not left the apartment, I would have slugged the guy. Gary and I would remain teammates, but we could never be friends again. Decades later Gary began sending me emails about being born again. I have not answered him. I like to tell Melanie I grew out of religion like clothes that no longer fit me. However, I never grew out of the stories of Saints and prophets. I have no doubt that Jesus Christ lived on this earth and was a prophet, as powerful as any other religions on earth believed in. I have read the Bible from cover to cover. I believe that Jesus Christ would condemn Donald Trump and his followers.

• • •

There are retired players who can recite chapter and verse, game by game of their seasons. Not me. Except for very special games, my entire ten-year basketball career is unclear. It's hard to explain. I'm not indifferent to remembrance. There's nothing I enjoy more than sitting down with teammates and gym rats, downing beers, and talking hoops. During those sessions snippets of memory pleasantly return in time for me to enjoy embellishing them. That's what old jocks do; you know. We take the art of embellishment to a higher level. "In my day we would say. . . And remember when you elbowed me?" This is also how legends begin. There were playground legends: Helicopter Hentz who could pick quarters off the top of backboards. There were family legends: Grandfather Lvov rushing across the street through a hail of bullets during the street fighting in Saint Petersburg to save a woman's life.

Perhaps my lack of remembrance about my basketball career in general has something to do with playing all my games being only in the moment, a routine that went like this: I would *enter locker room, shed my civvies, go to the toilet, throw up, put on my uniform, listen to the coach, sometimes space out, day dreaming about something totally unrelated to basketball, run onto the court for layups, still nervous, take practice shots.* All this on automatic pilot. But the moment the ref threw the ball up to start the game, all nervousness ended, automatic pilot turned off and intensity turned on.

From the time the game started until the game ended, the court became my world, and I was living inside the action. There was no crowd noise, no fans. There were only ten players and two referees in my world. When the game ended, it was like I stepped out of the action, like stepping out of one room into another. I can equate this to creative writing. Writers sit down at their desks and immerse themselves in their stories. I've been told by writer friends that sometimes they talk to their characters, and the characters talk back. Just as a player I was inside the action on the court, as writers are inside their story. At some point, they close their computer or put down their pen and step out of the narrative just like when the game was over.

By the time I sat down for my first post-game beer, I could not recall much of what happened on the court. If there ever was a sport designed for me, it was basketball, a sport that at its best, is played instinctively and being fully present when I played. When I tried playing basketball with my brain, bad things happened.

Like the time you scored a basket for the opposing team.

It is a story I've told my wife Melanie and her grandsons. Not that I wanted to relive the most humiliating game in my NBA history, but I believe it is an important lesson for youngsters to hear adults laughing at themselves. To the extent that this tale is meant to instruct what happened to me in the Boston Garden in a game against the Celtics could be considered a sports parable.

The Parable of Meschery's Folly

It's the third quarter. A Celtic player is shooting two free throws. I'm in position on the key ready to block off the Celtic player standing next to me. The free-throw goes up - a miss. I'm in the air, the ball in my hands. I land and look around, to my right, to my left. No Bill Russell in sight. I score easily and sprint back to begin playing defense, wondering why the Boston fans are cheering wildly. I'm in the paint, in a good defensive stance. Referee blows the whistle, "3 seconds in the key!" What? What? Tom Heinsohn, the Celtic forward I'm waiting to guard is looking at me, smirking. Coach Hannum is screaming for a timeout. Ref blows his whistle. I get to the bench, Hannum grabs my jersey. "Do you know where the hell you are?' he screams. Boston Garden? Alex shakes his head and points to the bench.

Boston fans are second only to the Philadelphia fans for getting on a player's case. That night the taunts, the laughter and the finger pointing was being directed at me. I had scored a basket for the Celtics and played defense when I should have been playing offense and being called for over three seconds in the paint. I was upside down and inside out.

• • •

The reason I was upside down and inside out has a name: William Felton Russell. It was the absence of Russell's long arms hovering over me that I once described in a poem I wrote about him as the *wings of an eagle* which caused me to score the two for the Celtics. Over the years, I have often been asked who was the greatest defensive center in NBA history. Handsdown, Bill Russell. It is possible, however: if Wilt Chamberlain had the desire to concentrate on defense, with his length and massive body, he could have eclipsed Russell. The comparison of the two legendary centers still goes on today.

Often the comparison strays beyond the game of basketball, which is where things become unfair to my teammate, Wilt. Compared to Bill, Wilt was dubbed a loser; Bill the winner. Bill was the cerebral one; Wilt the physical one. Bill, the fierce defender of his race; Wilt, the politically uninvolved. I knew both men. I admired both men. They were very different personalities. This is how I see them: Bill was the black man of the moment; Will was the black man of the future. Wilt believed he was the success story; Bill was still writing his story. Bill's story was of struggle and defiance; In Wilt's story the struggle is over and he's won. If this is true both men were symbolic.

• • •

Alex Hannum turned out to be one hell of a good coach. He was, back then, what today is called a "players coach." I'm not sure what that means now, but for teams in the Sixties it meant Alex would take our suggestions seriously; he never lied to us, and on occasion joined us for a few beers. That season he turned our pathetic previous season around and guided us to a Western Conference Championship. We lost to the Boston Celtics in five games. The last memory of that season is of me and Wilt drinking together in some of the clubs in the North Beach. I was drinking beer; Wilt was drinking scotch mixed with milk. At some point, Wilt left me sitting on the curb staring at passing cars. To this day I have no idea how I got home.

The season ended. Like a lot of NBA players in the Sixties, I looked for another job so I wouldn't have to live off what I could save from my Warrior's salary. I took a job selling cars at a local Ford dealership and quit the day Eddie Gottlieb called me on the telephone to ask me if I wanted to go to West Africa to coach.

WEST AFRICA
Summer of 1964

"Now, try to put on a black skin for five minutes.
I know that you find it hard to do, but there is
no other way to get the living feel for our situation."
Leopold Sedar Senghor

CHAPTER 20
TRAVELS WITH KC AND JOHN
Summer, 1964

Boston Celtics teammates Bill Russell and Bob Cousy were the first players the National Basketball Association sent to promote basketball in Africa. They arrived in the West African country of Senegal in the summer of 1963. Their coaching trip was sponsored by the United States Information Agency – the USIA. The following summer, I was selected along with John Havlicek and K.C. Jones of the Celtics, to conduct similar basketball clinics in Senegal and in four additional countries: Mali, Guinea, Ivory Coast, and Liberia. Except for Liberia the countries were French speaking ex-colonies of France. I could practice my French.

Our landing at the airport in Dakar, the capital of Senegal was memorable because it reminded me of a novel I'd recently read called *The Ugly American*, the theme of which I was not entirely ready to believe about my adopted country. What followed our arrival changed my mind. When we stopped at the gate and the door opened, a rush of humid air introduced the Senegalese custom officer, a smartly uniformed man, his skin the color of ebony, tribal scars on his cheeks. In precise Parisian French, he explained where passengers should go and what they must do once inside the terminal to clear customs. An American traveler standing in the aisle next to me, a businessman I presumed, nudged me, and said, "I didn't know these people spoke French."

K.C., standing on the other side of him must have heard it that way as well, as he gave the guy a sour look. "Yeah," I said, "How many languages do you speak?" I don't think he got my meaning, which was you are one dumb fuck.

The infamous slave prison from colonial days was located on the island of Goree, two km at sea from the harbor of Dakar. There, African slaves were kept in cells awaiting ships to take them to the Americas. K.C., John and I were given a tour of the prison, and I could see that K.C. was shaken by the still visible obscenity of manacles and handprints on the walls. Imprinted on one wall was a child's hand with two adult hands on either side, probably the mother and father, perhaps older brothers or sisters. It brought tears to K.C.'s eyes. K.C. said it was probable that one of his ancestors had suffered in this prison. As a white man, I could think of no response except respectful silence. John kept shaking his head. I could see he too was deeply moved and disgusted by this evil.

Although there was no reason for me to feel ashamed - the slavers and slave holders were not my descendants - I couldn't help but feel that every Caucasian far into the future would be left with the aftertaste of this rotten fruit.

The president of Senegal was Leopold Sedar Senghor, known not only as a politician but also as an important poet in the Negritude Poetic Movement which I would study later in my life in graduate school. I had already written a few poems that had appeared in an article in the sports section of the Philadelphia *Inquirer*. I remember wondering if being a poet was an asset for a president.

• • •

Years after I had retired, I was teaching *To Kill a Mockingbird* to my freshman English class and was reminded of President Senghor's words that white people needed to put on a black skin to "get the living feel of the black man's situation," or as Atticus Finch in the novel advised his daughter, Scout, to walk in another man's shoes.

• • •

Among the populations of the West African countries, we visited there were Lebanese, Arabs, and Asians, but very few whites, and those were leftover Frenchmen from Colonial days. It didn't take me long to discover what being a minority felt like. I never asked John how he felt. As for K.C., I caught him smiling at us when he didn't think we were looking. It was not condescension, but more like *he knew*.

In our travels from country to country, we were shocked by the lack of equipment and the rudimentary playing conditions of the courts. Some of the youngsters (boys and girls from ages ten to young adults) played without shoes, and the players with shoes mostly played without socks. Because there were no indoor courts, tropical weather affected time and duration of practices. In Senegal, which borders the Sahara, practices started early in the morning because the afternoons were too hot for strenuous physical activity. Further south, closer to the equator, the same hot conditions prevailed, but the afternoons at that time of the year brought tropical rainstorms, so heavy that the basketball courts would still be soaked the following morning and the players warmed up by brooming the water off the playing surface before we could practice.

In all the countries, the players were eager to learn. We had been told that the French introduced basketball to their colonies, something I found amusing, perhaps because I had a hard time imagining the French playing sports. Chefs and poets, okay, but not athletes. *Apologies to all French athletes, but that was my prejudice back then.* I had in my possession a small pamphlet entitled *Le Basket* that provided me with all the basketball terminology in French. *1. Jump shot = Shot en Suspension. 2. Hook shot = Bras roule.* They made sense to me as images, but K.C. and John laughed when I explained. *Shooting while suspended in air; the rolling motion of the arm.*

K.C. Jones and John Havlicek, my opponents during the NBA season, quickly became my friends. The African players liked K.C. right away, not only because he was black, but because he was gregarious and had an infectious sense of humor. John was more reserved, but so knowledgeable about the game and such a thoughtful teacher that he rapidly became known as *Monsieur L'Entraineur*, Mister Coach. They never called me coach, which makes me wonder today what those kids knew I should have known about my future coaching posts Often the younger kids had fun with my name, "Ma Cherieeee, Ma Cherieeee," they would chant and dance around, waving their arms in the air like helicopter blades. Like my name, my French language proficiency was the source of much amusement. I received compliments on my pronunciation, but was informed I needed some work on determining what was masculine and feminine. Some of the older guys turned my gender mistakes into a ribald joke. Several times I was asked if I knew the difference between past and present. I hoped that they meant the tense and not life. All in all, I managed by not worrying about being correct, figuring I could make up for it with body language. I might have gained some cred, however, for striking out on my own, exploring the local neighborhoods and downing a beer or two at the street bars, and on occasion, sampling the street food

On one of my outings, at a local market in Dakar, I asked two Tuaregs if I could take a photograph of them. Tuaregs are called the Blue People because of the indigo dyed robes they wear that stain their skin. They are a fierce and handsome people. It was impertinent of me, but what I saw were two warriors out of my childhood memory of stories in the Arabian Nights. Today, I would have asked to have a selfie with them, and they, being of a more techno educated generation of Tuaregs, probably would have been cool with the request and asked to have me text them copies so they could put it on their Facebook page, These Nineteen-Sixty variety waved me angrily away. Considering the swords dangling from their belts I did not pursue my request.

My collection of West African objet d'art began with that 1964 trip. After three separate coaching assignments in West Africa, there are a number of masks, half a Dogon door, a bridal spoon, and a bronze smoking pipe, which hang on our office walls. One rug, the center of which was leopard skin surrounded by black monkey fur hung in my high school classroom office for years. A student shamed me into taking it down, pointing out that the monkey fur came from a species that was endangered.

From Senegal, the three of us traveled to Mali. We coached primarily in the capital, Bamako, but traveled by boat northeast up the Niger River to the City of Segou for two days of clinics. If we'd continued north another couple of hundred miles, we'd have wound up at Timbuktu. I wish we had, as the name is often used to represent all things on the outer limits of life on the planet. I have always been interested in "outer limits." As an old man I guess I'll find out soon enough.

We flew from Mali to Guinea and settled into our hotel in Conakry, the capital of the country. The following day, we were driven to the practice site. On the way we drove past the harbor where a number of the docks were filled with snow plows. *Snow plows?*

GUINEA

On the way to basketball practice
our driver takes us past the docks
where he points to snowplows,

hundreds of them, lined up in rows
gray, rusting and useless. He laughs
and says, *regardez* what the Russians
send us. You Americans send us
basketball players. There is no snow
in our country, and all our children
play football. He flicks his cigarette
out the window. I do not understand
the ways of your governments.

Meschery, Tom. "Guinea," *Nothing We Lose Can Be Replaced*, Black
Rock Press, Rain Shadow Edition, 1999. University of Nevada,
Reno. Reno, NV

Like their northern brethren in Mali, Guineans became engaged and
enthusiastic devotees of the game of basketball. K.C. announced, "One day
there are going to be basketball players from Africa playing in the NBA."

"Maybe in a hundred years," John said.

It took only 17 years before a young six-foot-eleven Nigerian, Hakeem
Olajuwon, enrolled at the University of Houston. He would go on to play
in the NBA and lead the Houston Rockets to back-to-back championships.
He is now enshrined in basketball's Hall of Fame.

From time to time while watching a Houston Rockets game on TV,
the camera finds Olajuwon, dignified, graying slightly at the temples,
sitting in the first row observing and enjoying, and perhaps recalling
the two NBA Championships he helped his team win. Like me, he is a
naturalized citizen of the United States. *After a recent rant by President
Trump about African countries being shit hole countries, I read where
Olajuwon stated what Trump said was beneath the dignity of a president.
Beneath the dignity of any decent human being I thought. Olajuwon does
not sound as angry as I am, but then the 6'11" Nigerian is more dignified
than the Mad Manchurian.*

• • •

In the center of the square in Conakry, there is a statue commemorating
their country's independence from France. On the base of the statue is
inscribed the following words: *Pour Nos Soldats qui Tombait Pendant La*

Revolution. (For our soldiers who fell during The Revolution.) We were told by one of our embassy people this was a slight exaggeration as there was only one recorded death during the time the French left Guinea, and that occurred during the celebration when a bullet fired into the air returned to earth striking a person on the head. This sounded to me suspiciously like white man's fiction, but a member of the embassy assured me it was true.

Conakry sits at the tip of a peninsula. Our hotel faced a beach of palm trees and soft curling waves, dugouts and longer fishing boats lined up on the palm strewn shore, their hulls colorfully painted red, blue or yellow. At dinner time, fishermen would bring a basket of freshly caught fish onto the porch, and we could choose from their catch. The hotel chef would then cook the red snapper, called a *rouge* in French, and serve it to us with *pommes frites* – wedges of heavily salted potatoes baked crispy on the outside, soft on the inside. Avocados and mangos the size of nerf footballs would accompany the fish. I even came to enjoy the taste of *Fou F*ou, boiled cassava mixed with plantain and pounded into a dough, served smothered in *pili pili* sauce that should have come with a warning, *If you think Mexican hot sauce is hot, you haven't tasted the African variety.* KC and John tried it, but only once. There was a local beer. While waiting for our meals to arrive, a gin and tonic kept me company. I was also acquiring a taste for Gitanes, a French cigarette made with a dark, extra strength tobacco.

Liberia was next on our schedule. John and K.C. were happy to finally be able to coach without a translator. Liberia, we learned, was a country invented by the United States under President James Monroe, the purpose of which was to ship back to Africa all our slaves. Thank God that President was not completely successful, but many shiploads of slaves were transported to the territory that the United States had purchased for the establishment of a new country. The slaves named the country Liberty, and the capital, Monrovia after the U.S. President Monroe. Ironically, history records that upon arrival in their new land, the returned American slaves immediately enslaved the indigenous people and continued to dominate the government until an army coup led by Sergeant Doe toppled the regime on April 12, 1980.

The Liberians tried to scare us with stories of juju and leopard societies. *Do not go out at night, the leopards will get you.* While the Liberians might have been joking with us, there is no question that the general population of Liberians believed in witches. We witnessed a soccer match between two Monrovian club teams. One of the club teams forfeited the game because they were certain that their opponents had hired a witch to cast a spell against them. I was also entertained one night over beers in the hotel bar by a colonel in the army who related a story of one of the soldiers in his command who'd had his leg crushed badly during maneuvers by a tank. Instead of being taken to the hospital, he demanded to be taken back to his village. The colonel was positive the soldier would never walk again. Two weeks later, according to my storyteller, the soldier was standing in front of him, saluting and requesting to return to duty. His leg showed no sign of injury. *Village healers or magic?* In the history of the Firestone Rubber Company plantation, no native Liberian ever died after being bitten by a green mamba that lived in the rubber trees. This was not true for the American and European administrators who were bitten. The bite of the mamba is fast acting and usually lethal.

• • •

In Liberia, I fell in love with Enid Buchanan, a member of the Liberian women's basketball team, and the daughter of the Secretary of the Treasury. I'm uncertain that I can describe Enid's beauty accurately. After so many years, I'd be tempted to exaggerate. As I recall that night, our meeting sounds like a scene out of a movie. I have written this scene a number of different times in my mind.

The night is balmy, as are most nights in Equatorial Africa. The moon is full, the view from the balcony opens onto the beach, waves sweeping onto the sand, palm trees rustling in an Atlantic breeze. Enid is leaning back against the railing, a silhouette against the moonlight. I walk toward her. Up close, her skin is the color of ripe plums. She is wearing a red, black and green long wrap-around skirt and loose top. A traditional woman's head wrap of the same colors covers her hair. Her features are African, broad cheekbones, and full lips. Her eyes are light gray, with hints of sparkling green. We are face to face. She looks at me, expecting me to say something. I'm too stunned to speak.

I had never dated a black woman. I remember the thought entering my mind and just as quickly departing. I must have been staring because I remember she said, "What?" Would she dance with me? I asked her, and she accepted. By the end of the dance, I couldn't think of any reason why

I couldn't fall in love with her. My African travel scrapbook contains only one photograph of Enid. *I am certain I had more.* We are dancing the twist.

For the rest of my week in Liberia, Enid and I were inseparable. We made plans. She would travel to the United States. I promised her an engagement ring. We would marry. It would be difficult being an inter-racial couple; we understood that, but we thought of ourselves as strong-minded people. It *was* the Sixties, times were "a-changin'" Dylan reminded us. Many years later recalling the coup that brought down the Liberian government, I wrote this poem for my first collection of poetry about Enid.

MONROVIA

For Enid Buchanan

I remember thinking back that this was a country
of hotdog stands and transistor radios playing
rock and roll, and that the palm trees must have been
imported from Los Angeles, and the tin roofs
were like umbrellas over a beach of slums,
with open sewers, and the streetlights in Monrovia
worked only if the spirit moved them and evil spirits
were at work to make the poor poorer and the rich richer.

But, what the hell, I was young and in love
in this land of poverty with one of the rich girls,
with a beautiful set-shot, who played on the Women's
National Basketball Team. Her house was like Tara
in *Gone With The Wind*, white pillars, wrap-around
veranda. Her father was the Secretary of the Treasury.
Much later, back in the States, already retired
from the NBA, I read that her father had been shot
along with others by Sergeant Doe and his gang.
I refused to believe she too had been shot,

so I told myself that she'd escaped and was living
in Switzerland on the money her father had embezzled
from his poor country and that she was still beautiful.

Meschery, Tom. "Monrovia," *Nothing We Lose Can Be Replaced*,
Black Rock Press, Rain Shadow Edition, 1999. University of Nevada, Reno. Reno, NV

The last country on our tour was Cote D'Ivoire. Because it was an oil
producer, it was the richest nation that we visited. In Abidjan, the Capital,
we stayed in the luxury high-rise Hotel Ivoire. The restaurant and cocktail
lounge overlooked a huge swimming pool. In the hotel area were tree-
lined boulevards and outdoor cafes. Their national team trained in an
indoor arena. The Ivorian players had uniforms and Converse shoes. Their
skills were more advanced than the players of the previous countries we'd
coached in, but as I recall they played with less enthusiasm and were not
as eager to be coached. I found myself thinking it was time to go home.

After our last practice, the Ivorian coaches took us to the *Boule Noir*,
The Black Ball, a nightclub in one of the local neighborhoods. K.C. brought
the house down with his interpretation of Nat King Cole, and I spent
most of the night dancing the samba with an African maiden, who kept
whispering the various prices she'd charge Le Tres Grand American for
specific pleasures of the flesh. The experience reminded me of waiters in
restaurants explaining the evening specials. I decided not to place an order.

Enid and my engagement and marriage plans never came to pass.

CHAPTER 21
IF WILT CHAMBERLAIN CAN BE TRADED ANYBODY CAN

There were no untouchable players in the NBA. That was the message understood by all the players in the league after the 1965 All Star Game when the Warriors' owner Franklin Miuli traded Wilt Chamberlain to the Philadelphia 76ers, the new name for the relocated Syracuse Nationals. The reason generally accepted was that the Warriors were suffering financial difficulties and Franklin wanted to get rid of Wilt's huge contract. I was sorry to see Wilt go, but he was going home to Philly. As for basketball, I wasn't overly concerned because we had second-year potential super-star 6'11" Nate Thurmond to replace Wilt. Thurmond was already making a name for himself as a power forward, but his true position was clearly center. It would be a position that would earn him the title Nate, The Great and membership in Basketballs' Hall of Fame, the only NBA player ever to record a quadruple double. The trade didn't turn out well. Lee Schaffer. a versatile forward with a fine shooting touch, was the key player in the trade. He retired rather than come West, giving up a promising future in the NBA for a career in his father-in-law's business.

It reminds me that Phil Jackson, coach of the championship Chicago Bulls and Los Angeles Lakers was right when he said that "There is more to basketball than basketball," although I'm certain Phil was being more Zen than my practical interpretation of his words. I was sorry that Lee did not join our team. I admired his game. He and I were on the 1961/62 All-Rookie Team. Together, we would have been a tough combo to guard.

We did not make the playoffs that season after Wilt left.

But the next season turned out to be a memorable one. The previous summer, I had met Joanne Pritchard in Squaw Valley where I was coaching kids at the Warriors basketball camp. In the summer of 1965, we were engaged to be married in August, but not before I traveled to West Africa for a second coaching clinic sponsored by the USIA. It is not an exaggeration that both events changed my life dramatically.

BACK TO AFRICA
Summer of 1965

The world through which I travel,
I am endlessly creating myself.
Franz Fanon, author of *The Wretched of the Earth*

CHAPTER 22
COUP D'ETAT

The 1965 summer NBA All-Star Exhibition Tour began in Milan, Italy and ended in Beirut, Lebanon. We would be playing against Teams from Italy, Bulgaria, Greece, Romania, Yugoslavia, and Lebanon. At the conclusion of the exhibition games, I would fly from Beirut to Algiers, the capital of Algeria, to begin my second summer coaching basketball in Africa similar to the one I had done the previous summer, but with an expanded number of countries. I would be teaching with a different NBA partner, Sihugo Green, a guard for the Saint Louis Hawks and one time All-American from Duquesne University.

Basketball in Europe in 1965 was not the popular sport it is today. When we walked the streets of European cities, we drew crowds like we were a circus coming to town. Our elephant was 6-foot-10, Wayne Embry, center for the Cincinnati Royals. (The Royals are now the Sacramento Kings.) The gapping children hovered around Wayne, often trying to touch him to see if that huge body was real. I can attest to his realness, having been on the receiving end of many of his screens set for his teammate, The Big O, Oscar Robinson. I remember once colliding with Embry and found myself on the floor looking up at a wall of muscle. Bricks wouldn't have hurt as much. He was glaring at me. I leaped to my feet, but for once in his life The Mad Manchurian held his temper. As the European kids reached out to touch him, Wayne, a gentle man when not on the court, had nothing but smiles for those curious youngsters.

The owner of the Milan basketball team was also the owner of a winery. He had named one of its red wines after George Mikan, the Hall of Fame center from the Minneapolis Lakers. One of his white wine he named for the legendary Boston Celtic guard, Bob Cousy. *A nice, dry Pinot Grigio.*

After Italy, our team traveled to Eastern Europe: Yugoslavia (Croatia and Serbia), Bulgaria, Rumania, and Greece. I had never traveled to the Soviet Union because my mother feared for my life, but I got a good idea what it might be like while in Bulgaria. We were escorted everywhere in the city of Sophia, the silent, gray, and ominous capital, by an interpreter and at least two other sinister looking men and women, equally gray and joyless, never the same two, whom I assumed were the Bulgarian version of the Soviet KGB. They never smiled. It was creepy. I kept hearing my mother's voice: *They will arrest you and never let you leave.* I was seeing the KGB around every corner. When I think back, I believe I was frightened, but not panicking. As an American citizen and a member of an NBA tour, I had no need to fear. The images of secret police, brutal murders, gulags, unmarked graves my mother instilled in my memory like children's stories, must have never entirely disappeared. I was delighted when we left Bulgaria for Romania and its beaches on the Black Sea and topless European maidens sunbathing, and Tuica, a local plum brandy that I was informed, too late, should only be drunk in moderation.

From country to country, I felt our presence was helping to popularize the sport of basketball. Today, NBA team rosters are filled with players from foreign countries. Italy, France, Serbia, Spain, and many other European countries have sent players to the NBA. It gives me a good feeling to know I was at the forefront of this emerging development. Today, the NBA sponsors *Basketball Without Borders* and a West African professional basketball league. Currently 55 players in the NBA are either from Africa or have parents who are native Africans.

From Romania, our All-Star team flew to Athens for two days and ended our tour in Lebanon. In Beirut I won beaucoup bucks at *rouge et noir,* doubling down on black three straight times and feeling like James Bond. Back then, Beirut was a banking capital with casinos and hotels catering to the wealthy, not the war zone it is today. French was the lingua franca. I spoke enough French to feel comfortable asking for *encore de Heineken, s'il vous plait.*

At the conclusion of our tour, I boarded a flight to Algiers for the second leg of my trip. I was looking forward to going back to Africa but feeling guilty that I had left Joanne in California with all the wedding preparations. As I'd explained to her, I'd signed the contract with the United States Information Agency before I had proposed to her and couldn't back out without risking the displeasure of the NBA league office, damaging my chances for future coaching overseas. She understood. *I hoped.*

In Algiers, the capital of Algeria, I would meet Sihugo Green, my NBA traveling partner for the African leg of the trip that included the sub-Saharan country of Guinea.

Si and I conducted a number of basketball clinics in Algiers and played in a game against the Algerian National Team. To round out our team, we were joined by some guys from the Peace Corps who'd played high school and college ball. One of the Peace Corps guys, Chris Appel, was a guard on the USC team against whom I played in college. Si and I called him our ringer. We defeated the Algerian Nationals soundly. The following day's newspaper reported that three stars of the National Team hadn't played, due to illness, making it clear that their absence was the reason we Americans won. Face-saving, we were told by somebody at the Embassy. I had no way of knowing if such a generalization was true, but in a couple of later games, the same thing happened, the best player on the Algerian team conveniently happened to be injured and could not play against us. I wished the best player could have played against us. We both could have learned something from the experience.

The owner of a team we'd played against treated Si and me to lunch at his ranch, which was located in a fertile valley of orchards and alfalfa fields south of the capital. I do not remember his name or very much what he looked like except that he was taller than me and very thin. He was French, but a third-generation Algerian citizen referred to by the Arab locals as *Pieds-Noirs* (Black-Feet) They were usually disliked. My political consciousness was not raised at that time, but that summer I walked into the home of a pied-noir rancher and thought, now this is the way to live.

I'm in a Scheherazade garden of palm trees and fruit trees. Lemons and oranges hang from branches like Christmas ornaments. In the center of the garden stands a fountain built of mosaic tiles, the water arching into the air and cascading into a sparkling pool. Flowers of all varieties grow in bright ceramic pots. The estate itself is surrounded by Gunga Din-type adobe walls with an iron gate that could withstand an army.

His ranch has been in his family for three generations, he explains. The house is filled with antique furniture. The billiard room has both a billiard table and a pool table. The walls are covered by several different heads of some species of African antelope. There is a head of a leopard and what looks like a goat with horns like corkscrews. I fall in love with the kitchen with its gleaming copper pots and pans hanging from the ceiling within easy reach of the cook who, in my imagination, is Chef Meschery, recent graduate of Le Cordon Bleu, with apologies to my Aunt Maroucia.

The second floor of that lovely old building is all French doors opening onto balconies with grand vistas of farmland and orchards. And beyond those rich fields lay the unseen and seething Moslem slums. As I looked out over those fields, I had no idea how soon the landscape of Algeria would change.

Standing in that sparkling state-of-the-art kitchen, I was reminded that when I was a boy, my very dignified Aunt Marusia had nearly fainted when I announced that I was going to be a chef. In her mind, she was probably thinking of a short-order cook flipping burgers. She might have been okay with the NBA had she lived to see me in my uniform. And she might have cut me some slack if I'd turned out to be like the French chef who created Beef Stroganoff.

Si and I are treated to a traditional Algerian meal served on a round copper tray that could have been an ancient shield. A mound of couscous and raisins covers the tray upon which rests half a roasted lamb with grilled vegetables surrounding it. We eat in the garden, sitting in a circle on cushions around the table, gathering the food into our mouths, using only the left hand as is the custom and soaking up the juices with flatbread. I am back to my days reading adventure novels. At any moment Rudyard Kipling will appear. It occurs to me that I am a character in a novel that I'm writing about myself. We are offered cold beer or pomegranate juice. Si won't eat with his hands, so they give him a spoon. He eats sparingly. All the way back to our hotel in Algiers, I can't stop talking about the meal and house. The cook had given me the recipes. In my head I'm planning my future kitchen. Si complains of a stomach ache. There was nothing wrong with my stomach, but I had traveled in Africa and was used to the food. I was l already imagining Meschery the Chef using these recipes when he returned to San Francisco.

At the start of our trip, I'd asked Si, who'd played for the Saint Louis Hawks at the same time my friend Fred LaCour was on the team, why Fred had been cut. He just shook his head. "Saint Louis," he said and refused to elaborate. Sihugo was not an elaborating kind of guy. You could hardly call our communications conversations. By the time we left Algeria, aside from discussion about basketball, I knew little about my traveling partner, other than he'd been an All-American at Duquesne University and played for the Hawks. He was a character, one of the many I have met in my life. A number of nights I woke up to see Si sitting on the opposite bed, staring into the dark, smoking, the tip of his cigarette glowing on and off like some distant streetlight. It was unsettling to me.

Our coaching assignment took us a couple of hundred miles to the south-east of Algiers to the city of Constantine where we visited the ruins of the Roman city of the same name. On the morning following our welcoming banquet, Si and I stepped out of our hotel to walk to the office of the United States Information Agency where we were to meet one of the city's basketball coaches. The streets were deserted. A tank guarded by several armed soldiers stood on the corner. We continued walking. More tanks, more soldiers. It occurred to me that the USIA office might not be the best place to be. Si agreed, and we reversed course and returned to our hotel. In the lobby we were told that a coup had taken place during the night and the reigning government of Ahmed Ben Bella had been overthrown by the Army led by General Houari Boumediene. We waited half the day before we were told we could leave and return to Algiers. We were driven by an Algerian soldier in an open jeep with our escort, an American USIA employee. We were stopped numerous times at roadblocks to have our passports inspected. The closer we got to the capital the surlier the soldiers became. At the last roadblock, Si and I were ordered to step out of the jeep. Our suitcases were searched. The soldier patting me down was not gentle. Was I frightened? I must have been, at least a little, but I was under the impression back then that being an American would keep us safe.

When we arrived at the capital, we were informed that the national airport was closed. All foreign residents would have to be patient. No time frame for departure was offered. Si and I stayed mostly in our room, me reading, Si smoking. Considering how much he smoked, Si kept to a physical fitness regimen. Denied the outdoors for his morning runs, he jogged the halls of the hotel. When he asked me to join him, I declined. Excessive physical fitness was not my thing. And never was. Throughout my career I did my conditioning on the basketball court.

In the square outside our hotel, the protests went on for days and nights. The protestors were mostly students who favored the more liberal government of Ben Bella versus the strict Islamist regime proposed by the Army of General Boumediene. The students gathered, slogans were shouted over bullhorns, speeches were given. From my hotel balcony, it was hard to hear what they were saying, but I managed to pick out words like education, human rights, independence, and religious freedom. Trucks filled with soldiers arrived accompanied by water tankers. We watched from our hotel balcony as the students were being hosed to the ground. Pummeled by water, their bodies were tossed end over end until the soldiers carried them off like wet laundry to huge gray windowless vans. I felt sick to my stomach as I watched soldiers crush those innocent heads. It was a kind of violence that seemed completely unnecessary. What possible harm could these kids do if they were simply allowed to march and speak?

On the second evening of the protest marches in Algiers, a bullet sizzled past our heads and struck the hotel wall behind us. Si decided his bed would be a safer place to be. I continued watching from behind the window curtain, my view restricted, but the cruelty of the soldiers was disgustingly visible. I thought the students were extremely brave; the soldiers would drag away a number of students and more would arrive to take their place even though they knew that they would be hosed, beaten, arrested and possibly killed. I began to recognize a few of the protestors, or at least I thought I did. One young woman wearing a Red Crescent armband kept avoiding the fury of the water cannons, darting in between soldiers and protesters to attend to the fallen injured. I named her Florence Nightingale. I prayed that she'd survive. When I saw a soldier raise his rifle and shoot a young boy attempting to throw a rock, I knew that something inside me had changed.

At the time I could not imagine this kind of authoritarian violence happening in the United States. That is not the case any longer as the television screens fill up with Black Lives Matter protests.

● ● ●

After the third day of protests the airport opened, and Si and I flew to our next stop, Conakry, Guinea. We were booked into the same hotel in Conakry in which KC, John and I stayed the previous summer. After practices, I welcomed the wide veranda, the view of the palm strewn beach, the fishermen and their boats. Si preferred spending his free time on the Ship Hope that was docked in the Conakry harbor, hanging out with the American sailors. Maybe he felt safer there after our experience in Algeria.

I found myself once again hanging out by myself. I loved strolling down the streets, stopping at stalls selling everything from music records, soft drinks, clothing. There were the ubiquitous cigarette and matches stalls and the street food stalls selling their culinary wares that my curiosity dared me to try, the most exotic of which was *Chitoum*, beetles whose innards had been squeezed out and their shells roasted and seasoned with salt and pepper. They were crunchy and delicious. I thought it was West Africa's version of American potato chips.

It didn't take me long before I was back again sitting in a wicker chair with a gin and tonic watching the sunset and surf, the warm breeze from the Atlantic blowing over me, waiting for my *rouge* to be grilled. I was back channeling Humphry Bogart in *Casablanca*.

Si admitted he found it difficult to deal with the poverty. How can they live like this, he'd ask. I wondered why Si wanted to hang out with the African-American sailors when he could have been exploring Africa. I remember wondering if Si would look back and see the time as a lost opportunity to know more about Africa and his roots.

The elevators still didn't work. Our hotel room was on the seventh floor. I'd have a hard time at my present age and physical condition making it up those stairs three or four times a day. I was in NBA physical shape, so up and down I went, *pas de problem*. As much as I remember the basketball and the people of Guinea, I remember the rainstorms that blew in from the Atlantic in the evenings. It was June, and West Africa's monsoon season. The lightning from one of those storms struck the balcony outside my room one night and knocked me out of bed. I lay on the floor encased in mosquito netting like a cocoon, unsure what had happened to me. I have experienced rainstorms all over America, but the monsoon rains of Africa buckets you, drenches you through to skin and bones. The winds that accompany an African rain, if you are unfortunate enough to be caught outdoors, will buffet you off your feet. Man oh man, how those storms fascinated me. "*C'est manifique, n'est ce pas?*" one of the waiters asked me as I watched raindrops, the size of water balloons splash the windows of the restaurant. It was as if the rain was alive. I loved West Africa.

It's been decades since I've been there. I want to go back. Melanie says I'm too old, she reminds me, what if I got sick. I would call a Liberian native healer. It would not bother me if he or she would be called a witch.

Guinea was experiencing the peace of post-colonialism, which might be best described as shared poverty. What the Guineans lacked in material wealth, I quickly discovered they made up in *joi-de-vivre*. After Algeria, it caused my spirit to soar. The poorest country appeared to be the happiest. I had not read Chinua Achebe's *Things Fall Apart*. If I had, I might have sensed traditional African society already beginning to crumble. But that summer I was as much caught up in the post-colonial optimism as the Guineans were.

What kind of basketball players were the Guineans? A little bit better than the summer before, but not ready for U.S. colleges.

I returned to the United States, looking forward to being a family man. I figured my off-season trips to Africa would be over. But I was mistaken, my relationship with Africa did not end. I would coach there one more time.

CHAPTER 23
RICK BARRY COMETH

In August of 1965, back from Africa, I married Joanne Pritchard, a high school home economics teacher whom I had met the previous summer while I was coaching at the Warriors' Squaw Valley Basketball Camp, and she was working for one of the resorts in the valley. Because her father was a Methodist minister, we tied the knot at his church in San Leandro. My mother had originally been disappointed that we would not be married in the richly ornate and symbolic ceremony of the Orthodox Church. My mother finally managed to work out a narrative that since the missionaries in our internment camp were all Methodist, I was destined to be married to a Methodist woman and be married in a Methodist Church. All her life, as far as I could remember, my mom, Maria Vladmirovna Mescheriakova, adjusted her circumstances by inventing a story that fit her view and beliefs in her world

After the ceremony, Joanne and I left the church for a flight to Hawaii for our honeymoon. I prevailed upon her to stop at a local tavern where my friends were continuing the festivities, given that the wedding reception, being a Methodist one, had been dry. *How can you blame a bunch of beer guzzling jocks?* I'm reasonably sure Joanne was not pleased with that pit stop. I thought it was perfectly natural.

On December 24, 1966, our first child was born, a baby girl we named Janai. In Chinese, Janai means *One Who Loves*. The quietest baby in the world has turned into the most loquacious.

The 1965/66 basketball season was an improvement over the year before. Our year-end record was 35 and 45. We didn't qualify for the playoffs, but as we prepared to leave for the off season, we were in good spirits. There is a saying in sport: To check all the boxes. A team that checks all the boxes has all of the characteristics to compete. By strength, size, speed, skills, at every position, all the Warriors' boxes were checked. The two most important boxes filled were the center box that belonged to Nate Thurmond and the newly arrived box at forward that belonged to our first-round draft choice, Rick Barry. The other forward box checked was me, at the power position as the rookie Barry had clearly assumed the responsibility of the principal team scorer. The starting guard boxes were Guy Rodgers and Al Attles. The addition of Fred Hetzel, our other first round draft choice (the Warriors had two that year) and Keith Erickson in the second round plus other reserves Paul Neumann and McCoy McLemore filled out a roster that was finally competitive. From training camp, we all felt the excitement. Coach Hannum must have had to because the training camp was particularly intense even by Hannum's maniacal standard. Was he the coach?

There have been plenty of stories written about my temper on the basketball court, most of them I am not proud of. However, I was recently reminded of one incident from our 1965 training camp that I confess I enjoy revisiting from time to time. It was summed up in an excerpt from a Sports Illustrated article written about our Coach Alex Hannum after he retired from coaching. He was being questioned about Rick Barry, but the excerpt was really about me.

"Of all the rookies I ever saw break in, Rick Barry was the most special. It was something to remember, that first day as a Warrior, when he scrimmaged against

Tom Meschery, whom we called 'the Mad Manchurian.' After a while they were going after each other and ignoring everyone else. I was refereeing and I let a Barry basket go on a dubious play, but then I whistled a charging foul on Meschery when he came through Barry like the Normandy Invasion. Meschery went into a rage. It was so bad

I had to rearrange things so they were no longer guarding each other. But as soon as

Tom got the ball again, Barry left his new man, picked Meschery up, and stole the ballas he blocked the shot. Meschery was so enraged I had to call off the whole practice."

Many years later at one of the Golden State Warriors Championship Parades, I was reminiscing with Rick about this clash we had in his first training camp. He told me that Alex had it wrong. He'd been the one who'd come through me like the Normandy Invasion. I will allow those readers who will remember the way the two of us played to judge which version is most likely. I *do* remember telling Alex after that practice, "Coach, that kid, Barry's going to be a great." Considering that Rick Barry is enshrined in the basketball's Hall of Fame, my prediction was spot on. I didn't pass on this information to Rick at the parade. Why add more fuel to his already bonfire ego?

The rechristening from Mad Manchurian to Mad Russian came later. Part of it might have had to do with my habit of yelling at referees in Russian. If I lashed out at opponents, I did not spare the refs if I felt they made a wrong call. My temper began to cost me money. League fines in the Sixties were around Twenty-five to fifty dollars. (Today's fines for committing flagrant fouls or verbally abusing referees are approximately ten to twenty grand.) My checkbook was taking a hit. Knowing that my own personality would not suddenly turn docile, I got the bright idea of yelling at the referees in Russian. Who would know? It was a good strategy because the refs could not understand the Russian word, *sukin syn* (son-of-a-bitch in English) or the other Russian pejoratives that followed. For a while, it worked. I swore gleefully, sometimes smiling. My Russian experiment came to an end when Mindy Rudolph, the very senior and savvy NBA referee, after I yelled at him, squinted his eyes thoughtfully, smirked and gave me a T. I remember him saying something like this to me: "I don't understand Russian, Tom, but I don't like the way you're saying it." Word spread from referee to referee that if number 14 of the San Francisco Warriors spoke to them in any foreign language in an abusive tone, he would be assessed a technical foul. Years later, after I had become a teacher, I told this story to my creative writing students as an example of the importance of tone in their fiction.

I wish I could say I stopped verbally abusing the referees. I wish I could say they didn't deserve it. Some of them, at least. Occasionally I find myself back in time abusing the referees from my seat in front of the television set watching a game on NBA League Pass.

The adjective Mad that introduced Manchurian most likely had to do with my first-strike philosophy. When I think about how I played the game of basketball, full throttle, seat of my pants, turning fouling into an art form, I suppose I earned the sobriquet. At one time, Melanie, had been engaged in conversation in the parking lot of our local Safeway with a man who'd seen us together and recognized me. When Mel said I was her husband, the man offered this description of me, "He was one of the meanest sonovbitches I ever saw play."

I take exception to the word, mean. That implies a desire to harm, which was never my intention. I am over 80 years old and remain puzzled about my violent behavior on the basketball court. In what part of me did this anger originate? Did it have something to do with the self-conscious Russian immigrant part of my psyche that had me believing that the playing field was never equal for me? Was this the chip I carried on my shoulder into each game? Why was it only on the basketball court? Did the game give me permission to express my anger? Should I have considered anger management counseling? I have yet to answer these questions satisfactorily.

How is it that in the 24 years of teaching high school, I do not remember any time that I ever raised my voice in anger at my students?

Well, maybe a couple of times, but I was provoked. *Teenagers, you know.*

CHAPTER 24
MY BEST AND LAST SEASON
AS A WARRIOR

By the end of the 1966/67 Warriors training camp, we knew we would compete for an NBA Championship. It was not bragging; we did not take our opponents lightly. In the summer we were shocked to learn that Franklin Miuli, our owner, fired our coach Alex Hannum and hired Bill Sharman, the ex-Boston Celtic. There was no reason given for firing Alex that satisfied me. But there were rumors about a relationship between owner and coach that had soured, something to do with a shared interest in a certain woman. An *"Affaire de Coeur"* I thought. Romance has always interested me. In September the Warriors traded our star guard Guy Rodgers to the Chicago Bulls for Jeff Mullins and Jimmy King, two guards with very high skills that were not stars yet but only because they'd not had the minutes on the court. Mullins became an indispensable starter and Jimmy provided seamless back up. Al Attles, The Destroyer, remained at the other guard position. That season, Nate became The Great. We lost 37 games, but we won 44 and won the Western Conference by beating the Saint Louis Hawks. Need I say any more about my emotions in the locker after that final win, sucking on a cold one, a wide grin on my face. By then, the players, who'd made my friend Fred LaCour's life miserable, were no longer playing for the Hawks, but it didn't matter to me - the Hawks were still the Hawks. During that final game the fans in Saint Louis threw Snickers Bars onto the court because our star forward, Rick Barry, had made a commercial for the candy. I rarely ate candy and still don't, but if I do, my favorite is Snickers. I wish I could say that those Snickers aimed at our heads had something to do for my future candy preference. Who knows it might have. But it is the kind of detail that enlivens a story and stories were already a big part of my life.

For the NBA Championship, our opponent would be the winner of the Eastern Conference, the Philadelphia 76ers. As irony would dictate, the Sixers were coached by Alex Hannum and led by our ex-teammate, Wilt, The Stilt, Chamberlain. It is one of many ironies I've experienced in my life, which leads me to believe that the principle of irony governs most human behavior. One must learn how to deal with such often inexplicable twists and turns. When I was teaching, I made sure my students could recognize irony in the literature they were reading and was a frequent topic of class discussion.

• • •

It's the fifth game for the NBA Championship. The Warriors are playing in Philadelphia. We're down 3 to 1 in the series. We have been told that the 76ers management has cases of champagne in the locker room waiting to celebrate their victory tonight. For most of the game, the two giants, Wilt Chamberlain and Nate Thurmond battle, but by the start of the fourth quarter the 76ers are pulling away. We're down 96 to 84 and the 76ers look to be on their way to their locker-room and champagne. Coming out of our first time out, the ball is in my hands. I shoot from the top of the key and it drops - swish, then from different places on the court, another and another shot, nothing but net. It is an unspoken rule in the NBA, when a player is hot, his teammates feed him the ball. I am on fire and the ball comes my way time after time. I am in the zone, that remarkable surreal, miraculous place in sports in which everything goes right. There is no thinking, there just is. This is how basketball was for me.

By the middle of the fourth quarter, I had swished our team back into contention. From that point on, my teammates took over and we won. There would be no champagne corks popping in the 76ers' locker room that evening. On the flight home, my friend Bill King, our play-by-play broadcaster, and I found ourselves sitting in the first-class section drinking champagne. Teams did not travel first class back then, let alone fly in private jets as they do these days, so I have no idea how we wound up in first class seats. That win inspired several toasts. I was high on my success. No drug or booze could have made me any higher. I remember Bill often repeating about the night's game that I was hot. Many years later, remembering that game in Philadelphia and similar games in which I was smoking hot, I wrote this poem.

AUTO DA FE

I remember the game. I was on fire.
Shot after shot dropped.

Someone yelled from the stands I was hot.
I yelled *pass me the fucking ball.*

On the next move I burned my opponent
and scored. I was like those birthday candles,

the ones with the flames that never go out.
The arena was filling up with smoke.

Fans were holding handkerchiefs over their noses.
In the distance I could hear sirens.

I was too hot to care, I was reckless
like a kid playing with matches.

It was only a game of basketball,
but I would not recant the story of my life.

If you tried to stop me,
I'd just add more fuel to the fire.

Meschery, Tom. "Auto Da Fe," *Clear Path*. Random Lane Press, 2022. Sacramento, CA

Bill and I became loud, and a little drunk. Our assistant coach George Lee had to come up from second class to tell us to cool it. We landed at San Francisco International airport to a crowd of well-wishers cheering and waving Warrior banners. One of my favorite photographs is from the front page of the morning sports page of Rick, Nate, and me in the terminal, Nate in the middle with his porkpie hat and Rick and I on either side. Rick is holding his baby son, Scooter, and I am holding my baby daughter, Janai. My daughter looks terrified. I look like I have a hangover.

Sadly, we did not win the sixth game and the season ended. The Sixers finally got their champagne. That game would be the last game I played as a San Francisco Warrior.

SEATTLE SUPER SONICS
1967 - 1971

CHAPTER 25
SOUTH KOREA TO SEATTLE

In 1967, the fifth and last losing game of that NBA Championship was going to be the last game of my professional basketball career. Unbeknownst to the Warriors' ownership, coaches, and my fellow teammates, I had made plans to retire at the end of the season and take a position as the deputy director of the Peace Corps in the Republic of Korea. I would have completed my sixth season, and, despite our success, I felt as if I'd lost my enthusiasm for the game. Part of that had to do with Bill Sharman, our new coach, who I believed had made the game - particularly game preparation - too much like labor. Playing the game should have an element of fun as we practiced and played basketball. I don't know exactly when this shift in attitude toward basketball started. It wasn't that I'd lost my intensity. I was still The Mad Manchurian. It might have had something to do with starting to think about my future beyond basketball. It's likely that the idea of following in my mother's footsteps and being in the diplomatic corps had never left me.

As I reflect on those feelings, I understand why Steve Kerr, the present coach of the Golden State Warriors, stresses the importance of playing with joy. This is particularly true of professional sports with their long season and physical punishment that require some form of light-heartedness to moderate the stress. At the end of the 1967 season, I remember feeling more mentally exhausted than I was physically.

Was my criticism of Bill legitimate? Not entirely. Many of Bill's policies: two-a-day practices and shoot-arounds at noon of game-days are now normal procedure for all NBA teams. There was no video back then or power point, but had there been, Bill would have had us in front of a screen watching. It is understatement to say that Bill was compulsive.

My decision to retire led me to the office of Franklin Mieuli, the owner of the Warriors. He and I had a close owner/player relationship. We were both Bay Area boys who made good. I had to tell him my plans and to suggest a proposal that might make my departure more palatable for him, since I was certain my decision would take him by surprise. That year the NBA was adding two new teams, one in San Diego and the other in Seattle. Each of the present teams in the league would have to place two of their players on a list from which the expansion teams would select to fill out their rosters. I suggested to an unhappy Franklin that, since I was going to retire anyway, he could save one of his players by placing me on the expansion list. Franklin was upset with me, but wished me luck in my future career in international relations. I left Franklin's office confident I'd made the right decision. I would use this Peace Corps position in Korea to jump start my career in the diplomatic corps. *Like mother, like son.*

I returned home and enrolled Joanne and me in a beginner's Korean language course offered at Stanford University. Before the lessons began, the NBA expansion draft took place, and I was selected by the new team in Seattle called the Super Sonics. The team's coach would be Al Bianchi, a retired NBA player and a friend of mine. He called. I told him he had wasted a pick because I was retired. Al asked me how much it would take to un-retire me, something I did not expect. I thought he was joking, so I gave him a ridiculously high number. When he agreed, I remember saying, "You're kidding, right?" He wasn't.

A four-year no-cut contract at more than double what I was making for the Warriors was the price it took for me to *un-retire* myself. Considering the many decisions I've made in my life; I've never satisfactorily figured that one out. Did I return to the NBA because playing for Al meant a return to the joy of the game? That's the answer I'd like to believe, but I fear it would not be entirely truthful. It bothered me that I rejected the Peace Corps. If I hadn't, it might have segued into a Foreign Service career that I had long ago, entering college, planned on. But at the end of four years in Seattle, I would be thirty-one years-old, too old to reasonably take the Foreign Service examination. My guilt at the time about my decision would have lasted longer except that the years I played for the Sonics turned out to be marvelous years.

Joanne and I bought a Cape Cod style home on Mercer Island with a spectacular view of Lake Washington and the skyline of Seattle. Its back lawn was surrounded by blackberry bushes. In the summer the berries invited honeybees and small children with tin buckets. My daughter Megan and son Matthew were born in Seattle.

When we first arrived in Seattle in August of 1967, the sun was shining, perennials were still in bloom. Our backyard was shaded by evergreens, hummingbirds poised over Bee Balm. Comforting breezes came in off Lake Washington. For another two months, the sun continued to shine. I thought how perfect. Then November arrived.

And I changed my mind.

It rained or drizzled or threatened to do both through the first of the year. Someone remarked in one 12-hour period in the Northwest, you can see 12 shades of gray. Then, one morning I woke up with the sun shining into my eyes.

And I changed my mind again.

I had conducted a basketball clinic in Bellingham, a city north of Seattle and spent the night. I stepped out of my motel room into dazzling sunlight. The leaves of the trees were glistening raindrops from the previous night's downpour. The air was crisp and clean. I stepped into my car. I drove south on Interstate 5 towards Seattle and my home on Mercer Island. On my right was Puget Sound with its harbors and boats and ferries, some heading South to Tacoma, some north to Vancouver Island, Canada. To my left were the snow-capped Cascades. Ahead of me was Mount Rainier, its snowy peak shimmering in the sunlight.

A few days later the rains began again. But this time I thought, it's okay. The rain was a small price to pay for those glorious sunny days. I decided that those sunny days in Seattle were similar to rare and beautiful jewels kept under lock and key and brought out only on special occasions for public viewing.

If Seattle was a child in need of protection, Mt. Rainier was **its** bodyguard. Rainer's white capped peak looms up protectively out of the south. It is home to mountain climbers from all over the world. The spring following my first basketball season, my wife and I joined others on that mountain. We began our ascent from base camp at 10,000 feet climbing with pickaxe, crampons, and headlamp, roped-up - up, up, and up until breaking through cloud-cover, we faced the rising sun illuminating the sea of clouds and the distant mountain peaks rising into the blue sky. I can think of a few vistas I've seen that are more magnificent. On the descent, we were shown how to glissade (ski) down the mountain on the soles of our boots, using the handle of our ice ax as a rudder. It was surprisingly easy. By the time we returned to the basecamp, I would have had to play three NBA games back to back to come close to how tired I felt. I find it curious that today I can barely look out a window that is higher than two stories without feeling anxiety.

We drove home to Mercer Island. Lake Washington was sparkling. The air was fresh, the rhododendrons were gloriously in bloom. I decided I could live in Seattle all my life.

• • •

My Sonic teammates were good guys and good players, not great but solid. Walt Hazzard, our point guard came the closest to greatness except that he often succumbed to playing a form of hoop arrogance (hero ball) that convinces a player he can win the game on his own.

We didn't win many games on his own or on our own during the four years I played for the Sonics. Could it have been about the same percentage of days in the Northwest that there is sunshine?

My first game back to the Bay Area as a Seattle Sonic on October 13, 1967 was memorable for a number of reasons. Unbeknownst to me, the Warriors retired my Warriors' jersey number 14 at a ceremonty before the game. I remember standing, sort of shell-shocked, at center court as GM Bob Ferrick read the announcement to the crowd, who had already given me a terrific welcome-home round of applause when I'd been introduced in my new green and white uniform. I was already emoitionally on edge. Standing with me on the court were my mother, sister, my college coach, Jim Weaver, and my irracible high school coach Ben Neff. So many years later was I still his little sonavabitch? I watched as my number 14 banner was lifted into the rafters. As it slowly ascended I was ticking off all the city's playgrounds that I'd played in as a kid. Those asphalt courts so much a part of my childhood. I'd come a long way from that immigrant teen waiting patiently on the sidelines for the older guys to let me play. My number would be the first of other Warriors' numnrs to rise into those heights. At the time, #14, floating up by itself, looked sort of lonely. Today, it is still the only jersey number to have been retired while the player remained an active player in the league. This could be a good question for Jeopardy.

On that day, after the ceremony ended, the game began. The Warriors soundly defeated the the expansion Sonics. Tom Meschery did not play well. I guess, looking back, I can say it was a loss to remember.

The following season the Warriors bestowed another surprise honor on me. The team changed their logo from an Indian Headdress to the outline of the Bay Bridge it is today. For a year, my number 14 would appear on that logo to the right of the bridge, which ment it would be on every Warriors' uniform and everywher else the log was used. This lasted until the following season when a newly hired GM had it taken off. It's likely that he decided it was not helpful to have my number on the Wariors' logo since I was playing for the Seattle Sonics. In NBA history, no team has ever incorporated one of their retired players' numbers into their team's logo. Anotheer Jeopary question? Thinking back to that time, and my subsequent four years as a Sonic, for me and my family, Seattle turned out to be a good-luck-rabbit's foot.

Expansion teams in the NBA are usually able to scratch out a few victories, but not notable victories. Such was not the case for the inaugural year of the SuperSonic expansion team. On Thanksgiving Day 1967, we waxed the legendary Boston Celtics. I can still hear Bailey Howell, Celtic forward, raging at his teammates in his southern accent, "Shame, y'all, shame." For me, any memory of beating the Boston Celtics gives me the same satisfaction as watching reruns of favorite movies. I keep a few of my best victories stored on the rolodex in mind that I turn to on occasion when I want to remind myself that at one time I was not over 80 and that I possessed a finely tuned body and could play the game of basketball at the highest level.

Get the popcorn and let's play that scene again.

I am flying through the air. I reach out and block Wilt Chamberlain's shot. Whatever I do in the future will never equal that moment.

CHAPTER 26
TRYING TO PUNCH WILT

It's 1968, my second season as a Sonic. In a home game against the Los Angeles Lakers, I tried punching my old teammate, Wilt Chamberlain. Tried, as in made a valiant effort. (I don't have the faintest recollection of why I was so angry at him.) I might have succeeded had Wilt not placed his hand on my forehead and held me far enough away from him that the Mad Manchurian's wild punches hit nothing but air. I remember him scolding me, "Tom, Tom, what the hell are you doing, son?" It was a scene out of a comedy movie, *entitled the Mad Manchurian Goes Berserker* .

My Warriors' teammate Al Attle's voice is never far from my mind when stuff like this happened to me on the basketball court. *Tom's eyes would start spinning around and all hell would break loose.* There have been times in my life when he and I questioned my sanity.

• • •

Nineteen-sixty-eight was the year of the Summer Olympic Games in Mexico City in which Tommy Smith and John Carlos won Gold and Bronze in the 200-meter dash and raised their black gloved fists above their bowed heads during the playing of the National Anthem. Most of my white teammates including myself thought they were disrespecting the flag. I *do* recall, however, thinking it was damn brave of them to risk the crap that was bound to come down on them. The winner of the Silver Medal was Australian, Peter Norman. He had asked for a black glove so that he could stand with his fellow medalists, protesting Black exploitation and inequality, but no black glove could be found. Instead, he wore a badge that stated he supported Carlos and Smith's symbolic protest. He too was brave. I didn't know at the time how brave. Years later I watched *Salute*, a video about his life made by his nephew and discovered that the Australian Track and Field Federation had blackballed Norman for his solidarity with Carlos and Smith. Disregarding his winning trial runs, they barred him from future international meets.

America was experiencing anti-Vietnam War protests from one side of the country to the other. We would sit down to dinner and the TV commentator would say, "48 Viet Cong killed today, and 4 Americans died." It sounded to me like he was announcing athletic results. We didn't realize how horrific it was because it was presented to us like a game, not war, not death, but score keeping. Of course, now we can appreciate that we were being lied to and the North Vietnamese were actually winning.

Our nation was divided. So much of that time into the '70s reminds me of what we are going through today. The military being sent into our cities to intimidate Black Lives Matter protesters. In 1968, I was aware of the plight of African Americans, but I don't recall being outraged the way I feel today. I certainly should have been. Was there some reason I didn't feel outraged? I was against the war in Vietnam. While on the court, I was easily outraged, off the court I was, for the most part, passive. I began writing poems that expressed my opposition to the war. They were not good poems. But they did allow me to get inside myself. Poetry does that. It may have something to do with the language needed for good poems being so refined that the struggle to find the right word forces the writer to think more deeply. That kind of deep thinking was something that was missing from my life.

• • •

In August of 1968, our second Daughter Megan Ann was born. For the first six months she had to wear a coddle at night because her little hip sockets needed to become stronger. I couldn't imagine how uncomfortable that was to wear, but Megan never cried. Tough girl, I remember thinking, earning her name, which in Greek means mighty one. Meg turned out to be the best athlete of our three children. Maybe like father like daughter, we both overcame, in my case diseases, in Meg's case a potential physical disability.

In that same year the United States basketball team won the Olympic Gold Medal easily. They won without their best player, Kareem Abdul

Jabbar, who had refused to try out as his way of protesting racial inequality. Another brave protestor. I felt guilty. Yet I continued to do nothing.

• • •

It is the summer of 1969 in the backyard of our house on Mercer Island. Wilt Chamberlain is holding my three-year-old daughter Janai in his giant hands, his equally enormous fingers wrapped around her tiny waist. She looks miniscule. Janie looks frightened, Wilt looks delighted.

Recently, looking through old photographs, I came across this backyard photo and sent it to Janai. She emailed me that it brought tears to her eyes. *Dear Janai, who is in her forties, would still weep watching Bambi or Brigadoon.*

Wilt was in Seattle helping me kick off a City of Seattle Recreation Department summer basketball program for under-privileged children. The Dipper, who rarely got the press he deserved, came to Seattle, charged no fee, went through the ceremonial tossing up of the ball at center court, then squeezed into a referee's striped shirt. Instead of going home, he stayed and refereed for two additional days. There have been few articles written about Wilt's generosity. The Dipper kept his good works to himself like secrets he'd promised not to divulge. There are a whole bunch of little boys and girls who probably remember Wilt blowing his referee's whistle, patting them on their heads and escorting them to the free throw line. How many of them, I wonder, preserved Wilt's inscribed T-shirts? Wilt's signature is worth big bucks.

It is unfortunate that Wilt has always been compared to Bill Russell of the Boston Celtics. They are very different yet both were complicated men. I was asked once to compare the two. I said that Russell was Rembrandt and Wilt was Caravaggio, and like him a flawed and magnificent virtuoso. I admire both painters. I admire both centers.

• • •

After two years with the Sonics, Walt Hazzard was traded to the Atlanta Hawks. In return the Sonics received Lenny Wilkins. Basketball in Seattle just got better. Lenny was our player-coach. As a coach, he was a quick study. As a player he was a magician, a lefty who seemed to float instead of run. I was elected team captain and union representative. Although we didn't make the playoffs with Lenny leading us, we were a stronger, more cohesive team. Later in his life, Lenny Wilkins would coach the Sonics to the NBA Championship. Seattle would cheer and perhaps a few people would remember how it all started.

SLEIGHT OF HAND

For Lenny Wilkins
It doesn't matter how often our coach
tells us to over-play Wilkins to his left hand
he goes there anyway, with that slippery move
that looks to me as if he's skating. Somehow
he slips through the jam of players rushing
into the paint to impede his progress.
To no avail. It's a pass to Zelmo or a slick
floater. Exploiting our vanity for having been
born right handed, he flaunts his left.
If only it were once or twice a game, but time
after time he shows us how the trick is done,
opening the black hat to reveal the trap door
from which he pulls the white rabbit and then
closing it before we can learn his secret.

Meschery, Tom "Sleight of Hand," *Sweat: New and Selected Poems About Sports*. Black Rock Press, 2014. University of Nevada, Reno. Reno, NV

• • •

Off the basketball court, I was living the American dream: lovely home, a beautiful wife, two of the cutest children imaginable, (Matthew was not yet born.) and a good paying job doing something I enjoyed.

I made many lasting friendships in Seattle. In particular, Don Horowitz, a lawyer with an operatic voice. Now a retired Justice on the Washington State Supreme Court, we call each other to catch up, exchange book titles, and talk politics. Another friend from that time was Roger Sales, an English professor, a Shakespeare scholar at the University of Washington, who hosted a radio talk show about the Sonics on the local PBS station. Roger brought classics to sports broadcasting (You think I mean class. No, I mean classics.) For example, "It appears as if Meschery was compelled to shoot." Once, Roger described the way the Sonics were playing as "Much ado about nothing." And another time, as I argued strenuously over a referee's call, Roger quipped, "I do believe Meschery protests too much."

It was in Seattle that I was first introduced to modern poetry. And for this alone, Seattle will always hold a special place in my heart. In 1970, in my third year with the Sonics, anticipating my retirement from the NBA after 10 years, I wrote essays about my experiences playing professionally. The more I wrote, the more my wastebasket filled up with pages of forgettable prose. I turned to verse. The result was a book of poems called *Over the Rim* published by Saturday Review Press. I had a book signing at Nordstrom's Department Store and felt like a bona fide poet. A newspaper story called me The Bard of the Backboard, which alliterates nicely but means squat. As I learned later, feeling like a poet was not the same as being one. That same year, at a poker game hosted by Professor Sales, I met the recipient of the University of Washington's Theodore Roethke Poetry Chair, Mark Strand. Mark encouraged me to sit in on his writing class when the team was in town. Which I did, and discovered, both to my dismay and to my amazement, what modern verse was all about. It was not the Russian ballads my father read aloud or the religious verse my mother read to me. It was not the poems I remember from my college classes, the sonnets of Shakespeare, the rhymed couplets of Alexander Pope. Contemporary poetry was certainly not what I'd written in *Over the Rim*. Strand gave me the names of modern poets I should read; James Wright; Richard Hugo, Elizabeth Bishop. He told me to find poets whose verse I admired and copy them, and that soon I'd be copying myself. I knew instantly what he was talking about in basketball terms. As a kid, I would watch older players making moves, and if I liked what I saw, I'd copy them.

I started reading and copying James Wright. Elizabeth Bishop too. I liked Richard Hugo best. His poem *Missoula Softball Tournament* was the first time I saw how a poet made serious poetry out of sports. Hugo remains one of my favorite poets. But I felt intimidated trying to copy the way he wrote. It was like trying to copy the moves of Elgin Baylor. No way could I achieve those moves - *those lines*. But I stuck with it stubbornly, learning a little with each failed poem. It would take me many more years to begin to feel confident about my poetry. Somewhere among my memorabilia, there is a folder containing many failed poems and drafts of poems I never completed. I look at them occasionally to remind myself that my efforts weren't entirely wasted. Here I am in my eighties, and perhaps I am finally copying myself.

About time, wouldn't you think?

That early advice Mark Strand provided me was the single most important advice I could pass on to a young person who has hope of being a poet but with little idea where to start. Read your favorite poets, then pretend you are them and write a poem in their style. The style will be theirs, the thoughts will be yours.

• • •

That NBA season ended with a national tragedy: On May 4, 1970, Ohio National Guardsmen shot and killed four unarmed students from Kent State University who were part of an anti-Vietnam War protest. Forty-eight years later that massacre became part of a poem I wrote about Muhammed Ali, who had been banned from boxing for his stand against the War.

VIETNAM

Grass grows, birds fly, waves pound the sand. I beat people up
Muhammed Ali
What is Ali asking us to understand
that a right cross or a body punch is as natural
as grass growing or waves pounding the beach?

Or was the butterfly that stings like a bee
being more subtle, asking us to consider
infinitives as violence: to grow, to fly, to pound?

I was ten years old when I fought first,
tackling Howard Buckle and pounding his nose
until it bled and he cried, and I cried.

Twenty years later, I marched against the Vietnam War.
I held a Bird of Peace above my head. A cop
pounded the guy next to me with a club.

After that, violence grew into more violence
until a campus of students died on a grassy lawn
and a country wept. And a country cheered.

I was watching the Knicks and L.A. when I heard the news.
I forgot who won. I wanted to punch anybody.
My childhood anger had grown into an adult.

All the doves of Peace in my heart had flown away.
There was nothing to replace them.
Ali told reporters he had no quarrel with them Viet Cong.
It cost him the right to beat people up.

Meschery, Tom. "Vietnam," *Clear Path*, Random Lane Press, 2022.
Sacramento, CA

During the last game of the 1970-71 Seattle Sonic season, my last in
the NBA, the Sonics honored me at halftime. The team gave me a plaque
and goodbye gifts. Everyone in the stands wore a black paper cutout of the
bushy mustache I had grown a couple of years before, which had become
my trademark image. Ten years of beating up my body was enough for
me. Plus, at the beginning of the season, the Sonics had acquired Spencer
Haywood, an extremely talented forward. I surmised that this meant if I
returned for an eleventh season, I would no longer be a starter. I would not
have admitted it then, but today I realize my ego was not going to allow
that to happen. Considering that the year following my retirement turned
out so badly, it's a decision I regret. At the time, of course, I was unaware
of the future turmoil I would encounter trying to find a life outside the
protective chrysalis of the NBA. So, I had to admit that my knees were
starting to hurt, and I was no longer enamored of the travel and rigors of
the long NBA season. Time for the Mad Manchurian to hang it up. While
this is true, I never lost my love of basketball. How could I? It would have
been rejecting a part of myself.

What made the decision to retire easier was an offer to teach poetry from Evergreen State University, a brand new State school, located in the town of Olympia, which is just south of Seattle. The offer allowed me the perfect way to leave the game and move directly into a new career. What I didn't know about poetry, I felt confident I could acquire with hard work, staying one step ahead of my students until at some point I would surge ahead of them. I accepted the position.

And shortly thereafter I un-accepted the position.

I had not realized that my wife was eager to leave the Northwest. I think it could have been the many days when I was away on the road playing basketball and she was left at home often inside because of rain with two children and one baby. Our son Matt was born in April. When the Peace Corps, surprisingly, offered me a two-year-contract coaching in Venezuela, Joanne convinced me this would be an adventure we couldn't pass up. Much to the university's surprise and I suspect shock, I resigned the teaching position and signed on to the Peace Corps.

The season ended, and we sold our house on Mercer Island. We hired a mover, packed ourselves and belongings into our Volkswagen bus and drove to Donner Lake in the Sierra Nevada Mountains, where we rented a summer home. There, I waited for our traveling papers for Caracas, Venezuela.

And waited and waited.

COUGARS, THE WRITERS'
WORKSHOP & FBI
1971 - 1976

CHAPTER 27
CAROLINA COUGARS

. . . and I was still waiting.

It was August 1971, hot and dry in the Sierra, and I was nervously waiting for traveling instructions for Venezuela. I'd had my fill of swimming and hiking. I loved the family time, (my baby son Matthew was gorgeous) but I was getting antsy. I needed to work. If I had been more introspective at the time, I might have recognized how psychologically dependent I was on work. In retrospect, this is a bit shocking since I had always considered myself a sort of laid back person. I know that sounds odd considering how intensely I played basketball, how easily I was angered. Eugenio Montale, the Italian poet and winner of the Nobel Prize in Literature in 1975, wrote, "All we have to do is look in the mirror to see that we're someone else."

Whoever I saw in the mirror that August, waiting for the Peace Corps to contact me was in a state of stress. I wasn't sleeping well; I grumbled at my wife; I snapped at my daughters. I telephoned; they'd get back to me. I called again, same reply. The first week of September, I finally received a call from Washington D.C. It was not good news. President Nixon had cut funding for the Peace Corps. My coaching position had been eliminated. I was jobless and deeply regretting turning down the Evergreen College teaching position. I hadn't saved a lot of money. I wasn't panicking, but by mid-September I was on the verge of it. I was beginning to experience a kind of insecurity that had little to do with money and more to do with abandonment. After ten years, the NBA train would leave the station without me. I felt directionless. I was saved by a telephone call from Carl Scheer, the General Manager of the Carolina Cougars of the American Basketball Association, the NBA's rival league, asking me if I was interested in the head coaching position. I jumped at the opportunity. We packed our suitcases, and with our three little children in tow, flew to Greensboro, North Carolina.

Let me pause here to say I don't recall consulting my wife about this job. I don't remember if she was happy with the move across the country or not. I thought of it as salvation, she might have thought of it as more of an ordeal. Basketball wives back then lived solitary lives. I suspect they still do.

I might have saved myself some grief, had I'd been told or I had asked about the previous coach before signing a two-year contract with the Carolina Cougars. He had suffered a nervous breakdown. I might not have taken the position had I also known that the owner, Ted Munchak, would telephone me from his yacht after games with his unintelligible critiques. I would have had more second thoughts if I'd have been aware that 6-11 Jim McDaniels, the Cougars first round draft choice, projected to be the teams' savior, couldn't play a lick of defense, not a smidgen.

McDaniels, listen up, on D, one foot has to be placed in front of the other. Got it? Hey, McDaniels, listen, on D, one foot... here too?

And there was the incident that happened a couple of weeks into training camp that should have had me packing up the car and family for a quick departure: One of the minority owners following a couple of days of training camp invited me and my "missus" and the team to his country club, but "not your n..... players." I remember thinking what kind of job had I signed for? I only *had* four white players.

And there was the disgusting morning: After my first home game, I stepped out the front door to get the morning newspaper and found the house toilet-papered with a sign on the lawn that read: *Nigger Lover*, which I could only assume had to do with my starting five African Americans for the previous night's game. I removed the sign and as much toilet paper as I could before my kids woke up, but they saw enough, the little ones confused, my wife furious.

I remained the coach.

When I was in college, I had an annoying professor who never passed up the opportunity to quote a Greek or Roman philosopher. As I started writing about my year as a coach in North Carolina, I recalled one of his quotes by Sophocles: *I have no desire to suffer twice, in reality and then in retrospect.* Which is exactly what writing about North Carolina has turned out to be, one painful remembrance after another.

I'd like to believe I did not resign my coaching position because I wanted to prove that I could coach basketball, but the truth is that I persisted because there had been no other prospects available, and I needed the salary. Once again, I made an important decision against my better judgment.

It became increasingly clear to me that this was going to be a losing season. I had the painful realization that Tom Meschery, a ten-year veteran of the NBA, a one-time All Star, was a terrible coach. I had taken the position without any coaching experience - on any level. I'd thought at the time I took the job how hard could it possibly be? I was a 10-year veteran of the NBA. I knew my sport. Which was not entirely true. I knew my position. I didn't know the other positions. I didn't view the game holistically as a player and I didn't as a coach. I had no patience with players who didn't play with high intensity every single game. I accepted no excuses. The Mad Manchurian was back. Now he was the Mad Manchurian Coach. I kicked chairs, I threw chalk and towels and clipboards. The season that started out badly only got worse. About midseason, at one practice, my assistant coach, said to me in his profound southern drawl, "Tohm, the playaas' eeahs ah geddin smawll." Translation: "Tom, the players ears are getting small." Specific Translation: The players no longer give a shit.

By then, I was completely frustrated and depressed. From the start I had been uncomfortable with the ABA's 3-point shot that encouraged shooting from beyond 22 feet, something that did not exist in *my* NBA. I was a basketball purest. I believed it to be a bad percentage shot. I was a power forward. I taught the power game. I became moody, sulked and whined. When I looked in the mirror, I didn't like what I saw.

Thinking back to that dreadful year, it's a memory like a punch in the chest. I remember breaking my toe, kicking the bench after Wendall Ladner, my handsome, girl-crazy-Cajon-dive-for-any-loose-ball-forward, took a jump-shot just as he passed the frigging mid-court line at a crucial time when our team needed a basket. The missed shot and my toe hurt like hell. After the loss, I hobbled for weeks. I whined that the league's red, white and blue ball was cheesy. The ABA's wide open, hurry-up, brand of basketball was not for me. I may have been politically liberal, but as a coach I was a conservative. If I'd had any sense back then, I should have realized I was sowing the seeds of my own destruction.

If you know who you really are, no fakery, the Gods allow you to glimpse moments of greatness.

I should have seen that the upstart ABA was to the NBA as Buck Rogers was to NASA. Today's NBA owes its success to the innovations of the upstart league.

There would be no glimpses of coaching success for The Mad Manchurian. As the season drew to an end, Jim McDaniels, our team center, jumped leagues to the Seattle Sonics, my old team, coached by my old teammate Lenny Wilkens. I felt ambushed. True, McDaniels still didn't know which foot came before the other on defense, but he was all I had.

The losing season continued. About that time, I received a telephone call that my friend Fred LaCour had been diagnosed with cancer. Back then, the diagnosis of cancer meant painful death. The disease had spread rapidly. He was in the hospital and not expected to live much longer. Fred died before I could get on the plane for San Francisco. I mourned for Fred but did not mourn his passing as better the universe than the pain of a prolonged painful disease which very well could have been a metaphor for the emotional pain he suffered most of his life over his racial identity. In the beneficent universe he was saved from both.

I must be careful writing about Fred. It is so easy to sound maudlin. In some ways, my friend was heroic, refusing to give in to racists' view of him.

In New York City to play the Nets, starring the great Julius Irving. We got hammered. I went to dinner with Mark Strand. Mark listened to me complaining how unhappy I was. He suggested that I apply to the University of Iowa's Writers Workshop. He'd write me a letter of recommendation. I followed Mark's suggestion and was accepted into their MFA program for the fall.

Totally relieved, we sold our home and left Greensboro at the end of the season and headed for Iowa City. I think of my family leaving Greensboro, packed into our International Harvester Station Wagon, driving west over the Great Smoky Mountains toward Iowa. The back seat was down with blankets spread out and pillows for the kids to sleep on. From time to time when the noise from the back increased, I would take a handful of candy from a bag and throw it over my shoulder.. Whenever I think of that journey, I can't help laughing, thinking of the kids, scrambling for treats, the oldest, getting more than her share.

We left Greensboro early in the morning. In Ashville, we stopped to visit the home of the poet Carl Sandburg, whose poetry I had tried unsuccessfully to imitate in *Over the Rim.*

I was looking forward to Iowa and finding out more about poetry. By leaving coaching behind, I felt as if, in a way, I was making up for the poetry teaching position at Evergreen University that I'd passed up. After I earned my Master of Fine Arts degree, I would look for a job teaching poetry. Students would call me Professor Meschery. I would no longer be The Mad Manchurian. Perhaps The Mad Professor.

I had made two prior attempts to leave basketball behind. In both instances circumstances prevented me. It is what I wanted to believe. I didn't know it at the time, but upon reflection, there was only one circumstance and that was me. I wasn't ready. I do remember wondering if Iowa would be the catalyst to a different career. I was nervous heading into the unknown territory called academia. We made the drive to Iowa City in one day, arriving in the dark stopping at the first motel we could find with three sleeping children in the back blanketed with candy wrappers.

CHAPTER 28
JOCK OUT OF WATER
1972-1974

We purchased a midsize Victorian on a lovely tree-lined cobblestone street not too far from the university campus and moved in. It was late summer, hot and humid, the kind of damp humidity I remembered from my trips to Africa, but without the palm trees, beaches and the drums. But there were ponds filled with large-mouth bass and dark woods where morel mushrooms grew. I learned to cast into the reeds lining the shore where the bass lurked waiting for my bait. The morels were delicious thinly sliced, sautéed in butter, and served along with the grilled bass. Our house had no air-conditioning but lots of fans. Of that time, one of my favorite summer memories is of the evenings our three children ran around the front lawn catching fireflies.

At the start of that first semester, I had no idea what was in store for me. I could not have felt more out of place - *a jock-out-of-water*. The first terrifying morning, all new student-poets met for an orientation. Marvin Bell, one of the teaching poets, kicked the meeting off by asking questions to determine what we knew about poetry, poets, and specific poems. He made it feel like a game. It became a student competition to see whose hand could go up the fastest - trying to impress. With the first question, which was in what meter did Homer write the *Iliad*, I knew I was seriously out of my league. I sat in the back row feeling like the new immigrant kid with the bad haircut and short pants, sinking lower and lower in his seat, hoping the mean third grade teacher would not call on him. I recall some of the questions. *Can someone tell me who wrote Elegy for Jane? What was the title of Walt Whitman's most influential collection of poetry?* I knew that answer but didn't dare raise my hand. *What was inscribed on John Keats tomb?* A dozen hands shot up. I slunk lower in my seat. *Which American female poet was a fan of baseball?* I'd never heard of Marianne Moore. I'd never heard of most of the questions that afternoon, let alone the answers and left for home certain that I'd made a terrible mistake bringing my family from North Carolina to Iowa City. It was a feeling that lasted for months as all the student writers seemed to know vastly more about poetry than I did.

It was Marvin Bell, one of the teaching poets, who finally convinced me that I'd be fine, that my efforts at poetry were worthy, and helped me to understand what poetry demands of a poet. It was not just "voice" that young poets are trying to discover, but much more. A poetic voice, according to Marvin may be unique, but if it isn't honest, it does poetry no service. How right he was. I hated to admit it, but the poems in *Over the Rim*, my one and only collection of poetry were pretend poetry. Don't over think, Marvin cautioned. Leave your brain for later when you rewrite. Like Mark Strand told me years before, read poets. Marvin gave me more names. I went to the library. I spent more money than I should have in bookstores. I read.

It has been five decades since Iowa. In all that time, however successful my poems were, I've tried my best to follow the edict of Philip Levine: *Poems are forbidden from lying.*

After my first Iowa Writers class our teacher-poet Donald Justice suggested I read Flannery O'Conner's stories in *Everything That Rises Must Converge* and the poems of Caesar Vallejo. You can probably guess, coming out of my life as a professional basketball player, what I mean when I say those poems and stories made me feel like a stranger in a strange land. A year later, at a party I asked Donald why he chose those two writers. (We were between poker hands. He was winning. Justice always won.) He told me that I looked like I needed them. It sounded like I was ill, and he was prescribing medicine. I think it cured me. Not that I was ill, but Donald must have known or sensed I required something special to move me from the world of athletics into the world of literature. O'Connor and Vallejo remain two of my favorite writers. Vallejo wrote about dying on the streets of Paris. Donald Justice wrote about Miami. Many years later, I tried to imitate Vallejo myself, my death taking place on the streets of Sacramento. The effort never made it out of a first draft, but it brought back a lot of memories about my two years studying in Iowa City.

Of the teachers I had in Iowa, Helen Chasin provided me with the most practical help. I don't want to leave the impression the other teaching poets were not helpful, but they didn't provide the specifics about language that she did. And strategies about how to muddle through a poem that seemed stuck. She always provided me with specific examples. Helen told me she read more fiction and non-fiction than poetry looking for inspiration for her own poems. She encouraged me to do the same. Unfortunately, for me, Helen taught for only one semester.

Years later when I was teaching high school English, I conducted workshops for English teachers in our district. How to teach poetry often presents a problem for English teachers, even the most seasoned ones. I never failed to follow Helen Chasin's example. *Be concrete. Provide examples. Be specific.*

Marvin Bell became one of my mentors. I also remember him as a tennis opponent. Teachers vs Students: David St. John, a fellow student poet and I defeated Marvin Bell and Mark Strand. I, with my vicious serve, St. John with his stable backhand; the profs had no chance. It is possible that my eighty-two-year-old memory of those matches may not be entirely accurate.

It's your memory; you own it.

Damn right. We won in straight sets.

• • •

Stuart Dybek and Tracy Kidder, two of the married students in the fiction workshop we'd become friends with, advised my wife Joanne to submit two chapters of a novel she'd written while we were living in North Carolina. On the basis of those chapters, she was accepted into the Fiction workshop. This marked the beginning of her career as a novelist and her gaining independence in a way that was different from my very idealistic 1950s idea of marriage. I'm reasonably certain neither of us ever took the time to be realistic about what it takes to make a marriage work, both of us coming from dysfunctional families. Without a parental model , I chose to fictionalize marriage. Television provided me with the ideal American model.

• • •

Preparing to write my memoir, I'd read enough memoirists explaining their failed expectations, affairs, and broken promises to know that kind of memoir was not for me.

• • •

Another married couple we met at the workshop was Jon and Ruth Jackson. Like Dybek and Kidder, Jon was in the fiction workshop. Jon and

Ruth had a 3-year-old daughter, Sarah, whom they called Buzzy. Buzzy was a year older than our son, Matthew. Shortly after we met them, Ruth and Jon split up. Ruth had a day job, and we took care of Buzzy during the work week. Today, Jon lives in Missoula, Montana and writes the terrific Sergeant Mulheison detective fiction novels, and Buzzy is a successful writer of non-fiction and fiction. Her latest non-fiction book is called *The Inspirational Atheist*. Her soon to be released novel is *Die Beautiful* about a female French spy during the Second World War. Buzzy and my son Matthew consider themselves siblings and have remained close friends. I haven't told Buzzy this, but I've decided being an Atheist is the easiest way to avoid dealing with the far more difficult subject of the human soul, the existence of which every Russian is absolutely certain.

I remember Jon telling me that because Stuart Dybek was first generation Polish, and grew up in a Polish speaking family, he might have been better able to express himself if he'd written in Polish. "Stuart's genius," Jon explained, "is that he gets so much wrong in English absolutely right." I knew what Jon meant. I'd felt that way myself–writing in English thinking that if only I was fluent in Russian. In my case, unlike Dybek, I got much wrong.

Not too long ago, Melanie stopped in the middle of editing the memoir and said. "Tom, you wrote that paragraph in Russian. You gave me the most important part at the end and used 17 clauses to get there."

I begged to differ about the number 17. But I do not disagree with my tendency to use clauses. I have read enough Russian stories to know it's the Russian way with the help of the semicolon and dash. I comfort myself that, at least, I have no problem with the copular verb, which is left out entirely in the present tense in Russian.

I read somewhere that what you lose when you're not writing in the language of your birth is the natural rhythms of your adopted language. I thought it was like you were meant to play the oboe, but instead you were playing the trumpet. Conversely, I feel the rhythms of the Russian language but cannot write in it other than in simple sentences. All these years I should have been playing the oboe. I made a huge mistake as a boy refusing to continue my Russian lessons.

I am rarely in contact with Dybek and Kidder, but have maintained close ties with Jon Jackson. He critiqued my first attempt at writing a murder mystery. He did not give me high marks, but continued to encourage me. He is a great fellow and one of the few men I know whom I can say is a true

Renaissance Man: novelist, saxophone player, golfer, gourmand, singer, fly-fisherman, bird-watcher, radio commentator, aficionado of jazz vocalists, and repository of arcane information. Jon and I are both Scorpios, which according to astrology, marks us as the "Bad boys of the Zodiac."

• • •

My love of poetry began with my parents. My father's and mother's choice of poetry was, of course, not contemporary, or experimental. I watched my father weeping over the epic sagas of the Bogatyrs, protectors of the Russian borders, Russia's equivalent of England's Knights of King Arthur's Court. If he could weep over poetry, so could I.

Poetry was equally important to my mother, if not more so. It is likely that my talent, whatever that might be, is from the female side of her family, the Tolstoys. One of the most illustrious of the Tolstoy poets was Alexey Konstantinovich Tolstoy, a second cousin to Leo Tolstoy. Several of Alexey Konstantinovich's poems have been set to music by Tchaikovsky and Rachmaninov. My favorite is Tchaikovsky's Blagoslavyayu Vas, Lesa (I Bless you, forests) sung by Dmitri Hvorostovsky. **I have poetic genes.**

• • •

The University of Iowa was the home of the International Writers Program, run by Paul Engels, the first director of the Iowa Writers Workshop and his wife, Hialing Nieh Engle. Jon and I got jobs helping the international writers translate their poems into English. Our family finances were tight, so the additional paycheck helped. I was assigned to Sasha Petrov, a Yugoslavian poet who wrote in Russian. His poetry was questionable at best. Jon and I decided that he was a KGB agent there to keep track of the other poets from Russia and other Soviet satellite countries. Once that had sunk in, it made me a little nervous working with him. For a while I thought I might sabotage his work by making glaring errors in the translations until Jon told me my name would appear on the manuscript as the translator. I wisely decided against that idea.

Some of the poets I met in the workshop were damn good and became famous. There was the Slovenian poet, Tomaz Salamun. I didn't know what his poems were about, but decided I didn't need to for me to enjoy the imagery. It was like reading jazz. The freedom some of these writers from Soviet counties experienced in America must have been heady stuff.

As I recall, two of the international writers' ongoing themes were fast food and Las Vegas. When the Yugoslavian writers were ordered home, one of the writers set his manuscripts on fire in the wastebasket in protest. It might have been the emotional Ivan Kushan, a Croat fiction writer. The apartment neighbors were not amused.

Word got out that I had played in the NBA. The assistant coach of the university basketball team recruited me for their club team. With my addition we easily defeated the rest of the teams in the league. One of the teams we competed against was a bunch of American Studies graduate students, led by 6'11" "Big John" Wiston, who'd been the starting center at Yale University and a feisty point guard, Charlie Dee. As the season progressed, I found it strange that the guys on my team took such pleasure defeating these grad students. There were other teams that provided us with more competition. SoWhat was it? It was 1972 maybe they thought it would be unpatriotic losing to the long-haired radicals.

I wound up hanging out with Big John and Charlie and their gang of radicals after our basketball games because they were interesting. They were deeply committed to leftist politics and, depending on the amount of beer consumed, provided each other with numerous unique strategies for improving the country's ills. I drank and listened and occasionally nodded my head in agreement. I didn't recognize it at the time, but they were changing the way I viewed America. I had already been rethinking my traditional view of America, so I was receptive to their ideas. Big John quit his graduate studies the next year and departed for Missoula, Montana, the state that in 1917 had produced the radical IWW (Industrial Workers of the World, called the Wobblies) where he was dead certain the next uprising of workers was imminent. *By God, it wasn't going to happen without Big John.* Charlie completed his degree and moved to Milwaukee and taught American history and the history of the Vietnam War at Milwaukee Technical College. He became one of the leaders of the teacher's union and activist in Wisconsin's Progressive wing of the Democratic Party. He retired in 2012. If there is anything I need to know about politics these days, I call Charlie. He always responds with the current news, unless he's off in the backcountry of Wisconsin cross-country skiing or shooting some wild-ass rapids, challenging any river that might dare to take his life. He's 72 years old and still doing physically daring stuff.

It was during my second year in the workshop that I began to notice my basketball game was slipping. I shouldn't have been surprised. By 1975, I was 37 years old and four plus years removed from NBA competition. It is best described in the following poem I wrote that became part of the poetry collection that was a requirement for my MFA degree.

WILLIS REED
Center for the New York Knicks 1975 NBA Championship team

You limped onto the court
and made sports history. I limped
to the kitchen for a beer
feeling this pain not in my leg,
but in my heart. Only four years
out of the league and already
my body breaking down. A simple
maneuver with the lawnmower
and I heard the muscle tear. No
thanks to you, I'll probably hear
somebody at work tomorrow
say, look at Willis, only one
good wheel and able to out-play Wilt.
Horse Laughs, then the bright eyes
of the dandelions staring
from the lawn, daring me to return.

Willis Reed; *Nothing You Lose Can Be Replaced*; Black Rock Press; Rain Shadow Edition; University of Nevada, Reno, Reno, NV 1999

• • •

At the end of two years, in May of 1974, I turned in my final manuscript of poems and the University of Iowa conferred upon me the degree of Master of Fine Arts. If this sounds a little formal, that's how I want it to sound. I'd bet I'm the only NBA player who ever earned an MFA in poetry.

Melanie received her PhD in education from the University of Oregon in 1993. Her license plate reads PhDDuck. Mine reads: WAYER14.

CHAPTER 29
PORTLAND TRAILBLAZERS

My MFA degree completed, I began looking for a job. Jobs teaching poetry were not plentiful, and none came my way. Out of the blue, Jack Scott called. I knew Jack by his reputation. He introduced himself as the athletic director of Oberlin College. He wanted to know if I would be interested in applying for the head basketball coaching job. If poetry didn't want me, I could fall back on basketball. I drove from Iowa to the college in Ohio. Oberlin's reputation as a liberal college put all other liberal colleges to shame. Jack told me hiring was purely a democratic process. I asked him what that meant. The players interview the candidates and pick the coach they want, he told me. He added input, but he didn't interfere. I was cool with that. Why wouldn't they choose an NBA player and an ABA coach? That's what I thought. That didn't happen. After I had been rejected, I asked Jack where I'd screwed up. I hadn't, he answered. The players felt they'd be more comfortable with an African American coach. My memory is a little foggy and Jack Scott has passed away. Anyway, if there were two blacks on the team, that left 13 white boys who turned me down. Racial profiling? I have to admit I thought of it that way, until I reminded myself that as a white man, I really had no right to complain. What did President Senghor say about putting on black skin for five minutes?

• • •

Not too long after my Oberlin rejection, still suffering from my bruised ego, Lenny Wilkens, my Seattle SuperSonics teammate and friend, newly hired as the head coach of the Portland Trail Blazers, called to ask me if I wanted to be his assistant coach. I didn't need to think long to say yes. I needed a job. I had a family, and our bank account was running low. I figured the job would be a good one. The Trailblazers had the No. 1 pick in the NBA draft, and selected Bill Walton of the NCAA Champion UCLA Bruins. Owners and management were excited at the prospect of a Trailblazer team centered around one of the best college centers who ever played the game of basketball.

My wife, Joanne, had been admitted into the workshop in fiction writing. She was starting her second year toward earning an MFA. She and our kids would remain in Iowa City. If I had been paying more attention to what was happening with Joanne , I would have been better prepared. I was very much unaware of any problems at the time.This decision would turn out to be a disaster for our marriage.

• • •

Thinking back to that time, I have come up with a theory why Lenny chose me as his assistant. Here's how I imagine it happening.

Owner: "You know Walton is pretty damn controversial, Vietnam protester and all that."

Wilkens: "But I haven't seen a center with his skills since Abdul-Jabbar."

General Manager: "Long hair. A real hippie. Doesn't eat meat. What the hell is that all

about?"

Wilkens: "I know a coach who can relate to Walton. Maybe we should hire him."

Owner: "Yeah. Who's that?"

Wilkens: "Tom Meschery. He played NBA basketball. He writes poetry."

General Manager: "Poetry? Okay, that makes sense."

Has writing poetry ever procured any basketball coach a job? I may be unique, the first and the last. Granted, this scenario is a product of my imagination. The Trailblazers were not worried about Walton's basketball skills, but they were extremely nervous about the Big Redhead's political activities.

Bill Walton was no doubt a superb center, possibly the best all-around center I had ever seen, even to this day. Unfortunately, at that time in his life, he was constantly injured due in part to being a vegan with hopes of becoming a *Breatharian*. He was so skinny, in my imagination he looked like a seven-foot Ichabod Crane. The team without him couldn't win. This led to frustration which culminated in Assistant Coach Tom Meschery taking out his own frustration by trying to punch Sydney Wicks, one of the star players on the team, for smart-mouthing the Mad Manchurian once too many times. I landed a punch on Sydney Wicks, one of the star players on the team. He didn't. And at 6'8" and 240 pounds, he probably would have done me considerable damage had the players not broken us up. My temper had embarrassed Lenny and the organization, and I had to apologize to Wicks. I did it with my fingers crossed behind my back.

• • •

I have never been a fan of the FBI, as was much the case with Herbert Hoover's 1974 version of the FBI. I have started to change my view of the FBI since President Trump started picking on them.

In my second season in Portland, I was interviewed by two agents of the FBI, a distinctly unsettling experience. It was all about Walton.

Walton was part of the anti-Vietnam War movement. At a party Bill threw for friends and political activists, the FBI set up cameras just off the perimeter of Bill's property and were filming all the attendees of which I was one. I joined the group solidarity giving the agents the middle finger. It felt right to do it. *Screw J. Edgar.* The next day as I was about to leave my apartment for the Trailblazers' office, the doorbell rang. When I opened the door, I was facing two men with crew cuts (I kid you not, crew cuts.) wearing dark suits with white dress shirts and black ties. The only part of the FBI attire that was missing were the hats. In my mind I was thinking, *gotta be Rosencrantz and Guildenstern.* They questioned me for about an hour. They made it clear that they knew I was a naturalized citizen, which I never doubted was intended as a threat to me. Before they left, they offered me a chance to provide information on Walton and the people living with him, especially Jack Scott and his wife, Micki, who were well known to the FBI. I declined the honor. From that day on, I figured my name would be inscribed on J. Edgar's hit list. They left me feeling dismayed and sad. I loved America, even during its disastrous war in Vietnam.

Many years later, it was Jack Scott who drove Patty Hearst across the country from her hiding place in Pennsylvania, to evade the FBI arrest warrant order demanding she turn herself in to the Los Angeles Police Department.

It is fair to say that my two years in Portland moved my views towards progressive politics that had begun in Iowa City.

I do not believe, as President Trump does, that our country's FBI is part of the so-called Deep State. Not even in the height of Director Hoover's reign did I believe the FBI was as evil as the Soviet's KGB (Committee for State Security.) Not to mention Putin's present day secret service, the Russian FSB (Federal Security Service). I grew up with my mother's accounts of murdered relatives. I hear my Russian friend Dmitri talking to me over the phone from Saint Petersburg about the Soviet he grew up in where friends and neighbors disappeared overnight, never to be seen again, or about dissidents returning home from gulags, their bodies and spirits broken. He might have been talking about the present Russia under Putin, which is increasingly looking like the old Soviet Union.

• • •

I love the Rose City. Its rivers, its closeness to the Pacific Ocean, its tidy neighborhoods, even its rainy days. I made lifelong friends in Portland. Peter Sears, who was teaching creative writing at Reed College. Peter was not only a terrific poet, but he was an amazing teacher. The enthusiasm he displayed for his students and his subject became a model for me when I began teaching years later. I never whistled the way Peter did when he approved of a student's recitation, but I followed his example in my own way by pumping my fist or making some inane sound of excitement. I met Oxford Scholar and Stanford track star, Dell Martin, who was living in Bill Walton's commune, and Bill's advisor, Jack Scott, a sociologist and political activist who was advising Walton (his detractors called him Walton's guru). Larry Colton, an ex-MLB pitcher for the Philadelphia Phillies and high school English teacher, and I renewed our friendship in Portland. I'd met Colton a year before. He'd organized *The Portland Conference on Sports and* had flown me in from Iowa. Along with me, there was Bill Russell, Althea Gibson, NFL coach Chuck Knox, Olympic Gold medalist Olga Connelly, my old college nemesis, Darrall Imhoff and Dave Meggyesy, a star linebacker for the Saint Louis Cardinals, who'd recently written a book called *Out of Their League,* an expose of NFL football that had rocked the sports world. Colton was going for a conservative liberal divide among the participants. By then my view of politics was decidedly liberal.

I found out later that Larry had been married to Hedy Lamar's daughter. Hedy was my boyhood fantasy. Her and Rita Hayworth. And Ingid Bergman, And. . . *So many Hollywood actresses populating my boyhood dreams.* Difficult was the word Larry used to describe Hedy. Larry left teaching to write books. His *Counting Coup,* the story of a girls' basketball team on a Blackfoot reservation in Montana was nominated for the Pulitzer Prize.

It was in Portland at a poetry reading that I was introduced to the poet, Morton Marcus. I might never have met my mentor if I hadn't taken the assistant coaching job with the Blazers. Without Morton, I would never have published my first authentic collection of poetry. He mentored me through each poem with suggestions and criticism. Morton died two days after my birthday on October 28, 2009, both of us Scorpios. Melanie and I never miss The Morton Marcus Memorial Poetry Reading in Santa Cruz every November. Morton's literary accomplishments were many, but my feelings for him can be summed up in this poem I wrote for him.

A LITERARY MEMOIR

For Morton Marcus (1936-2009)
Is this where poetry starts, Mort,
with a jab and a right cross, uncle
in your corner, trainer and cut-man,
Jewish Mafia gunned down,
and all the intervening years
you tell me about fighting with words?
Some wins, some draws, few losses
but enough to cost you friends and family.

I have no problem seeing you in the ring,
a welter-weight with quick hands,
jabs that keep your opponents off balance,
no dancing, moving straight forward,
accepting two punches for one,
what you believe it takes to write.
You got to get bloody, you say.

We are sitting together a month
before your death. We have done this before
talking late about sports and poetry,

sometimes forgetting there's a difference,
your punches, my hook shots,
a game I played that you admired,
a poem you wrote that knocked me out.

Meschery, Tom "Literary Memory," *Sweat: New & Selected Poems About Sports*. Black Rock Press, 2014. University of Nevada, Reno. Reno, NV

In Morton Marcus' *Writings on Writing: Musings from Notebooks and Articles*, Morton said one of his goals was to "live at that pitch which is near madness but disciplined by art." *Dear Mort, my own on-the-court madness was never disciplined and as I look back on it, so unnecessary.*

• • •

As it turned out, at the end of the 1973/74 Blazers' season, Lenny Wilkens was fired, along with his coaching staff of one: me. I drove to Truckee, California, a small railroad town near the border of Nevada within driving distance of Lake Tahoe where the summer before I had purchased a house, and where Joanne and the children were waiting for me. My professional basketball coaching career ended, but I hoped perhaps I could save my marriage.

FALSE STARTS & JUST PLAIN SCREWUPS
1976 -1985

CHAPTER 30
TRUCKEE RIVER BOOK & TEA

Over the years of hooping, in high school, college and through the NBA, the game became a way of life. Much of my identity was wrapped up in being a professional basketball player. After I retired it took me years to find something that I felt would be as meaningful and as exciting that I could devote my life to. I retired from the game with no template for the future. Jobs were always available if earning a living to support your family was your only criteria.

I recall many of the players of the 50's, 60's worked at second jobs following their basketball seasons to make ends meet, which allowed them to move from the NBA into banking, insurance, sales, and marketing. This was the case for many of the white players but not the black players for whom such employment was not readily available and a great deal more difficult to obtain. Not impossible as in the case of Dave Bing of the Detroit Pistons who went from being a clerk in a bank to owning his own steel mill.

More daunting than finding a regular paying job was finding employment that would fill the adrenaline packed vacuum of playing professional sports. Pro athletes are not the only ones who have found it difficult to deal with this void in their lives. I talked to a friend who danced for the Joffrey Ballet, and she told me lots of dancers, once retired, missed the kind of daily high that dancing provided them. I spoke to a basketball player from my generation, now deceased, who told me he became a professional gambler because it was the only way he could experience the same kind of rush he did playing in the NBA. Today's NBA players are paid handsomely so that their financial futures, barring any misfortunes, are assured. But I'd be willing to bet, even Michael Jordan, a billionaire and owner of the Charlotte Hornets doesn't on occasion yearn for the thrill of flying through the air for one of his spectacular dunks.

Later in my life, reflecting on my difficult transitional years, I wrote this quatrain. I wrote it in the style of one of my favorite poets, Gerard Manly Hopkins.

GERARD MANLEY HOPKINS

Leave basketball behind, can you?
As your age tells you, leaving
Without a sigh, no whys, will you?
Without looking back, or, to mourn.

Meschery, Tom. "Gerard Manley Hopkins," *Clear Path*, Random Lane Press, 2022. Sacramento, CA

• • •

The years beginning in the fall of 1976 were filled with several failed test careers. The first of my attempts came in Truckee, CA after moving down from Portland to reunite with my family. A storefront became available on the main street of the Old Historic District. A bookstore sounded to me like a good way for two readers and writers to earn a living. Joanne agreed, although she had other plans for that year. She had earned her MFA in fiction from the Iowa Writers Workshop and received a Wallace Stegner Fellowship to Stanford University for the coming year to continue writing her first novel, *In a High Place*. She would live in Palo Alto while I stayed behind to run the business. And care for our three children. I was fine with childcare and was looking forward to it.

On one side of our future bookstore was *The Squeeze Inn*, a breakfast restaurant that was well on its way to omelet nirvana and on the other side the local newspaper office. I set to work immediately. The store came together quickly. I had a sign carved out of wood that read *Truckee River Book and Tea* and had it hung perpendicular to the brick-front so that customers could easily see it as they walked down the sidewalk. I could jump and touch it like the basketball rim I'd left behind. *I still had hops.* I felt good. The air at altitude 5890 feet was fresh. It was a glorious yellow aspen mountain fall. I looked forward to winter snow. I was excited about being a bookman. As I envisioned it, tourists would return home after skiing in the Sierra and tell their neighbors about the charming bookstore in Truckee that served coffee and bagels in the back of the store.

Bookshelves in our store lined the walls downstairs. One bookcase with shelves on either side stood in the center of the floor. On one side of the store entrance, I constructed a brick hearth and installed a pot bellied stove. Laying the bricks myself made me feel like a real working man, none of this privileged NBA life. In the back of the store, we built a tea and coffee bar.

I hired a carpenter to build stairs that led to a loft, where the children's section would be located. The railing of the stairs was constructed out of one length of redwood, and it curved in waves up the stairs. On the wall facing the railing were shelves displaying our self-help and spiritual books. I thought of it as my Baba Ram Das section. I could have named it my Carlos Castaneda section just as easily since his *Teaching of Don Juan: A Yaqui Way of Knowledge* turned out to be the store's best seller.

It was the 70's. Many of the new arrivals to Truckee were men and women fleeing the big city for a quieter and politically understandable life in a small town. Some were liberal activists who had come to believe that the best way to effect change was from the bottom up. They were all good-hearted people and easy going, and we soon made many friends. They were excited that there would be a bookstore in their town.

It's a crisp fall day in 1976. Inside The Truckee River Book and Tea's opening day party, shoppers browsing, some curled up in front of the pot belly, leafing through books. A tea bar takes up part of the back of the store. We serve an assortment of teas, coffee, and bagels with a variety of spreads. The cream cheese pimento spread is a big hit. I am standing behind the cash register thinking that a book-food combination store will guarantee success.

I was sort of right, and I was very wrong.

Shortly after the store opened for business, Joanne departed for Stanford on a Wallace Stegner Fellowship. I was not unhappy to see her leave. I was hoping the separation would relieve the stress and possibly put our derailed marriage back on track. Sometimes, when you look back on your life, you feel like slapping yourself to get your own attention. I did not imagine at the time that it would have the exact opposite effect.

With Joanne gone, I'd dress the kids in the morning and watch them from the window of our home on the hill, trudge, skip, run or, in winter, bundled in their parkas, slip-slide down the hill to Donner Pass Road. The school bus would pick them up at the corner in front of Ernie's Bakery. On wintery days, Ernie, the baker, would meet the children of the neighborhood with freshly baked donut holes and hot cocoa. Is it any wonder my children believe they grew up in a magical place? Once the kids were out of the house, I'd have my coffee, then head down the hill and open the store. I loved going to work. I'd unlock the door and I swear I could smell the aroma of books.

On some weekends, Joanne returned to help with the children and the store, but for most of the first year, it was me and three little ones. I remember those months as some of the best of my life, buying books, talking books, recommending books, serving tea and bagels in the back of the store. Our store was connected to the Squeeze Inn next door, a popular breakfast and lunch restaurant. Sometimes their customers would come in carrying their plates and sit and read at the bar or at one of the small tables across from the bar. From time-to-time NBA fans would come into the store, and we'd talk hoops, that is, those who remembered me. It was only 1976, five years since I retired from playing. Was I already in the past tense? I signed up for an amateur basketball league that played on the high school court in the evenings. All I needed was a babysitter, and I was back to being a gym rat. It is curious when I think of it that playing in these amateur games I played hard as I always did, but I never got angry. So, it was not the fury of the game that caused my bouts of anger in the NBA.

• • •

What then could it have been? *Sweat without stress?* Nothing that simple I figured. Why I played angry in the NBA has been something I've always longed to understand. I had read somewhere that a certain amount of anger is necessary for survival. As a child in Japan, I had certainly been exposed to enough bodily threat that surviving must have meant a lot to me.

If that was the case, one answer to the question could be that I was far more insecure about my game and my life than I understood, so every game, even team practices menaced me. If I didn't play well, would I lose my starting role? What came next? Being traded. Being cut? Basketball supported my life. What would I have done without it? The greater question being, who would I have been without it? I considered this a real possibility. Luckily, I thought, I had survived basketball and was now living the ideal, less stressful life. To hell with the money, the glory, the endorphins, I'd get my rush drinking coffee and becoming a rich bookstore owner.

• • •

My home life consisted of making dinner for the kids. I always liked to cook. The kids and I ate together at our large dining room table. After dinners, the kids in their pajamas, (oh, man were they cute) all of us on the couch, Matt on my lap. We'd watch some show on the smallest television set on the planet, or I'd read to them. *The Camel Who Took a Walk* and *Pop Corn and Ma Goodness* are children's books that come to mind. And *Will You Be My Mother* and *Frog and Toad*. They never failed to find the worm in Richard Scarry's *Cars, Trucks, and Things That Go*.

• • •

In the second year of owning the bookstore, Joanne returned and took her turn selling books, but she was completing *In a High Place which became an award winning first novel*. Ruth, our friend from Iowa City, with her daughter, Buzzy, moved to Truckee. Ruth took over the tea and bagels part of the business. A born raconteur, Ruth turned the back of the store into a local's club. In my second year, I sold the lot we owned on Mercer Island in Washington to keep the bookstore afloat. We were losing money, but I kept at it, loving the book part of the business, and hating the business part. Why didn't I cut my losses after the second year? I can only hazard that there exists in me a singularity of purpose that is not always a rewarding trait.

• • •

Peter Guber, one of the two principal owners of the Golden State Warriors wrote a book *Tell to Win* in which he states, "Today, everyone is in the emotional transportation business whether they know it or not. Success is increasingly won by telling compelling stories. . ."

The following meeting in the bookstore is the first paragraph in the story of my future marriage to Melanie Marchant. Melanie and I reflect on the first moment we set eyes on each other *whether we knew it or not*. Did it actually happen? We believe so. Mel paints portraits. She says she never forgets a face.

You came into the store with your kids just off the mountain from skiing.

You were young, blonde, and gorgeous.

You flirted with me shamelessly.

The other way around, Melanie.

I was a married woman; I would never have flirted.

Three decades later both of us divorced, we would meet and marry, what do you make of that?

You were very tall and had dimples.

Like the detectives in my favorite mystery novels, I do not believe in coincidences.

• • •

Year three of the Truckee River Book & Tea would be its last. I finally had to admit that I was not a good businessman and the store, after expenses, was draining our limited financial resources. If all that was required of being a bookman was purchasing books, recommending books, getting excited over new titles and authors; if all that was required for being a coach was having played the game. *You get my drift.* By the summer, the shade of my balance sheet looked like blood. I sold the store at a loss and for the rest of the summer sat at the kitchen table smoking cigarettes, drinking coffee, and feeling sorry for myself.

CHAPTER 31
MAN WITH A LUNCH BUCKET

My second attempt to recover from the life of professional basketball was not much of an attempt, but rather an escape. Joanne's first novel, *In a High Place*, had sold and her advance from Simon & Schuster against royalties helped financially, but not enough. It is my recollection of that time that I considered getting back into the NBA, that there had to be a job, perhaps with the Warriors, perhaps as an assistant coach, perhaps as a scout. But I had made a promise to Joanne that my traveling days were over. As our savings continued to diminish, I yearned for the financial security that the NBA had provided. I resented my promise.

I remember feeling guilty. I was a captive of the 1950's culture that taught boys that fathers were sole providers, and that they knew best. It was my responsibility, and I was failing. I've wondered if this belief of dads being sole providers is stronger in immigrant males. At least for my generation of immigrants, the answer would be yes. I'm sure it weighed heavily on my father that he could not provide for his family. I know it weighed on me.

For a while, I painted houses. Now I was a *real* working man. I packed my lunch bucket in the morning and drove to Reno to meet the painting contractor. I climbed ladders, scraped old paint, applied an undercoat, brushed on new paint, cleaned brushes, and arrived home exhausted. I had become the kind of working man that my father would have understood. For two months of that time, I came home to my studio apartment in Reno because Joanne and I had separated.

This was not the labor of sports, but pure physical labor. The beers didn't go down as well. By the third month, I was back living in Truckee, giving

our marriage another try. When it didn't go well, I left for a month to paint
houses with my friend Dell Martin on the Oregon and California coasts.
Dell and I had met in Portland. We shared a love of sports and poetry.
Dell's sport was track. At one time he was the fastest sprinter on an excellent
Stanford University track team and had competed against the likes of John
Carlos and Tommy Smith. With Dell, the painting was less like labor. We
talked poetry; we listened to PBS. We talked hoops. We even played some
hoops after work, both of us still in spattered painting pants and shirts,
playing on an asphalt court, not unlike the playgrounds I played on when I
was in high school. We played all comers. We kicked butt.

Finally, no matter what kind of narrative spin I put on the importance
of an honest day's labor, I felt diminished and miserable.

My reaction, as I look back on it, would puzzle today's immigrants
who look upon labor and a daily paycheck as a worthy goal. It shames me
that I thought of myself as special. My father labored, first on the docks
of San Francisco and later long hours repairing false teeth, never earning
enough, knowing without my mother's earnings our family would have
been in dire straits. And what kind of labor did he see his son doing?
Playing basketball? Did I think that made me worthy? I should have been
more sympathetic to my father. It's taken writing a memoir in my old age
to admit my appreciation for him is long overdue.

I wish my father had lived to read this poem I wrote for him:

JOURNEYMAN

For my father
I admit sleeping in late at the Hilton,
Ordering room service,
Handing out big tips while other men
Are opening their lunch buckets. I know
you would have scolded me:
Что это за работа для мужчины?
(What kind of work is this for a man?)
Old immigrant, I admit all of this
too late. You died before I could explain
newspapers call me a journeyman.
They write I roll up my sleeves

and go to work. They use words
like hammer and muscle to describe me.
For three straight years on the job
my nose collapsed. My knees ached,
and I could never talk myself out of less
than two injuries at a time. Father,
you would have been proud of me:
I labored in the company of large men.

Meschery, Tom. "Journeyman," *Nothing We Lose Can Be Replaced*, Black Rock Press, Rain Shadow Edition, 1999. University of Nevada, Reno. Reno, NV

CHAPTER 32
SCREWUPS ONE & TWO

First came a job teaching English and coaching varsity basketball at Wooster High School in Reno, Nevada. I didn't have a teaching credential, but I had enough education credits that I was hired on a provisional contract. I figured to be a better coach at high school than I was as a pro coach. I wasn't. It did turn out, however, that I was a good English teacher. I could have stayed on at Wooster High, but. . .

That's when I did something really dumb.

What happened next would take extended hours on a counselor's couch for me to explain. At the end of the school year, 1982, the Continental Basketball Association, the CBA, a mostly East Coast minor league, unaffiliated with the NBA, expanded to the West, and a franchise was purchased by a group of Reno businessmen. They offered me the head coaching job of the Reno Bighorns. I took the job and resigned my teaching position. My decision did not turn out well. The Big Horns wound up last in its division. My coaching stunk, and in the spring of 1983, the Bighorn franchise went bankrupt. Then I made another foolish move. The commissioner of the CBA, Jim Drucker, offered me the position of deputy commissioner.

When I think back, I was about to make the worst decision of my life, and by then, I'd already made several bad ones.

I signed a contract and left my family in Truckee with the promise that I would faithfully send them a monthly check. My girls were in their junior and sophomore years in high school. I drove across the country to the league office in Philadelphia, rationalizing all the way that I was doing this for my family. But I was floundering and frightened of failure, so this move was about me and who I was.

As I examine my behavior during those times in retrospect, (what would memoirs do without the word, retrospect?) **I must** admit that my identity and ego without basketball was more fragile than I thought. I needed to examine the source of that frailty: My parents were Russian, which meant I was, but I was born in Manchuria, no longer a country. I arrived in the United States as a Displaced Person. In America I was labeled an Immigrant. I would have to wait for years to be a citizen. When I became a citizen, the McCarthy Period began, and I was called a commie. Who the hell was I? I was clinging to that part of me I knew best - the basketball part of me and not doing a very good job of it.

It would take me many more years before I could answer the question, who was I? I flogged myself through seven months being the CBA'sb Deputy Commissioner, a job for which I had no training, living in a less-than-attractive singles apartment, listening to the zany promotional ideas of James Drucker, my boss, one of which was the Million Dollar-Half-Time-Half-Court Shot; and traveling to small franchise cities evaluating teams and administrations. There was much glad-handing with team owners, many of whom knew very little about basketball, while I knew virtually nothing about sports administration. There were conversations about team finance. I felt ignorant but did nothing to improve my ignorance. My gut must have been telling me it would be no use.

The only bright spot during my tenure with the CBA, and I mean *the only* one, occurred on Easter weekend when my teenage daughters, Janai and Megan, flew into Philadelphia to visit me. My sister, Ann, at that time, an advertising executive in New York City, took them shopping for spring prom dresses. On Saturday night, the three of us and Ann attended the midnight service at the New York City Cathedral of the Lady of Signs, and they saw Mikhail Baryshnikov. They still talk about that sighting as if they were ornithologists and the famous ballet dancer was an exotic, rare species of bird.

I resigned my position in March of 1985 and drove home back across the country, smoking one cigarette after another, knowing I'd lost another year of my life and that there would be no job waiting for me. I was a failure, a man who could not support his family. What every man in my generation grew up knowing he must do. In my case, father did not know best. I had some serious decisions to make.

I had not been unhappy being a teacher. I would give it a second try. However, it would take a return trip to West Africa before my teaching career began in earnest.

AFRICA REVISITED
Fall of 1985

People create stories create people; or rather stories create people create stories.
Chenua Achebe

CHAPTER 33
POTO POTO TIME

The USIA needed a French-speaking coach to conduct basketball clinics in West Africa. I needed a job. I applied and was hired for the position. The contract was for four months from September through December of 1985. I flew to Washington D.C., met with my employer, the United States Information Agency, taped an interview in French and a few days later boarded a flight for Paris. I did as much sightseeing as I could. The Eiffel Tower, the Champs-Elysees, the Arc de Triomphe. I ate at an outdoor café. I smoked Gitanes again. It is shameful to remember that as I sat at that café, smoking, and sipping brandy, looking out at the bustling streets of Paris, I had felt free of my family responsibilities. The next morning, I boarded a flight to Niamey, Niger.

The Niger Sports Federation must not have received the message that a well-known former NBA player was arriving. Instead of a hotel that befitted me , I was housed in a student dormitory. I didn't complain even though the room was spartan and the shower hardly worked. It was not too unlike my dormitory room in college without the crucifix on the wall.

I was pretty sure they had no idea that I was an NBA basketball player when I was driven to the practice and discovered the women's team instead of the men's. The men's national team, I was told, was playing in a tournament in Senegal. I was two decades removed from the last time I was in West Africa, but I hadn't forgotten the response to all such dilemmas. "Pas de problem," I said and introduced myself to the women in my flawless French. Their response to what must have been some gross grammatical error was a lot of hand-covering-the-mouth giggles. I was not offended. Language is the art of communication and by the end of practice we were doing fine. The young women were reasonably skilled and by the next day I decided I would not have had as much success with the men.

In the center of the dusty dormitory courtyard stands a single tree that might better have qualified as its skeletal remains. Every day after practice, I sit in the minimal shade of that tree and play checkers with the Chinese gymnastic coaches. None of them speak any English or French, but we manage and have a heck of a good time. They laugh a lot and I laugh a lot. They crack up every time they say, "King Me!" My prowess at checkers is clearly not legendary. Our checker playing comes to an end when a Chinese official informs me that the coaches no longer wish to play checkers with me, something I know is untrue. This official is very solemn and comically scary, like a Peter Lorre villain out of a 1950's film noir. What he means to say is that he would no longer allow the coaches to play checkers with an American war-mongering capitalist. I could show him the balance in my checkbook to assure him I'm by no means a successful capitalist, but I suspect he would not see the humor in that.

Niger was a dreadfully poor country. Still is. But one afternoon I was driven through a neighborhood of gated homes facing broad streets lined with palm trees with gatekeepers. These homes would not have been out of place in the priciest neighborhood in Miami. I was told this was where the rich of Niamey and the foreign diplomatic corps lived. No open sewers in sight. I was not so young anymore, past thirty, and becoming more politicized. Poverty, wherever I encountered it in Africa or in the United States, made me feel ashamed.

Next on my tour was the Republic of the Congo.

When I played in the NBA, flying from city to city, air travel never frightened me. This was about to change. I boarded the Air Mali twin engine turboprop at the airport, the destination, the Republic of the Congo's capital, Brazzaville. I'd traveled on twin engine turbo-prop commuter airplanes on my previous coaching trips to Africa, so I wasn't nervous. That is until our pilot entered the cabin wearing jeans and a T-shirt, one sleeve rolled over a pack of cigarettes, like a character out of the movie, *The Wild Ones*. When he emerged from the cockpit later, with his uniform jacket on, in jeans, to say a few words about our flight, I was not reassured. He spoke French too rapidly for my basic comprehension. For all I knew he could have just announced his impending plan to drive the plane to the ground like a dart and take us all with him.

As our airplane roars into the air, the pilot at the controls, I feel the first twinges of fright, followed immediately by full-blown fear of dying. We barely clear a grove of palm trees at the end of the runway and rocket into the clouds. People on the plane are screaming and children are crying. Much to my relief, we survive and level off. The ride turns smooth. My fear subsides. Clear skies and smooth flying the rest of the way. I feel almost normal as we approach our destination. Then comes our descent into the Brazzaville airport. The airplane begins to lurch from side to side, as if it has lost all sense of its aeronautic footing. My fear doubles down. I am certain the plane would miss the runway. Once again, the crying begins as well as invocations to the deities. Certain that this time it's death, I start thinking of my children conjuring various images of them in my mind: My daughter Megan, as a 10-year-old at her first swim meet; my oldest daughter, Janai, sprinting 100 meters, her blonde pony-tail flying in the wind; my son Matthew in his yellow and white Little League uniform throwing fastballs to me in our backyard; all three of my children floating down the Truckee River in inner tubes. Those images sustain me through several harrowing air-bumps, until the wheels slam onto the tarmac and the plane taxies to a stop in front of the terminal. The Gods of all faiths are being credited with our survival. I am crediting love. No thought of your wife?

Since that time whenever I have had to travel by air, I have relied on imagining Melanie, or my children and more recently, my grandchildren during take offs and landings.

• • •

There is a final flight into the universe that is fast approaching that at my age I can no longer ignore. I think I'll use this strategy when the time comes.

• • •

The following poems are short images, mostly my first impressions about each of the countries in which I coached on this trip.

BRAZZAVILE: Republic of the Congo, 1985

Entering the airport, the soldier
guarding the passport booth
can't be more than fifteen years old.

He's holding a rifle at port arms,
a cigarette dangling from his lips.
Above him, a banner in red print reads:
A Bas Les Americans! Down With Americans!
"Don't worry," the Embassy man says,
"They don't mean basketball coaches."

Meschery, Tom. "Brazzaville, Republic of the Congo," *Nothing We Lose Can Be Replaced*, Black Rock Press, Rain Shadow Edition, 1999. University of Nevada, Reno. Reno, NV

It made me nervous seeing several teenage soldiers wearing wrap-around sunglasses, holding weapons bigger than they were. I felt as if I was in the middle of a James Bond movie. The Charge d'Affaire who met me at the baggage claim could not persuade me that as a basketball coach I wasn't in any danger. It turned out he was right. The Republic of the Congo was a country of bizarre contradictions. The government maintained a precarious and cynical relationship with both the United States and the Soviet Union. For financial consideration, they spied on both superpowers, which profited them immensely. The proof was noticeable in the shop windows filled with Russian and American products. It seemed everybody in Brazzaville was riding a brand new motorbike or moped. On the other side of the Congo River was Zaire, previously called The Democratic Republic of the Congo, a capitalist country, whose president was the Dictator Mobutu Sese Seko, supported by the United States CIA according to the widely accepted rumor. It was a horrifically poor country.

On the wealthy side of the Congo River in the rich Republic of faux Communists, I was introduced to a uniquely African time management strategy.

POTO POTO TIME

They will arrive for practice in their
own good time called Poto Poto.
I am standing on an empty court
looking nervously at my watch

which is what Americans do.
The sky is darkening and the wind
is rising. It is monsoon season.
It could rain for days and days.
The backboards growing darker,
and still no players on the horizon.

Meschery, Tom. "Poto Poto Time," *Nothing We Lose Can Be Replaced*, Black Rock Press, Rain Shadow Edition, 1999. University of Nevada, Reno. Reno, NV

Eventually the players would show up. No apologies. I'm a quick learner. I acclimated to Poto Poto time, kicked back, after which the players and I got a lot of work done on the basketball court. When I returned to the United States, I remember writing to Saint Mary's College suggesting a scouting trip to West Africa might turn up some potential prospects. There were already African players enrolled and playing in American colleges. In 1984, Hakeem Olajuwon of Nigeria, who played for the University of Houston, had been the NBA's # 1 draft choice of the Houston Rockets.

Most evenings after practice, I'd take a taxi to a Vietnamese restaurant that overlooked the Congo River. I'd sit on the veranda, drink Tsing Tao, a Chinese beer, served in sweating-cold quart bottles, eat crispy summer rolls of shrimp and pork called nims and watch islands of lily pads floating down the immense river toward the Atlantic Ocean. Once, I saw a small white deer standing on top of a lily pad. I took it as a sign. In the distance I could see the smog shrouding the high-rise buildings of Kinshasa, the capital of Zaire, a country that was as remote from democracy as our planet is from Pluto.

During the Second World War, the headquarters for General Charles de Gaulle's Free French Army was in Brazzaville. It was to Brazzaville at the end of movie, *Casablanca* that Humphry Bogart and Claude Rains were heading to join up to fight the Nazis.

I left The Republic of the Congo feeling the citizens of this country were better equipped to deal with the stress of time and schedules, they simply didn't take them very seriously. You arrived when you arrived; you performed what was required. You were not a slacker. The hour hand of the clock should not dictate your life. I took this lesson with me on the rest of my trip and back to the United States. In America, It is difficult to run your life on Poto Poto time. I found that out quickly enough. But I did manage to slow down. If I didn't stop to smell the roses, I at least stopped occasionally to admire them.

• • •

My next coaching assignment was in the country of Burkina Faso. The country had started as the Republic of Upper Volta. Its President, Thomas Sankara, had renamed it Burkina Faso. It too claimed to be a Communist country, but unlike the Republic of the Congo, Burkina Faso was desperately poor. The capital where I coached was called Ouagadougou. I liked the sound of the word and found myself often repeating it aloud. You had to move your lips over the syllables to pronounce it correctly. The team practiced on an outdoor court. The players were not as advanced as some of the other West African teams, but they were hard workers and surprisingly punctual..

HAKEEM OLAJUWON

aka Hakeem the Dream

In Africa each morning practice starts
with warm-ups. The youngest on the team,
perhaps sixteen, always the first waiting for me,
sits in the thin shade below the backboard,
reading the latest article about Hakeem.
We stretch hamstrings, then slow jog
around the court. He keeps pace, all the while
talking about The Dream. "Dis donc," he says,
"With The Dream we would defeat Senegal
and be champions of West Africa. Que
pensez vous, entrainerur?" What do I think?
I can't think about anything other than the red
and smoky sun rising over the opposite basket,
the heat already sweating my shirt, and how
the rains suddenly begin halfway through practice.
I shag his jump shots, the ones he swears

are like Hakeem's. He says he too will attend
The University of Houston, later play in the NBA.
"Vous m'assistez?" But his shots are ugly, too flat;
I nod my head, whatever I can do to help –
my best shot. I'm in the country of Burkina Fasso.
Its name means Land of Up-Right People.

Meschery, Tom. "Hakeem Olajuwon," *Nothing We Lose Can
Be Replaced*, Black Rock Press, Rain Shadow Edition, 1999.
University of Nevada, Reno. Reno, NV9

I conducted a two-day clinic in the city of Bobo Dioulasso located in
the mountains west of the capital, close to the border of the Ivory Coast, a
country in which two decades earlier John Havlieck, K.C. Jones and I had
coached. I could have caught a train in the morning and been in Abidjan
by night, dancing in the Boule Noir, the nightclub I remembered fondly
from my first trip to Africa.

My final coaching assignment, early December, was in Mali, a country
I had also coached in twice in previous years. Poor Mali. These days its
northern provinces are being terrorized by the Boko Haram, Islamists.

*It is Sunday afternoon in Bamako, Mali toward the end of my coaching
stay, I take the day off to go exploring. I borrow a jeep from the embassy
and depart the capital for a drive in the countryside. On the outskirts, I
stop to take photographs of some buildings that I was told were excellent
examples of the architecture of the French Colonial period. I am clicking
away when two jeeps suddenly appear out of nowhere, roaring toward
me. In Africa, appearances out of nowhere are not uncommon. You can
be driving through a vacant landscape of sand and thorn bushes, not a
village for miles, and spot an old man or woman squatting in the shade
of a single Baobab tree or walking by the side of the road. Maybe a goat
nearby.*

*When the jeeps come to a stop, soldiers leap out, pointing rifles at me.
They are yelling, "Interdit! Interdit!" What isn't allowed? I don't get it. The
officer, a young man wearing wraparound sunglasses, so I can't see his eyes,
demands my passport. I give it to him. Then, he holds out his hand for my
camera, which I refuse to give him, until one of the soldiers places the muzzle
of his rifle against my temple. The camera or my head – it's an easy decision.*

I am now thoroughly frightened. The officer demands to know why I'm photographing a military installation. I had no idea that they were military installations. That answer does not satisfy him. I am hurried into a jeep and taken to the recently photographed military installation that up close looks like Tara, the mansion in "Gone With the Wind." For the rest of the morning, I am interrogated. I stand in front of the officer's desk. He will not allow me sit. I tell them repeatedly "Je suis un entraineur Americain de basketball, travaillant avec l'equipe nationale Malienne. An American basketball coach working with the Malian national team.

"Non, non, vous ete un espion, CIA, CIA,"

They think I'm a CIA spy. My fear is growing with every "espions" and my Non, non, non! My continued requests to call the American Embassy are ignored. Finally, the officer in charge shakes his head. In sorrow or in anger, I'm uncertain. I've decided this officer is related to Idi Amin. The thought is not comforting. I am taken to a jail cell in the basement where I remain all afternoon in a cell with no windows and no air-conditioning. Spiders (big, black and scary ones) and cockroaches are my companions. I call the spiders Armageddons. I call the cockroaches disgusting. There is only an army cot to sleep on and it's filthy. It's a long night of imagination: I am Edmond Dantes imprisoned in Chateau d'If. I am Ivan in a Soviet gulag in Solzhenitsyn's One Day in the Life of Ivan Denisovich. I am Fabrizio, sentenced to 12 years in a tower prison, in Stendhal's Charterhouse. I don't want to sleep. There are critters. It's inconceivable that an American would be treated this way. Finally, in the morning of the next day, someone at the American Embassy comes to my rescue.

At the embassy, I was furious. I demanded to know how this could have happened. My passport was in order. Clearly, I am not a spy. One foreign service officer said it might have been my birthplace, Harbin, China, that confused them. Another said, you know it's Africa. Which reminded me of the last lines in the movie, Chinatown, "Forget it, Jake, it's Chinatown."

I never did get my camera back.

Despite that terrible night, Mali remains one of my favorite West African countries and Bamako, one of my favorite West African capitals.

Philip Pillsbury, from the Embassy, with whom I'd become friendly, convinced me to join him one evening for music and dancing in a village outside the capital. Nothing he explained, started before 10 or so and didn't hit its stride until midnight. He picked me up at my hotel at 11 p.m., and we took off in his jeep. A few miles outside the capital, he turned on to a gravel road and soon the forest closed in on either side of us. I was imagining wild beasts. Phil drove like he didn't believe in torturous road conditions, darkness, or the beasts that were about to overtake us. We hit a railroad crossing, and the jeep flew into the air. We landed wheels on either side of the track. Stuck. If a train came along the jeep was toast. I had walked far enough away from the collision to feel safe. Phil remained seated in the jeep. He didn't seem concerned. I asked him what we were going to do, imagining a night of lions and leopards checking out the white meat. "Pas de problem," he said. Not a problem? In all my trips to Francophone countries in West Africa, pas de problem was, and probably still is, in use. Perhaps it was a continent's casual way of dealing with its insurmountable difficulties.

As it turned out Phil was right. A half hour or so later, I saw lights. A group of men approached with lanterns. Phil talked to them. Soon four men at each end of the jeep began chanting "Ally Oop, ally oop!" It sounded like the name of the caveman cartoon character from the funnies I had read as a child. But what they were really saying was in French, Allez meaning let's go and in English, up – Allez Up! They lifted us off the tracks, then all piled into the jeep and we drove to the village, which was no more than 10 minutes away around the bend in the road. The rest of the night we danced and drank and listened to drumming and woke up at dawn with hangovers. On the ride home I asked Philip how they knew. He shrugged. After I was back in the United States, I tried to contact Phil, but was told he no longer worked for the U.S. Government. I later heard that he had been forced out of Foreign Service for being too close to the native population. *Gone native* was the expression. I recall his saying that he was working on a book on grammar of the various Malian languages. My last night in West Africa was Christmas Eve.

CHRISTMAS IN BAMAKO

Coaching basketball in Mali is easy,
celebrating Christmas Eve in eighty degrees
around a tinseled palm tree is not.
Where I live in America, there's snow
in the mountains and my children
are opening their gifts. Moi,

Je n'ai pas de cadeaux a leur envoyer,
not even, myself. My Malian players
believe Jesus was just another prophet,
not as important as Muhammad,
so tomorrow I've scheduled practice.
When I return home, I'll tell my children
about these players and about a desert
country with palm trees not unlike
in the country where Jesus was born
sometime in the heat of summer.

Meschery, Tom. "Christmas in Bamako," *Nothing We Lose Can Be Replaced*, Black Rock Press, Rain Shadow Edition, 1999. University of Nevada, Reno. Reno, NV

FROM AT RISK TO ADVANCED PLACEMENT
1986 - 2005

*"I cannot be a teacher without exposing
who I am."*
Paulo Freire

CHAPTER 34
IN THE BASEMENT

Fall 1986

Those who can, do; those who can't, teach. Whoever said these words never spent a day teaching in a classroom on any level of education, let alone an alternative education classroom full of truants, potheads and high school malcontents with anger management issues.

It was in such a classroom at the age of 48 that I started my 19-year teaching career at Reno High School. It began in the basement of the building as the only teacher in a newly organized federally funded program called Alternative Education, designed to serve students who could not or would not function in a traditional classroom. These were not students with disabilities; these were students designated as *At Risk*, often referred to by some teachers as the *knuckleheads*. Did I know what I was getting into when I applied for the job? Not really. I had driven down from Truckee, looking forward to my first day in a classroom. I was happy to be employed. Let me rephrase that; I was overjoyed. This looked like it could be a long-term career. I could support my family. I had a secondary school teaching certificate. I had a contract with the Washoe County School District. For a number of years, I had felt like a loser. Those days were behind me. Briefcase in hand and lesson plans in mind with a newfound energy and feeling a little like I did as a rookie on my first day on the court, I entered the building **and** walked down to the basement to my assigned classroom.

Throw the ball up, start the game.

I walked in the door. There were no windows. In front of me were rows of student desks. Empty, except for one in which there was a body slumped over the desk, head in arms. I couldn't tell the gender. He or she appeared asleep. I thought of Robert Frost saying, "I am not a teacher, I am an awakener." As I stepped forward to do the awakening, I caught a whiff of a nasty odor coming from the body. The body belonged to a young male.I could see vomit seeping out from under the arms of his leather jacket. My first decision as a high school teacher was not an intellectual awakening, but a call for school security that arrived promptly to haul my first ever student away. My second job as a teacher was to clean up the vomit that seemed to be a visual mixture of pizza and chow-Mein. The sub-text aroma was whiskey. Walking back from the utility closet with a mop, bucket, and paper towels, there was no doubt in my mind that the National Basketball Association was far behind me.

In my four years in the basement of Reno High School, I suffered no more spewing. I did experience some extremely difficult kids - some drunk, some drugged, most of them angry about their lives. For every basement success I enjoyed, I could count on ten failures, a miserable percentage. Imagine if an NBA player shot 10% for a season, he'd be out on his butt playing in a D League. But Alternative Ed was not a sport, although there was plenty of gamesmanship required to teach teenagers who despised education and authority, and in too many cases, themselves.

The federal government provided half the budget for Alternative Education, whose informal label was *A School within a School*. I was given a free hand to spend. I bought computers- just as they were beginning to be used in education.

And I bought a pool table.

I recall one of my colleagues saying, "You're kidding, right? You put pool cues in the hands of angry teenagers."

My idea was simplicity itself, if a kid finished his or her assignment in class ahead of time, he or she could play pool. I bought a sofa and floor cushions. I bought a small refrigerator. Most of my students came to school hungry and smelling of tobacco. I served orange juice and blueberry muffins. Their culinary tastes were not ready for bran. I taught all five core classes, even mathematics, which was a little unnerving. In basketball, there are player-friendly coaches. I saw myself as a student-friendly teacher. My students as a whole were not teacher-friendly.

But some, like the following girl in my poem, were achingly adorable.

SONNET FOR A FUTURE BEAUTICIAN

Lord, give this little girl what she wants.
Her dream is so modest: that hair
will be beautiful and perfectly styled,
that she will possess the knack, the light touch
by which all strands will bend to her command,
sweep back or lightly fall over one eye;
that she can also manicure on the side,
hold her customers' hands gently
in and out of a cleansing liquid,
listening to their stories while she files
and decorates, cutting back the cuticles.
For this little girl, Lord, let hair
be heavenly set and on those slender nails,
allow pale half-moons to rise forever.

Meschery, Tom. "Sonnet for a Future Beautician," *Nothing We Lose Can Be Replaced*, Black Rock Press, Rain Shadow Edition, 1999. University of Nevada, Reno. Reno, NV

In my second year, the principal hired an additional teacher for Alternative Education. His name was Aubrey McCreary. He was also hired to coach the varsity basketball team. That of course meant the two of us talking hoops when we should have been paying more attention to the students. I wound up helping him with the team.

Help, but not coach, no way.

Aubrey and I became good friends. After Aubrey retired from teaching, he became a physical fitness trainer. Two of his successes were NBA players Derrick Fisher and Paul Milsap.

Years later, both of us out of teaching, Aubrey and I would reminisce about our time together in Alternative Education. Over a few beers.

Did I remember the kid with the Burger King?

How could I forget?

One boy was in the habit of returning from lunch break still eating his Double Whopper even though it was against the rules to eat in class. I kept taking the burger away from him. This dance went on for about a week. The day Aubrey was asking me to recall was the day I took the burger away and was about to toss it into the trash next to my desk when I heard the student behind me call me a muthafucker. The distance between my desk and the boy was about 30 feet. I wheeled around, gave it my best pitching form and let fly. The burger hit the kid square in the face, tomato, mustard, burger meat, lettuce and all the condiments dripping from his chin. Best pitch I ever threw.

What about Quiet Girl?

She was a tiny thing. Barely spoke, skinny, cute smile, frizzy brown hair, dimples. The school counselor had enrolled her in our class halfway through the semester. She kept to herself, kept her head down, did her work. Two desks away from her sat a mean foul-mouthed biker chick, who made it her mission in life to bully the quiet one. Aubrey and I did all we could to stop it, handing out detention slips to the biker chick, reporting her to the vice-principal of discipline. She'd stop, then start again. She was addicted to meanness.

Aubrey was smiling, waiting for the punch-line he knew was coming, and it came - big time and not a play on words.

After Biker-Chick directed a particularly vicious comment at her, the quiet, gentle-one leaped from her chair onto her desk, bent her knees, let out a howl, and launched herself though the air over the desk that separated them. I remember her body horizontal to the floor. Frozen in place behind our desks, we watched as Quiet-One's fist hit Biker-Chick on the jaw, causing her to fall backward over her chair to the floor. We're talking comic book Super Woman. A split second later, Quiet-One had her fingers around Biker-Chick's throat, slamming her head into the floor before we arrived to pull her off the dazed Biker Chick. Quiet-Girl hyperventilating. One of us said, "Holy shit!"

• • •

In my third year in Alternative Education, the principal added a science teacher, George Kerr, who was already on the faculty. Aubrey had taken over the math instruction. I now taught only history and English. George taught us how to deal with administration. I remember the moment well when he told us, "Boys, it is easier to get absolution than to get permission." This dictum resulted in the Three Amigos of Alternative Education, unbeknownst to administrators, managing to appropriate a lot of additional classroom materials. For the rest of my teaching career, I followed George's philosophy.

These were the stories Aubrey and I could laugh about because they were by no means some of our most difficult and horror stories from our time as teachers of At Risk kids. From alternative education teachers, I have heard even worse stories. When I think of people who denigrate the profession of teaching, I would love to talk to them after they spent a week teaching in an alternative education classroom.

There were also stories that were desperately sad. By the time these kids arrived at our basement, they were already so broken by poverty and drugs and parental ignorance or abuse or neglect that all you could do was weep for them. The most horrific were the cases of sexual abuse. A school counselor told me the percentage of children that recovered psychologically from such violence was low. The statistic couldn't have been made clearer to me as I was part of a parent teacher conference for one of my students. The scene remains fixed in my memory.

I'm in the principal's office for a truancy intervention for one of my sophomore students, a wisp of a girl, who'd be mistaken for a seventh-grader. A row of freckles bridges her nose. She needs braces. Also in the room, on either side of her across from the principal, sit her mother and father. I have read the reports. It is not spelled out, but it is evident from the language that her father is the student's abuser. The implication is horrifying. But we're not here for that heinous behavior, but because of the girl's truancy. Not about the abuse, for God's sake. Her counselor and I are sitting off to the side. Every time I look at the father, the fury inside me grows. At one point in the intervention I watch, horrified, as he places his hand on his daughter's knee. I can see her little jaw clench. I want to grab this youngster and rush out of this room and find a place for her to live safely, away from this sadism.

Within a month the girl and her parents moved out of our district. She would go to another school. There would no doubt be another meeting in another administrator's office.

• • •

In my years in the basement of Reno High School, I don't believe there were enough student successes to count on the fingers of one hand. I would like to say that those few successes made up for the rest of the failures, but that would be untrue. Toward the end of the fourth year, I began feeling like Eeyore, *Winne the Pooh's donkey pal,* who walked around with his head down, a dark rain cloud hovering above his head.

Then, the dark cloud burst, and light shone through. I was chosen to be a senior Advanced Placement English teacher. I began with a little help from James Joyce.

CHAPTER 35
THE DEAD

My escape from the basement of Alternative Education and its sad cadre of students came in the nick of time. The 81-year-old legendary Senior AP English teacher, Mrs. Muth, announced her retirement. Before her position could be offered outside the school, the teachers in our English Department, of which I was marginally a member, had to be given the opportunity to apply. As I recall, no one wanted to follow The Legend. As a relatively new teacher and suffering from Alternative Education blues, I applied, interviewed, and was hired for the job. It turned out that I was damn good at it. There are AP classes in virtually all high schools in America, and many marvelous teachers. My tenure as much as I'd like to think of it as spectacular, was nothing out of the ordinary, not like surviving the firebombing of Tokyo, playing professional basketball, or coaching in West Africa. I am aware of the irony that a Russian immigrant who arrived in this country barely speaking English stumbles into a career teaching British Literature to gifted high school senior students.

Of the many years that I taught British Literature in AP English, it was that first day in front of my students that remains the most memorable because it set the tone for all the classes of all the marvelous years that followed.

I stood in front of six rows of questioning faces. Behind me on the chalkboard I had written my name in large block letters. I was holding a book of short stories by James Joyce in my hand.

First days in high school are normally reserved for seating, reading syllabi, explaining goals, discussing classroom rules, dispensing textbooks, and filling out forms. After the bell rang to start class, dispensing with an introduction, I opened the book to the last story entitled *The Dead*. I explain: *An Irish professor and part-time book reviewer, Michael Conroy and his wife, Gretta attend a family dinner on the Feast of the Epiphany. After the dinner, back in their hotel room, Gretta confesses to her husband that a song sung earlier during the dinner reminded her of a young love, Michael Furey. At the time of their romance, Gretta was about to be sent to a boarding school. On the last night before her departure, Michael Furey stands outside her window in a winter snowstorm and serenades her with that same song they heard at the dinner. From that night's cold, Furey, already in fragile health, becomes ill and dies. Gretta falls asleep and Gabriel remains standing by the window staring into the winter night thinking of his wife's youthful romance of which she had never before spoken.*

With that brief introduction, I said this: "And now, I am about to read the last paragraph of this story. It is arguably the best paragraph ever written in the English language." That got their attention. Halfway through, I felt tears forming in my eyes. By the end of the paragraph with *snow falling generally all over Ireland*, I came to the last sentence: *His soul swooned slowly as he heard the snow falling faintly through the universe and faintly falling like the descent of the last end upon all the living and the dead.*

As I closed the book, tears were streaming down my cheeks.

I do not remember what happened next exactly, but I'm reasonably certain my students were stunned watching their new AP teacher, all 6-foot-6 of him, weeping over words. Me, I couldn't have been happier. I have had only one epiphany in my life, and that morning was it. I had finally found a substitute for playing basketball. The next 15 years teaching AP came as close to the thrill of playing hoops as I could have possibly imagined. Teaching those bright students provided me with the kind of intensity and daily satisfaction that I had counted on as an athlete. Teaching was not physical, but it was certainly mental, and definitely visceral. Each morning I drove down the mountain on interstate 80 from my home in Truckee, reviewing my lesson plan for the day. It was like preparing for an NBA game, except I didn't need to vomit. If my lesson plan didn't work, there was the next period to do better: *one game at a time, one classroom at a time, one student at a time.* For each class, I had to bring my A game. I was well on my way to thinking of myself as a teacher, which meant stopping thinking of myself as a basketball player, which in turn had kept me from thinking of myself as an immigrant or someone displaced or a failure. The problem with such thinking is that your job or career is not who you really are. Whether consciously or unconsciously, in my sixties, I was nonetheless trying to figure that out. It would be another decade before I got an answer to that question.

It is during this time that my grandfather, Vladimir Nikolaevich Lvov reentered my life. In October of 1990, Richard Pipes published *The Russian Revolution*. I was busy teaching AP, trying to stay one lesson plan ahead of my brilliant students', so I don't remember rushing to the local bookstore. When I did, I found information in it about my grandfather. After reading the chapter entitled *The October Coup*, I was deeply hurt for myself and especially for my mother, who believed to the day she died that her father was a hero and a saint. Professor Pipes wrote about my grandfather Lvov's role in the Kornilov Plot. The plot was an attempt by the Commander and Chief of the Russian army, General Kornilov, to take control of the Russian Provisional Government following the abdication of Czar Nicholas the II. I had grown up believing my mother's account that her father's sole purpose was to bring together the two conflicting sides. Pipes labeled my grandfather a troublemaker who exacerbated the discord between General Kornilov and the Prime Minister. Pipes claimed that my grandfather misled the Prime Minister into believing the General's goal was a coup d'état. I read with alarm descriptions of my grandfather: "great personal charm but naïve;" "questions about his sanity;" "unreliable;" "temperamental." In a footnote, Pipes quotes Nabokov Pere: "Vladimir Lvov was untrustworthy." In another footnote: "Nikolai Vissarionovich Nekrasov - Kerensky's *eminence grise*: claimed that Vladimir Lvov saved the revolution by exposing Kornilov." Nobokov was referring to Kornilov's plot to overthrow the Kerensky government.

But for whom, I wondered.

That question remained unanswered. I thought of how unhappy my mother would have been to read these accounts about her father. Would she have believed them? I doubt it. Knowing my mother's imagination, she would have devised another alternate narrative. When it came to her father, my mother was by no means objective. But then, neither was I.

When I was young, my mother's theories about her father and brother's secretive activities behind the Iron Curtain found fertile ground in my imagination. My sister never believed. "Oh, Mom," she'd say and stalk out of the room.

I don't recall discussing Pipes' evaluation of my grandfather with my sister. Possibly because I was far too absorbed with my teaching. There was the poetry of John Donne to explain, Milton's epic simile. One student quipped, "Mr. Meschery, I could graduate before one of his similes end." *So smart, so quick, they were.* There are times I remember some of the things those teens said, and I laugh out loud. And there were senior A.P. essays to correct. And students already requesting college letters of recommendations. I placed *The Russian Revolution* along with Grandfather Lvov on the shelf. I did not take the book down until I had retired from teaching and was thinking of traveling to Russia.

• • •

The Japanese camp commander in the film, *Bridge on the River Kwai*, often preached to his prisoners, *be happy in your work.* I was teaching - immensely happy. At the same time, I was deeply unhappy in my marriage. By the start of the Nineties, Joanne and I were living apart. The kids were off to college. She'd rented a house in Cal Pine, a small town north of Truckee that she regarded as her writing studio. She had now written a second novel *A Gentleman's Guide to the Frontier* that was selected as one of four novels for the Pen-Faulkner Award. She was working on a third novel.

While she wrote in her cabin, I remained in our large family home in Truckee. Often during those years, I'd drive to the Bay Area and across the Golden Gate Bridge to the bayside village of Sausalito and bother my friends Bill King and his wife, Nancy, with my marital woes.

Bill King was the voice of the Warriors when I played. In the 90's he was the radio play-by-play voice of the Oakland Athletics. And what a voice he had, deep and strong and full of emotion. He became the older brother I never had. He was a gourmand, a landscape painter, a Slavophile, a devotee of the ballet and opera, and captain at the helm of his beloved ketch, Varuna. When he wasn't on the road, he was fussing aboard Varuna, chipping or varnishing, and admiring her, like an adoring father. Bill loved the scent of varnish.

Bill and Nancy kept pressing me, when was I going to stop whining and file for a divorce. I suppose I was a coward, fearful I would lose my children. I do not discount, however, like the knight in John Keats' poem *La Belle Dame Sans Merci*, I was still in thrall with Joanne.

I didn't always visit Bill and Nancy when I was depressed. Many times I drove down to Sausolito because being with my two friends was a joy, at a time when joy in my personal life was at a minimum. I would arrive and Nancy would immediately place a tall gin and tonic in front of me and pour rum and coke for herself and Bill. We'd talk hoops, or about saving whales, or about a particular Russian poem Bill loved. Often, we talked about ballet, a subject dear to both Bill and Nancy's hearts. Bill was the voice for the San Francisco Ballet Company's performance of *Peter and the Wolf* under the directorship of their friend Michael Smuin. Smuin's wife, Paula, I discovered, was in my class at Grant Elementary School, a skinny little thing who grew up to be a beauty and danced for the New York City Ballet.

In the eighth grade graduating class photograph I'm the tallest kid standing in the back row. Paula Tracy is the smallest kid in the front row.

If I thought of Bill as the brother I never had, what was Nancy? For a start, dramatically beautiful with raven hair, high cheekbones, and gray-green eyes. Smart and sensitive, there were few environmental causes in which Nancy was not actively supporting. I didn't need another sister. But to call Nancy simply a friend would not be quite accurate. Like half the Warriors players, fans, and Sausalito sailors, I suspect I was secretly enamored with her.

As I'm writing this, I remember the day in October of 2005 when Bill's daughter, Kathy called to tell me that Bill had thrown an embolism while in the hospital for a hip replacement adjustment and died. I have a hard time believing Bill is dead. Whenever I watch any of the three major sports, no matter who the broadcasters are, I tune out their voices and hear my friend calling the play by play. I wrote this poem and read it at his memorial.

IN MEMORIAM, BILL KING (1927-2005)

(After *Jubilate Agnos* by Christopher Smart)

My friend, you are speaking and we hear pictures.
For you are sitting courtside or above the game.
For the action is moving from left to right on the dial.
For someone is rising to shoot a miracle.
For the referees are dying in your microphone.

For the air is tumbling with punters' kicks.
For your call, Bill, leaves the tailback no choice
But to believe in the hole that opens as you speak.
For someone has hit a home run beyond Toledo.

Meschery, Tom. From the poem, "In Memorium, Bill King (1927
- 2005)" *Sweat: New & Selected Poems About Sports.* Black Rock
Press, 2014. University of Nevada, Reno. Reno, NV

The poem goes on for several stanzas more, but Bill is in my mind:
*It is the bottom of the ninth, the score is tied, the Athletics are at bat.
Bill is sitting in the announcer's booth overlooking the Oakland A's ballpark,
leaning into his mic, crouched and leaning forward over his chair, like a
jockey over his horse waiting for the race to start. The batter hits the ball, and
it is arching toward the center field , a possible home run - going, going, gone
– Bill screams, "Holy Toledo!"*

For I hear you reciting in Russian
The poetry of Pushkin and Ahkmatova.
For we are together on a train racing across Siberia.
And we are drunk on vodka, and we are weeping.
But I will keep you like a voice in my heart.

Bill and I made a pact that when we were old and retired, we'd travel
across Siberia together
    on the Big Red Express the way my mother's family did during the
Bolshevik Revolution, just the two of us, one Russian, one Russophile
from America's Midwest. I'd write poems; Bill would paint landscapes. We
would both drink vodka, listen to the balalaika. And weep a lot.
    For I hear you now railing against the politicians.

We need your voice, my friend. Things are dire in this country.

• • •

While I was teaching Advanced Placement student, I also taught one
period of freshman

Proficiency-English. Proficiency was the designation for students that needed extra help with the basics. They were a challenge. Our district policy was to mainstream students from

the Special Needs Center and students from the English Language Learners center. I had a number of Downs Syndrome students whom I adored. Never any discipline problem, and they always wanted to please. One boy competed in the Special Winter Olympics. He won a Gold and a Silver in two downhill races. He wore both the medals around his neck for the rest of the semester. The English Language Learners fell into two groups: those that didn't want to learn and those who did. It couldn't have been simpler. And it was easy to see the difference between the two groups. The former were filled with anger and distrust. The latter full of enthusiasm and belief. Breaking through to the angry group was damn near impossible.

I tried to use my own experience as an immigrant to convince them how important education would be for their future, especially learning the English language. I used my family history to impress them. My father, I told them, was never able to master English and was relegated to employment that did not pay the bills. My mother, who spoke English was the wage-earner in our family. I used every anecdote in my immigrant playbook to no avail.

Of these students, I can count the number that I succeed with on one hand. I thought of myself as an excellent teacher. Teaching fit my personality the way basketball fit my personality.

By the time I retired I felt I'd done a good job except with these kinds of immigrant students.

Why I could never get through to them still bothers me. Whatever language I was speaking, it was not theirs. I worried what would happen to them. How difficult their future would be.

In basketball, I was never good at accepting losses. It took me a long time after I retired to stop visualizing the worst and imagining something positive happening for them.

CHAPTER 36
RAZOR WIRE

While I had discovered the joy of teaching bright, engaged, and curious AP students, I had not entirely given up teaching at-risk students. For a couple of summers I taught poetry at the Reno juvenile detention center. My students were incarcerated teenagers ranging in age from 13 to 17. Every morning, I began class by having the guards, stationed one in each corner of the classroom, open the windows of the room. The kids enjoyed watching the guards obey orders. After the windows were open, I asked all the students to place spelling and grammar in the palms of their hands, modeling how to do it, and throw the twin culprits of their failed classroom experience out the window. After a few of these demonstrations, and the idea firmly in their minds that I wouldn't pay attention to rules of spelling or grammar, they wrote with the kind of freedom that comes with leaving jail behind – *if only they'd had wings of angels* - and produced some startling poems, well not exactly poems all the time, but honest imagery of deep emotional experiences. I loved those kids, although many of them were there because they had committed serious crimes, from selling drugs to robbery and worse.

One of my favorites was a teenage girl who wrote love poems that a young Elizabeth Barrett Browning would have been proud to have written. After a week, curious about her, I asked a guard what she was in for. "Murder," he said. The information was so heartbreaking I nearly quit the job.

Melanie once said that poetry can save the lives of children. She went on to explain that poetry allows children to learn to think freely, adding that was true of all the arts. Her point about saving children hit home. I knew firsthand that poetry can save the lives of convicts. Shaun Griffin, a poet and friend, taught a poetry workshop in the Nevada State Penitentiary for Men in Carson City. Over the years, I joined Shaun in prison along with Gaelmarie Pahmeier, a creative writing instructor at the University of Nevada, who wrote poems that were only exceeded in excellence by her fabulous cowgirl outfits. I'm reasonably sure that I speak for the three of us when I say that the sound of steel doors clanging behind you as you make your way through the walls and halls of prison is both frightening and sad. The workshops themselves were neither sad nor frightening. The men were eager to learn. I felt that the time they spent with us was, in their minds, time spent outside the prison walls. Most of the men who wrote poems in the workshop were hard-boiled cons. Shaun and his workshop published a penitentiary literary magazine entitled *Razor Wire* that included book reviews, poems, essays, and art. Ishmael, poet and artist, released finally after two decades behind bars, continues to write and paint. His sketches for the magazine, mostly portraits, which are rendered with clarity and beauty. He and Shaun communicate as do many of the other men who've been released. When I think of poetry as the conveyor of freedom, I'm reminded of Shaun's description of his first few workshops in prison: The first time we read *Strunk and White* it was like chloroform. I could do nothing to save them from the ruin of independent clauses.

Shaun sends me copies of *Razor Wire* which I read with pleasure. I am grateful for his service to these men whose lives would be substantially more difficult without his belief that they could fly over the prison walls if they had the wings of poetry. The same wings I remember thinking the poets that I helped in the International Workshop at the University of Iowa yearned for so that they could fly away from the repressive regimes of their countries. Those men and women were as incarcerated within the borders of their own countries as these prisoners were behind the walls of their prison.

CHAPTER 37
THE STUPID BOWL

George Gutekunst, the owner of the five-star restaurant, *Ondine's*, in Sausalito, invited friends to his home for his annual NFL Super Bowl he dubbed Stupid Bowl party to watch the last standing teams square off. If I was asked to rank stupendously fun events I enjoyed in my life, George's parties would rank near the top. Bill, Nancy and I never missed the annual Stupid Bowl. I would drive down from Truckee, and together, the three of us would drive to George's home in Sonoma. George's parties came with his scrumptious personally slow-cooked short ribs, excellent wines, and conversation with writers, poets, chefs, ballet dancers, athletes, teachers and unrepentant Commie longshoremen, long retired but still feisty for The Cause. I was no fan of Communism, so I kept my mouth shut. The aging Commies tolerated me because I was by then a committed Democrat who believed in certain specific elements of Socialism -- a weeny position in their eyes, but they cut me some slack because they were also big Warriors fans. As for the football game, I don't remember anyone watching the game let alone rooting for either of the teams when there was politics, poetry, and art to discuss. Occasionally, if the game was even marginally close, a few guests would wander into the living room and watch the last quarter. I'm pretty sure I never did.

Gutekunst is a German name, and George looked every bit the German beer meister: short, rotund, bald with a beer belly with fair skin and ruddy cheeks. As tradition dictated, the booze flowed and George cooked, while regaling his guests with stories from his days as owner of Ondine's, his waterfront restaurant in the quaint bay side village of Sausalito a few miles north after crossing the Golden Gate Bridge. I can only guess how many of these parties I attended and how many interesting stories George told, but you could count on two stories he always told that are fixed in my memory. The first was the time he kicked Frank Sinatra and his entourage from his restaurant for bad behavior. Mr. Blue Eyes was drunk and insulting. George gleefully described how he stared down Sinatra's bodyguards. And the second story was his discovery of Beryl Markham's autobiography *West With The Night*, which had long been out of print. He'd begin:

It was John "Bumby" Hemmingway, the son of Ernest and my fishing buddy who turned me on to Markham. While the two of us were on a fishing trip, sitting around the campfire – we might have been drinking. I'd brought a hellava bottle of scotch - Bumby recommended that I read the letter his father wrote praising to high heaven Markham's writing. Praising contemporary writers was not something the old man did, so this was unusual, admitting his father had probably been smitten by Markham.

Gutekunst was addicted to the parenthetical expression.

As the short ribs simmered, George would recount how he immediately went to the public library, found the book mentioned in the letter and read it in one sitting. According to George, he immediately booked a flight to Kenya. In 1983, Miss Markham was still alive.

I used my powers of persuasion to talk her into giving me written consent to republish. As soon as I flew home, I visited Evan Connell to see what he thought of the book.

The Evan Connell George was referring to was the author of *Mrs. Bridge and Mr. Bridge*.

Connell read it and approached Berkeley's North Point Press. It became a bestseller and a TV movie, *A Shadow on the Sun*.

Depending on George's mood, the hyperbole grew or diminished from Stupid Bowl to Stupid Bowl depending on the amount of booze consumed. The short ribs were always perfect, succulent meat falling off the bone, George's highly decorated rhetoric floating through the air, arguments about politics, talk about new novels, new poets.

Being part of these discussions was heady stuff for me. Sure, I had earned an MFA. I was an English teacher and I wrote poetry. But I can't say I was confident discussing poetry or art, or other "intellectual" subjects. All the years while I distanced myself from basketball, I hadn't entirely shaken the image of myself as a jock. So, as the conversations deepened into greater esoterica, I kept my distance, listening carefully in order to remember and learn. Many times there was something interesting or a subject related that would help my students. Classrooms, I'd tell them, are not the only places to learn.

• • •

At every Stupid Bowls there was Milt Wolff, who in 1939 at the age of 23 was the last commander of the Lincoln Brigade of the XV International Brigade during the Spanish Civil War. When I knew Milt, he was in his late eighties or early nineties, with a slender ropy-tall body, a barely wrinkled face, piercing dark eyes, and long gray hair, topped by a black beret. He wore a red bandana tied around his neck in the fashion of the Communist partisans he led against Franco's Fascists. His autobiographical novel, *Another Hill*, was published by the University of Illinois Press. Milt died on January 14, 2008. With his death, another backdoor to history closed. I used to ask my students, "Can you name the last commander of the Lincoln Brigade?" And they'd answer, "What's the Lincoln Brigade?" *AP students, no less. Argh!*

• • •

It occurs to me that I've been lucky to have spent most of my life with people in sports, education, and the arts. I'm not excluding other professions from their share of good people. I'm simply saying I haven't had to deal personally with many assholes, and I believe this has to do with the occupations I've chosen - or more likely have chosen me. I believe this is particularly true of teachers. My two daughters, Janai and Megan, are teachers. My wife, Melanie, is a retired teacher, her daughter Emily is a high school counselor, and Em's husband, Greg, is an elementary school teacher. We could use more male elementary teachers like Greg. In twenty-two years of teaching at Reno High School, I can recall only two or three teachers who were unlikable, and I attribute this to their unexplainable and obvious contempt for teenagers. I could never figure out why, if they didn't like teens, they'd chosen the teaching profession in the first place. Summer vacations can't possibly count as an answer.

Today as I think about my years teaching Advanced Placement Senior English, not all halcyon, but always exciting and meaningful, I am encouraged that there are enough bright young people enrolled in high schools' AP classrooms in every city and town in this country that I do not despair for future generations. I like to believe that the students I taught in AP are now the millennials who are embracing more progressive, social, and economic thinking. They'd be just about the right age, and they'd be just smart-alecky enough to affect real change.

Melanie says I'm an optimist. She may be right, but if you want to be a teacher, you'd better not be a pessimist.

• • •

It is May 26, 2020. It's been a year since the memoir *The Mad Manchurian* has been finished and sent off into the darkness of the publishing world. So far with no takers. I am not discouraged. On television I'm looking at the streets of Minneapolis filling up with Black Lives Matter protestors. They are protesting the death of George Floyd at the hands of police. Such a great percentage of the protestors are young people, black, white, brown, Asian, many multi-racial. They are the faces of the future. I hope that the students I taught are among them.

As a teacher, I had what in professional sports today, is called a *platform*. I hope I made good use of it. I hope that along with the subject I helped to instill in them a social conscience.

• • •

When I retired from teaching in the spring of 2005, a couple of my student-jesters, remembering their returned essays with comments in red ink, gave me a box of green ink pens. With a note of such subtlety: *To Save the Environment.* Another student (Was his name, Charles?) gave me a case of Smithwicks, an Irish beer I'd mentioned once to my class that I'd discovered on a trip to Ireland, which I could not find in the United States. I immediately went to my computer and changed his grade from an A- to an A.

Under my desk is a large Rubbermaid container holding my memorabilia, mostly basketball or family related. Along with my sports albums, is a binder containing the seating charts for each of my years teaching AP along with photocopies of each of the class graduation pictures out of the school's yearbooks. By cutting a pasting, I have my students sitting in their assigned seats, as Shakepeare said, looking at me with their shining morning faces. I peruse these seating charts far more often than I look through my basketball stuff.

I come to certain students and stop and remember and smile and laugh. There is Troy who would not budge from his position that Samuel Taylor Coleridge's poem, Kubla Khan, was a metaphor for an orgasm; Sally with her beautiful singing voice and sensitive mind whom I desperately tried to match- make with my son; Lisa, political activist, story teller, oh so confident; Rachel, the young Emily Dickinson in the Chautauqua performance I narrated; Jarod Park whose "Lego" essay got him into Harvard and later found a need for his Korean heritage, and Danielle, gangly Danielle who dared the universe to laugh at her candy-cane striped knee socks, her magenta bows and tassels, her costumes of many rainbows. Look at me, she was saying, I am brilliance.

And brilliant she was, and is, today, a doctor caring for the suffering. I no longer miss walking onto the basketball court, but I miss walking into my classes and greeting my students in Bambara: E*e ni sogoma*. And the students rising to their feet and responding, the way I had taught them how the West African students did depending on gender: *Nba or Nse - Ee ni sogoma*.

I enjoy listening to tales from my basketball past, but I miss listening to my students excited voices discussing a poem or essay or griping about having to memorize the first 42 lines of the *Prologue to the Canterbury Tales* in the original Middle English, then listening to them recite in front of the class, delighting in their performances. Most of them, that is. Some remained terrified.

I miss handing out year-end awards for academic excellence as well as some goofy awards that the devil in me created, such as the following:

THE WIFE OF BATH AWARD
FOR
THE MOST SEXUALLY INAPPROPRIATE
COMMENT OF THE YEAR

WINNER'S NAME_____
Thomas N Meschery
Advanced Placement English
May 10, 2002

Somewhere in my memory is a letter written by one of my students that told me that reciting the *Prologue to the Canterbury Tales* had helped her impress a boy in her college class who was now her fiancé. I wish I could find that letter, and I wish I knew if they ever married.

Those kids - they were such heartbreakers.

From time to time I'd hear from students, a phone call, email, cards at Christmas. *Brilliant, eclectic Sylvia what new career have you decided to conquer?* But I don't hear from them so often anymore. That's okay. After a certain amount of time, teachers like parents, should be remembered mostly at late night family gatherings over too much booze or at high school reunions. I could imagine my students after graduation at such class reunions embellishing my teaching theatrics to the point that I wouldn't recognize myself.

I don't have students anymore, but I do have my Warriors. Not exactly my students. Not my children either since the Warriors have been adopted by the entire Bay Area. But I can live with being one of many with parental feelings for the team.

While I was still teaching, I had already published a collection of poems, *Nothing We Lose Can Be Replaced*, and on its merits along with my work teaching poetry, I'd been inducted into the *Nevada State Writers Hall of Fame*. As they say in sport, I had Big Mo – momentum for my future career as a poet.

Joanne and I divorced in the summer of 2004. In the spring of 2005, at the age of 67, I retired from teaching. I taught high school for 22 years. I told myself I was ready to devote the rest of my life to writing poetry. In June, as I drove away from Reno High School for the last time, lines from Alfred Lord Tennyson's poem, *Ulysses*, came to mind:

How dull it is to pause, to make an end
To rust unburnished, not to shine in use
As though to breathe were life.

I was not about to rust. I followed the premise of Tennyson's poem and wrote. Poems mostly, but I tried, with a sort of why not give it a try attitude, my hand at writing a novel. Completed, I sent it to detective fiction writer Jon Jackson, a friend from the Iowa writer's Workshop who lived in Missoula, Montana. He sent back the manuscript with these words on the title page: "Meschery, I thought you could write better than this." I wasn't offended. Having survived being called sonavabitch for four years by my high school basketball coach and a pinko by Russian haters during the McCarthy period, and any number of expletives my NBA opponents called me, and a few mumbled threats by referees. The Mad Manchurian had a thick skin. Who needed fiction? I was a poet. As it turned out, much to my surprise by 2016 I had written three manuscripts of fiction with sports themes, none of which had attracted the attention of an agent, and a year later started work on a mystery novel. The only reason I can think of for these books must have something to do with being one stubborn sonavabitch.

But back in those months in 2005 following my first failed attempt at writing fiction, I was happy to devote my time to poems. It was poetry through the fall and winter. Joanne and I were living separately. I remained in the family home in Truckee. I called Bob Blesse of the University of Nevada's *Black Rock Press* who had published my first collection of poems and explained my present project, a *New and Selected* collection of sports poems. He liked the idea and told me *Black Rock Press* would be pleased to publish it. I began work. By the New Year I had several completed poems I was happy with. I was looking forward to writing more.

OVERTIME
2005 to the present

CHAPTER 38
MULTIPLE MYELOMA

In September of 2004 as I was beginning my last year teaching, I was assaulted by a case of shingles, a painful adult form of chickenpox. The verb *assault* best describes the kind of dreadful pain this virus inflicts on a person. My rash arose with such fury that the skin on the entire left side of my body turned into a pink sheet of electric currents. The only way I could sleep was to lay on the couch in the living room, stripped to my waist – a pillow beneath my head, without a blanket because anything touching my skin would ignite the pain. Of all the types of music I enjoyed, the blues to Sixties rock, to African songs, to classic orchestras; operatic arias managed to calm me into fitful and grateful sleep. Number one on my list was the Pearl Fishers' Duet sung by Jussi Bjorling and Robert Merrill. It is only through hindsight that I recognize now that my choice of music was a gift left to me by my father.

It is Saturday morning in our apartment. As is his habit, every Saturday, my father is sitting in his easy chair in front of the radio. My sister is sitting on the floor next to him. They are listening to the Texaco sponsored radio broadcast from New York City of the Metropolitan Opera. I would join them but without enthusiasm. I wait, feigning interest until I see they are in raptures, and I'm out the door with my basketball under my arm.

• • •

I intend to burn CD's of *The Pearl Fishers Duet*, one for every member of my family and close friends. I do not want a memorial. In my will I have asked them all to play the CD. That's all. I think my father would approve.

• • •

Shingles is the physical alarm bell of a weakened immune system. In my case, it was like the medieval town-crier fulfilling his job description. In early January of 2006, sitting across the desk from an oncologist, I heard the diagnosis, Multiple Myeloma, a cancer of the white blood cells. Then I listened to the dreaded word, "incurable."

Ask any person who's been diagnosed with cancer how they felt the moment they'd been told. Select from the following responses: heart racing, legs weak, trouble breathing. In my case, all of the above. But I also felt angry that my body had betrayed me. That may sound silly to some, but I had been a professional athlete. My body had fought through 10 NBA seasons. I was a "power forward," in the early Sixties, one of the best to play the position in the league. I never saw a rebound that I wasn't entitled to. In 1962, I led the NBA in personal fouls and remained in the top five in that category for the rest of my career. I was involved in multiple fights, some of which I was proud of, most not so much. I missed only six games my entire ten-year career. My jersey, #14, is one of only six retired by the Warriors, and hangs from the rafters in Oracle Arena next to Wilt Chamberlain. This body - *tough as nails*, a sportswriter once wrote - would not dare let me down. My body should have been strong enough to withstand any disease. Cancer quickly proved such arrogance an illusion.

Yes, that was me, feeling faint and wobbly. And totally pissed off as the Mad Manchurian was known for on the basketball court but now it was the medical court and cancer.

• • •

I was first treated with a new drug, Revlimid, then recently approved by the FDA that within six months took me into remission. Without enough data to guarantee the longevity of remission my oncologist suggested I go through the traditional white cell transplantation.

Of that time leading up to my successful autologous transplant, I remember with gratitude how my three children rallied to support their dad. Janai and Matt accompanied me to the hospital for doctors' visits. The night before my procedure in U.C. Davis University of California Cancer Center, Megan and I went to dinner and afterwards to see *Blood Diamond* at the theater next door to the restaurant. After the successful transplantation while I was recovering in an isolation hospital room, my oldest daughter, Janai, took it into her head to inform every living person

I ever knew and perhaps encountered casually while standing in grocery lines that The Mad Manchurian was in the hospital and would love to receive get-well cards. Nurses brought in bags. I felt like a rock star.

I spent Christmas of 2006 in the hospital. There was a small, decorated Christmas tree in my room. I was given lots of steroids, the result of which turned my face into a balloon. By the end of December, I was discharged from the hospital. I will always remember my doctor's words, "I need your bed for someone really sick." His way of assuring me I was in remission with at least five years of guaranteed life ahead of me. I felt cured, even though I knew at some point in my life the cancer would return.

If this memoir was only about my cancer, I'd entitle the book, *Remission*, which is the medical condition I've been in for the last thirteen years. That is not a challenge or competition Melanie reminds me. And I remind myself to be grateful for the years I've been given living with her.

I wrote the following poem after an hour in an oncology ward getting my monthly bone strengthening infusion, thankful I was not receiving chemotherapy.

COATRACK WITH WIGS AND HATS

Wigs hang down one after another
from the top, suggesting beauty
and renewed health: Jet black to tempt
all Russians matrons with an earlier age
in which there was admiration instead of pain.
Brunettes from chocolate brown to sepia.
One with a streak of auburn sets it apart
for the daring. Blondes for the blondes
because, despite the drip, drip, drip
of poison, they might have more fun.
I'm drawn to the flaming red
of Magdalen's hair in a painting I saw
in the Sant'Agostino Cavalletti chapel in Rome.
the child Jesus in her arms, such suffering
transported from the 17th century to ours
in the face of the woman sitting across from me
wrapped in a warming blanket.

Further down, hats for the gentlemen:
Derby, porkpie, a Stetson for the visiting cowboy –
too far from the purple sage to be of use, except,
perhaps, as a doctor's wish to lighten our hearts.
For the Rastafarian, a tricolor crocheted tam,
no longer needed, dreadlocks gone, while the head
still needs to be protected from the cold.
A black beret for the professor of ancient history
or the French poet, missing only the accessory of a cravat.
Two Oakland A's baseball caps. One of the Yankees.
 I'm wearing my old Warriors cap.

I was bald before my disease,
but I'm thinking a change of headwear might
better fit the mood I'm in, not athletic
but sort of spiritual. How else to feel
sitting in the middle of such courage.
The Rasta tam would work and Bob Marley's
reggae would follow naturally, wouldn't it.
It might help us to listen to a tune or two:
Get Up, Stand Up; *Redemption Song*.

Meschery, Tom. "Coatrack, Hat & Wigs," *Clear Path*, Random
Lane Press, 2022. Sacramento, CA

CHAPTER 39
BASKETBALL REDUX

*The Roman Goddess Fortuna Redux was trusted
to bring back those far from home safely.*

During the 23 years I taught English at Reno High School, I don't remember paying much attention to the NBA. The most time I invested in basketball was trying to make my last-minute selections for March Madness, which, considering my failure to ever come close to a winner, gave credence to the word, mad in Mad Manchurian. If I saw an NBA regular season game that interested me, I'd watch. Mostly, I reserved my enthusiasm for the NBA playoffs and finals: Bird versus Magic. Michael Jordan versus any team, usually the Knicks or the Jazz. The Spurs. Kobe and Shaq. I was a fan, but not a dedicated one. I didn't have a lot of time to spare in those days. I had a family to think of (three kids who would be in college at the same time), which meant earning an additional paycheck teaching classes at Truckee Community College teaching an additional two nights a week, over and above the 5 classes per day I taught at Reno High. And when our shaky finances needed a boost, I taught a film class on a third night. The schedule was tough physically, but not a real hardship as I loved movies, particularly those *Film Noirs* that reminded me of my childhood sitting in the dark of San Francisco theaters mouthing the words of my anti-hero-heroes: Richard Widmark as crazy Tommy Udo, "*I wouldn't give you the skin off a grape.*" And that scene that has remained in my memory as one of my favorites: James Cagney as the American secret service agent strapped to a chair, spitting in the face of his Nazi torturer, the actor Richard Conte, in *13 Rue Madeleine*. I believe that my enthusiasm for those old movies rubbed off on my students as I often heard them imitating the voices of the actors and actresses. It is my belief that to be a successful classroom teacher you must be wildly enthusiastic about your subject. All the other teaching can be learned or acquired with time and On the Job Training.

As memories go, I am struck how much of a man of the 1950s I was and still am. Sometimes it seems to me that the rest of the decades of my life played virtually no part in my growth as a person. I know this can't be entirely true, but the feeling persists. Do other immigrants feel as frozen in the decade in which they arrived as I did?

• • •

In Seattle, Mark Strand had introduced me to poetry. In Iowa I began to study and write poems. During the years 1986 to 2005 while living in Truckee, I was busy teaching **and** writing poetry. Basketball became sort of an afterthought. On the few occasions that I wanted to drive down to the Bay Area to see an NBA game, my requests for tickets were met with a kind of grumbling approval. The new owner of the Warriors, Chris Cohan, and his administration did not appear to be interested in their retired players. (These days we're called legends.) I wound up feeling as if I were begging and stopped asking and stopped going.

It is with a nod to the principle of irony that it took getting cancer for my love of basketball, in particular the NBA, to return. After leaving the hospital, I remained quarantined for three months in my house in Truckee, with the Sierra Mountains that loomed protectively over our little town. To occupy my time, my son, Matthew, purchased an NBA League Pass for me. It allowed me to view all the NBA games of the season. Confined to my mountain home, I watched a lot of pro games. Sometimes, I started in the afternoon and turned off the TV after the final evening game. I'd been away from basketball a long time, and was prepared, like a lot of my generation of basketball players, to be critical of the "new" game, like the kind of guys who keep referring to "back in my day." *Yeah, a man of the Fifties, I could have been one of them.* It wasn't that I was unaware that the NBA game was evolving from the sport I played in my era. I had watched the Bird/Magic match-up and the following Michael Jordan Bulls championship success and the fantastic teams coached by Gregg "Pop" Popovich in San Antonio. I was like a father who'd watched his children grow up but was shocked one day to discover they were adults and leaving home.

It surprised me how much I enjoyed the way these new adults played. For the better, I thought. Certainly, more exciting.

What attracted me first was the speed and aerial acrobatics. Once some of the players jumped, they never seemed to come down. I could not imagine myself flying through the air the way they did. It's not that there weren't highflyers when I played. I remember Jumping Johnny Green, and Billy "the Kangaroo" Cunningham. There were those playground legends of the time I never saw personally but heard of from players who crossed their hearts when describing what they saw with their own two eyes: Herman "Helicopter" Knowlings, picking quarters off the top of backboards. And there was the playground legend, Jacky Jackson, who, like Paladin in the TV series advertised, *Have Gun Will Travel*, had his own card made: *Have Converse, Will Jump.*

But the NBA players I was watching in the winter of 2007 in my confinement all had hops, even the white guys, who for generations were ridiculed for a lack of jumping ability, a pejorative referred to as white man's disease.

But what finally brought me back full circle was the simplicity of the 21st century NBA variety of basketball. The sport resembled the game I played in my youth, the playground games of three-on-three called Hunch, so pure: *Pass and cut; pass and screen away; pick and roll; pick and pop, winners' out, sun going down, balling in the shadows until night falls, dribbling all the way home, right hand, left hand, spin dribble at the fire hydrants, reverse direction straight to your front door.* The only things missing was a finger in the air testing for wind direction and the familiar chung of the ball passing through chain link nets.From a sport of set plays, the modern game of basketball had returned to its original playground roots. I found it compelling. Watching the games made me feel young. *I'm not kidding.* And, then much later in my life in 2015 came the Dubs, those splendid young Warriors. *The way they played, my God! I close my eyes, and I am 13 years old on the outdoor courts and gyms of San Francisco, feeling the game, every muscle and bone of my now weakened body aching with pleasure.*

By the time my quarantine ended and before the 2007 NBA All Star Break, my oncologist formally announced I was in remission. My future life span was uncertain, but I knew I had at least five years and with a little luck a few years beyond that to live. I began planning the trip to visit Russia, the birthplace of my parents. It was a promise I made to myself if I survived my cancer.

CHAPTER 40
THE MOTHER COUNTRY

Predely maevo yazyka est' predely maevo mira
The limits of my language are the limits of my world.
Russian Proverb

Three years after the cancer diagnosis in early August of 2007 my flight to Saint Petersburg took off from San Francisco International Airport. Perestroika had swept the hated Communists from power. This time, my mother, had she been alive, would have approved the trip. I flew into Pulkovo Airport and was met by my friend Dmitri and his lovely wife, Tania. The year before, Dmitri telephoned me and introduced himself as a now retired professional basketball player for Spartak, the Euro League team from Saint Petersburg. He'd read online about my Russian background. We became telephone friends. I was excited to meet him in person. We drove into Saint Petersburg. He took a circuitous route through the city pointing out important monuments, government buildings and churches. We drove past the Cathedral of the Saved Blood with its spectacular blue dome. He drove to another church. The one the Lvov family attended; he told me. We would have stopped, but I was too exhausted from the long flight.

During my stay in Saint Petersburg, I would live with a host family. I planned to take a four-week Russian language immersion course at the Derzhavin Institute.

The Derzhavin Mansion which houses the language institute, is a building of exquisite beauty overlooking the Fontanka Peka, the principal tributary of the Neva River that runs through the center of Saint Petersburg. **The mansion** was designed by the Lvov family ancestor

Nikolai Aleksandrovich Lvov. Lvov was also a friend of Derzhavin and related to him through marriage. In the 18th century, Derzhavin was Russia's most celebrated poet and Lvov, the country's most celebrated architect. Derzhavin had married Mashinka Dykova, Lvov's wife's sister. Both women were reputed to be stunningly beautiful. I was able later to verify the claim when I saw a portrait of Mashinka that hangs next to her husband's portrait in the Tretyakov Galleria in Moscow.

• • •

I rode the underground to my first morning class. A female administrator(all the staff and owners were female) interviewed me to see in which language level section I should be placed - beginner, intermediate, or advanced. We sat facing each other. There is an unmistakable Russian face that hints of Tartar ancestry that looked back at me. "We shall converse in Russian," she said, and I will know." She asked questions. I answered. The questions were mostly about my family, my life: why had I signed up for the course. What was I going to do in Russia? Did I like Saint Petersburg? Nothing very complicated. I understood and answered correctly. So much of what we discussed, I almost knew by heart, that even to myself, I sounded fluent. My Russian pronunciation has always been solid. At the end of a half hour, she enrolled me in the advanced class. Who was I to question her that this might have been a teensy bit above my level of linguistic expertise? I took my folder and briefcase and joined the advanced class that was just starting. It is safe to say that I was by far the oldest student in the class. Ten minutes into the class, I wanted to cry. I barely understood one word. At break, I found the supervisor and begged her to place me in the intermediate section. She did. The intermediate class was difficult but did not bring me to tears. However, my teacher, a Slavic blond beauty, would occasionally stop the class and say to me in English an exasperated voice, "Are you listening, are you listening?" Hubris would not allow me to request being placed in the beginner's level.

• • •

Russian women in their twenties and early thirties are often tall, blonde, and *slender with a curvaceous figure. I approve* entirely of slender, curvaceous females of any nationality. It was a pleasure to watch them walking along the streets of Saint Petersburg. How they managed on six-inch heels to navigate the crumbling city sidewalks remains a mystery to me. It is said of Russian women that after 35 their curves begin to resemble potato sacks and their legs fire hydrants as they begin the slippage into the babushka stages of their lives. This may have been true of women of my mother's generation – there is anecdotal evidence as well as family photographs of this generalization of all Slavic women. But based on my time in Russia, this no longer appears to be true for modern Russian women. A couple of the teachers at the institute were in their forties and looked more like sunflowers.

It might have been presumptuous of me, but I asked them about dating in Russia. My teachers were unanimous in their belief about Russian men. They are *peyanee* – drunks – they told me, swiping their fingers up under their chins, a sign in Russia for drunkenness. This, of course I recognize as another huge generalization, but I assumed my teachers knew about the subject better than I did. They continued by saying if they wanted men, they'd fly to Spain or Italy. Lucky, the men of Spain and Italy.

As I learned, those teachers represented a growing female entrepreneurship in the new capitalist Russia. I was surprised how many shops and small businesses were owned by women. True, but with this caveat: All large corporations and financial institutions were firmly in the grip of Russian males – read Oligarchs. Read Putin and his buddies.

• • •

There was a series of three articles in a Russian sports newspaper dating back to 2007 entitled *Tomislav Nikolaevich Mescheriakov, the First Russian in the NBA*. The first two articles in the series were written in the United States before I traveled to Russia. The last two articles were written and published while I was there.

Twice after my Russian lessons ended, I met the reporter up the street at a pub with a British football theme. The interior was festooned with banners of the Premier League teams and three televisions were showing matches. All the cheering was in Russian. The beer on tap was Baltika, hardly Fuller's London Porter. I remember feeling as if I'd walked onto a movie set. Although my classes had improved my Russian, I was not fluent, but I managed the interview, and the reporter was pleased with my effort. After the second article came out, I noticed that from time-to-time passengers on the subway staring at me. When I was young and playing in the NBA, people recognizing me in public was not unusual. Already an old man, so many years past my glory days, it was a little startling. As a rule, Russians do not publicly display emotions, at least not when they're sober. Years of Communism had conditioned them to remain stoic unless in the company of relatives and friends. By the publication of the third article, passengers on the subway began smiling at me and nodding. I smiled and gestured back. Occasionally when I felt brave enough, I ventured a word or two in the Mother Tongue. I felt very Russian.

After the course ended, feeling more secure about my spoken Russian, but by no means confident, I took the train to Moscow. I stayed with my cousin Nikolai Lvov, named for his father, my mother's older brother who in turn was named for our ancient relative. Nikolai lived a few miles beyond the Moscow ring road in a house that had once been his dacha, having signed over his larger Moscow apartment to his son and daughter-in-law. Nikolai, an amateur carpenter, had remodeled his dacha, the Russian name for a summer home. I could not find a reasonable plumb line anywhere. His dining room addition, he proudly called *Mon Plasir*, my pleasure, with its numerous windows looking out on a large vegetable garden, left me thinking Mon Plasir would not be *plasir* during a Russian winter. Luckily, I was visiting in summer, and the breeze that found its way through the numerous structural failures was warm. I could only imagine what temperature Mon Plasir would be in a Russian winter. Whatever skill Nikolai lacked as a carpenter; he made up for as a chef. We realized we shared a common love of cooking.

I often make a *Rassolnik* (pickle soup) the way he showed me. It's heavenly. Not to mention a Borscht, a delightful *Shti*, a cabbage and sauerkraut soup, and *golubtsi*, stuffed cabbage rolls that would make any person of Slavic origin salivate.

One evening while Nikolai and I were sitting around the table in *Mon Plasir* having dinner, a delicious *pirozhok* (potato and meat pie) that we washed down with shots of vodka, Nikolai told me how he and our cousin Lev (Leo) Lvov met for the first time. Lev and I had no knowledge of each other. This is his story.

• • •

Our family name of Lvov and all other names of families associated with the Tsarist nobility had been dangerously unpopular with the

Communist rulers, so I lived under my mother's maiden name. I was still a baby when my mom divorced my birth father, Nikolai Lvov, your mother's older brother. She remarried a member of the Communist party, perhaps for love, but probably for her own safety and my safety. I grew up with his name. After 1986, with Mikhail Gorbochev in power, there was an attempt by a fledgling Society of Nobles to bring families of the nobility together. Most of whom, if they'd managed to stay alive, had changed their family names. The conclave was advertised in the newspaper that on such and such a day at the Moscow Metropol Hotel there would be a meeting for men and women who wanted to reclaim their old family names and meet relatives they might not have known existed.

I went because I was curious and signed in under my real father's name, Lvov. The person at the desk told me that just a few minutes earlier another man had signed in under the same name. He escorted me to the man. That's how I met Lev, our cousin.

• • •

My sister Ann had traveled to Russia several times. In her last visit, she had traveled by car with our cousin Nikolai, accompanied by Alla, our cousin Lev's wife. Nikolai drove his car from Moscow to the province of Samara to the Krotkovo family estate. This estate was where my mother and her brothers had been raised. The Krotkovo estate was a two full day's journey from Moscow and would not fit into my schedule. I instead explored the Lvov family estate a couple of hours from Moscow close to the city of Tver and near my cousin Lev's village home where Nikolai, Lev and I would meet.

On the drive to Lev's house, Nikolai and I stopped in Tver, at the city square to pay homage to the statue of the patriarch of the Lvov family, Nikolai Alexandervich Lvov. I explained to Nikolai that NBA teams erect bronze statues of their greatest players. Michael Jordan's statue stands in front of the United Center Arena in Chicago and one of Magic Johnson graces the front of Staples Arena in LA. I meant it as a joke. His response was *Ya ne dumayu chto Nikolai Alexandrovich ne zanimalsya sportom. So he wouldn't have paid much attention to sports?* I guess our exalted relative would have been too busy being a genius.

Lev with his wife, Alla, lived in a two -room wooden house straight out of a Turgenev novel in which the Russian peasant life was idealized.

Our cousin Lev met us in his heavy work-shirt and trousers tucked into high boots, looking the part of an 18th century Russian peasant, which was possibly the effect he was seeking. Why Lev chose to live in a two-room wooden house with no plumbing, after his children had offered to buy him an apartment in Moscow, is a question my cousin Nikolai said remained unanswered. He suspected it had to do with Lev's romantic fantasy that the peasant represented the soul of Russia. His wife Alla was not as romantically inclined to the rigors of peasant life as her husband. As soon as winter came, Alla would leave for an extended trip to visit her daughters, one in Moscow and the other in London.

Alla was the family chronicler and the unpaid guardian of the nearby Lvov Mansion and estate. In her account of her trip to Krotkovo, my sister describes her as a tiny gray haired bundle of energy and a walking oral history of the Lvov family. Alla has published a book on the Lvov ancestry and is working on the second edition with all her new findings. She has worked on our family history for fifteen years and is the one who has brought so many members of our family together. My sister writes that for the last year she had been in touch with Tatiana Petrovna, Director of the regional museum in the village nearest Krotokovo. The museum had established a room preserving the history of the pre-revolutionary estates and the families who owned them. My sister wrote before her trip to Krotkovo: *We will be the first descendants of one of these noble families to visit. We will stay two nights at Tatiana Petrovna's home, and we have been told that the red carpet is being rolled out for us.* I could not imagine why the descendants of serfs and servants would be this interested. To me, it sounded like American slaves welcoming back the descendants of southern plantation owners. I say this and bite my tongue, knowing my sister will not be happy with this analogy.

I loved my sister's story of her visit to Krotokovo, a journey from Moscow of approximately 1,500 kilometers. Especially the part about the lack of amenities along the route which required my very distinguished sister, archivist of our noble ancestry, to seek the convenience of bushes on the long journey. In her own words, "How do I explain to my dermatologist how I got poison oak on my butt?" The Krotokovo estate was at one time an elegant two story building, the walls of the first story made of local granite, the second story built with lumber from the nearby forest. The second floor of the mansion burned during the revolution. The first story survived and with a new roof is now a regional hospital. Not far from the hospital is a lake that my mother always referred to as the pond where she would spend her summer days with her watercolors painting and dreaming her teenage dreams.

• • •

Alla took me to visit the Lvov mansion, a not so distant and pleasant walk from their home through a grove of birch and maple trees. Alla explained that Maple trees contained the souls waiting to be reincarnated, pointing out as proof their five fingered leaves. *Given the opportunity, Russians will never pass up talking about the soul.*

Having been neglected for close to a century, the Lvov mansion was in remarkably good condition. Marble columns protected the entrance to the white two-story building. It sat neglected in a field of weeds but the remains of a landscaped garden was still in evidence. I could see where at one time a circular drive brought carriages to the white pillared entrance. Some of the windows were boarded up, the ones that were uncovered were too dirty to see through. The French doors on the second floor opened onto balconies. To see the Lvov mansion as it was back in its day was left to my imagination; thus, I imagined the windows glowing with light, waltzes being played inside a brightly lit ballroom, men and women dressed in their finery, dancing. Servants offering zakuski (hors d'oervres) and flutes of champagne. It was a life of great privilege. Not far away were the wooden homes of the peasants.

• • •

Lev was the only son of my uncle *Vanya,* - Johnny - whom my mother died believing was alive in the era of the Soviet Union working to bring down the Communist regime. It was a belief that I grew up with, a family legend that had at its roots in a few facts and a lot of my mother's fantasies.

According to Lev, the story of his father, my uncle Vanya, was not so cloak-and-dagger. He explained that his mother and father had been living in Shanghai. She had left her husband and taken Lev and his sister back to Russia in the early thirties. At that time, many Russians who'd fled during the revolution, were seduced by Joseph Stalin's promise that they could return safely to Russia, and all would be forgiven. There is a marvelous 1999 French movie about that tragic time called East/West starring Oleg

Menshikov and Catherine Deneuve. Lev's father had followed his wife and been arrested. Like many of those depicted in the film, he was executed. Lev's mother was sent to a gulag, and he and his sister were raised in an orphanage. I was sitting in Lev's combination living room and bedroom, drinking vodka and eating zakuski (snacks) with his wife, Alla, and cousin Nikolai. I was listening to Lev's account of his father's tragic fate.

At the same time, I am hearing my mother's voice: *Vanya spoke many European languages and three different Chinese dialects. The Soviets were delighted to employ him.* My mother's voice continues on in my memory. I recall feeling somewhat schizophrenic.

"Had your father ever been a spy?" I asked Lev.

Never, Lev replied but added not as far as he knew. This reply would have left the door open for my mother, had she been there, to firmly advance her version of her brother's life. She would have felt it important to clarify: *It was only a rumor that her brother had been shot.* And she would have gone on to explain in detail her brother, Vanya's, clandestine activities.

History is always personal.

Family history is also anecdotal.

One afternoon, while Nikolai and Lev had gone for a walk, Alla said to me, "You know that your grandfather was a saint." I did not ask her why because I'd heard the story of my grandfather's saintliness often enough from my mother while I was growing up. *Your grandfather saved the Orthodox Church.* Rather than commit, I nodded. Alla nodded back.

My time spent with my cousins cleared up much of my family's history for me except for what happened to Grandfather Vladimir Lvov. What they knew was this: After he had escaped Russia, our grandfather lived in Paris. Of this, we were all in agreement. According to Alla there was evidence he wrote for a Russian émigré magazine. One account of him I had read, and put forth, claimed that he was indigent and homeless. My cousins soundly rejected that possibility. *Not our noble grandfather!* Based on what they knew for sure, or what they thought they knew, sometime in the "1930s", Grandfather Lvov returned to the Soviet from France, was arrested, and exiled to the city of Tomsk in Siberia. My cousins assumed that our grandfather had been executed and was probably buried in one of Stalin's mass graves. This part of the story was speculation.

Toward the end of my visit, Cousin Nikolai took me to Botova, the site of one of those mass graves on the outskirts of Moscow not far from his home. A huge white cross stood at the top of a stone platform in the middle of five hectares of grave mounds covering who knows how many bodies. Some say as many as 50 persons per day were executed at that site. Twenty thousand in one year. I remember feeling anger first, then a deep sadness for all those peoples' lost lives. As we left, Cousin Nikolai made the sign of the cross, and I did too, even though I was no longer a practicing Orthodox Christian. The religion I grew up in was alive in this cemetery, and I honored it by crossing myself in the Orthodox way, from right shoulder to left rather than left to right as the Catholics do. It was a little thing, but it seemed right to me. It would have pleased my mother.

I returned to Saint Petersburg to spend my last week visiting with my friend Dmitri. Dmitri could have written a history of Saint Petersburg. He was particularly proud to take me on a walking tour of the Taurida Palace where the Duma – the Russian Senate – had held its official meetings during Czarist times and in the early days of the post-revolutionary government. He took a photograph of me standing on the stage at the podium, one hand raised over my head as if giving a speech. This was the exact podium, Dmitri informed me, from which Lenin and Trotsky spoke. I was able to sit in the seat designated for my grandfather, Senator Vladimir Lvov. I remember getting the chills as I sat down. I remember asking myself if my grandfather had also stood at that podium, and what kind of speech he had delivered. Was he eloquent? Did he speak to defend the Revolution? Did he support the arrest of the Tsar or argue against it? My mother believed he supported the monarchy. Then she claimed he supported a Constitutional Monarchy like the British. She also told me he supported the Social Democrats, which was more in line with all the history books I'd read up to then in which my grandfather was mentioned.

I took a tour bus on my own to visit the Tsar's Winter Palace. There was supposed to be an English translator aboard, but he or she never appeared, and I remained frustrated all the way, trying to keep up with the speed of the guide's historical recitation, which included numerous references to the 17th century Russian poet Alexander Pushkin, considered Russia's Shakespeare. I had read *Evgeny Onegin* in translation and knew some of the more famous lines in Russian by heart. Somewhere in my memory there was a line Pushkin wrote, *I want to understand you/ I study your obscure language.* Was that what I was doing in Russia, trying to understand the country I was born *of* but not *into*? As an American, I was distant from my roots, but as an immigrant, not nearly distant enough.

I remember being revolted by the opulence of the palace. The Amber Room is mind blowing in its extravagance. One look at it and you could understand why the Russian people needed a revolution. I visited the boarding school close by where the young Alexander Pushkin lived and studied. I have a photograph of me, standing at the open door to his room pointing to his writing desk. On the return trip there was less history, but more Pushkin. Many of the Russian tourists had long sections of Pushkin's poetry memorized, and they were delighted to entertain us. It was okay that I didn't understand all of it; I enjoyed the rhythms and how enthusiastically they declaimed the lines. I listened and looked out the window at the landscape of plowed fields and birch forests that had been the home of my parents and grandparents and the family ghosts of all of my relatives.

· · ·

Together with Dmitri's beautiful wife, Tania, we drove to their dacha north of Saint Petersburg. It was September, mushroom hunting season, an almost mystical experience observed by nearly all Russians. As we entered a densely forested landscape, cars were parked on either side of the highway. Mushroom hunters, Tania explained. Dmitri parked the car. We were going mushroom hunting, he told me. A Russian saying my father had told me came to mind. *To be afraid of wolves is to be without mushrooms.*

I was given a basket and pointed in the direction of the forest where Dmitri assured me there were no wolves. But maybe a *leshi*, the horned forest deity in Russian folk tales my mother used to read to me as a child. And, perhaps, deep in the forest, a hut belonging to a woodcutter and his two small children, and a bearded father telling a tale. How I loved those Turgenev short stories.

The three of us split up, giving ourselves a half hour to pick as many mushrooms as we could find. Before I departed Dmitri said, "Don't forget, one who is noisy scares away mushrooms."

I hunt and pick and am surprised that despite the many people tramping through the forest, it is remarkably silent. I think centuries of fallen leaves cushioning the sound of our shoes. I make up my own Russian saying: A silent forest produces more mushrooms. I return a half hour later with a full basket, proud of my haul. I give my basket to Tania, who proceeds to throw most of my mushrooms away, making a face as she tosses. Poisonous, she keeps repeating as each one sails back into the quiet forest. When she is finished, they both start laughing. I join in the fun but feel as if I've just failed my Russian 101 final.

• • •

To be truly Russian, my friend Dmitri explained, I would have to go to the Banya to be cleansed with, as he put it, "light and hard steam." Which I interpreted, at the time, would be analogous to the Irish describing rain as soft and hard. How very wrong I was. Late September was the start of banya season all over Russia. Dmitri took me to his private club. (There are numerous public banyas) I was made aware of the layers and layers of ritual involved in a Russian steam bath. The basics began with an initial full body scrub, with soap, done in a warm shower with a banya-master, using gloves that felt like sandpaper on my skin. The steam bath came next. The temperature was initially bearable, but the heat increased with each bucket of water thrown into the furnace, until finally the heat became barely tolerable, but I remember at the time, despite the heat, my body tingling all over with pleasure. During the steam, the banya master fluttered birch branches over my body. I was told that this increased the waves of heat, which it did. Out of the hot steam, I was led to a cold pool and told to jump in. I was glad I had a strong heart, but my heart, I daresay, was unprepared for the shock. In the NBA, I was not known for my speed. But my speed exiting the cold pool would have qualified me for the Olympics 100-meter dash.

Following my icy bath and surviving my near heart attack, Dmitri escorted me to a side room where we sat, rosy and toweled, at a table with other rosy and toweled men of approximately our age. Those broad Russian faces, those sturdy Russian bodies were the size of refrigerators. We ate black bread, cheese, herring in sour cream, piroshki (baked buns filled with meat and rice) We spread caviar on triangles of toast, washing the beluga morsels down with shots of vodka. They told jokes; they poked fun at each other. They laughed at my pronunciation, but by now into my sixth week in Russia I could be understood. Following this feast, I was told tradition called for a final steam and thrashing of birch leaves and a last dunking in the icy pool before, of course, a good-bye round of vodka. I was sated and slightly drunk but made it through the final steam and final shots of vodka. Thus, I was baptized a Russian by steaming, rosy-faced Russian men. Any one of them could have been my father. I imagined my dead father among the living and wept openly. The men hugged me and patted me on the back. It didn't matter that I was an old man crying because, as Dmitri assured me, for Russians, it was okay to cry anytime, anywhere, even in the Banya.

• • •

At the tail end of my trip to the Motherland, as September turned into October, I was invited by the Russian Basketball Federation to attend the opening tournament of the Russian Professional Basketball League. The tournament was played annually in honor of Vladimir Kondrashin, the celebrated and deceased basketball coach of the USSR team that defeated the U.S. team in the 1972 summer Olympics in Munich, and his star player, Alexander Belov, also deceased. Belov was the player who made the winning basket in that disputed overtime victory. When the buzzer sounded at the end of the fourth quarter of regulation, the American Olympic team was ahead by one point, the Americans believed they had won and began to celebrate. However, the official timer had made a mistake and ended the quarter with several seconds still remaining on the clock. Over the protest of the U.S. team, the game was restarted. In the remaining seconds the Soviet team was awarded the ball out of bounds. The ball was thrown the length of the court, caught in mid-air by a leaping Alexander Belov who touched the ball off the glass for the win. The United States team refused to accept the silver medal. I have always believed our Americans should have shown more sportsmanship.

The day before the opening game of the Kondrashin Tournament, the players of that famous Soviet gold medal-winning team, their families and friends - Dmitri and I included - bussed to the graveyard to honor their deceased coach and star player. Honoring meant bringing tables, chairs, plates, glasses, and enough food to not only feed us but any mourners that might be visiting other gravesites. And, of course, enough vodka for endless rounds of toasts.

A public service message for any traveler to Russia: Do not try to keep up with Russians drinking vodka. You will find the following morning extremely painful.

During the cemetery festivities, one of the players from that celebrated team, Ivan Edeshko, took me aside and said. *"Znayou, Znayou,* (I know, I know), all bad clock and timer, but *pochemou* (why) didn't your coach put a player to guard me out of bounds? I see clear pass down the court, and I very accurate throwing ball?" His English was understandable. The not-so-subtle implication was clear: Hank Iba, the Olympic basketball coach of that team, was a *dourak,* the Russian word for moron. I had to agree with him.

I couldn't remember eating and drinking as much in my life as I did that afternoon. I would not argue with my cousin who told me that Russians celebrate death better than life. Which raises the question: is there such a thing as too much vodka? Since this is my story, I reserve the right to withhold how I felt the next morning.

At half time of the opening game, an official asked me to address the crowd. Ten thousand fans or more packed the arena. Knowing my Russian was not good enough for an extemporaneous speech, I was terrified, but to refuse was out of the question. Dmitri patted me on the back and assured me the people would appreciate my attempt to speak Russian. As I was being escorted to the center court. I tried to piece together something in my mind that I could say, which wouldn't sound completely idiotic. The public address announcer introduced me as the first Russian to play in the EN-BEH-AH. He stated my American name, then repeated my Russian birth name, Tomislav Nikolaevich Mescherikov. Then, he handed me the microphone. The applause was polite. I remember pausing, then throwing all caution to the fates, I began. I thanked them for inviting me to the game. I praised the brand of basketball I'd just witnessed. I told them I was proud to be the first Russian basketball player to have played in the NBA. As I finished and walked back to my seat, enjoying the applause, I realized that for the second time in my adult life, I spoke Russian fluently.

• • •

The first time in my life I spoke Russian fluently happened in 1989 after my mother's burial. The funeral party had returned from the cemetery to my mother's San Francisco apartment for the funeral feast. At some point, my sister asked me to telephone two of our mother's friends who had not been informed of our mother's death. They did not speak English. I argued that her Russian was better than mine. Ann claimed she was too emotional to be able to do it. Reluctantly, I placed the calls. The calls took, perhaps, no longer than three or four minutes each, but for that brief time I spoke fluent Russian. After I got off the phone, my sister said it was a miracle. My mother would have had a different interpretation. Russian is in your blood; she would have reminded me. Twenty three years later in Saint Petersburg with 10,000 Russian basketball fans applauding, I walked back to my seat smiling and thinking how right my mother was and why a country's language is referred to as The Mother Tongue.

I wish I'd told my mother that she was right about language being in the blood before she died but I didn't have any proof of it, before she died in 1981. Her death was sudden. I was living in Truckee at the time, so I was unable to drive down from my home in Truckee to be with her. I did get a chance to sit by her hospital bed, holding her hand, her soul already departed. She was 86 years old. I thanked her for everything. For my sister and I, her strength had been everything.

Today, my Russian language skill is better than it's ever been but remains rudimentary. Too often, listening to someone talking to me in Russian, I must plead, "*Pazhlesta, gaveritse medlino.*" "Please, speak slowly." There are also times I overhear Russian being spoken in a grocery store or in a restaurant, and I understand every word. It's unnerving.

• • •

While Melanie is editing the Russian sections of the memoir, I bring out photographs of me and my two cousins. Our likenesses are stunningly similar. I show them to her. She tells me the three of us would be mistaken for brothers. In the photograph, we are standing outside the wooden home where Lev and his wife, Alla, live. It is in a village within walking distance of the Lvov family estate and equidistant from our great relative, the architect, Nikolai Lvov's Leaning Tower. I have a photograph of that tower that is dangerously in competition with the famous tower in Pisa.

• • •

On the flight leaving Russia, I tried to evaluate and consider what these last two months in Russia meant to me. Was I leaving Russia as my friend Dmitri questioned if I felt more Russian than when I arrived? Had the *baptism of steam* worked? It was 2007. I had lived in America for sixty-two years. Over those years, especially the formative ones, I had done everything I could to be an American. But as hard as I had tried, I had the feeling I'd fallen short of my goal. It was something I couldn't rationally explain. Discussing that feeling later with a friend, I'd explained it to him this way, "It feels like my clothing doesn't fit properly." He replied, "Like your underwear is biting you?" It was meant as a joke, but he was right. Like the collar of my shirt was too small.

These thoughts were in my mind as I watched out the airplane window, at the landscape of Russia disappearing below me. I tried to think if I had felt more natural, more myself in Russia. I decided that I had not. So where did that leave me? In the air. That is *not* a joke. I thought of my mother, something she told me a long time ago, which I had used in a poem in my first book. I couldn't recall what age I'd been when she'd taken me aside and sat me down on our couch as she did whenever she wanted to impart something important to me, and said, "Tomishka,I knew the minute I left Russia when I was nineteen, no matter where I lived, I'd always be displaced." On the flight leaving Russia, a country I would probably never visit again, I wondered if, like my mother, I too would always feel displaced.

• • •

My flight had me stopping in Spain where I would with my daughter, Megan, and her family for a couple of weeks. Megan was on a Fulbright Fellowship, living in the southern city of Granada. I changed planes in Madrid. Meg met me at the airport in Granada, and we took the bus to their rented house in the Albayzin, the ancient gypsy quarter of small squares and serpentine cobblestone alleys that wind through the hillside neighborhood. It was late September, already cold in Russia, but shirt-sleeve weather in southern Spain.

• • •

Meg was my athlete. She played basketball in high school and college and would throw a wicked elbow if needed to ward off an opponent. She is tall, broad shouldered and beautiful, a description that has not changed over the years. My two weeks in Granada were pure pleasure. I observed my two granddaughters, Grace and Ruth, becoming bilingual. Meg's husband, Brendan, and I took a Garcia Lorca bus tour, the only two men among twenty-five female Spanish school teachers, many of whom would, upon request, recite Lorca's best-known poems from memory. It reminded me of the bus tour I took from Saint Petersburg to the Winter Palace, listening to the Russian tourists reciting the poetry of Alexander Pushkin. I couldn't imagine Americans visiting burial sites of famous American poets, like Walt Whitman or Robert Frost, let alone spontaneously reciting lines from their famous poems. The official site of Lorca's burial is under an olive tree. The unofficial site and the one more likely, is in a common grave in a hillside ditch.

• • •

I became accustomed to the Spanish tradition of eating well at noon followed by a siesta. I listened to flamenco. I visited the Moorish palace, The Alhambra. Outside its entrance I was accosted by an extremely persistent gypsy. I finally gave up five bucks and extended my palm to be read. She told me that I would live a long life, but I should give up sadness.

• • •

I arrived home to Truckee in time for Thanksgiving, the day after Thanksgiving, a family affair that included my ex-wife, I suffered a bout of depression, borderline suicidal, a combo that I attributed to the final realization of a failed marriage, the diagnosis of terminal cancer, and the feeling of intense displacement and loss of some part of me that I'd left behind in Russia and would never be abel to reclaim.

• • •

The depression lasted two horrible weeks. Medication didn't help. I progressed through it using a strategy of intense exercise that I had relied upon in my past to overcome hard times. Instead of basketball, I spent hours in the gym on the stationary bicycle, pedaling furiously, like an adult version of the boy in D. H. Lawrence's story, *Rocking Horse Winner*, force-feeding endorphins. At the beginning of December 2007, I came out of that dark tunnel, exhausted, alive, lonely, and determined to do something about it. At the suggestion of my son, I began perusing on-line dating possibilities - *It's no biggie, Dad, everybody is doing it.*

Thanks to my son, I met Melanie Marchant.

I see my future wife's gorgeous face on the online photograph she posted, although I must confess I questioned whether the photograph wasn't of a younger Melanie. That suspicion was dispelled on our first date.

CHAPTER 41
OUR FIRST DATE

Given that my parents' marriage was, at best, a marriage of convenience and at worst a tragic mistake; and that my 38-year marriage had ended in an unhappy divorce, it is a head- scratcher that I ever entertained being married again. Luckily, I didn't allow failure to influence me; otherwise, I would never have permitted myself to love Melanie.

For our first date, Melanie had selected a Turkish restaurant named *Ganouls* in Sacramento. I drove down from the mountains. Despite driving directions. I got lost and arrived late. As I approached, I could see a woman with her back to the window talking to the maître d'. I could also see through the window that the restaurant was full, the tables covered with whitetablecloths. On the center of each table rested a long-stemmed red rose. Then, I remembered – it was Valentine's Day. I wanted to slap myself. I checked my embarrassment and opened the door. The waiter looked up; the woman turned around. She smiled, then stuck her tongue out at me, stamped her foot, and pointed to her watch.

I was charmed.

The waiter looked relieved. That night, over dinner and a surprisingly excellent Turkish wine, I gave her a copy of *Wild Geese*, a poem by Mary Oliver. Why that particular poem? Perhaps it had something to do with the first stanza in which the poet says, ". . . you do not have to walk for a hundred miles through the desert repenting,' a reminder to myself I was coming off a stressful divorce.How many years since the divorce? Melanie gave me a Batman Valentine's Day card. Consider these gifts as representative of our personalities.

Melanie and I have finished dinner. She has invited me to her condominium. I follow her in my car. I walk in the front door and see a wall of icons leading up the stairs: saints and angels, as beautiful as any I remember from the Orthodox church that I attended as a child. Whose icons? I ask. Hers. She'd painted them. My first thought is that it could not be a coincidence that we met each other.

It is worth telling because it is both charming and darling (two of Melanie's favorite words) and because food has always been an important part of my life that Melanie led me upstairs past the sacred icons to her bedroom, and we sat on the floor our backs cushioned against her bedstead in front of her very old TV set, and she put on a video called *Ratatouille*, a cartoon about a rat that turns into a chef. I thought of my youthful desire to be a chef. I thought of my Aunt Maroucia. I held Melanie's hand as we watched. That night, I drove home to Truckee knowing I was in love.

I have attempted over the years to make ratatouille with only marginal success.

• • •

When I realized after the first couple of dates that this might turn into a committed relationship, I screwed up enough courage to tell her.

"Myeloma is an incurable form of blood cancer," I stated.

Melanie shrugged off "incurable." She told me that she knew lots of people with cancer. It sounded to me as if she considered cancer a religion like, I know lots of Baptists. I realized she was unwilling to allow something as insignificant as a terminal disease to stand in the way of what she believed might be love. Melanie never once considered that she might be linking her life to a fragile and temporary future. It never entered her mind that she might wind up caring for me if my white cells weakened, and I became bedridden.

"We are all temporary," she'd said, as if she was talking about employment. I remember smiling at that whimsical way of thinking about death. Over the years, I have come to understand that it was not at all whimsical, but an acceptance of death as a transitory condition. In her words, if you're tuned in to death, it allows you a glimpse into the future. *It's like after you finish a novel and there are a few pages of the author's next book that you can read.* I remember asking what if a person didn't like what they read. Her response was typical Melanie, "You have to be tuned in better."

Cancer is not a way to start a marriage. But we chose to, and it soon became clear that turning our lives over to the universe was the best way to live in the present.

CHAPTER 42
WE WERE MARRIED IN A GALLERY

We were married on Valentine's Day, 2009, in Melanie's living room. She wore a white tuxedo; I wore a black tuxedo, with studs and everything. Melanie and I exchanged wedding bands that had belonged to my parents, resized to fit us. They were classic 18-karat rose gold. Inscribed inside the rings were the names of my parents: Masha and Kolya (diminutive for Mary and Nikolai). Before our wedding, Melanie and I had our initials inscribed inside the rings. During the marriage ceremony, I passed my father's 14th century bronze Russian icon given me by my father, to my son Matthew. My mother's sacred icon of the Virgin, in my sister Ann's possession, will go, after her death, to my oldest daughter, Janai.

• • •

On our first trip to New York City to visit my sister, Ann told us a friend of hers had recently given her the gift of a free consultation with a well-known spiritualist. The woman contacted our mother who wanted Ann to know she was fine and enjoying her life in heaven. Ann remained skeptical until the spiritualist told her that our mother was delighted that Melanie and I were wearing hers and her husband's "rings." There is no way, my sister stated, that the spiritualist could have known about the wedding bands. I believe in spirituality, but not spiritualists. I was delighted by this revelation. Since my mother was alive when my ex-wife and I were married, we had selected our own rings, but both of us stopped wearing them. Wearing my parents' rings made me feel that whatever love they might have felt in their early marriage, and lost, our love would make up for.

There are no walls in our condo that do not have paintings on them or nooks and crannies without some form of art. It's a gallery, Mel says. I like that we were married in an art gallery and live our daily lives surrounded by art. The two major settings of my life have been the basketball arena and the classroom. Now in my old age, I live within an art gallery.

I wouldn't mind living inside a poem.

CHAPTER 43
HOW MELANIE CAME TO BE KNOWN AS THE FABLED

Melanie Marchant Meschery, my wife of the last thirteen years - my love, and my friend is my editor and principal critic. As I write, her voice is always in my head or sometimes in my ear as our desks stand an arms-length from each other in our office. I'm in the habit of shortening her name to Mel, which she's not crazy about. I have a perfectly beautiful name, Melanie, she reminds me.

And sometimes I refer to Melanie as The Fabled, a sobriquet that was bestowed upon her in New York City in October of 2016, when we were visiting my sister, Ann. The airline tickets were Ann's birthday gift to me so that we could celebrate together. On the 26th of the month, I'd be 78 years old. Melanie and I gladly accepted my sister's generous gift of travel to New York City, with its museums (There is not enough art in the world to satisfy my wife). My sister had reserved a room for us at a hotel, which she referred to as the hovel. A name that did not inspire a lot of confidence in us, but turned out to be clean, comfortable and affordable, with a view of the Hudson River. Included in the trip was dining at Ann's favorite Russian restaurant, Uncle Vanya's. Fine art and perfectly prepared borscht were ways to ignore the fact that I was slouching towards eighty like it was frigging Bethlehem. My wife and sister got along as they loved the same person. There was also mutual respect by two women who'd achieved independence at a time when women were treated as second-class citizens. My sister had selected Melanie as one of several judges for her annual fall Gracie Mansion Art Show. Mel holds a BA in art, an MA in art, and a PhD in Education . She is an artist in several mediums herself, and she appreciated my sister's recognition of her expertise.

Ann had been telling her good friend, David, that I was her older brother. I was okay with the fiction, since David had doubtless figured it out anyway. Militsa Mescheriakova or Ann Meschery, as she was known in the business world, is an exceptional woman. She was crashing through corporate glass ceilings before the metaphor was created. After a long career in the advertising industry, she'd dropped softly and elegantly into retirement on a golden parachute. I love my sis, but I didn't always love her as much. There was a time in our middle years when she was a devout conservative Republican, *fiscal conservative* was how she put it, and I was a liberal Democrat. Our differences turned into years of jaw-clenching arguments. One afternoon's particularly heated exchange resulted in her saying, "Tom, I never knew how stupid you really are." I remember it shocked me. Our political standoff wouldn't have changed, I suspect, except that after retiring, Ann took the financial reins of the non-profit Russian American Youth Orchestra, and witnessed first-hand how the arts were marginalized by her beloved political party. By no means did she become a liberal, but she did resign from the Republican Party *and became more independent in her voting preferences.*

This trip to New York City provided us with the opportunity to meet with Philip Spitzer, of Spitzer Literary Agency. He had read my first attempt at a memoir, *Seasons Past, Power Forward* and had been shopping it to publishers. The frame of the memoir was the 2015-2016 NBA Golden State Warriors basketball season, with running commentary on the magnificent Warriors team that had won the NBA Championship the previous season. The manuscript included my thoughts about the present game and players, flashbacks to my own life both as a professional basketball player that spanned ten years from 1961 to 1971, and my various careers following my retirement from the NBA - teacher, traveler, writer, and amateur chef. I was excited, anticipating good news. *A six-figure book deal. Why not?*

We met Philip Spitzer for lunch at Docks Oyster Bar. Spitzer was the only literary agent - out of approximately 20 agents I'd submitted to - who'd agreed to shop my memoir. He had not offered me a contract to be my agent yet. But I was optimistic that our meeting might change that.

Philip had arrived ahead of us and was already seated. He was about my age, in his seventies. He looked the way I imagined all male literary agents should look, short, slightly portly, and wearing spectacles, with an embracing personality. (Embracing, of course, meant embracing my memoir.)

Philip waved to us. As we approached, I was sad to see walking crutches leaning against the table. I presented Philip with a signed copy of my recent collection of Poetry, *Sweat: New and Selected Poems about Sports*, published in 2014. The book, with a cover Mel had designed and painted, was selling well for poetry. I hoped the gift would add a little to my cred as a writer of prose, the chasm that exists between the publication of poetry and fiction notwithstanding.

As we looked through the menu, Philip regaled us with stories of his family's safari in East Africa, which I enjoyed, having coached on and off in West Africa for several summers during my years in the NBA. I'd never made it to the east side of the continent because those countries, ex-British colonies, didn't play basketball. The more Phil talked, the more I liked him.

I could tell that Mel was also charmed by Philip and he definitely was taken by her. He asked her about art. He promised to check out her website. He told us that he'd seen me play basketball in Madison Square Garden. He mentioned something about a near fight I'd had with Willis Reed, the Knicks fearsome 6'10" Hall of Fame center. I hadn't remembered being that careless with my life, although I *did* take a swing at Wilt Chamberlain, a man much larger that Willis. *Talk about carelessness with your life.*

After we ordered our meals and the waiter left, he produced an email from his coat pocket and showed me the rejection from Gerald Howard of Penguin/Doubleday:

Thu, Sep 29, 2016 11:30 am
Phil, I'm figuring I must be one of the few people in publishing who would snap to when Tom Meschery's name is mentioned and who might have watched him play even on television. . .

Skip to the crucial closing sentence:

Anyway, I'll have to pass on this, but thank you for the look.

According to Philip, Gerald didn't like all the basketball stuff, and thought the book would be a whole lot more interesting if I'd kept to my own story. As Gerald stated: *I really had no idea that he had this exotic and fascinating White Russian background – and a blood connection to Leo Tolstoy even!*

I'd been hoping *Old War and Peace* would impress a publisher, but apparently not enough. My Russian roots and early immigrant life had been chronicled often during my athletic career. My place of birth is one of the questions in the sports category in the board game, *Trivial Pursuit*. I've always thought that was cool.

The letter rejecting my memoir was definitely *not* cool.

My athletic career, a series of successes from high school through the NBA, had not prepared me for the failure that literary agents were delivering to my ego like Mike Tyson body blows.

Philip told me not to be discouraged, that Andre Dubus' *House of Sand and Fog* was rejected over one hundred times before he sold it. The book went on to be a finalist for the National Book Award. Given my age, anecdotes about how long it takes writers to get their books published did not cheer me up.

Philip inquired about my novels. I explained that I'd written five, three that could be considered "literary fiction," one young-adult novel and one mystery, all waiting for the right publisher to accept them. Philip told me he was willing to read my manuscripts and I told him I'd send him a manuscript as soon as I got home. Considering my numerous rejections, I was surprised by my excitement. *Here I come, National Book Award!*

We said our goodbyes to Philip outside the restaurant. He promised he'd get back to me as soon as he read the manuscript. We walked away to catch the bus that would take us to THE MOMA. I had put the memoir *Season Past, Power Forward* where it belonged, in the past. Wrote it off as a learning experience. With Philip's voice in my head, I felt like a fiction writer, soon to be rubbing shoulders with some of Philip Spitzer's famous clients, Michael Connelly and James Lee Burke, both writers whose detective novels Mel and I read and enjoyed.

In the cab on our way from Docks Restaurant to the MOMA, Melanie remarked Philip was a love. She was thrilled that he was willing to read all my books.. She had edited 2,100 pages, on average of seven revisions, which came to a total of approximately 14,700 pages, an effort that can only be called heroic. But I think the real reason she thought Philip adorable is that he made a point of telling her how he enjoyed the way I'd portrayed her in the memoir, as if she were my foil, providing the reader at just the right moment with *witty asides and intelligent remarks,* at which point he stated, "From now on you shall be referred to as 'The Fabled'." Melanie bowed her head, as if she'd been knighted. Later, my wife, usually known for her modesty, told me she'd gladly answer to The Fabled, but at some point in the future she'd like for her title to be "The Mythic."

On the airplane home to Sacramento, Melanie suggested that I should write a new memoir, limiting the basketball stuff and focusing more on my family history and other non-athletic areas of my life. My answer was "Not a chance. No more memoirs for me."

At home I sent Philip my novel, *Dolby*. Weeks, then months passed. 2017 began. No word. Emails and phone calls went unanswered. All my efforts writing fiction, some seven years, felt wasted. There they all were, my many manuscripts one on top of the other in a corner next to my desk like fuel for a bonfire of vanities. One match, and I would have burned down the house.

Fuck prose. I went back to writing poems. They felt like good friends that had been out of the country. "Welcome home," I said.

Not that Melanie didn't support my poetry, but she had another idea. By the spring of 2017, my wife had persuaded me to give writing a new memoir a try. Perhaps persuasion is not quite accurate, more like wrestling me to the floor until I cried uncle.

"Talk less about basketball and more about your life and family," she'd said. "Growing old together. There's romance there. Write about battling cancer. Write about literature."

Okay, I was always a battler. The term power-forward didn't exist in the NBA before I came into the league. Perhaps I exaggerate some, but you get my meaning. Melanie patted my cheek. "Get started," she ordered. My wife taught for years at Sacramento City College. When she says, "Get started," about anything, it's with the voice of authority. That day, she tapped her wristwatch, taped her toe. I opened my computer. The title would come later.

After that trip to New York City, I've often referred to Melanie as The Fabled: *The phone rings; it's my wife's son. He asks for his mother. I respond: "The Fabled will be right with you."*

CHAPTER 44
BALLBOY

In the fall of 2012, Melanie and I were living in Alameda, an island city connected by two bridges and a tunnel to Oakland. We were three years into our marriage, experimenting with the idea of moving permanently to the Bay Area, which for me would have been completing a full circle. In Melanie's case, one of the enticements had to do with living close to three of California's most important art museums. We were renting a garden apartment below a Victorian owned by our friends Dell and Pat. The street address was on Versailles Avenue, which elicited this comment from Mel, "We're living in France," *If only we were.* On our many trips to Europe over the years of our marriage, we had decided Paris was our preferred home away from home, preferably in the hilltop district of Montmartre, near the Dali Museum and a cute little square in which Melanie imagined setting up her easel.

Memories such as these make the exhausting and often painful writing of a memoir pleasurable.

Our Alameda experiment failed because a year later, Mel's aging mom needed our attention, and we moved back to Sacramento. In the fall of 2011, however, the possibility of returning to my roots took a surprising turn. It started with a telephone call from the Golden State Warriors' office. The person calling introduced himself as Rick Welts, the COO of the Warriors. After I acknowledged, he asked me if I remembered him. I recalled photographs of Welts in the newspaper, a handsome youngish looking man, but certainly older, given his status. Easy smile, neatly attired. I admitted I couldn't recall. His answer: "I was the ball-boy for the Sonics when you played." I might have uttered something like "Well, for Christ's sake." I did say something about coincidence. Welts wanted to know if I'd like to have lunch. Delighted, I replied, and we set a date. Before getting off the phone, he said. "You know, you and Lenny (Lenny Wilkins, our star guard and Sonics player-coach) were the only players who treated the ball-boys with any respect." After the call I spent some time on the computer Googling Rick. I found out that the "ball boy", a graduate of the University of Washington and working in the Sonics office, had been hired by the NBA and was responsible for developing NBA Properties that is now a multi-billion-dollar enterprise, for which he was considered the league's wunderkind.

Three days later Rick and I met for lunch at the Marriott Hotel in Oakland. The Warriors offices and practice rooms were located on the two top floors of the hotel. I took the elevator up and was admitted into a long hall leading to the practice gyms. On one side was a row of windows. Opposite the windows the wall displayed bigger than life images of the best retired Warriors' players. And there I was. I stopped for a moment to remind myself what I looked like when I was young and in shape. It was slightly depressing. Before lunch, I was introduced to Rick's staff at a meeting and provided with a tour of the practice facility. There were immense photographs of all the retired jerseys on the walls. Rick explained that Joe Lacob, the executive owner of the Warriors, had decided that, unlike the previous ownership, the Warriors under his watch wanted to embrace the team's history. Every player that played significant minutes for the Warriors would be welcomed at games. Tickets and parking would be provided. I decided on the spot that Lacob was thinking in terms of the sport, fans, and community, not just money. Over the years that thought has proven correct. I looked forward to meeting Lacob and his partner Peter Guber, whose film company had produced many of my favorite movies.

Rick and I had lunch and reminisced about Seattle and the Sonics. We both felt horrible that Seattle no longer had a team. It was like there'd been an eviction and a family home had been lost. Rick was interested in what I was doing in my retirement. I told him that I'd originally set out to devote myself to writing poetry. Ironically, because I never saw myself as a fiction writer, it turned out that I had begun writing a novel. It was a story about a guy in his late thirties whose only experience playing basketball was in high school and at men's fantasy basketball camps. My protagonist was in training attempting to make it in the NBA. Rick was polite, but I could tell skepticism when I saw it. His skepticism was providential considering this was the novel *Dolby* that I'd sent to numerous literary agents and received an equal number of rejections, including Philp Spitzer's silent rejection.

When I taught my high school creative writing class, we discussed the idea of *willing suspension of disbelief* that allows a reader to believe something is true even if it seems impossible, an absolute requirement if writing fantasy or science fiction. But also, when reading the great epic poems and stories of the past, Homer's *Odyssey*, The *Tales of King Arthur and the Round Table*, and my favorite, the Old English epic, *Beowulf.* I personally didn't believe my tale was that impossible. Why couldn't a thirty-year-old male be fit enough to make it into the NBA? It was a plot that probably originated in my own deep sense of yearning to be that same physical creature at my advanced age that I was in my thirties.

Rick was excited about the Warriors future. At the time we had no idea how fabulous that future would be. I drove home feeling that, perhaps, I had not entirely left my past behind. I remember saying to Melanie when I returned home, "You know, I feel like a Warrior again."

Melanie and I were invited to Warrior games. As Rick promised, there were tickets and parking space, and we were made welcome. Often Raymond Ridder, the Warriors' Public Relations Director, would ask me to speak with reporters or to groups of season ticket holders. "You are like family," Raymond said, echoing the words of Rick Welts.

After the third or fourth game Melanie and I attended, I remember feeling that the Warriors and I were about to start a renewed friendship. That feeling has proven true. As of this writing, # 14 was back with his Warrior family in The City where he first learned to play the game on its multitude of playground courts. Again, I was the immigrant boy with his ball, testing the wind before he shot, knowing the cracks in the asphalt as he dribbled, hearing the faint future accolades of a ten year career in the NBA coming from the spectators watching from behind the playground fences.

On January 17, 2017, Melanie and I attended the groundbreaking ceremony for the new Warrior's state-of-the-art Chase Center Arena. As COO, Rick Welts was responsible for the prodigious task of seeing the project to completion. While we watched giant cranes dominating the skyline, and acrobats dressed as construction workers somersaulting through the air, the title for an article or a book about Rick came to mind: *The Ball-boy Who Became an NBA Legend.*

Next to Rick stood Joe Lacob watching with an expression on his face that might have been similar to a father's watching his child being born. And next to him was Bob Myers, the young GM whose job it had been to put together the players who'd dominated the NBA for the previous four years. And Steve Kerr, who trained those basketball magicians who entertained the Bay Area from Oakland's Oracle Arena and would again from this state of the art Chase Center Arena in San Francisco. It was there, sitting and watching these men that I wished Bill King was alive and with me, two old timer Warriors, player and broadcaster. Perhaps it was my ego, but I felt when this arena was finished, part of it belonged to me.

• • •

It didn't take me long after Rick Welts and I met to feel grandfatherly towards the Warriors. It didn't hurt that my old team soon became *The Dubs* and won three out of four NBA Championships. *Proud grandpa.* Melanie and I took our grandchildren to games. Mel took photographs of me and the kids with my jersey banner 14 hanging in the rafters above us. All right, I'll say it again: *Proud grandpa.*

I was asked once what it was about the Warriors that made them special for me. The answer was easy: The Warriors had a coach who spoke about joy, the most exquisite shooter there ever will be in Stephan Curry, an undersized power forward in Draymond Green who, like me when I played, was asked to do the dirty work, and an assistant coach Ron Adams who loved poetry and emailed me Poems of the Day and had known Philip Lavine, one of my all time favorite poets.

I mention the following only because it is historic. Rick Welts became the first openly gay sports executive. When Rick came out, he opened one of the front doors to history that had been locked so long, entered, looked around, ascertained the danger, decided it was worth it, and kept walking bravely into his new home - freedom. That's courage.

• • •

In the summer of 2017 after the Golden State Warriors won their second NBA Championship, the last article in the *Sports Illustrated* issue honoring the team was dedicated to my life and career. It was entitled: *Poet in Motion*, written by Jack McCallum, one of the magazine's senior writers. The poet part was accurate, the motion part was not so much. I was living with an arthritic knee and a cranky spine. It was a splendidly written and flattering article. I felt like. . . what? Perhaps like returning to your family home after being away on a long journey and finding your childhood room exactly the way you left it.

I wondered how other NBA retired players reacted to their past glories. I didn't want to seem maudlin about seeing my name in print, my NBA successes resurrected, but I had to admit to giving in to pride, to reliving those days in my mind. When I spoke of this to Melanie, she asked me if it was like watching a silent film. Ego is *not* something *The Fabled* tolerates.

Nor should I. Except on occasion I have, as the following story illustrates.

In 2014, I had both my arthritic shoulder joints replaced. Maybe the arthritis was the result of too many hook shots. *Bras roule, French: circular motion of the arm.* I remember telling Mel's grandsons Jaxon and Max something like wait until my shoulders heal, boys, and I'll show you what a great shot looks like. The operations were a success and allowed me to regain full range of motion.

The time comes to live up to my promise to the boys. I lead the two young basketball aspirants to their parents' garage driveway where there's a basketball standard. The ball feels good in my hands. I let it spin off my fingers a couple of times to get the feel, spin it on one finger to show off, then I step back 15 feet, the distance from free-throw line to hoop. I give the boys a nod. They smile. I wink. It's Meschery on the line for the game winning free-throws. I'm Mr. Clutch. I eye-ball the distance. I settle into a perfect stance, elbow directly under the ball. I execute, my arm extending at a 45 degree angle the way I was taught so long ago. My wrist snaps, the ball leaves my fingertips perfectly, flying in an arc toward the rim, seams rotating backward – a perfect arc, a splendid arc, a divine arc. It travels majestically for about four feet then its majesty fails and the ball, as if it is too exhausted to continue its flight, falls short of the rim by about a foot. Three attempts later, and no closer, I realize that, yes, I have new shoulders, but I don't have the strength. I had not taken into consideration that for the last 15 years or so, I hadn't shot a basketball.

The boys were kind.

There is the following story about me that Melanie told her grandson, John Clark:

We're at a game last season against the Rockets, in which Thomas was being honored as one of the Warriors' retired Legends. We were sitting courtside. Before the game began, Rosalyn "Ros" Gold Onwude, the Warriors on-court analyst, crossed the court to say hello to Tom. Roz was the star basketball player for Stanford University as well as a top scholar. She is also beautiful. As she stepped toward Tom, holding out her hand. He rocked forward in a futile effort to rise from his seat, but his knees would not permit him. He didn't do any better with his second effort. Then Roz reached down and took Tom's hand and pulled him up to a standing position.

John-Clark's response was predictable: "No way dude."

I was not the embarrassing kind, but this incident made me blush. There I was looking into the twinkling eyes of a stunning young woman who'd just helped a power forward to his feet.

CHAPTER 45
TRAVEL

During the time Melanie and I were doing our on-line courting, three topics came up over and over again: our children/grandchildren, our art, and travel. So far, I think we've done a pretty good job sticking to these priorities. (I suppose I should have included the NBA as a priority, but that's sort of been exclusively my thing.) Not exclusively, Melanie would argue.

Who do you think watches the games with you and listens patiently to your game analysis?

Our families and our art are second nature to us, so do not require planning the way travel does. Before we met, Mel and I had already done a lot of traveling. I had told Mel about my summers coaching in West Africa and touring Eastern Europe as part of an NBA All-Star team. Melanie recalled her year living in Florence, studying for her master's degree in art. She'd also taken several extended trips with friends and one with her mother and daughter, Emily, to Europe, mostly to the countries that border the Mediterranean. We decided as long as we were physically able, we'd continue to travel. *No retirement village living for us.* Both of us agreed that being limited to living with our own age group would be like eating at the same restaurant every day, no matter how much you enjoyed the food, eventually you'd become tired of it.

In the summer of 2008, the year before we married, we traveled together to San Juan, Puerto Rico, for an NBA Retired Players Association conference. The association is better known as The Legends. We were given T shirts with NBA Legends printed on them. Currently, the Players Association has not reprinted the shirt. I have worn mine until it might be best used as a dust rag.

I spent time at the conference with many of my old opponents and teammates. There was Earl "The Pearl" Monroe, the spinning, bobbing, infuriatingly difficult player to guard. He was a playground legend before he became an NBA legend. I recall someone telling me that The Pearl's arrival on the local playground courts elicited awed whispers from the onlookers of, "Jesus is here."

EARL THE PEARL

For Earl Monroe
In the rec leagues
they called me Black Jesus.
When I walked onto the court
the crowd parted like the Red Sea.
In college, someone found a rhyme
and I became a Pearl.
I guess I've been a mixed
metaphor ever since.
Today, when I back a player
down toward the paint
and spin into my shot,
I know before the ball leaves
my fingers it's going in.
At that moment I can heal lepers,
raise the dead.

Meschery, Tom "Earl the Pearl," *Sweat: New & Selected Poems About Sports*. Black Rock Press, 2014. University of Nevada, Reno. Reno. NV

How many times had I thought, I'd block The Pearl's shot only to miss by a fingernail. I'm not the only one who'd been embarrassed by Earl I'd wager. *All of you out there, raise your hands!*

Today, I watch future super star, Ja Morant, and think, *it's The Pearl all over again.*

I drank a beer with Dick Barnett, one of the oddest and brightest men I've ever met. These days, Dicky Barnett is Dr. Richard Barnett, PhD. There are many fabulous basketball Dicky Barnett moments. This one is mine:

Los Angeles: closing seconds of the game. Warriors up by two. Dicky with the ball, dribbles to mid-court, lets fly a jumper, and as the ball sails through the air, turns to Chick Hearn, the Lakers broadcaster at the announcer's table and says, "Baby we Ah in O-Va-Time." Swish.

I can't remember who won that game but we're talking about memories, such heroic moments make wins and losses, not only unimportant, but irrelevant.

I had considered naming this memoir *Overtime*. But it works better as a section title since as at my age and my medical condition, I am living in overtime.

Don't forget me. I'm living in overtime too, Melanie reminds me. I reassure The Fabled I won't forget

My Warriors' teammates Rick Barry, Fred Hetzel, and Jeff Mullins were in San Juan, along with Jim Barnett, not a teammate, but in retirement, the Warriors' splendid TV color commentator.

During those four days in San Juan, I forget how many photographs of grandchildren were passed around. Ours were, of course, the most beautiful and handsome and destined for greatness.

As much fun as the reunion with old comrades was, there were simply too many break-away meetings that were offered to improve our diminishing physical and cognitive abilities. It was a reminder I didn't really want. By that summer, my cancer was in remission, but it was always in the back of my mind. I was already wearing a hearing aid in my right ear and thinking I should buy one for the other ear. I wished to hear less about prosthetics and more tall tales about our heroic past accompanied by more pina coladas.

CHAPTER 46
EUROPE

Our first trip to Europe together was in the summer of 2012: a cruise through the Adriatic and Mediterranean sponsored by Saint Mary's College as part of the college's sesquicentennial celebration. Melanie provided a personal theme: the two of us would seek out every painting by Caravaggio to be seen in the cities we visited. We accomplished our goal, except for one painting in Naples. The Bank Intessa, where *The Martyrdom of Saint Ursula was* on display, was closed the day our cruise ship was docked there.

Melanie had become my personal art historian. She has very strong opinions about artists. Her favorite three painters of all time are DaVinci, Michelangelo, and Rembrandt. She calls them The Big Three. She told me that early in our relationship, and I'd replied I thought The Big Three were Magic, Bird, and Jordan. I remember Mel giving me an unmistakable pathetic-jock look.

We returned from our cruise and immediately began saving for our next trip. I was holding out hope that I could convince Melanie that it would be to West Africa. Here's what Melanie said to dash my hopes. I'm paraphrasing, "I'm too old to get Ebola." Mel is not a fearful person, but she does possess a healthy paranoia gene. I'll let the following poem I wrote about her explain her paranoia.

CASSANDRA

For Melanie

Sometimes, I feel as if I'm living in Troy, and Cassandra aka, girlfriend,
soon to be wife, is pronouncing certain doom throughout the house and
out into the neighborhood. And where am I?
I am somewhere within the walls of her fears: mutant germs
ready to spring from the clothes I wore to the hospital; the truck
turning on my right (her side) about to send us into oncoming traffic,
and the thieves and rapists who will strike the minute I forget
to lock our front door. You have been living in the country too long,
she says. Life in a city is not as safe as before. Life in not safe
in her kitchen either. Botulism resides in the refrigerator
or beneath the sink. She refuses to name whatever she believes
lurks in the pipes waiting to leap out onto her dishes.
She purifies them in water hot as lava. Wear rubber gloves, she says.
And outdoors, remember, the world is blooming with allergies.
Wear a mask; you will save yourself thousands in doctors' fees.
When I tell her she's being paranoid, she answers, did Priam listen?
Did Hector? Look what happened to the Trojan Women.
It is clear I cannot convince her, and never will. The omens
are too strong, and all around us, and far too many to ignore.
Remember The Wooden Horse, she says. And suddenly I understand
the extent of her love for me; that she could have left me outside
the gates of her city, but has risked her life to let me in.

Meschery, Tom. "Cassandra," *Some Men*, Black Rock Press, Rain
Shadow Edition, 2012. University of Nevada Press. University of
Nevada, Reno. Reno, NV

• • •

Since our 2012 cruise, Melanie and I have traveled to Europe three
more times, twice with an art group. The first trip left May 20, 2017 was
to Athens and the islands of Mykonos, Santorini and Folegandros. Travel
drawing was the focus of the trip. We were being taught Travel Drawing, a

method of recording travels by quick sketches, done mostly graphite or ink, but sometimes in colored pencil. Not an artist, I drew along with Melanie. I didn't do too badly and remembered that at one time in Elementary school my teachers thought I had artistic ability. Mostly I enjoyed the sights and food and wrote poems.

Our second trip was also an art tour to Italy's Cinque Terre, then to Florence and Rome. The instruction on this trip was about watercolor. On this trip I devoted most of my time instead of painting which I was not good at, to writing poems. The poems are, I believe, worthy. Someday, I might try to put a collection of poems together about our European trips.

FLAWED BEAUTY

"I love imperfections."
Lady Gaga

Before you're tempted to draw in pencil,
think first of your family, of their slight
imperfections: your uncle's wandering eye,
the gap between your daughter's front teeth,
the ears of your cousin that look like sails,
your brother's nose too large for his face.

Would you love them any other way?
Would you, if you'd had an eraser
at birth, altered the mistakes, the ones
you think of now as endearing?

The way you're tempted today to do,
looking at the face in front of you,
at the spot where your pencil shook
because the night before you drank
too much red wine. Your desire to draw
his lips full and sort of pouting, slips,
from its intention, and becomes, what?
An abstraction in need of repair.

This is the reason beginners should never
begin drawing in pencil. The temptation
to use the eraser is too great. Begin in ink,
a medium that's unforgiving but instructive.
  Whatever the pen gives you, you cannot
take back: a crooked line below the eye,
an earlobe bent at an odd angle.
What is it listening to, the ocean,
Chopin's adagio for strings?
Think of such flaws as birth.
Move on to the next line.
Try not to lift your pen.
Think only of beauty.

Meschery, Tom. "Flawed Beauty," *Art Lessons*. From a manuscript
in progress.

Our second art trip ended in Rome. The rest of the art group flew
home, but Melanie and I stayed behind in Rome to visit more museums
and churches. From Rome we flew to Barcelona.

• • •

I am not a religious man, but I do believe in the importance of a
spiritual life. Back in my days in college I'd sat quietly meditating before
basketball games in our chapel dedicated to the Virgin Mary. And once in
West Africa in the Republic of the Congo, walking by an empty field, I came
across an outdoor shrine to that same virgin and stood among the trees
shading the shrine. I felt she was there to remind me of the importance of
the spirit. Both of those times could not compare to the intense feeling of
spirituality I experienced in Barcelona sitting in the architectural wonder
of Antoni Gaudi's Basilica, *La Sagrada Familia*. It is a structure of both
natural landscape and technological engineering. The interior is all color,
light and shadow. We sat in our pew, and I felt I was not my body. That
is different from saying I was not inside my body, or that I was outside,
viewing myself as some people describe near death experiences. My body
was simply not there. Since I have never felt that way before or after. It may
remain my one and only true spiritual moment.

When we left the Basilica, I pointed to an apartment building across the street from the basilica. I told Melanie we should move here, rent one of the apartments. We could visit *La Sagrada Familia* every day. Had we both been unwilling to leave our children and grandchildren behind, we might have become expats.

The following day, we flew to Paris where my granddaughter, Grace, my daughter Megan's oldest, was planning to meet us. She was in Normandy on a Rotary Exchange and would take the train up. After her first day of visiting, she asked if we minded if her Brazilian friend joined us. He was visiting friends in Paris, she explained. He was teaching her Portuguese. He could stay with her. Was there something a grandfather should know, I remember asking. She had assured me it was "nothing like that." They were only friends.

Your children grow up. Then your grandchildren grow up. At some point in life it might be time to think more of the spirit.

My favorite photographs of the trip are of Grace and Melanie in the Tuileries Garden sitting on a bench with their watercolors painting, my wife the accomplished professional artist and Grace on her way to the same artistic heights.

Grace spoke fluent French. When we were having lunch, a waitress told her she could not tell her French pronunciation from that of a Parisian, a high compliment from any Parisian. They can be pretty smug about their language. Grace's presence brought our second trip to Europe to a fitting and satisfying conclusion.

Sitting together, admiring family photographs, such a simple act. but in a county these days so full of chaos and political strife, so peaceful. Our minds register our children and grandchildren, our family trips to the Grand Canyon or down the Mississippi River, or to see the Redwood forest - those memoires are universal. *Look there's Johnny at 12 driving the tractor; Margarita at her Quinceanera, Steph Curry's first ever jump-shot.* In albums or these days stored in cell phones. Such memories bond us.

CHAPTER 47
DEAR MR. MESCHERY

It wasn't long after I met with Rick Welts and began my renewed relationship with the Golden State Warriors that I received an envelope with my Warrior rookie trading card enclosed along with a letter requesting I autograph the card. This may not seem noteworthy as I am a retired NBA player, but I was in my seventies at the time and had not received a request for an autograph in decades. After I retired from the NBA as a player and coach in 1976, I continued to receive requests from autograph-seekers, but within a few years all requests for my autograph ceased. This signature request came as a surprise. Like the detectives in mystery novels, I enjoy reading, I'm suspicious of coincidences. I reasoned that this new request had to do with a recent local newspaper article about my life in retirement. However, the envelope was addressed out of state, so that wasn't likely. I signed it and mailed it off. A month later, another autograph request arrived in the mail. And after that several more. Suddenly, I began receiving one or two every other week. All the years that I'd been teaching high school, I had been so far removed from the NBA that the thought that my card was desirable to a collector puzzled me. For a man my age I had to admit it was a bit of an ego boost. When Melanie and I moved back to Sacramento from Alameda, I figured our address change would put an end to this phenomenon. It did not, a mystery that I attributed to networking between trading card collectors: *This dude signs cards, this dude doesn't, don't waste a stamp.*

Most autograph collectors send a short complimentary note along with either my Warrior rookie card or my Sonics card or both to be signed. They include a return self stamped envelope. If there is no envelope, the request is not filled. At which point I begin to separate the collector from the trader. I am suspicious of those requests that state the petitioners were fans from my playing days. Most fans from my days are getting pretty long in the tooth for collecting autographs of childhood favorite athletes. Such petitioners, I assume, are in the business of collecting and selling trading cards. A trader can make a nice return on investment, and sometimes, if he or she is lucky, a significant profit, even trading cards of lesser-known athletes, such as myself. I discovered that a 1961 Fleer Philadelphia Warriors rookie card unsigned is worth approximately $21. 60. Signed, the same card in mint condition is selling for $199.99 on eBay. Some traders disguise themselves, writing requests supposedly by a boy or girl, or by a father wishing to start his son on the collectors' path *that gave him such pleasure when he was a boy, etc, etc.* I've become pretty good as Mark Twain once said, about ferreting out fakers.

Some requests are just plain weird or unusual. One I received recently was from a retired high school teacher. He wanted the signed card for his son as a surprise. He explained at length, and I mean all the way to the bottom of the page, detail after detail about his son getting into a terrible automobile accident and almost losing the use of his legs, and how his son, of whom he was exceedingly proud, had recovered beating the odds that were stacked against him. I was reasonably certain this was not a professional trader but a proud dad. I autographed the Sonics trading card and added an autographed rookie card. There are some requests for autographs that touch an emotional nerve.

From another teacher, I received this request:

Dear Mr. Meschery,
My name is Ebbie Shores and I teach 3rd grade reading at Wattsburg Elementary Center in Erie, PA. My students are learning how to write friendly letters. Their assignment is to write a letter to someone famous and ask for their autograph. I complete the assignment with them every year. I chose to write to you because I admire you for playing professional basketball. When I was young, I dreamed of playing in the NBA, but it was not meant to be. Only the most talented athletes go on to play professionally. You got to the NBA by combining your talent with hard work. I bet it is an incredible feeling to run out onto the court for the first time in the NBA. . .

How did I feel? The memory of my rookie year in Philadelphia is not entirely clear. I don't recall even if that first game was in Philly or on the road. I do, however, vividly remember how I felt a year later running out onto the court for my first game as a San Francisco Warrior. It was my homecoming. I would be the first homegrown professional basketball player on the first San Francisco NBA team. Prior to the game in the locker room, I thought briefly of how *first* had meant so much to me growing up, being *first*, being chosen *first*. I'm certain that this obsession I had to be first had a lot to do at the time with being an immigrant kid trying to be an American. At that homecoming game that was played at the Civic Center in front of a sparse crowd, I saw myself running out on the court as the *First Warrior*. I had butterflies, of course. I always did. For the rest of my career, I felt those fluttering wings in my stomach. But for this game it was butterflies and barn swallows and red-tail hawks. I'd already vomited, something I also did throughout my career before games. Describing it today, I would say I felt as if I was a character in a movie running toward a destination that because of the camera lens continued to be out of reach no matter how hard I ran. When I described this to my wife, she replied, "Like the scene in *The Graduate* when Dustin Hoffman is running to get to the **church**." Exactly, and like him, suddenly there I was on the court, and I heard people from the stands calling my name. On my first layup, I tried to dunk, and blew it, the ball rattling off the rim. How did I feel? My God, I was both shaken and elated. The next layup, I *did* dunk. It was not a dunk worthy of today's high-flying dunkers, but I saw a few of my Lowell High School teammates, members of my tribe, standing on the sidelines cheering my very ordinary effort.

Dear Ebbie Shores,
That's how I felt...

• • •

The most surprising letter I've receivedcame from Chris in Arkansas. After I read it, I remember saying aloud: *you gotta be kidding.* I inspected the card. It was tattered at the corners and stained:

Dear Mr. Meschery,

In Vietnam, I carried your sports card with me for what I hoped would be luck. I was wounded Christmas Eve, 1968 and again New Year's Eve. Most of my cards made it home in better shape than me. We found sports cards in the rubble of bombed-out villages during our ground sweeps and, to our amazement, we often found cards on the bodies of dead VC... most surprising and very eerie.

Sincerely,

Chris _____

In 1968 when Chris was in Vietnam, I was halfway through my seventh season in the NBA and my first season with the expansion team, the Seattle Sonics. American soldiers were shooting Viet Cong, and I was shooting hoops. As I looked at this card five decades later, I was reminded of Tim O'Brian's gripping tale of the Vietnam War, *The Things They Carried*. The collection of linked short stories was a Pulitzer Prize finalist and National Book Critics Circle Award finalist. The American soldiers in the story carried all manner of talisman: comic books, a lucky pebble, a Viet Cong thumb, a hunting hatchet. I remember imagining my card kept in Chris' breast pocket was just enough to deflect the killer bullet like Wonder Woman's bracelets. I thanked Chris for his service to our country. I signed the card. I looked through my container of memorabilia and found one of my pristine rookie cards.

• • •

Melanie and I are in our office. I have just finished signing two of my Warriors rookie cards and one of my Sonic cards and placing them in their return envelopes. Melanie has a theory about my being discovered by trading card collectors. She says it has to do with art. She reminds me that dead artists are worth more than the living variety. At my age, I get her point, but I'm not amused.

CHAPTER 48
POETRY

I wrote my first poems in 1964. Sandy Padwe, a sports reporter for the *Philadelphia Inquirer*, and later a feature writer with *Sports Illustrated*, and professor at Columbia University, published a couple in the sports page. If my teammates thought it odd that I wrote poems, they never mentioned it. I suspect the incongruity of my writing verse and my on-court "Mad Manchurian" personality was not lost on them. They were aware of my temper so, apart from a few jokes, they kept quiet.

By the time I had finished my MFA at the University of Iowa in 1974 and was writing poems consistently, I could tell the difference between average poetry and inspired poetry. Later, as a literature teacher, I often wondered if "minor" poets understood that their poetry did not stretch the imagination or did not leave readers with a deeper understanding of the world around them. Did these poets consider themselves *Understudies to the Stars*? Were they satisfied riding the poetry bench? I thought of Charles Lamb, who was no slouch as a poet, but was not in the same league as his contemporaries: Wordsworth and Coleridge.

Until I was well into my graduate studies in poetry, I hadn't known, nor had I really cared, how many Americans were writing poetry. After I began subscribing to poetry magazines, I realized how many people were writing verse. The poets with real talent stood out. In this way, they were not dissimilar to the best basketball players in the NBA. I decided I would not mind playing in poetry's D League. I have not changed my mind, even though I believe that over the years I've become a better poet and at some point, could find a place at the end of the bench in the poetry big leagues.

It is noteworthy, although not surprising, to mention that there is a great deal of difference between what a superstar poet is paid compared to superstar professional athletes, and it is ridiculous to hope that at some point in the future this disparity will shrink.

If it is odd that I compare poets to basketball players, it shouldn't be. It has always been easier for me to see the world through the lens of sports, and particularly of basketball. The basketball players I love to watch most are full of surprises. The same is true for the poets I enjoy reading the most. Another way to describe it is that there is a kind of misdirection, not unlike the moves some athletes make that seem to have little chance of success but in fact succeed. *How the hell did he do it, you ask yourself, as the shot drops and the crowd rises to its feet and roars its approval.* I have read poems that do exactly the same thing. Halfway through the poem, I ask myself what the hell is going on here, but later it happens: by God, it was a fake right, run left, and I finish the poem and find myself roaring with the same kind of joy that often accompanies a magnificent basketball move. Whenever that happens, it occurs to me that I'm a better fan of poetry than I am a poet. And just so I stay true to the sports theme, I'd buy season tickets to any of Robert Hass' poetry readings, front row courtside no matter the price of admission.

• • •

Melanie reminds me I need to write about the time at a Warriors promotional function when a fan continued to question me about writing poetry, "Why?" as if it was not something he associated with his idea of athletes or manliness. She thought he was expressing concerns about my sexual orientation. I tried to be polite. He continued to badger me, and I felt myself getting increasingly angry. I can't remember how it ended it. I might have just walked away.

I'm always on the look-out for good poems. Friends send me poems. One of my best sources for poems is Ron Adams, the assistant coach of the Golden State Warriors. Before the NBA, Ron coached at Fresno State University where Philip Levine taught poetry. They knew each other. I'm enormously jealous because I'm a huge Levine fan. Levine is a starter on my Poetry All Star Team. Probably a two-way guard – Levine can play both ends of the court.

I search the internet for poems. I browse in bookstores. The doctor's or dentist's office are always good for two poems in the *New Yorker*. I open the magazine wondering what I'm going to find. I'm like a birdwatcher anticipating the sighting of an Ivory Billed Woodpecker or the San Clemente Loggerhead Shrike. More likely I find the more common Barn Swallow or Steller's Jay. That's not necessarily disappointing. I usually find something in the poems to like, even if it's only one line. When I find such a line, I'm in the habit of writing it down and taking it home with me. It's like finding a penny on the street, a sign of good luck. I store my discoveries in a folder. Sometimes such *found* lines lead me in the direction of a poem of my own.

There are mornings when I wake up with the beginning of a poem in my head and rush, sleepily, to my desk to write the lines down, certain that in the morning the start of an amazing poem will be waiting for me. Nine out of 10 times it turns out to be a let-down. I had a similar experience playing basketball. The Warriors played a Sunday afternoon game in Baltimore against the Bullets. It was the fifth game following four successive games on the road. I was exhausted. For the first time in my career I took three bennies (uppers) before the game. Back in the day as they say, bennies or greenies were always available. That afternoon I played, collecting massive rebounds and scoring double-digit points - or so I thought. After the game I looked at the stat sheet ready to be impressed with the results of my heroic effort. Instead, on the stat line next to my name I saw two rebounds and four points. And I'd fouled out. I didn't recall fouling out. This would have made a shitty poem. I'm not equating poetry to uppers. *Well, maybe. Let me think about it.*

There is a case to be made for an amazing experience in poetry. In sports, it's called the zone; in poetry it's called inspiration, a state both poets and athletes find themselves in, in which success flows without thinking. Naomi Shihab Nye wrote a poem that speaks about turning oneself over to that moment. She explained to a group of students that you begin by believing your poem will end in a Buddhist temple in twilight, but the poem ends up taking you to the dog races. According to her, that was where the poem intended to go in the first place. I met Naomi in Santa Cruz when she came to read at the annual memorial poetry reading for my friend and mentor, Morton Marcus. She, too, is a basketball enthusiast so we discussed the strange mental state in which basketball players and poets often find themselves. I wrote the following poem for Naomi.

THE ZONE

For Naomi Shihab Nye

I know it's a stretch, but for me,
writing a good poem is like being "in the zone."
Words appear: the sky turns aquamarine
whether you want it to or not, clouds,
darkening at the edge of the line, may
or may not grow into a storm or a half rhyme,
or into a jump shot from the top of the key,
or into just the right metaphor or perfect form.
It is what you expect your body to do is learn
on the court. It is an act of acceptance
that governs the flight of the ball
into the net and the words as they drop
like rain into the line. You give yourself up
to the zone. You give yourself over
to the muse. Surely, you can't make
every shot, surely one couplet will not scan.
Even so, the poem will end where it must:
riding your motorcycle along the coast,
waiting for a gondola in Venice,
or taking the winning shot that seemed
impossible with one tick left on the clock.

Meschery, Tom. "The Zone," *Clear Path*, Random Lane Press, 2022.
Sacramento, CA

• • •

The Zone is in my recent chapbook *Time Out*. All the poems in it have
to do with basketball.
I wouldn't mind being the Poet Laureate of sports poems.
Counting only those poems that have been published, I have written
237 poems about sports. Is this a record for poetry written on a single
concrete subject like motorcycles or wind chimes? I'm thinking of
the Guinness *Book of World Records*. I see myself in an office in the

Smithsonian, down the hall from the Poet Laureate of the United States. *I walk to his or her office. I say, "Hey check out this sestina I wrote about the curve ball."*

Where I see myself in reality is in our office most mornings writing, Melanie sitting at her desk ready to be editor or critic. It means we're here. We're together. There is no need to say anything about our age. Together is enough until one of us, probably me, does the do-us-apart-thing. In which case, I tell Melanie I'll wait until she catches up.

Outside the window, over the rooftops, the tall redwoods and my favorite crows, two Armageddons, assaulting the sparrows. Crossing our parking area, a flock of wild turkeys. The strutting males, their tail feathers up like fans, look like Kabuki dancers. It is a view I can almost count on every morning. Where Melanie and I live, Campus Commons, close to Sacramento State University and the American River, there are walking paths cutting through green space and two small man made lakes. Here are ducks and Mary Oliver's *Wild Geese*. Depending on the time of day, Mel is painting. I'm writing. We are answering Mary Oliver's question about what we are doing with our "wild and precious lives."

• • •

Melanie says, poetry strikes her differently depending on how hungry she is or whether she has to use the bathroom. My wife has a droll sense of humor. Recently I finished a poem that I'd been struggling with for weeks. Mel had read the earlier versions with little enthusiasm. This time I asked her what she thought. Her response: "You pulled that out of the trash can, and I didn't even have to throw myself in front of it." There are times Melanie says stuff that requires some thinking. I finally decided it was a compliment. But I reserve the right to reassess.

A lot of professional athletes have excelled in their sport as well as their art. I remember going to see the paintings of Bernie Casey, the 49er's wide receiver, at an exhibition in Los Angeles with my teammate Nate Thurmond, who'd graduated from Bowling Green University with Bernie. I was blown away by Casey's abstracts. Mike Reed of The Cincinnati Bengals played the piano with the Cincinnati Symphony and wrote an opera about football. Tom Heinsohn of the Celtics, with whom I battled for many NBA years, is a fine landscape artist in the style of Andrew Wyeth. Waymon Tisdale, before writing and recording 8 jazz albums, had a 12-year NBA career. I recently saw a marvelous abstract painted by Serena Williams. Two pro boxers of international reputations, Manny Pacquiao and Oscar de la Hoya are singers and have albums. De La Hoya was nominated for a Grammy.

Just as there are gym rats in basketball, there must be the equivalent rodents in the halls of poetry. You can count on every city big and small, suburbs and small towns having them. They are called poetry societies or writing groups. Sacramento has one called The Sacramento Poetry Center, SPC. Every Monday night at 7 PM, the Center offers readings by featured poets followed by an open mic that allows anyone in the audience signed up to read one of his or her poems. The open mic can sometimes be difficult to listen to as some of the poems are not very good. But open mic is intended to encourage poetry. Poetry needs a fan club. The more poets and people who enjoy poetry the better. When I was teaching high school, I once suggested to my high school principal that I wanted the school's cheerleaders to come into my creative writing class when my students were reading their poems, and lead cheers before and after each reading. I'm sure he didn't take me seriously, but I was dead serious.

When I lived in Truckee, a bunch of us local poets came together once a month as the Jibboom Street Writers. We met in my house and brought potluck. There was my son-in-law, Brendan and his fellow carpenter, Jim Beggs, who on various nights brought me to tears with their verse. And Russell Mann, a nurse and ex Green Beret who wrote of stealth in Guatemala's jungles, and Cathee St. Clair, a painter of miniatures and painter of poetry, and other locals, each one of us representing the active world that exists all across the country. We printed our own anthology. It sold well in our town's bookstore. The profits covered the printing costs. Publication signals success in the world of poetry. We received no prizes except for the praise of our mountain neighbors. That was enough.

A couple of years ago, I told my friend Dell that I'd give up writing poetry entirely if only I could write one transcendent poem. I had in mind *Animals in Winter* by John Dennison, a man who never wrote another poem in his life. It is a poem about children living alone without parents and the animals who care for them. Dennison was a social worker at an orphanage. It is a poem of exquisite compassion. Who knows if I would have followed through on my promise?

So far, my poetry has not reached transcendent levels. But neither had my basketball as a pro. I was good, considered solid, a hard worker. I made the NBA All-Star Team in 1963, then for the rest of my career joined the ranks of Understudies to the Stars. That's not so bad. There were times in my 10-year career when the stars didn't show up, and I had to take over shining brightly. I've had plenty of 20-point games under my belt. I don't think I have the equivalent 20-point-poems under my belt. But I'm not finished writing yet.

• • •

It is the evening of Saturday, September 15th, c. 2016, The Creative Writing Program of Saint Mary's College is sponsoring a poetry reading with Tom Meschery and Robert Hass, Poet Laureate of the United States and my Gael classmate. The reading hall seats are filled, standing room only. As protocol demands, I read first, three poems, one of which is based on a quote from one of Hass' poems called Dragonflies Mating: . . .and I'd bounce/the ball two or three times,/study the orange rim as if it were/which it was, the true level of the world/the one sure thing. Then it's Bob's turn. He startles me by recounting the college "soiree" where I was seen hanging out of an upper-floor window in Dante Hall.

I remember the poem but not the incident. Maybe that's the whole point of drunkenness.

Following this expose, Bob reads from three new poems-in-progress. There are few poets in the world who can take incredibly complex philosophy and turn them into poems of sensual clarity. When you read a Hass poem, you find yourself going back to it over and over, finding new pleasures each time.

I must admit, being in Bob's company, I feel like a star. I never felt like that in Wilt's company. Or in the company of Rick Barry, a star of a slightly lesser magnitude. At the end of the reading, there is a Q & A session. The moderator joins Bob and me on stage. The moderator asks us questions and takes questions from the audience. At the completion of the Q & A, Bob and I are asked a final question. "As poets working so closely with words as you do, I wonder if you would tell us your favorite word." The moderator turns to me, "You may start first, Tom."

I am terror stricken. My one word compared to Bob's one word. I'm thinking this is like going one-on-one against Michael Jordan. I won't have a chance. But I can't humiliate myself. I think through a list of wonderful words, none of which seem to be remarkable compared to the single word Bob will surely select, that perfect, glorious word, which upon utterance would blow my paltry effort off the face of the planet. Then I remember Mark Strand, my early mentor and teacher, going on and on in a class about how much he loved the word crystal, how it appealed to so many of the senses. Strand too had been a Poet Laureate. Aha, I think. I turn to the moderator and say, "Well, there are many words I can choose, but I like the word Crystal." The audience claps politely. The moderator turns to Bob. Bob looks at me for a moment sorrowfully, then looks out into the audience where his wife Brenda is sitting. "My favorite word," he says, pausing for dramatic effect, "is Brenda." The audience, mostly women, who know Brenda as Bob's wife and professor at Saint Mary's College, sigh audibly followed by resounding applause. As the applause lessens, I turn to my wife in the audience and say, "I'm sorry, Melanie."

Bob laughs, along with the audience. Together we walk down from the stage and are joined by our wives. Brenda approaches me and says, "Okay, Tom, who is this Crystal, anyway?"

"Yeah," The Fabled says. "Who is this floozy?"

On the ride home, Melanie asks "You didn't really hang out the window?"

"It was Rimbaud," I say. "What else could I do?"

CHAPTER 49
ONCOLOGY

Although I taught Shakespeare's *Seven Ages of Man* to my high school seniors, I have never committed wholeheartedly to the Seventh Age. However, since I began writing my memoir, the thought crossed my mind that there was some truth to his circular idea about life. For Tom Meschery, part of it was about health. I began my life as a toddler in Harbin, Manchuria infected by one dreadful disease after another, followed by a lifetime of strength and health, while in old age once again falling prey to numerous types of diseases, cancer being the most dramatic. First, it was a liposarcoma in my right calf about the size of a nerf football that had beendetected while I was teaching high school. Fortunately, it did not metastasize. The tumor was removed, and I underwent radiation, which left nerve damage in my foot. No more dunking the basketball. *Hell, I never had that much hops anyway.* I was in my fifties, not exactly Shakespeare's second childhood yet, but closing in.

Then in 2006 came the Myeloma and a year of drug therapy and a white blood cell transplantation.

By 2017, my remission from Multiple Myeloma had lasted longer than doctors were willing to predict. Ten years at that point. Medical science notwithstanding, I attribute my longevity to marrying Melanie Marchant. Although less than logical, I believed then and I still do, that there is one remedy for physical and mental illnesses that works across the spectrum of scientific medical treatments, and that's love.

According to my sister, however, it may have been love, but she was of the belief that it was Our Lady of Iversk, our family icon, that was the deciding factor. I prayed for you; she told me. My sister is a strong believer in our Orthodox faith. She believes our family icon can produce miracles. Her belief dates to 1812 and the following family legend. Nikolai Krotokov, my ancestor on my mother's male side, an officer in the Tsar's army, was being sent with his unit on a military assignment. His mother blessed him with our family icon and gave it to him to take. In those days there were no trains in the region of Samara and people traveled in carriages or on horseback. It was early spring, but the rivers were still frozen. When the travelers were in the middle of the river, all of a sudden, the river ice began breaking up. Horses and carriages went down under the ice. Clutching the family icon, Nikolai started to jump from icefloe to icefloe until he reached shore. When he returned home, he had diamonds placed around the frame of the icon and on the halos of the Virgin and Child. Over a hundred years later, those diamonds saved his descendants from starvation when during the revolution and subsequent refugee years, our grandmother exchanged diamonds for food and clothing.

> My father said our icons were like family.
> Still, we couldn't save them all, only the smallest
> sewn into the linings of our clothes:
> The Lady of Iversk I hid in my brassiere,
> the boy Saints Svetapolk and Svetislav
> sewn in the hem of my skirt. Each time
> I walked I was a moving church.
>
> In Harbin, safe at last, we made our homes or tried.
> There was no work. To live we pried the diamonds,
> one by one from the halos of our Saints
> for rent, warm coats, shoes that never seemed
> to keep the northern Chinese winter out.
> Next, we sold the Saints themselves,
> like slaves. Their gold brought just enough
> to see us through one year.

Meschery, Tom. From the poem, "Small Embrace," *Nothing We Lose Can Be Replaced,* Black Rock Press, Rain Shadow Edition, 1999, University of Nevada, Reno. Reno, NV

• • •

On a spring morning in 2019 Melanie and I drive to my oncologist to hear the results of my six-month blood test. We sit in his office waiting for him to arrive with the results. I remember Melanie touching my shoulder. The gesture comforts me. I need comforting because these six-month visits to the doctor always remind me of how I originally reacted after I was first diagnosed, like watching a rerun of a scene in a movie in which the protagonist suffers a horrible death. I have always been good at playing the stoic, so I'm sure Mel has never guessed the extent of my anxiety. Will this revelation make Mel more solicitous of me? I doubt it. The Fabled does not do drama.

Fifteen minutes pass by before Doctor Laptalo arrives. We go through pleasantries, after which he turns on his computer and peruses my results. As usual, Doctor Laptalo's face reveals nothing. A few minutes pass. Finally, he leans back in his chair and explains to us that my recent blood test has detected the M protein. My stomach clenches into a fist. I feel Melanie looking at me. I keep my eyes on Doctor Laptalo. After another perusal of his screen, he assures me that the indicator was barely noticeable, a mere .006 on my oncological Richter scale. Relief? Not exactly. The knot in my stomach is still there but has loosened some. I ask what the significance of this numerical presence means, steeling myself to hear the worst. It's part of my personality that I've always wanted to hear the worst first - about anything: You've been traded to the Lakers. I hate the Lakers. Thank God I never was.

Doctor Laptalo points to his computer screen. The significance at this point, he explains, is minimal, other than to reduce the time between blood tests from six months to three months. He assures me, I shouldn't be alarmed. In his words, the cancer appears to be growing at a very slow pace. "More like the tortoise, than the hare," he says.

As a retired English literature teacher, I appreciate the analogy. As an athlete, however, I would never want to be labeled slow. But a slow-growing cancer? It gives me great pleasure to imagine my cancer as a fat, clumsy and uncoordinated turtle waddling to the finish line 15 years from now. That would take me to the age of 93 and, as my wife's distant Native American relatives would say, a good day to die.

After scheduling my next appointment, we returned to our car and headed for home. I found myself gripping the steering wheel too tightly.

I try to relax. I remembered saying to Melanie who'd been silent since we left the doctor's office.

"Should I tell my children about this spike?"

"Yes," Melanie said "When there is a spike. This is not a spike; it's .006. You're going to live."

My wife looks at life clearly, while the world through my eyes has always been a little lopsided, as if one leg of my thinking is shorter than the other.

The NBA provides five minutes for an overtime period. The universe, I decided, would measure out how many years I had left. The day we were married, I promised Melanie that I would live ten more years. The day we drove home, I promised Melanie that I would live another ten. Being optimistic is the only way to live with cancer.

"You'd better, Mel said, "or I'll kill you."

CHAPTER 50
SAFEWAY

Melanie hates to shop for groceries. This is beyond my comprehension. For an immigrant such as myself, who remembers what hunger felt like as a child, pushing a cart down the aisles filled with an abundance and variety of foodstuffs is culinary Nirvana. How can Mel claim to be poor dirt farmer's grandchild from Oklahoma and not want to visit the greengrocer, the deli counter, the butcher, the bakery – ah the aroma of freshly baked bagels.

I am also the principal cook in our home. For me, cooking is a form of meditation. I rarely use a recipe, although I love perusing cookbooks. I cook the way I played basketball, instinctively. I do not bake. When pies or muffins are required, Mel bakes.. Baking requires paying attention to measurements, a fourth of this, one eighth of that. Too many fractions for me. I equate my cooking to playing hoops and Mel's baking to being a coach. I have no doubt that's why I was a horrible coach, my disdain for mathematics, which goes back to my third-grade teacher.

We are members of our Sacramento Food Co-op, but our closest market is Safeway. It's where I most often shop. It must have been in 2009 in the first year of our marriage on my shopping trips to Safeway that I met Jesus and Paul, after which shopping for groceries at Safeway meant more than shopping for groceries.

Jesus and Paul are not the Messiah and the Christian Saint. They are aficionados of bounce, devotees of swish, prognosticators of athletic outcomes, and NBA true believers. If that is not enough, they are our local Safeway cashiers who somehow found out that I'd played for the Warriors. Over the years we have developed a relationship and grocery shopping turns into discussions about hoops.

Paul checks my groceries and gripes about his favorite NBA team, the Portland Trail Blazers. He has been on this same rant about salaries and players since I started shopping at the store. The enormous NBA salaries irritate Paul the way I assume the wealth of Russian nobility irritated Lenin.

I have lived through numerous NBA seasons with Paul lamenting the fate of his Blazers. He is like the town crier of Pompeii pronouncing doom about the coaches and players. He would shake a roll of paper towels at me as if it were my fault. I have maintained a receptive and kindly face. I take fans seriously. They may have no idea about how professional basketball works from coaching decisions, trades, draft choices, and ownership financial considerations, but their continued patronage at the ticket box and in front of the television has something to do with my retirement benefits.

The Trailblazers made the playoffs in 2018, and gave Paul finally something to cheer about, but not for long as his team was defeated in the first round. Paul was no longer working at Safeway at the start of 2019, which was a shame because his beloved Trailblazers made it all the way to the Western Conference Finals versus the Golden State Warriors. The Dubs swept the series, which might have been too much for Paul to bear.

My favorite cashier is Jesus. a supernova Warriors fan, and a law enforcement student at City College who I discovered to my astonishment was able to recite the first 50 lines of Chaucer's *Canterbury Tales* - in the Middle English, a difficult task that I required of my AP seniors.

How my students hated it, and later loved it when they would return years after graduation and show off, proudly declaiming the lines in front of my desk. Over the years I taught, did my students believe me when I stated that memorizing The Prologue would get them dates in college? Did they believe me when I told them about one of my female students who wrote to me after graduation from junior year at the University of the Pacific to tell me, "It worked." She was engaged to this "dreamy guy." Some of them did believe. Teenagers are easily persuaded of just about anything when it involves romance.

So, I'm always tickled whenever I arrive at Jesus' counter to hear: *Whan in Aprille with its shores soote, the drought of Marche is perced to the roote,* followed by his giant smile, followed by, "How about them Dubs?" Jesus never misses the opportunity to point out Warrior success to Paul. I feel sorry for Paul having to suffer the slings and arrows of Jesus's basketball comments.

Often Jesus hail's me from the "15 and under" items counter. "Tonight," he yells. "We kick Lakers' butt." Or the Rocket's butt. Or Clippers'. I respond with the victory sign. In turn, Jesus sends the V for victory sign in Paul's direction, and Paul raises his middle finger at Jesus. I'm reminded of two ships at sea signaling each other.

On game days, I'd leave Safeway with a full bag of groceries, thinking, yeah, baby, it's *Guacamole and chips. And, perhaps, a cold cerveza.*

And another Dubs victory.

As of last year, Paul is no longer working at our Safeway. I miss our back and forth. I hope in these troubled economic times, he has a job. Jesus remains at the checkout counter, ready with his take on the Warriors and always ready to recite Chaucer. It is the 2019/20 season, and the Warriors are playing poorly. But we both remain optimistic about the future.

Jesus and Paul are moved to other stores or other jobs. My Safeway basketball buddy is Antwan, one of the baggers, a special needs young man who is a huge Warrior fan. He spots me coming into his line and waves. I say those Warriors screwed up last night, and he'll repeat what I said and smile. He's as good a worker as the store has. He also likes the local NBA team the Kings. "The Kings looking good," he says. I repeat, looking good, Antwan.

CHAPTER 51
CAL GUYS

In 2012 when we were living in Alameda, my friend and one time University of California Bears' foe, Bill McClintok invited me to be his guest at The Cal-Guys Luncheon. He explained that ex-players from that 1968 NCAA Basketball Championship team and other Cal athlete-alums gathered at the Alamo Country Club, east of Oakland, had lunch and updated each other about their lives. The luncheon was held every three months on the third Thursdays of the month. The California Bears was the same team that had kept my Saint Mary's Gaels from playing in the 1958 NCAA Final Four, which should have been a good reason for me to stay away. I agreed because Bill was a good guy, and he promised to buy me beers.

My first lunch was fun. Since then, I have become a regular and long-time foe have turned into friends. Not long after that first lunch I attended; the group opened the lunch to other jocks from colleges in California. We were mainly athletes from the fifties and sixties, all were local Bay Area sports legends: Ken Flowers, Bernie Simpson, Mike Farmer, John Burton whose basketball legend was enhanced by the eight years he was a congressman in the House of Representatives. I could name many others, the way I could name important points of interest on a map of my life. We swapped stories of our past, some slightly exaggerated. We figured out what was wrong with the new generation of athletes. We talked about our grandchildren. Each guy was allowed three minutes by rule to speak. Our de facto leader was Ned Averbuck, a guard on the championship team, who is part Mexican and Jewish and a liberal of the Socialist variety, which made for great fun and occasionally a little tension because most of the guys were conservative. It made sense that talk of politics was not allowed.

Until 2016, I wouldn't have thought this would be a problem, but since a few of my fellow jocks might have voted for Trump, a political discussion might have become heated, and in my case, given how I felt about Trump, might have turned into a Mad Manchurian moment.

• • •

Occasionally a 40-year-old slipped through the cracks and joined us for lunch. And more recently a grown grandchild showed up to make us feel truly ancient.

We commiserated with each other that our bodies were breaking down, and we were all suffering degrees of pain, which, when remarked upon, sounded like bragging. Or, as one of the guys pointed out, like a competition. *Bound to compete; we're athletes, aren't we?* I had to do some thinking about that. Were more points awarded for the greater the affliction?

A few of the Cal Guys had serious heart conditions. Some that included me were battling cancer. Dementia was not a popular topic. Some guys had graduated from the Fourth Quarter of Life and joined me in Overtime.

Any old athlete with a pulse, Melanie remarks.

• • •

It cannot be a coincidence that at the same time in 2012 I was being brought back into the bosom of my Warrior family that I was also reconnecting with a brotherhood of college and high school teammates and adversaries. I have tried never to miss the Cal Guys Lunches. I had to admit to something that I never would have when I was in my fifties, a time when I saw myself exclusively as a teacher and writer, that I enjoyed being around basketball players and athletes of my generation. I felt comfortable around them. George Selleck, star guard for Stanford, began attending. Don Bowden, the first American to run a sub 4-minute mile, was a regular. *What stories!* Maybe it was the stories that kept me going to the Cal Guys lunches. History, someone once told me, is best understood anecdotally. I told McClintock once that being with the guys was like comfort food. Bill's response, "meatloaf."

• • •

One of the more fascinating guys who attended the luncheons was Joe Kapp. Joe played on the Cal basketball team, but he was better known as the quarterback who took Cal to the Rose Bowl and went on to a stellar pro career in the NFL and CFL. The only time I played hoops against Joe was in summer league games, and I recall receiving a couple of crushing elbows from him. I can't swear to it, but I'm pretty sure Joe smiled after he hit me. Joe was a combination of loveable joker and dangerous hit man. When I first attended Cal Guys, it was impossible not to realize that Joe's thinking and comments were all over the place. He was like a boat without a rudder. At the last meeting he attended, Joe grabbed me by the shoulders, wrapped his arms around me and drew me in close, then whispered the word, *soul*, into my ear. I had no idea what he meant, but later I believed I did and wrote this poem:

SOUL

For Joe Kapp

Yesterday, among men of my generation of athletes, gray haired, aging and aged, Joe Kapp, wild man, Mexican/Indian, famous for his exploits on the football field, still wild, there like the rest of us to honor a great dead coach, embraced me. And I embraced back, hearing him whisper in my ear the word, *Soul* as if he was imparting to me a special secret he'd discovered on his journey into the valley of dementia. Too many *knocks on the old noggin, fuck it who gives a shit, didn't we have some good times?* Was he telling me I had a soul or that souls were present in this room, wafting through the air with the bravado stories of our heroics? *Oh, that we were ever so young and athletic and destined for greatness.* Was he pouring from the cup of his mouth some special knowledge into my ear, a warm and blessed liquid? O My Soul, was that you, coming to me when I least expect it, announcing your existence among so many good men, through the mouth of this man, shaman of expletives, high priest of stories and fists, and laughs, and beers and hijinks that I recall left us all breathless, filled with good humor? O Joe, quarterback, who never ran out of bounds because only gringos do, wild, violent Joe, have you given me a parting gift, a piece of the eternal puzzle?

Meschery, Tom. "Soul," *Some Men*. Black Rock Press, Rain Shadow Edition, 2012. University of Nevada, Reno. Reno, NV

• • •

Darrall Imhoff, my nemesis from college would have attended Cal Guys but lived in Oregon. I wouldn't have minded seeing him. I might have even apologized for my mean-spirited thoughts about him. He was a worthy foe. Darrall suffered a heart attack and died. We stood for a moment of silence for him and Coach Pete Newell who'd also passed. On the drive home that day I remember thinking I couldn't shake the negative feelings I had about being overlooked for the Rome Olympics. It gnawed at me that I missed the chance to represent my country, to stand with my hand over my heart and watch the American flag rise over the Roman Colosseum and to wear a gold medal around my neck.

Melanie reminds me that by then I was no longer overly patriotic. She was right, of course, but Patriotism need not be the faux jingoistic kind of patriotism that several politicians express, and I find so ridiculously phony. By the time I was attending the Cal Guys, my feelings about Patriotism had changed from its youthful exuberance to a more mellow feeling of gratitude that America had provided me safety and opportunity that I might not have had elsewhere.

Darrall Imhoff remains a touchstone along that athletic journey. Melanie reminds me that you can only lose so many touchstones before you start losing your direction.

At the Cal Guy Lunches, as promised, McClintock buys me beers. When we were young, we drank beer like Samuel Johnson drank his tea - in oceans. Bill has somehow been able to continue to handle his brews. It just makes me pee. But to decline a beer might cause McClintock to question my manliness.

At one of the lunches, the Cal sprinter Eddie Hart, who'd earned a Gold medal in the 4 x 100 meter race in the 1972 Munich Olympics, announced the completion of his memoir, *Disqualified,* about those fateful games when Black September Palestinian terrorists kidnapped and assassinated the Israeli wrestling team. It was also the Olympics in which the U.S.A basketball team lost for the first time in Olympic history.

• • •

My elementary school and high school was 60 percent Jewish. Most of the owners of NBA teams when I played were Jewish. I grew up with my mother's belief that the Jews were the chosen people. One of the more intriguing of my mother's family myths was that the woman who birthed the maternal side of the Lvov family was a Jewess, thus all succeeding mothers in the maternal line would be Jewish. Since my sister is unmarried and has no children, all claims to a Jewish heritage would end with her. I've never thought to ask Ann if she ever considered this. I did examine our Family Tree to see if there was a direct line of females from the first mother to my mother and was unable to verify my mother's claim. I would be perfectly happy if it were proven true that I possessed Jewish blood. There would be a blending of two culinary traditions I adore. Don't get me started on blintzes and matzo ball soup.

CHAPTER 52
VALENTINES DAY

Despite my parents' marriage being an imperfect model, I grew up believing in marriage. The 1950's traditional American kind that would impress an immigrant teen watching television, like *Father Knows Best* and *The Adventures of Ozzie and Harriet*. As a child-immigrant, most of my belief system had no cultural roots so these TV shows were part of American culture for me. I do not doubt that my entire generation of males were similarly impressed by these shows.

When my marriage failed, it took me a long time to figure out what was happening to me. You would think a 38-year failed marriage would have turned me against the institution. Instead, I clung to the belief that a loving couple was the best way to live life. One love, one dear friend, a companion.

Melanie and I promised that whatever time the universe gave us, we would make up for the love my parents did not have for each other. As sentimental as it is, it is a promise we don't take lightly. I have no doubt that Mel's and my marriage will succeed. I found my other half in Melanie. As Mel's laconic grandson, John-Clark, often eloquently says, *I'm good - we are both good.*

• • •

When some of my graduated senior students asked if I would marry them, I went online and became a Universal Life Minister. I gave the couples "poetic" weddings. Lots of readings from some of the best love and marriage poems. One that never failed to enter into the ceremony was Shakespeare's 116th sonnet that starts out, *"Let me not to the marriage of true minds admit impediments. . ."* Impediments is such a polite word, nothing like the barriers that confront couples in real life. I also used Neruda's Sonnet 17: ". *. . So close that your hand on my chest is my hand/ So close that your eyes close as I fall asleep."* Or if the couple wanted a little spirituality, I'd have them read Elizabeth Barrett Browning's Sonnet 43, to each other, alternating parts of the poem they chose together ahead of time. *Not a dry eye in the wedding party.* My favorite line in Sonnet 43 is a couple of lines in the middle: *I love thee to the level of every day's/Most quiet need. . .* It's how I feel about Melanie, and I recite these lines to her often. In my student weddings, I always said something about the circular symbolism of the rings.

One of my favorite weddings was the one I performed for two of my daughter Megan's friends, the sweetest women imaginable and, not to make too much of it, terrific basketball players. I read from the ancient Greek lesbian poet Sapho. To this day, their same sex marriage is solid, and they have raised two fine sons.

How frightened in general some people are of change. A couple of years ago I read an April 19, article in *Psychology Today* By Nigel Barber PhD and conducted at the University College of London. It answered that question for me.

Self-professed conservatives students had larger Amagdalas than self-described liberal students

The amygdala is an almond-shaped area of the brain that is associated with fear and anxiety.

It certainly provides scientific evidence that conservatives are mostly motivated by fear. Fear of what? Of their shadows? I am reminded that during the McCarthy Red Scare, the senator and his evil associates began a hunt for homosexuals. As a kid I was not aware of this. I was having enough trouble with the *Red* Scare. Now, as I think of it, this information only reinforces my idea about the deep-rooted fear of change that must exist in all conservatives.

• • •

Every Valentine's Day, Melanie and I celebrate our marriage at our favorite restaurant, Banderas, which serves the best grilled artichokes this side of Castroville, the Artichoke Capital of the world. Our ritual is always the same: We are seated and order our customary *Gray Goose* martinis two olives. While we wait for our drinks, we acknowledge our marriage by reaching across the table and hooking our little fingers together, so our wedding bands are next to each other and repeating the names of my parents engraved inside our rose-gold bands, "*Masha ee Kolya.*" When our martinis arrive, as we have done every year, we toast our children, then our grandchildren.

CHAPTER 53
GRANDCHILDREN

Our office is on the second floor of our condominium, its windows overlooking cedars and redwoods rising behind gray-tiled rooftops. Our desks are within arms' length of each other, close enough to hold hands. I do not exaggerate when I say that if Mel and I wrote down the top 10 characteristics we wanted in our mates, the score would read 10 out of 10. That this marriage of true minds occurred as we were heading into old age is a miracle.

OLD MAN HANDS

For Melanie

I'm looking at my old-man-hand, blue veins
showing through rice-paper skin, blood
bruises like ink blots. I turn my hand over
and examine my palm. Younger, I think, flesh
still pink, my life-line curving around my thumb,
but at eighty, who knows for how long.
My index finger is arthritic and looks
somewhat like a waning moon. I can't palm
a basketball any more. My old-man-fingers
can no longer make a free-throw. Tell me
if that isn't pathetic, unable to propel
a 22 ounce ball fifteen feet into the air.
When my old-man-hands were young-

man-hands, they could grab a ball
out of the air, or out of my opponents' hands
and fling the ball the length of the court.
There are moments in my life when I still
hear an arena of many-hands clapping
for my young-man-hands. On my office
wall hangs a painting of a left hand
by Terry Miura. It drops gracefully down
from a cloudy background. The knuckles
suggest it is the hand of a mature male.
How I envy its agelessness.
I remember as a child in the midst of War,
among the ruins of Tokyo, I saw
a child's hand poking out of the rubble
that would never become an old hand.
Looking at you, I believe it's true what some say
that you can hold your loved ones' life
in your hands. As I'm doing now, my old-man-
hand reaching across for your old-woman-hand.

Meschery, Tom. "Old Man's Hands," *Clear Path*, Random Lane
Press, 2022. Sacramento, CA

My desk faces the windows. Melanie's desk sits at an angle. The two
corner walls behind her desk are covered with African masks, my favorites
being half of a Dogon door and a beautifully carved antelope head smoking
pipe, all of which I collected over three coaching trips to West Africa.
Some, like the door, are old and valuable.

Family photographs line the top of Mel's computer desk. Mel and
I work long hours with the faces of our children and grandchildren
looking down on us. There's Emily, Mel's daughter, as a young adult,
blonde hair, styled *au courant*, giving the camera a "sultry look," now
a public-school counselor. There are wedding pictures of my three
children, one I like especially of my Matt and Megan standing on either
side of my smiling oldest daughter, Janai, on her wedding day. Another
favorite of mine is a photograph of Mel and her son, Grant, when she
was in her forties, he in his twenties. He looks Hollywood handsome.

She looks more like an older sister than a mom, but her smile says proud mother.

There are some photographs of our grandchildren in our office, but the majority at various stages of their lives decorate the door of our refrigerator. Between us, we have 13, six on my side, seven on hers, although one of Melanie's grandchildren, her beloved Berkeley, Grant's 18-year-old first born, while away at the University of Colorado, fell asleep one afternoon and never woke up. Parents never recover from such tragedies and neither do grandparents. Berkeley had inherited Melanie's artistic talent. Years have cushioned the grief, but there will never be enough years.

I wrote John-Clark, Berkeley's younger brother, a poem about a time before Berkeley's death when he and his father, Grant, and I attended a Warriors game in Oracle Arena. After the game, I took the boy back into the players' tunnel to get autographs.

John-Clark doesn't just love basketball, he adores it. When I coached him, he listened. Unlike his older brother, the form of his shot was perfect. John-Clark had limited speed and physical versatility, something to do with a childhood hip problem. It kept him from making his high school team. A damn shame because he had a natural shooting eye and was instinctively an adept passer. John Clark is grown and in college. But earlier in his life, I often thought of him with a basketball under his arm heading to the courts in the schoolyard behind his house. It reminded me and my fellow high school gym-rats off to our favorite San Francisco courts. My hope for John-Clark is that he won't quit playing hoops but continues to "gym-rat." Pickup games might be the purest form of the sport anyway.

• • •

Not only did John-Clark get the autographs of each of the players as they emerged from their locker room, but Steph Curry autographed his basketball and the Curry jersey his father had bought him at halftime. I stood off to the side and watched amused, remembering the after-game moments long ago when it was me signing autographs and waiting to have my photograph taken the way Curry was waiting patiently. Some pro athletes can be brusque and arrogant. Not Curry, who Mel says is every mother's son and by extension every grandmother's ideal grandson. John-Clark's dad was so nervous taking the photograph that he almost dropped the phone. It was amusing to see Grant, who is normally a guy very much in control of the situation, far more nervous than his son. Grant had the jersey framed, and it hangs in John-Clark's bedroom. John-Clark has a photograph of it posted on his phone, viewed jealously by his schoolmates.

ON THE BASKETBALL COURT BEHIND YOUR HOUSE

For John-Clark, in memory of your brother Berkeley

He listened, cocked his arm and shot the ball
his way no matter what I said. You knew,
didn't you, John-Clark, watching from the sideline
where younger brothers are assigned to stand
in the shadow of the older one, that he was stubborn.
You knew the way all younger brothers know
that their older brothers know everything,
leaving nothing for their younger brothers to say,
except with a smile, "I could've told you, it's Berk's way
or the highway." I wish I could say, hearing of Berk's death,
that he took the road less traveled, to ease your pain,
my friend, my basketball buddy, grandson
with a knack for picking winners. You listened to me
and shot the ball the right way. I told you, Berk's elbow
stuck out like a chicken wing, and you laughed
and later in life, your brother still alive in Colorado
and you in the backseat of your daddy's car
driving home after a Warriors game,
you clutched Steph Curry's signed jersey to your chest
and said, "Berk is going to be soooo jealous."
I thought what you said was soooo hilarious
because, isn't this what brothers do, have done
from the beginning of brothers, compete, knowing
it's got nothing to do with loving each other.

Meschery, Tom. "On The Basketball Court Behind Your House," *Time Out*, Finishing Line Press, 2020. Georgetown, KY

I don't know if my poem helped John-Clark, but Mel's family, me included, have circled him like a wagon train to protect him from whatever pain might befall him. I'm betting that John-Clark has what it takes to figure things out and go on with his life. But he is so quiet that it's hard to tell. His response to most questions is "I'm good."

When I listen to the way NBA players torture the English language during TV interviews, I grit my teeth. To me a double negative is like listening to a fingernail scratching across the surface of a chalkboard.

Melanie's response: *You are dating yourself, my dear.*

Melanie believes that ending criticism with an endearment makes it okay. Ha!

Mel's grandsons compete with my granddaughter, Carson, for refrigerator space, but they are losing ground because her mother, my daughter, Janai, loves photography and guess who her favorite subject is? Mel's grand-boys, in order of age, are Max, 18; John-Clark, 17; Jaxon, 14; and Wyatt, 10. Most of the stages of their ages are represented on the refrigerator door, Jaxon either in a basketball (in one shot, palming basketballs outstretched in either hand) or in his football uniform, looking Hollywood-handsome. Dark and mysterious Max, kneeling in his football uniform, one of the most earnest youngsters I've every met. Wyatt who shuns traditional sports (a shock to his athletic parents), looking like he can't wait for the next chapter of whatever fantasy novel he's reading. My middle daughter's children, Grace and Ruth, have their own, less noticeable spot on the refrigerator because their parents do not send us pictures often. Grace is a marvelous artist. As it has turned out, so is her younger sister Ruth. But while Grace is mostly a right-brained thinker, Ruth works on both sides of the brain, which would qualify her to be either a nuclear scientist or the next Georgia O'Keefe. My son Matthew and his wife Eleese started producing babies late, so there are not as many photographs of their three boys: Leo, named after our famous relative, Leo Tolstoy; Moses, named after Moses Malone, the Hall of Fame NBA center, and Van, named after Van Morrison, the rock star. The naming of his children accounts for three parts of my son's personal history: His Russian heritage, his dad's basketball, and his own passion for music. My passion for basketball translated to my daughter, Meagan, who started for her high school team and was known for her rugged play. *Humm?* My passion for basketball did not translate to my son. Matthew was a good junior high player, a solid ball handler and accurate shooter. I had some hopes of going to high school basketball games and cheering for him. It was not to be. One afternoon during the summer between his eighth grade and the start of his freshman year in high school, Matt came to me. I was standing in the kitchen. "Dad," he said, "In high school, the basketball team and the jazz band practice at the same time. Would you be terribly disappointed?" I can't recall being disappointed. I figured it took some courage and a sincere love of music for Matt to ask me the question. Music has been my son's passion ever since. He had a college band and after graduation from Brown University, an acid rock band called *Cleveland Lounge* that had some brief success in Japan. His final band, a hip hop band called *OPM, was* number one for a week on *Top of the Pops* in England. He still receives a royalty check every once and a while for the song he wrote, *Heaven is a Halfpipe,* which is a sort of skateboarder's anthem. He no longer has a band, but he and his wife, Eleese sing and write music. They live now in Nashville, Tennessee, a perfect place for this musical couple.

It amuses me to imagine my son standing in his kitchen sometime in the future and his son Leo coming up to him and saying, "Dad, in high school, the jazz band and the basketball team practices at the same time. Would you be terribly disappointed if I chose basketball?

It is not surprising that many of today's NBA players have retired NBA dads. Steph Curry and Klay Thompson are two current examples. It is not unusual in any family that children follow in their parents' footsteps. Both my daughters are teachers. How many famous CEOs have grown up with businessmen dads? This may have to do with parental modeling and/or careful guiding. But some parents have been known to push, prod or excessively influence their children in the direction they desire. I never pushed my children into sports, but I was tempted to with my daughter Megan, who was a water baby. By the time she was ten, she was competing in local swim meets and destroying most of the competition, especially in the butterfly where she swam like a dolphin. I knew I was looking at a possible Olympic swimmer. In order to achieve this goal - mine but not necessarily Megan's - our family would have had to move from Truckee to San Jose where there were national swimming clubs. We remained in Truckee. Meg did not continue swimming. As an adult, she occasionally reminds me that I am to blame for her broad swimmers shoulders. She's joking - I think.

A few refrigerator photos are of me in my NBA days, which I

occasionally study the way I would an artifact from an earlier civilization. There is a sweet photo of Nate, "The Great" Thurmond and his beloved wife Marci, and one of Barbara Lewis, Wilt Chamberlain's sister, with her husband, Elzie, who played for the Harlem Globetrotters. Al Attles and his wife, Wilhelmina, are there. My teammate Al was the toughest pound-for-pound player in the NBA. It is possible that having Al guarding my back provided The Mad Manchurian with the courage to battle any NBA opponent. Such an admission might tarnish the Mad Manchurian's tough guy reputation, but it would be untruthful not to mention it. At the center of the fridge is a photo of Melanie and me, at Oracle Arena, with my retired number hanging in the rafters behind us.

I suspect in most kitchens in this country there are refrigerator doors covered with family photographs. At the top left hand corner of our refrigerator where there is space not taken up by family and friends, Mel has placed a picture and a quote by Mahatma Gandhi: *There is no God higher than Truth.*

CHAPTER 54
NEW YORK CHAPTER OF NOBLE RUSSIAN FAMILIES

Although my sister Ann is whole heartedly an American, she relishes being born into Russian nobility - on our mother's side, the Tolstoys and the Lvovs. A few years back, she was invited to a gathering of the New York chapter of Noble Russian Families. She telephoned with the news. I could hear the excitement in her voice as she described all the dignitaries. As a progressive liberal, I was tempted to say something about the gratuitously wealthy, overindulged, noble Russian families that ruled Russia prior to the Bolshevik Revolution, (our family included) but decided against spoiling her fun. Besides, considering I'd rejected most forms of capitalism, it was up to Ann to maintain our family status as a protector of wealth.

Before the Bolshevik Revolution, the nobility of Russia owned or controlled close to 100% of the nation's wealth. *Of what country does this remind you?*

The magnitude of such a disparity between the rich and the rest of Russian society was made startlingly clear to me when I was looking through my mother's papers after her death and came across a series of letters written to her from her favorite cousin, Nikolai Tolstoy who was an officer in the Tsar's army fighting on the Austrian front during the First World War. This particular letter was written from Saint Peterburg to my mother who was on her family estate in the province of Samara. The letter was translated by my mother and copied into her memoir.

September 2, 1914

Dearest Mashinka,

I arrived on furlough just in time to attend the ball Countess Kleinmichel gave for the beau monde of Saint Petersburg. Ladies with hair dyed blue waltzed with half naked cavemen. What buffoons. I saw Princess Xenia Alexandrovich among them with her beautiful daughter. Later, women dressed as fish swam on the floor over yards of blue satin while men with fishnets tried to catch them.

Why royalty still exists in the 21st century seems not only ridiculous but dishonest.

Melanie's interest in the British royalty is curious to me since her roots are what the Russian "nobles" would have classified as common. Once, early in our relationship, my sister was going on and on about our noble Russian relatives. Melanie listened patiently then when asked by my sister, about her heritage, stated that her family was descended from "dirt farmers and horse thieves." This descendant of dirt farmers and the descendant of nobility have remained good friends. Mel reminds me of a quote by Will Rogers: *There are two things for which a person cannot be held responsible: 1) who his parents were. 2) where he was born.*

In the summer of 2007 when I was in Saint Petersburg, I visited the address of my maternal grandfather, Vladimir Lvov's second home, an apartment at 34 Liteinaya Yletsa (Street) in the Nevsky Prospect, one he kept for the times he was required to attend sessions of the Duma. Standing in the park across the street, I recalled my mother describing playing as a child among the trees of the park with friends and in winter throwing snowballs and building snowmen. This same apartment that my mother loved so much, whose interior she described so faithfully, was, before her parent's residence, inhabited by the mysterious and dreadful Siberian monk Rasputin. According to my mother, her parents brought in a priest to perform an exorcism before they would move in. It is also a family story that our grandfather was part of the plot to assassinate Rasputin. There is no historical evidence of this, except considering my grandfather's deep religious faith, it makes sense that he would have despised Rasputin and helped in the evil monk's demise. I never questioned the veracity of this story. All of my life, until recently, my grandfather Lvov was a superhero, a combination of Batman and Superman when I was a youngster and a fierce Anti-Communist when I was a teenager. He was a role model for me to look up too and respect. I drew strength from the stories I heard about him. Grandfather Lvov was a big part of our family legend.

It was from one of the windows of the Lvov residence in Saint Petersburg that my grandmother witnessed the street fighting of the 1917 Bolshevik Revolution. An entry from my mother's journals recounts one such moment:

Petrograd,
July 6, 1917
Shooting into the air. Signs saying: Down with the Duma
and the Council. . . Well my dear, I did not escape from
the smell of gunpowder. Until late at night Papa could
not come to our apartment where I was in turmoil because
the Bolsheviks were firing machine guns. . . Bullets were
flying continuously in pursuit of the poor Cossacks who
galloped away in all directions. . . there was nothing they
could do since they were armed only with sabers. I was
alone and prepared to die, praying to God to forgive my sins.

After my grandfather V.N. Lvov's arrest and subsequent escape to Paris, my grandmother and her children remained behind in the Province of Samara on their family estate in Krotkovo. They remained there until the approaching Bolshevik army caused them to flee the ancestral home to safety across the Ural Mountains to the Siberian city of Omsk. My mother's brother, Nikolai Lvov, the oldest sibling, already a soldier in the White Russian Army, remained behind with his troops. He was later wounded and captured by the Bolsheviks. When Omsk became unsafe for White Russians, my grandmother and her children boarded a train and traveled across the winter landscape of Siberia to the Manchurian border and crossed it to safety. That winter trip across Siberia as described to me by my mother became part of a family poem:

We knelt on the shores of Lake Baikal
and pressed our faces against ice to see
fish we'd read about as children, trapped

below the frozen surface, their scales
magnified as clear as fingernails. Aboard the train
missionaries, thinking we were praying
to something heathen in the lake, threatened
us with forests filled with Trotsky's partisans.

Meschery, Tom. From the poem, "Small Embrace," *Nothing We Lose Can Be Replaced*, Black Rock Press, Rain Shadow Edition, 1999. University of Nevada, Reno. Reno. NV

Non-Russians were unaware that when frozen, the ice of Lake Baikal was so deep and transparent that a person looking down through the ice could see the ice-bound fish asleep in their cryogenic beds awaiting the spring thaw.

One question I asked my mother and never received a straight answer from her was why her father, Vladimir Nikolaevich Lvov, free in Paris, never located his family. Surely, he must have known that a great number of Russians escaped to Manchuria and settled in Harbin. I therefore assumed there had been some counter-revolutionary reason behind his reticence. Even when my grandfather's lack of interest no longer made any sense, either rationally or imaginatively, I could not find fault with him. It would have been a betrayal of my mother's unquestioning loyalty. More importantly, for me, it would have diminished the hero of my childhood.

• • •

Given how much my sister and I knew about the maternal side of our family, we both wished we'd known more about our dad's side. I have only three photographs of my father, one of him wearing his military uniform, the other in civilian clothes taken outside our home in Harbin, and the third much later in his life, in a family photograph at my Saint Mary's College graduation. In it, he looks proud, but he's wearing dark glasses, so I could be wrong. Bemused, possibly. My sister has a photograph of my father's gorgeous twin sisters. They possess the same dark complexion as our father. I bear little resemblance to my swarthy father, a descendent of a famous Cossack, but as a youngster I was thrilled to be related to a Cossack warrior. Even though it seems unlikely, I continue to accept this myth of my father's origins because in the story of my life my dad deserves a little status. He had to live with all my mother's exalted relatives, whose history she was in the habit of reminding him of from time to time.

Bless his heart, Melanie says.

• • •

In 1992 my sister Ann, while visiting Ireland for the Wexford Opera Festival, was surprised to find that the principal female voice was a soprano named Marina Mescheriakova. Ann managed to get an introduction and discovered that Mescheriakova's family had lived in the same region of Samara where our father's family was from. Mescheriakova's family, like so many families in the early years of the Soviet Union, destroyed family documentation that might make them suspect in the minds of the Soviet secret police. Ann and Marina decided that despite any clear evidence, they would be cousins. It was possible. While our family always believed that my father and his brother Orest were the only boys in the family, it turned out there was a much younger male sibling, Ivan who had survived the revolution. **That boy could have been Marina's grandfather.** When Cousin Marina Mescheriakova came to the San Francisco Opera to sing in *Don Carlo*, I met her briefly backstage. I remember thinking she looked like our father's sisters from a photograph of them. The reviews of Marina's performance were off the charts. Last we heard, Mescheriakova was retired and living in Vienna.

I thought of my teenage sister and our father sitting in the living room listening to opera. I saw myself lying on the couch in my home in Truckee suffering from shingles and listening to arias. Opera was in our blood.

CHAPTER 55
GYM RATS

My friend Barry Cummings and I were gym rats through high school. Gym rats are basketball players that find their way into gyms after the doors are locked and lights turned off so they can shoot hoops for another couple of hours in whatever light will not attract outside attention. Sometimes flashlights on the floor had to do. I remember playing in such light, sometimes having to imagine where the hoop was as I shot the ball from distance. Later in my life, this became a strategy I applied to practicing free throws. I always shot a few with my eyes closed, sensing rather than seeing the hoop. If I had turned out to be better than a 75% lifetime shooter, I could have packaged the idea and sold it. I would have called it sensory shooting. That sensory living became part of the way I conducted my life seems not at all surprising.

My group of gym-rats joined me on the court of Saint Vincent de Paul Elementary School gym: *Toso, Harrington, Randall, Luchese, and Cummings - these names are like street signs in a neighborhood so I would not lose my way*. Later, there were my college gym rats: Prescott, the Caranica twins, and Fred LaCour who, given his basketball mania, might have qualified him as the Bay Area's most accomplished gym rat. There wasn't a locked gym Fred couldn't find a way to get into.

After his retirement, Barry Cummings and his wife, Terese, moved from San Jose to Placerville, in the foothills east of Sacramento. Barry and I began meeting for lunches and trips down memory lane. I occasionally receive emails from another of my gym-rat friends, Bob Randall.

To: tom Meschery meschery14@gmail.com

Hey Tommy – just curious about something: when we were at Grant, as I recall, we came to school early to play whatever sport was in season. every day. for 3 years. There were four of us who got to school so early. It was still dark outside. Sometimes it was raining and dark. We didn't care. We scaled the fence.

I read the email, closed my eyes and there we were, hooping, Bobby and I. If I were to advise youngsters what they needed to do to become great basketball players, I'd tell them they would have to climb fences in the dark and play in the rain.

You couldn't help but like Bob. He was short and skinny and sort of looked like a mouse. He played like a tough little rat. When he emails me, he calls me Tommy. I hate being called Tommy. The only guy who called me Tommy was Tommy Heinsohn of the Boston Celtics, and we were NBA foes for ten years punching it out on the court every chance we could.

I pause mid-paragraph **to** apologize to all my NBA opponents I punched, elbowed, or attempted other forms of bodily harm. A memoir can also be a confession.

Sixty-five-years later, I guess Bob was paying me back for calling him Bobby. But I shouldn't hold that against him. I admire Bobby's devotion to the sport of basketball. Unlike most gym rats, he never stopped playing basketball as he got older. All the while he worked in the postal service, until he retired a couple of years back, he played some form of amateur hoops. I knew this because he'd send me clippings from newspaper stories that described his winning a state-wide 65-and-older basketball One-on-One Tournaments, as well as H-O-R-S-E contests he won at 70 and free throw-shooting competitions. I cannot rationally explain how jealous I was of him. No way could I have accomplished what he did at a similar age.

There were other old-timers like Bobby, still hooping. Guys like Jim Barnett, the Warriors long time color commentator. At age 60, he was playing in Sixties-and-Over tournaments. I'm not sure if Bobby will like this poem I wrote for him, but that's the result of him calling me Tommy.

BOBBY

For Randall

It's worth mentioning that he was small for his age
and scurried around the basketball court
like a mouse, a pet if we had held him in our hands
and gave him comfort. But we often ridiculed him
for the little gestures that he made with his fingers
on either side of his mouth where whiskers
would appear in our thoughtless imaginations.

It is worth mentioning that he carried letters
and stood behind the counter of his post office
and sent our important missives to their Important
destinations, all the while keeping faith
with those years on the basketball court.

Most of us grew fat, our legs turning to mush,
so that we could hardly run, in my case walk.
Bobby won championships shooting hoops,
Sixties and Over: Seventies and Over:
Three on Three; Free Throw Shooting;
H.O.R.S.E.; bringing home medals and trophies.

It's worth mentioning that Bobby never forgot
a single moment on the court or any player
that was worthy of his admiration. His memory
brought him joy and those accomplishments
whether so slight in our youth, in his old age,
grew larger into a garden of delight.

It is worth mentioning that few men his age
(What is he now? Eighty?) can sight over the ball
measure the distance to the hoop and score
as if the distance between his eye and the rim,
however difficult, were the measure of the man.

It is worth mentioning that we are not so far removed,
from our youthful venality that we can not
be forgiven, which Bobby has done with every
shot he swished the net because it was the sport
          we played together, and he guarded us so tightly.

Meschery, Tom. "Bobby," *Clear Path*. Random Lane Press, 2022.
Sacramento, CA

I found myself engaged once again with the sport of basketball. Not just the NBA, but college basketball. I even watched some high school games on television and marveled at their precocity. When had an entire generation sprouted wings? I continued to purchase a yearly NBA League Pass, so that I could watch games that were not on the major television channels. Much to my wife's amazement I looked forward to the NBA college draft and began tuning in to the television broadcasts of the various NBA Summer League games. Just curious about the rookies I replied when she asked.

It is to Melanie's credit that she has never complained about my resurgent basketball madness. If it's the Warriors, she usually watches with me. Mel was a fast learner. It didn't take her long to understand the basics and enough of the nuances that we could talk hoops. I once told her she was my basketball buddy. *What every wife wants to hear was her reply.* Lest I give you the impression that Melanie abandoned the esthetic side of her nature for the athletic, I offer you this as an example that she hasn't: A few years back we were watching a Warriors game. It was probably 2015, the first year the Warriors won the NBA Championship. Nature called, and as I left the room, I jokingly told Mel to call out **to** me a play-by-play. This is what I heard: *Curry dribble-drives down the right side of the court, passes to Thompson. Green sets a screen, and Harrison Barnes is looking very handsome tonight.*

In the words of hoop-land: *You see what I'm sayin?*

• • •

And there were Barry Cummings and Bob Randall taking me all the way back so that I began remembering gyms and outdoor playgrounds, where before you started you placed your finger in the air to see which way the wind was blowing so you could adjust your shot. How were all these people and memories possible?

I said to Melanie, "I guess I never left basketball."

"Did you ever really want to?" she answered.

The answer should have been clear to me a long time ago. "No," I said.

• • •

Sometime during this period of my life, I found myself going online and checking my ten year NBA stats. I recall that the first time I did it was after watching a Warriors game. Could these tired, old legs have been able to grab rebounds, shoot baskets, and guard opponents at a professional level? I wondered if other old athletes questioned the authenticity of their past performances. The stats confirmed that I'd played pretty damn well. I was happy to know that fact. Based on 48 minutes per game, for ten years I averaged 12.7 points, 8.8 rpg and 75% from the free throw line. It confirmed that I had scored 9,904 pts, 96 points shy of the prestigious 10,000-point club. *If only I'd known or cared, I would have taken a few more shots.* Or maybe I wouldn't have. I don't recall paying attention to my stats. when I played. I was never asked why not. My answer was that after the game in the locker room, while the guys were checking out their numbers, I was too busy trying to locate the beer bucket to bother with statistics. *You've got to have your priorities straight.* In a 48-minute game of professional basketball, a player who participates fully in the game loses 50 to 150 fl oz.

Scrolling down, I discovered a 36 minutes per game statistic. I liked the look of it. Thirty-six minutes was a more realistic number of minutes I actually spent on the court. Based on 36 mpg, I averaged 15.2 ppg, 10.3 rpg and remained consistent at 75% from the charity stripe. According to these numbers, I was a career double/double player. All right, I thought, I had played better than *just pretty well.* The thought occurred to me that there might be a statistic about the number of on-court fights or fouls committed in a season. I hoped not. Much to my relief, there wasn't. I found a separate statistic for playoffs in which I discovered, much to my delight, that I improved my scoring to 16.3 ppg and my free throw accuracy to 80%. I'd always thought of myself as a clutch player, here was the proof. I am not embarrassed to admit after that first time I have returned several times to visit my stats. A lot of the players after every game perused the final stat-sheets - checking out their numbers. But here I was closing in on 80 years of age, doing the same thing - checking out my numbers. And feeling proud of myself. For an immigrant kid, I hadn't done too badly. That night, I went to bed hoping to dream about playing basketball. But the lights in the arena remained dark.

CHAPTER 56
BARRY AND TERESE

Barry Cummings, one of my gym rat pals, was never big enough to play high school varsity basketball, but played well on the junior varsity team that in the Fifties was called the 130's. There were 120's and 110's as well, teams calculated by increments of weight, age, and height designed with the democratic notion that all boys should have a chance to compete on a team. Barry enrolled at Saint Ignatius. By my senior year we'd lost touch. Then, in our old age, Barry moved to Placerville and we renewed our friendship.

The last time I saw Barry Cummings, we were in a booth at *Frank Fat's*, a Chinese restaurant that was located about halfway between his home in Placerville and mine in Sacramento. Like me, Barry had turned 80. It had been two years since Terese, his college sweetheart and wife of 50 years, had died. She'd been suffering from dementia. After a broken hip operation, she languished in a convalescent home for a few months, then died – peacefully Barry had told me. I remember our conversation well.

"We watched television together and now that I watch television alone, I find myself turning to her chair and asking her a question, or for an opinion."

"Does she talk back?" I'd asked.

Barry had looked up at me over his Chinese chicken salad to see if I was being serious. I was, but I was not sure Barry could tell.

"No," he said, "but it doesn't matter. It keeps me from being too lonely."

Barry's oldest son and his family lived only a few miles north of him, but they, like other families raising children, were busy living their own lives. His other three children, two daughters and the younger son, lived on the other side of the state in San Jose.

At our lunches, Barry and I solved all the problems in today's game of basketball: *They carry the fucking ball. They have no idea how to block off the boards.* From there we made our way through all of the touchstones of our gym-rat days, the guys that could have made it but didn't, *but boy could they play the game.* Always a part of our lunch was our, *If only stories. If only* he hadn't been so small and light, he would have made high school varsity. *If only* so and so had not been so lazy, if only what's his name hadn't had a drinking problem. *If only,* you know, hadn't committed suicide, he would have been an All American tight end. . . We turned from *"if onlys"* to our playgrounds and gyms. *Remember the low ceiling at Salesians? Then at JK, so close to the backboard, you were scared to drive in for a layup. The dismal lighting at Anza. The wind at Pacific Heights.* Barry's mind was a photo album. *Remember that blonde chick that used to hang around Funston?* Modern women do not like to be referred to as barnyard birds, but for the sake of our 1950's masculinity, I never corrected Barry.

We usually ended our lunches by checking off the old Saint Vincent de Paul gang that Barry kept in touch with, and I hadn't been in touch with any of them. I would ask how they were doing. And Barry's standard reply; *Not getting any younger.* We could have been any two old farts having lunch at a restaurant in any town and city around the country. *One asks the other "How ya doin?" "Not getting any younger. Pass the Ketchup."*

Over coffee, Barry told me about the day Terese had been moved from the hospital to the convalescent home. She was well into dementia by then. I could tell by the sparkle in his eyes this was a story he enjoyed. Two firemen, he started, had moved his wife from the ambulance to her room, which was shared with another woman also suffering from dementia. Barry said that when he entered the room, Terese began to talk about how handsome the firemen were. "Handsomer than me?" he'd asked. "Oh, my, yes," she replied. Barry joked that he would go bring one back for her. The old woman in the other bed raised her finger and said, "One for me too."

As we left the restaurant, Barry was smiling over that memory. I told him as we parted not to be concerned if he woke up one morning and the aroma of coffee was wafting from the kitchen. Barry looked at me, like really? Thinking about it. Then he nodded.

At home, while Melanie was eating Peking Duck and banana cream pie that I'd brought back for her, I told l her about Barry talking to Terese. I added that in the unlikely event that she died before me, I'd be glad to talk to her. If that turned out to be the other way in which she died first, Mel promised she'd continue to help me drive. I told her I could do without a back-seat-driver from the spirit world. A mouthful of banana cream pie saved me from The Fabled's response.

Later that afternoon, I checked my email and got this from Barry:

Fr: <u>cummings</u>
To: <u>meschery</u>
Hi Tom
I told you I have good neighbors but getting together with a friend of 65-70 years brings me more joy than can be put into words. Thanks.
Terese said to say hi. I think.
Barry

Do I believe in spirits, or was I simply trying to comfort an old friend? The thought that I would pass into the universe and never see Melanie again is too much sadness to consider. When I told Melanie this, she said to take heart, her favorite artist of all time, Alice Neel, in her old age, remarked in an interview, "Nearly all of the people I talk to now are dead."

"I talk to Berkeley," Melanie added about her departed and beloved grandson.

There is much about The Spiritual we don't understand. A couple of years ago, a friend from college, Peter Fitting, visited from Toronto. We had dinner together. Peter was a professor of French Literature at the University of Toronto and a dedicated atheist. He demanded to know why Melanie would paint icons. I thought he was just being curious, but Mel thought that he was being hostile. Later, after we'd left Peter at the restaurant, she said in her defense, "I bet Peter never had an angel visit him in a dream." Not a lot of people have, but I'm willing to believe in the appearance of angels whether awake or in dreams in the same way that I believe in all forms of beauty. The poet John Keats said it best, Beauty is truth and that's all we need to know.

Barry had a stroke in the fall of 2019 and died. In one form or another, Barry and Terese are together again.

CHAPTER 57
MY EIGHTIETH

Melanie Scotch taped my birthday card to the inside of our front door to remind me that Sunday, September 8th, 2018, was my birthday celebration at the Campus Commons' clubhouse. *As if I could have forgotten. As if I wouldn't have liked to.* The correct date of my birth was the 26th of October. I had agreed to have my celebration early because Buzzy Jackson, who grew up with my children in Iowa City and Truckee, and whom I often referred to as my spiritual daughter, had scheduled her son's Bar Mitzvah on October 26. I did not mind. Doing it this way, I allowed myself almost two additional months to relish being in my seventies. *We octogenarians are sly devils.*

By the time Mel and I arrived at the clubhouse, the hors d'oeuvres table was set and Edith Piaf was singing *La Vie en Rose.* The Little Sparrow's voice has always given me the chills.

A month before the celebration, my son had asked me what songs I wanted. *Je Ne Regrette Rien* came to mind but decided for this occasion it was inappropriate since there was plenty I regretted in my life. Sinatra's *My Way* is often considered for octogenarian celebrations, which has always struck me as the height of arrogance. So many times, "My way" had turned out to be the wrong way. Mel and I decided on a medley of songs from our wedding day celebration. I added a few favorites from West Africa: Johnny Clegg and Savouka, Baaba Maal, and the incomparable Salif Keita.

I have given a lot of consideration to how much to write about my eightieth. So much family, my darling three children - Janai, Megan and Mathew, with spouses and grandkids, Mel's equally darling daughter Emily and her husband Greg and their three sons, and Mel's son Grant and

John-Clark. My three kids organized most of the celebration, and Mel's brood kicked in to help. Family friends and my friends from the world of basketball, teaching, and poetry came to join me. I have never been sentimental about birthdays and have often forgotten important family birthdays. I have rejected celebrating most of my own days of birth, but I suppose if you reach 80, it's worth some kind of shin-dig. That I didn't request Russian food should not be interpreted as anything meaningful. I was happy for good old American ribs and coleslaw. We *did* toast with Russian Vodka, the good kind, White Gold. The toasts went out to all - family, friends and especially to Melanie and basketball buddy. I wished my sister, Ann, my fellow traveler from Harbin, Manchuria to America, had been there with us. She was planning a longer visit for Russian Easter, so she'd passed on this quick, birthday trip.

Looking back on this 80th birthday, I think the word "dazed" might well have described the state I was in for the entire afternoon. There were stories about me. Most of them I couldn't remember being a part of. *No, I don't remember trying to break your arm Barnett.* My fellow teacher, Aubrey McCreary, was there with his stories of the two of us in the basement of Reno High with the "bad" kids. There were gifts. Buzzy Jackson gave me a T-shirt with the portrait of Dr. Kwame Nkrumah, his face on the front of the shirt. Nkrumah was the George Washington of Ghana when British colonial rule ended. Melanie whispered, "Africaaaaa," in my ear. I never traveled to Ghana, but my son had. Larry Colton, my friend from Portland and one-time Phillies pitcher and fellow writer, gave me a Portland Beavers baseball hat as a friendly reminder that I was old enough to recall those long ago Pacific Coast League seasons sitting in the bleachers of Seals Stadium watching my childhood heroes. *Where have you gone Joe DiMaggio?* Bob Stanley, the Poet Laureate of Sacramento's gift was a poem:

Pop Quiz , Multiple Choice
for Tom Meschery, Happy 80th Birthday!

What's tougher?

- Getting stopped by the Japanese navy on a boat when you're three years old and spending four years as a prisoner of war, or

- Boxing Wilt Chamberlain out of the lane in the fourth quarter in a game with twenty lead changes on the road, or
- Trying to explain the correct structure of an essay to a class of sixteen-year-olds on a hot spring day, or
- Realizing that you miss the touch of the ball so much you still feel the spin on the bounce pass in the dream, or
- Being the immigrant kid who couldn't talk at first so you ran faster played harder learned the language better than they did like all the kids with the funny names like Popovich, Iguodala Barbosa, or the names that got changed like Joe Kapp, or
- You, known for being the tough guy, and then waiting so long to learn that what you loved most of all was to tell the stories, to make moments that your readers, your friends, your listeners, would *remember* – poems in the moment – the inbound pass, the screen, a dribble-step-back-fake-and-jump shot to score because you've always been a great shooter, Tomislav Nikolaevich Mescheriakov, you've seen the world and youstill want every poem, every story, every moment to make its point: *swish.*

When I was called on to speak, I could barely think of a word. I should have thanked every single person in the room but all I could think of was what I said about Melanie.

"You saved my life."

As I sat down, Melanie whispered, "And don't you forget it."

Do you understand why I continue to be charmed by this woman?

The festivities ended and cleanup began. Mel and I were sent on our way. As we walked back to our condo, something Bob Hass wrote came to mind: *Poetry is a way of living, a human activity, like baking bread or playing basketball.*

I woke up the next morning thinking that I would have to consider myself old from now on. Why had I not considered 79 to be old? I admit to certain eccentricities.

• • •

On Election Day Tuesday, November 6, 2018, Democrats took control of the House of Representatives. Melanie and I were ecstatic. Finally, there might be some oversight of the machinations of President Trump and his minions. For progressive liberals like us, this was worth cheering even with the Senate still in the death grip of Republican Senator McConnell.

New Year's Day, 2019, arrived and quickly became February 7th and my scheduled appointment with my oncologist. As usual, I was nervous. As usual, Melanie was calm. Doctor Laptalo announced that my M protein remained steady. No need for any intervention. I do not take such positive results for granted. I was aware that the calendar was not my friend. I drove home that morning forcing myself to think of anything instead of cancer. It could have been Melanie, my grandchildren, poetry, but I remember it was basketball. How many times, I asked myself, since my remission ended the previous spring when my mood darkened about my disease, had I been comforted by Steph Curry's three pointers, Draymond Green's rebounds, Klay Thompson's clutch shots? *My sport - in my blood – my comfort food.*

Mac & Cheese, Melanie calls it.

CHAPTER 58
LE GRAND TOUR AVEC BERNIE

Being a member of the Octogenarian Club is a daunting realization for any person. I believe it is more daunting for people who are programmed by what they do for a living to be more "in the moment" such as professional athletes. Ballet dancers and test pilots fall into that category. Daunting, but to be honest more scary. For that reason I was happy that Melanie and I decided to head back to Europe for what could possibly be our last big travel adventure. This trip that would last 6 weeks would not be an art tour, but one we would take on our own, *shleeping*, as they say, from country to country, hotel to hotel, starting in Amsterdam, then on to Paris, Milan, Florence and finally to Athens. We named this trip Melanie and Tom's Grand Tour *Avec* Bernie, Bernie being a 12 inch Senator Bernie Sanders' look-alike cloth doll that Melanie had purchased online. Senator Sanders was in the Democratic Primary hoping to be the Democratic Party's choice to run against President Trump in November. Being Senator Sanders' fans, we decided to introduce our favorite political candidate to Europe. He sat with us in restaurants, traveled with us on buses and in taxis, marveled at paintings and sculpture with us in museums. Everywhere we roamed, our Bernie was greeted with smiles and thumbs up, except at the Parthenon in Athens, where a scowling security believed the doll was not appropriate for a sacred site. If Bernie Sanders were running for political office in the countries in which we traveled, he'd win hands down. Or so our liberal political imaginations told us.

• • •

We began our trip in Amsterdam. Our hotel was the Max Brown. Our room was so tiny that with my wingspan I could outstretch my arms and almost touch both walls. Looking up from my bed close to the ceiling was a small basketball backboard and hoop. It was sort of spooky as if somehow someone at the hotel knew I'd played basketball. Bernie loved the Rijksmuseum. At the Van Gogh Museum, I sat transfixed in front of his painting *Wheatfield with Crows*, thinking about the winged Armageddons of my childhood in the internment camp and my friendly crows at home. Melanie wanted to know what I was smiling about. It's history, I told her. Old age is a history lesson, be it through the back door or the front. Bicycles rule the streets of Amsterdam, and I almost was run over twice.

From Amsterdam, we took the train to Paris. We stayed once again at our charming little *Hotel Lautrec Opera*, in walking distance from the *Louvre*. We decided if we could not live across the street from the La Sagrada Familia, in Barcelona, we'd live in the Mont Marte across the street from the Dali Museum. I came very close to buying a pack of Guluois and starting smoking again. I'd join the rest of the French who have never heard of lung cancer.

On Friday the 13th, we flew from Paris to Milan. Our shuttle driver took us by way of Singapore picking up extra passengers, so we missed our flight and had to take a later one, for an extra $500. We almost didn't make it to Milan. I'll let Melanie tell that story that is proof that Friday the 13th never fails to deliver.

EXCERPT FROM THE FABLED'S TRAVEL DIARY

Our flight was postponed three times and when it finally took off, was forced to return to Paris' Charles de Gaulle because the landing gear wouldn't retract. Our landing at Malpensa was uneventful and we sought a taxi, having become disillusioned with shuttles and shuttle drivers.

The taxi driver we drew was lean and bouncy and way too friendly: read aggressive. He told us he was 47 – had celebrated his birthday the day before, that he had a daughter twelve years old of whom he was "jealous."

He seemed unable to tolerate two seconds of silence and spent the hour-and-fifteen-minute- seventy-five-mile trip from the airport thumbing pictures on his telephone of his daughter, his music list, and the news. Of all of this performed while driving 120 km an hour and turning around to make constant eye contact with us, his victims. Then he told us he wanted to come to the U.S.A., to Texas, so that he could get a gun and kill. *sigh*

• • •

The turn around in midair back to Paris brought back memories of a flight in Africa when I was certain I was going to die. In this case, if death was on its way I was prepared for it to go down holding Melanie's hand and thinking of my grandchildren. As for the last comment by our crazy Milanese cabbie, I had told Melanie she shouldn't be shocked. Most Europeans thought of us a nation of gunslingers. It's what I'd practiced to be as a boy with my cap pistol dreaming of the Lone Ranger.

Testosterone, Melanie had stated with another sigh.

• • •

As much as our previous trip to Florence was an art story for us, this trip turned into a basketball story: The general manager of the Berchielli Hotel in Florence, Massimo, drove us to his neighborhood athletic club where his son, ten-year-old, Ricardo, was practicing with his team. I had agreed to observe and provide observations and suggestions and speak about the NBA. We arrived and I saw it was not just Ricardo's team, but several teams sponsored by the club. Europeans do not have athletic teams in schools, so all sports happen in private athletic clubs. The club's managers and board members were there. The stands were filled with the boys' parents. It was a bigger deal than I'd expected, and I suddenly felt as if Massimo had exaggerated my NBA status. I was long retired from the NBA. *Long in the tooth*, one might also say.

From a seat at the scorer's table, I watched the teams practice. I don't know what I expected, but what I got was an energetic and concentrated practice, surprisingly well organized and efficiently executed for such a young age group. After the skills practices ended, the teams played full court games. Once again, I was impressed by their advanced play. I thought back to Milan and Rome in 1965 when I toured with my NBA All Star teammates. Were it not for size and strength, one of these teams composed of 11-year-olds would have beaten those Italian adult teams. Watching these boys, I understood why basketball skills had advanced so fast from 1965 to 1995 when the first Italian basketball player, Stefano Rusconi, played briefly for the Phoenix Suns.

After practice, there was a Q&A. session. The boys sat on the floor in front of the stands, their parents behind them. They asked questions, and so did their parents. Ricardo asked what advice I would give them about playing basketball. I was expecting a question like that and dreading having to answer it. I began by saying that they should start out playing a lot of sports and find the one they enjoyed playing the best. I followed that up by saying to never play a sport because someone else wants you to. I looked up in the stands at the parents. I expected some frowns, but saw a lot of nodding of heads. Then I said if they wanted to be really good, like Danilo Galanari, they would have to give up a lot of their social life. Parties and things like that, I said. Massimo translated and the parents looked joyful. The kids were looking at me with their very earnest faces.

I gave out my business cards with my jersey number 14 on them to all the boys. The cards had my email address. If they had questions about the NBA, I told them, they could email me. I ended the session by telling them to think of me as their NBA grandpa. I liked the idea of having 40 or so Italian grandchildren.

When we returned home to Sacramento, Melanie planned to create a photo album of our trip in which Bernie Sanders would look out at an admiring European audience. We were hoping Bernie would be the Democratic nominee who would defeat Trump in the 2020 Presidential election. As Mel's good-old-boy-brother once said, *hope springs external.* Massimo and I continued to email each other. From time to time, I received an email from Florence that began with, *Dear Grandpa Warrior.*

The Grand Tour might be our last hurrah traveling on our own. The following year because of the advanced age of my back and knees, (my mind clear as a bell, thank you very much.) we'd have to settle for a cruise. Our thinking was Turkey, Crete and Israel.

"While we're still young," The Fabled snarked.

CHAPTER 59
RUSSIAN EASTER 2019

On Thursday April 25, 2019, my sister Ann flew in from New York City to celebrate Russian Easter on Sunday. She brought with her Hiroshi Hara, the director of photography for her documentary *An Uncommon Woman*, the life of *Rhoda Levine, the librettist and author of childrens' books.* Hiroshi accompanied Ann because he'd convinced her that they should produce a documentary of me. He said it should be called *The Mad Russian.* I considered telling him that *The Mad Manchurian* would be more accurate, but it was his project and speculative anyway. When my sister told me about this proposal over the phone, I was skeptical, but Ann was excited about the prospect. Ann remains high on my list of "can-do" people, so I won't be surprised if the film gets made. Considering my age, he'd better get started. Ann stayed with us, and Mel's son Grant graciously opened his home to Hiroshi.

Hiroshi filmed for three days before flying home, while Ann remained for an additional three days. The first day of filming took place in our condominium and on the grounds of Campus Commons. The second day, Hiroshi, Ann and I drove to the Bay Area to film those places important to our lives growing up. We began at Saint Mary's College because it was on our way. The old arena in which I played, now used for intramural sports, was open, so we were able to film the interior. My retired jersey number 31 was the only banner hanging on the wall. The other retired Gael numbers were missing. Didn't that mean the old arena belonged exclusively to me? If I was not exactly a legend in the NBA, I decided I was as for Saint Maryls. I hummed the first few lines of the school anthem, *The Bells of Saint Mary's* and felt a little foolish.

From the college, we drove to San Francisco to film the three Russian Orthodox Churches associated with our family, first, the Holy Virgin Cathedral on Fulton Street where we worshiped after we had arrived in the United States and where Ann and I took after-school Russian lessons, followed by the American Russian Cathedral of the Holy Trinity on the corner of Van Ness Avenue and Green Street. Our next stop was Mel's Drive-In for burgers and shakes and memories that Hiroshi recorded of nights my friends and I spent at Mel's, the quintessential teen hangout after movies or parties. Mel's music selection had songs from the Fifties and Sixties. Booths and tables appeared the same as they were when Bobby Randall, Barry Cummings and I hung out there. I found The Platters' *Red Sails in the Sunset* and selected it.

Well fed on burgers and nostalgia, we drove to the first apartment my sister and I lived in when we came from Aunt Maroucia's farm to San Francisco, a three-apartment flat on Clay Street. Ann and I sat on the front steps and reminisced while Hiroshi filmed us. As we were talking, a young couple exited the door that led to our old apartment. We explained to them what we were doing. They were happy to talk to us about the neighborhood. They owned the apartment. I restrained myself from asking how much they paid for it. Ann, ever the businesswoman, had the couple sign a release form, so we could use the film of them. I walked to the corner and looked up Baker Street. In the distance I could see the uber-steep block between Jackson Street and Pacific Avenue that I walked up and down every day of elementary school and, once, because I'd been dared, hurtled down on roller skates.

We filmed at the original Lowell High School at the corner of Masonic Avenue and Hayes Street that had been turned into a continuation school. The present-day Lowell High is a magnet school located in a neighborhood closer to the Pacific Ocean. Ann sat in the car, while Hiroshi kept the camera on me standing in front of the red brick gymnasium where I practiced for four years and reminisced about those high school basketball days. I heard Coach Neff's voice, *Meschery, you little sonavabitch.*

We did not attend the three-hour Easter midnight service. Hiroshi wanted to but, as we explained, there is no seating in an Orthodox church, and my sister and I were too old to stand three hours on our feet. The other option, kneeling, would put me in the hospital. *How did those ancient babushkas of my memory of childhood church services do it, I wondered.*

On Sunday morning we all drove to my daughter Janai's home for the Easter meal. Hiroshi filmed and interviewed my children and grandchildren. There were Easter eggs. My daughter Janai and her daughter, Carson, had colored them the way Russian refugees in Harbin did when they had no money for paint, using scraps of colored cloth. Janai, who is a history teacher and of my three children the most invested in our Russian traditions, explained the process. The results were something that looked like a Jackson Pollock painting. We ate *pelimini* (meat-filled dumplings), *piroshky* (baked buns filled with meat or cabbage), and Beef Stroganoff. There was beet salad. And pickles. I had been notified earlier by my Americanized children that herring in sour cream would not be appreciated. I brought a *kulich*, a traditional Russian Easter bread, like a fruit cake, but not as dense. My mother used to bake kulich in MJB coffee cans. It was one of my mother's few culinary successes. I can still smell the aroma of the baked *kulich*, just out of the oven. Janai placed the *kulich*, its dome covered with white frosting and decorated with candied sprinkles, in the center of the table. Around its base, she placed the brightly colored eggs. There was vodka and toasts. *Would Russians be Russians without vodka?* The better question might be would Russians have survived their history without vodka?

After my sister returned to New York, she emailed me that Hiroshi told her of a person he knew in Japan who would try to find the location of our internment camp and the hospital that took us in after we were bombed out. I liked it that *The Mad Russian*, if such a documentary ever materialized, would be directed by a Japanese American. I thought of my childhood friend Magnase Nagase. He would have thought that was not a coincidence.

• • •

Sadly, this June there will not be a 2019 Golden State Warriors NBA Championship Parade. A tired and injured team lost in the 6th game to the Toronto Raptors. I will miss the parade. I will miss taking my granddaughter Ruth to it. Next season the Warriors will be playing in the Chase Center, their new state-of-the-art arena in San Francisco. I'm looking forward to seeing the team back in The City where I first played as a San Francisco Warrior. One night, not long after my sister left to return to New York City, I woke up from a night's sleep and remembered that I had dreamt something about basketball, a subject that should not be unusual, except I dreamt the entire dream in Russian, the only time I had done so since I was a child. Since then, I have been dreaming more and more **in** Russian.

CHAPTER 60
NOT SO SAINTLY

In early November, 2019 I received an envelope from my friend Dmitri in Saint Petersburg. Enclosed was a three-page letter dated 1933 written by my grandfather Vladimir Lvov from his exile in Tomsk, a city in Siberia. In the accompanying note Dmitri explained that he had obtained it from a childhood friend who worked in the Tomsk central library and had accidently discovered it in an old file. To say I was surprised would be an understatement. I stared at the tiny Russian script, at the date, at the official looking stamp at the top of the first page. My first thought was of my mother. Wouldn't she have been thrilled to read a letter from her father? An actual communication. I could only imagine what information this letter contained. A firsthand account of the last years of his life? I read enough Russian to know there was no salutation to wife or children, but maybe, later in the letter in his own words, he would express how much he had missed his family. I too wanted to hear his history, in his own words what had actually happened to him. I needed to know, not what my mother believed, or my relatives surmised, or historians deduced, or his political opponents concluded. It startled me to realize that after eighty years I yearned for a grandfather. I began to read. The Russian cursive was so tiny that it would have taken me much too long to translate. The next day I hired a Russian graduate student at Sacramento State University to translate.

When the completed translation arrived. I read it slowly, making sure I understood each sentence. At first, I was puzzled. Then my confusion turned to disbelief. By the time I finished reading and re-reading the three pages I was angry. I read the letter a couple of times more to make certain I had not missed some subtlety, but I hadn't. The truth contained in the letter would have brought my mother to tears. Vladimir Nikolaievich Lvov, Ober-Procurator of the Holy Synod, and Senator in the Russian Duma was not the counter-revolutionary my mother believed him to be, although that was what this letter indicated he'd been arrested for. Nor was he a saint, nor a family man. There was not one mention of his wife and family. No, my grandfather's letter was not written by a counter-revolutionary. It was written by a Communist true-believer, innocent of the charges for which he was arrested, insisting he remained a faithful member of the Communist Party, pleading for his life. *A Communist? For God's sake. My grandfather?* The Saint who protected the Orthodox Church - a Communist atheist? Here was the father my mother and I idolized, the grandfather whose exploits behind the Iron Curtain supported me during the McCarthy years. The man who even through my adult years I revered and considered the Patriarch of our family. Here he was listing all his accomplishments on behalf of the Communist cause. Reading them made me sick to my stomach.

1) Disintegration of Wrangel's army, for which the monarchists threatened to murder me.

2) I was the first one to urge the Parisian press to recognize the Soviet Republic and this campaign had a colossal success.

3) I advocated international help to the victims of famine of 1921 – without any contributions offered by the SB's [transl. note: socialist revolutionaries and Mensheviks.

4) Openly stated the rightness of the October Revolution and Bolshevik Party. All of these actions provoked a resolute furious reaction of all of the emigrants.

What I didn't know, Wrangel's army, the famine of 1921, I researched on the internet. The facts were all there. That night I hardly slept thinking of my mother's disillusion and horror had she known of her father's betrayal. I thought of Nikolai and Lev, my cousins in Russia and their families. I thought of Alla, the dedicated family historian. I thought of the night before I left Russia in the summer of 2007, in Nikolai's dacha, all of us sitting around the dining table in *Mon Plaisir* toasting our revered Lvov ancestors down through the centuries, shot after shot of vodka, finishing bleary-eyed, raising our glasses of vodka to our grandfather, Vladimir Nikolaevich Lvov, his name on our lips like a sacrament.

According to the letter, our grandfather returned to the Soviet Union in 1922 at the request of V.I. Lenin? *Lenin, Lenin. Are you kidding me! That date – so early - so startling.* It was our family's belief that he'd returned to the Soviet in the 1930s. In 1922, the Red Army was not yet in complete control of Russia. It was possible that his wife and family had not yet crossed the border into Manchuria but were still somewhere in Siberia. Grandfather Lvov could have attempted to locate them. *Goddamn it, why hadn't he? Didn't he care?* There seemed no rational explanation. Upon his return to the Soviet Union, according to his own words he was not considered a threat to the revolution. If he'd been friendly with Lenin as the letter implied, he would have had the resources to search for his family. Were the Tolstoys correct that he didn't attempt to find his family because he'd married another woman in Paris? *Jesus H. Christ!*

Melanie suggested that my grandfather's letter could have been a pretense, trying to save his life, so he could continue his work as a counter-revolutionary. How else, she'd argued, to account for such a radical ideological transformation? "Double agent," she whispered. I could hear my mother agreeing with her, whispering back, *"Da, da, Double agent."* Perhaps. It would have been nice to believe this, but I couldn't. To me, it sounded like someone trying to save his skin for no other purpose than to stay alive. I was heartbroken.

I hesitated to send my sister a copy of the letter, but I did. A week later I got her response:

Fr: Ann
To: Tom

Well, I read this letter but, I must say, I need to read it again thoroughly a couple of times to totally grasp what it is saying. It adds yet another layer to the mystery of our grandfather. So much about his saga and Ultimate fate is contradictory. . . According to a quote by the British Ambassador at the time VN Lvov was "either a saint or a total madman."

Dr. Pipes writes about VN's sojourn in Paris and describes his crazy writings

and says that he eventually died as an indigent on the streets of Paris. We now know that to be untrue. Next, we know from our cousins Lev and especially from Nikolai, discovered in KGB files, that were opened to scrutiny at Lubyanka that VL was working to overthrow the Soviet regime (he was designated as "an enemy of the people" along with Nikolai's father and Lev's father (Nikolai pere and Vanya). This ties more closely to the arrest and accusation against VL in the letter.

I really want to think a bit more about this. Will get back to you,

Ann

• • •

Weeks went by. I was wondering why I should waste my time concerned about the life of my long-departed grandfather. I never knew him. Perhaps, from the start, he was a fictional character in a novel that I should never have opened.

Thank God, I thought we'd never hear the end of him.
As always, my wife, The Fabled, pulls no punches.

But I was not through with my grandfather Lvov. Or perhaps, I should say my grandfather Lvov was not through with me. One morning, I woke up from a dream of him, the circumstances of which I couldn't recall, but with an immense sense of gratitude for him, fictional or real, who'd helped me as a boy to survive those cruel 1950's of Senator McCarthy's Red Scare. When I needed it most, Grandpa had my back. He would remain legendary in my mind.

I said, "Thank you," and went back to sleep.

• • •

November 7 2020
From: Tom

Dear Ann,
We survived McCarthy and the Red Scare, and we've now survived Trump. What a relief. All we have left to do is survive COVID. As the final votes were being counted, and it looked like a certainty that Biden would win, I thought of us as immigrants at the time McCarthyism came to an end. Trump's policies from the start infuriated me, but what the absolute breaking point for me was his attitude on immigration. As I remember writing to you, that's when things became personal between him and me. I

believe The Mad Russian would have had an elbow or two for him. Do you remember how you felt the day we arrived by ship and passed under the Golden Gate Bridge? Our dad was waiting for us. We would be Americans. I am not sure if I've ever stopped trying to be an American and just been one. No need to comment on this, as you never seemed to question who you were. I have always admired your toughness.

Love,
Tom

• • •

The evening the media declared for Biden, Melanie and I opened a bottle of champagne. I had gone to the market, my Warriors COVID19 mask securely in place, and purchased Italian Fontina, Fois Gras *avec les truffes*, hard Italian salami, a loaf of black bread and a baguette. We celebrated Joe Biden and Kamala Harris's victory virus free, tucked safely away in our gallery home. We wished we could have shared our cheese board with our families, but we are of an age that is most at risk. And, as I promised Mel - 10 more years. At the age of 82 that might be a challenge. Even so, I remain, as I have throughout my life, cognizant of my high school basketball coach admonishing me, as he did long ago on the basketball court and as he has done from the beyond at other moments in my life, his words, crafted to fit the moment:

Stay alive Meschery - you little sonavabitch!

CHAPTER 61
DOUBLE OVERTIME

January 7, 2021
To: Ann
From: Tom

Daragya, Melitsa,

After watching yesterday's attack on our capital played over and over again on all the news channels, I have fallen into a serious depression. Melanie says it's not just this treasonous act, but all the accumulated anti-democratic acts over the last four years that just now have caught up to me. I suppose I should not have looked back. But I'm not encouraged by looking straight ahead at a country so divided either. Melanie says that having taught art history for so many years, she has come to the conclusion that one of the big problems with America is its lack of cultural history to give it any sense of what and who we are as a nation. She believes we are the *Dis-United Tribes of America.* Haven't the last four years been examples of tribalism at its worst? I ask you, wouldn't that be the height of irony that we are in the same place as this continent was before the coming of the white man? And I daresay our indigenous people knew far better who they were than we do. No need to respond. I'm heading to the medicine cabinet for my Xanax and will try to sleep for the next week or so.

February 24, 2021
Fr: Tom
To: Dmitri

Dear Dmitri,

Regarding your concern for me, don't worry about my censorship. I worry more about you having someone reading my emails to you, so I don't mention anything about your government. Trump is gone. Soon, it is possible he'll go to prison for tax evasion and fraudulent business practices. Biden and Harris are good people. They will do their best to help our country become a better place to live. The entire world must do better. Melanie and I got our second vaccine shots and are now at 94% safe from the virus. Have you and Tania had your vaccine shots yet? Young people will be the last to get shots. I can understand for your daughter's sake why Tania would want to immigrate to Canada. Canada is a better choice these days than the United States. The landscape and weather are more like Russia and its politics is more progressive than America's. But I understand completely when you say you cannot leave Russia. Your flesh is the earth that is Russia. We return to the earth or our ashes do. I have never felt completely American, nor have I felt completely Russian. I told you once that my soul is Russian but my heart is American. For most of my life I've felt caught straddling the divide between the two cultures. I suppose the question I've wanted answered is can I be both? I've finally come to believe no, I can't. Which, although I am a naturalized American citizen, leaves me without a country. It does not leave me, however, without an identity. I will be remembered for the various lives I've lived: husband, father, basketball player, teacher, poet, and novelist. But of all of them, I will remember myself mostly on the basketball court. The Basketball court is my country, its borders the familiar end-lines and base-lines. It is a country that I know best and from which I can never be displaced.

With all my love,
Tomislav Nikolaevich Mescheriakov
Cumachedshe Pycckee
(The Mad Russian)

· · ·

With the help of anti-depressions and the determination not to watch any political news, I recovered from my depression that had started a few days after the attack on the capital. My anxiety subsided into a low grade feeling of discontent with the American body politic. During my depression I could barely read let alone write. By early spring, I began writing again.

Life, of course, was anything but normal as COVID continued to mutate and threaten the world. Melanie and I have done our best to stay safe as have most people who are not anti-vaxxers. But the vaccines were working, and people were beginning to feel they could once again be with each other, spending more time with family, and hugging again after 2 years.

My daughter Megan visited with Grace and Ruth, my granddaughters. We didn't wear masks. Having lived in Spain as grade schoolers, Grace and Ruth speak fluent Spanish. Grace is fluent in French and Ruth is well on her way to fluency. Between coffee and pastries, I spoke to them in my halting French, and they smiled, indulging my attempt at grandfatherly solidarity. Not to be outdone, Melanie raised one finger and announced she too could speak French. "Avec," she said proudly, and we all laughed.

Melanie and I have now started meeting with her two grandsons, John-Clark and Jaxon for occasional Saturday brunches. The boys and I talk hoops. Jaxon talks about his goal to be a firefighter. Melanie is excited because John-Clark has decided he would like to try his hand at drawing.

Life is better run to, not from.

• • •

My numerous rejections by literary agents of my memoir and my three sports novels had soured me on agents, so I sent out my first attempt at a mystery novel *A Brovelli Brothers Mystery: The Case of the '61 Chevy Impala*, to publishers that advertised they read manuscripts directly. I was not overly confident. Melanie reminded me by way of encouragement that Tony Hillerman was rejected 36 times before his first Lieutenant Leaphorn and Sergeant Joe Chee Navajo mystery novels were accepted. I'd reminded her that I'd heard that before in New York City from literary agent Philp Spitzer. It didn't gladden my heart then; it didn't impress me now. Much to my surprise I didn't have to wait for more than two rejections.

On the morning of April_____ 2021, I received a call from *Epicenter/ Coffeetown Press* out of Seattle, Washington. The woman on the phone introduced herself as Jennifer McCord. She was an associate publisher and editor and she loved my amateur sleuth novel. I'm not exaggerating that I felt slightly faint hearing the word love used to describe my writing. I would not have thought of it at the time, but it is one of the truths in the business of professional writing, whether fiction or nonfiction, that what a writer needs to succeed is one person, agent or publisher, to love his or her work. It is especially true, as in my case, that Jennifer McCord followed up her praise with a contract proposal for the mystery and for two sequels, which would make a total of three novels. Yes, I'd be delighted. Delighted, I repeated, delighted. I might have used the word delighted more often than that. If I were trying to sound like a cool author I should have controlled myself but I couldn't. That I had already published five books of poetry skipped my mind as I imagined the significance of authorship. The word author doesn't seem to apply to poetry. You're not an author of poetry, you simply are - a poet. After we hung up, I thought of all the mystery and detective fiction writers Melanie and I had read over the years, Tony Hillerman at the top of our list, but also Ian Rankin, Donna Leon, Peter Robinson, Michael Connelly, Sue Grafton, and Henning Mankell. I was now one of the bench players on their team. If I kept writing, I might someday be a starter.

When the contract arrived on May 5th, I was delighted to sign it immediately and had it back in the mail the same day before they could change their minds.

I returned home from the post office and told Melanie that with two more mysteries to write, I better get busy. There was only so much time on the game clock.

My wife, The Fabled, said, "Your life is not a basketball game."

"You could have fooled me," I replied.

• • •

The good news didn't stop. I had sent Jennifer McCord my memoir. She'd read it and wanted it too. Later, even more surprisingly, after reading the manuscripts of my three sports novels, she wanted *The Kid Has Hops*. By now, I was no longer given to fainting spells. I was gloriously happy. Melanie was right. My life was not a basketball game, but so much of the language of sports, like the Russian language, is in my blood that I can't but think of my life in terms of athletics. Every morning, I sit at my computer and write. It is not unlike all the years I spent on the basketball court. These days my wife quips, she knows where to find me. When I was a youngster growing up in San Francisco on days when I was not in school, my parents knew where to find me, on one of the many playground basketball courts of San Francisco - as they say in today's language of sports – hooping.

• • •

3/4/22
Fred Hetzel
to me

Loved the article in this morning's NY Times. (Not to mention the handsome photos of two very photogenic athletes.) However, I need to refresh your memory that it was Al Attles not Uncle Wilt who saved you from one altercation with Zelmo Beaty. During the brawl, Keith Erickson and I had ringside seats from under the scorer's table.

Please say hello to the "Destroyer." and many thanks for the memories.

Best from Fred

The article my teammate from our Warriors' 1965 season is referring to is the one published on Tuesday, March 2, 2022 on the 60th anniversary of Wilt Chamberlain's 100 point game. Three days before, Melanie and I were chauffeured from our home in Sacramento to the home of my Warrior teammate Al Attles in Oakland. Al and I were the two highest scorers after Wilt. Sitting together on a couch in Al's living room, we listened to a recording of the last quarter of that fabulous performance and remembered and commented. It was great fun, as often nostalgia can be. Or not, Melanie adds.

On our drive home from Al's, I thought about our 1961 Philadelphia team. Of the starting rotation, Al and I were the only players still living. The Times' reporter had described both of us as legends of the game. The logo of our NBA Retired Players Association is an orange basketball with the word *Legends* on it. For many years I taught British literature, filled with stories and epic poems that combined both legends and myths, like the Tales of King Arthur and the epic of Beowulf. Unlike myths, such as Beowulf, which are stories invented to instruct us about life, with no basis in fact; the sources of legends are based to some extent on truths. There was, in fact, a Celtic Warrior called Arturus from which the legend of King Arthur grew. Through telling and retelling, the truths became larger than life legends. I could understand how Wilt Chamberlain and other superstars of sports could be legends. But did Wilt really pick a silver dollar off the top of a backboard? Why not? He was *Wilt, the Stilt*, already legendary by the time he reached high school.

I did not claim legendary status except, perhaps, as it applied to my part in our Russian family history. I could imagine a chronicler of our family writing about the grandson of Vladimir Nikolaevich Lvov, himself a legend, explaining how that frail diseas- inclined boy in Manchuria wound up in America as a professional basketball player. The chronicler was not me, he had added the word *frail*, which I was not, having been born weighing 14 pounds and sturdy throughout infancy. But I was, in truth, the unwitting host of several serious diseases. So, you see, already, my story had begun its journey toward legend. On my father's side of the family, he descended from the legendary cossack warrior Matvai Mescheriak who helped conquer Siberia? How had that legend begun? How far had I kicked the ball in my elementary school during recess? Over the schoolyard fence was what I remember. But much later in life at a dinner get-together of some of our elementary school graduates, assured me that kicked ball wound up not only over the fence but into the street where it struck a passing car. At another time, the first punch I threw at Clyde Lovellette that I remembered missing was retold to me as bloodying Lovellette's nose. Had I really blocked Wilt's finger-roll in preseason camp in my rookie year? I knew I did , but at a team sponsored banquet in which Al Attles was the speaker, my teammate called Wilt's attempted shot a dunk, which made my effort far more difficult - the stuff of legends. Was I a legend because I was an NBA player who wrote and published poetry and novels? It was certainly unusual enough that a number of newspapers had written about it in terms that made me out to be a far more important writer than I was. Recently Melanie and I were leaving a restaurant, and as we passed a table, a person at the table said, "That's the NBA player who writes poetry." Someday, who knows, I might hear, "Hey, there goes the old NBA player who won the Pulitzer Prize."

Now that would be something worthy of a legend.

The End

CHAPTER 62
THE END

A recent article written by Jason Quick in *The Athletic* is a welcome relief from the stories that have been published about me: Manchurian born, immigrant Russian, survivor of a Japanese internment camp, etc, etc. This article is about life in my old age. It is about my wife, Melanie and our love story. It is about a new career I have embarked upon in my eighties as a mystery writer, and it is about staying one step ahead of cancer. It comes at a time in our lives when Melanie has joined me as a member of the over eighty club.

Oh, say it isn't so.

It is as much her story as it is mine. For this, I'm immensely grateful to Jason for writing it with such sensitivity. *Melanie says she wants to adopt Jason.*

The article begins with me in my office working on various writing projects. I'm referred to as *The Poet*, not the NBA basketball player, ex-Golden State Warrior and Super-Sonic and not the high school English teacher, which was my career for 24 years after my NBA days were finished. According to the writer, *The Poet* is usually found every morning in his office *tidying up his memoir or working on his new mystery novel*. Jason ends by saying, *but then there is his poetry – there is always his poetry.*

Jason is right about poetry. I have been writing poems most of my adult life. Like basketball, poetry is as much a part of me as the skin in which I live.

As Melaine often quips, she always knows where she can find me, watching hoops or sitting in front of my computer. However, this morning, the writer is wrong. I *am* seated in front of my computer, but

I am *not* working on my memoir or my third mystery novel. I am not writing a poem. What I'm doing is trying to craft a response to a recent email from Dmitri, my dear friend in Saint Petersburg, Russia, who has informed me of his plan to take his daughter - my God-child - and secretly leave Russia. The word he uses is *Pobeg* - escape. It must be done secretly because Vladimir Putin, the dictator of Russia, has closed the Russian borders because more and more Russians are fleeing this autocratic state. Especially the men of an age to be inducted into the army to fight Putin's illegal war against Ukraine. As of today, that war will be beginning its second tragic year.

I'm frightened that Dmitri is attempting to leave his homeland too late. It would have been better had he decided to take his family out of Russia a year earlier with his son, who is now safe in Finland. But I sense in his writing that Dmitri is desperate and is willing to take the risk. So, what else should I say to my friend that might be meaningful?

I might begin by telling him that I completely understand his fear because we in America are approaching a presidential election and facing the horrifying prospect of another Donald Trump presidency. One that will bring with it his commitment to autocracy. One writer recently labeled it, "Christian Authority."

I consider the possibility that the writer had the Inquisition in mind.

I want to say to Dmitri that we, too, are living in scary times, even as we have just passed through some of the scariest times in our country's recent history. But I'm guessing Dmitri would not be very sympathetic. As he wrote to me once, "You only had Trump for four years, we have had Putin for twenty-four years."

Dmitri's plan will take him and his daughter to Kazakhstan first. From there Dmitri believes it will be easier to reach the west. That's where he will leave his daughter and her mother and return to Russia. He mentions that, on his return, they might shoot him. He sounds unconcerned about the prospect. I shouldn't be surprised. In a much earlier email, Dmitri explained he could never leave his native land. Dmitri is a retired basketball player for the Saint Petersburg Spartak of the Euro-league, he's turned Russan mystic in his old age. I've told him he belongs in a Dostoyevsky novel. He says he prefers Turgenev, and I counter with Tolstoy. I remind Dmitri of these conversations in my letter. I add that I would prefer he not wind up a *Dead Soul*. I know he'll appreciate the reference to the title of the Gogol

novel. I write, be careful. I write *pozhalyta*, please. I stare at my screen.
I do not touch the send key. I feel that if I send this email, Dmitri will
vanish from the earth. This does not make any sense, except I'm feeling
very fragile lately. Melanie feels the same way. We both agree we shouldn't
watch so much news, but then we do. We're like two kids frightened at a
horror movie, opening and closing our fingers over our eyes.

I press the send key and watch the computer screen turn momentarily
dark as my letter makes its electronic flight to Dmitri in Saint Peterburg.

I whisper, "Good Luck, *moy brat.*"

My brother.

• • •

At the end of March, Melanie and I flew to New York City for my
sister's eight-eighth birthday. Accompanying us was my daughter Megan
and her husband Brendan. They were going to visit their daughter Grace,
but also as a kindness to us, helping us make our way through the intricacy
of airports and the streets of Manhattan. Grace is the same young woman
who spent time with us in Paris, whose fluent French kept us from
getting lost on numerous occasions. Grace lives in Brooklyn and works
as a cataloguer for Swann's antiquarian auction gallery, her dream job. My
son, Matthew, flew in from Nashville to join us for my sister's celebratory
dinner at her favorite Russian restaurant *Marie & Vanna's*. And celebratory
it was. Militsa Ann Mescherikova no longer takes airplanes, so this was
the opportunity I had to embrace her. This thought flies in the face of my
sister's belief that she will live to be a hundred.

Ann and I toasted our Russian ancestors. The vodka was ice-cold
Beluga. None of that popular French vodka, thank you very much. As we
downed our vodka, my head spun with images of our life together: years in
the Japanese internment camp, the fire-bombing of Tokyo, growing up in
San Francisco during the McCarthy period, our personal political divide
and our reconciliation, together still, Tomislav Nikolaevich and Militsa
Nikolaevna. We made certain that there was enough vodka left for a toast
to honor our grandfather, Vladimir Nikolaevich Lvov executed by the
Bolsheviks, an uncommon man, buried in a common grave somewhere
in Siberia.

• • •

Melanie and I returned to our Sacramento home knowing that nothing had changed in our country since we departed a week ago. But I *will* remember that I had embraced my sister, if this turns out to be our last time together. And that I had the chance to thank her for giving me Mishka, her teddy bear, and having had the courage, as American bombs dropped around us, to rush back into our burning internment camp to save my teddy bear from the flames. And that she showed me how to stand up to ignorant people who were prejudiced against Russians and immigrants.

And that Melanie and I once again had been together in the Metropolitan Museum looking with pleasure at the Rembrandt paintings.

And that the hot dogs sold on the streets of New York City were as tasty as ever.

A week after Melanie and I returned from New York City, I received an email from Dmitri, informing me that his request for a travel visa to Amerca was turned down. The officials in Khzakstan felt he was trying to escape Russia. I remembered the time he and I walked through the Saint Petersburg Tikhvin Cemetary in the fall of 2007, stopping at the graves of Dostoevsky, Mussorgsky, Glinka, and Tchaikovsky, the day before I was to leave Russia and fly home to America, and Dmitri telling me that this would be a good place to be buried.

• • •

The Mad Manchurian is scheduled to be published in October at the start of the next NBA season. I will be watching my Warriors in whatever iteration of the Dubs they will be. I am planning more mystery novels and Melanie and I are collaborating on a collection of poems about Art. I am writing the poems, Melanie will do the sketches. All of our children are healthy and so are our darling grandchildren. There is more life yet to be lived.

POSTSCRIPT

SACRAMENTO — The poet has been upstairs in his office, tapping at the keyboard on various projects. Most of his mornings begin this way ... so much work to do. Some days he tends to <u>his blog</u> — his most recent subject the NBA All-Star Game — and on other days he tidies up his memoir that is nearing publication. Or he may put the finishing touches on another of <u>his mystery novels</u>. And of course, his poetry. There is always his poetry.

Much of his poetry chronicles his remarkable life. He was born in Manchuria to Russian parents and lived in an internment camp in Tokyo during World War II. After moving to America as a youth, he became an accomplished professional basketball player who did more than just start alongside Wilt Chamberlain, including his 100-point game. He was a 1963 All-Star and the first player to have his number retired by the Golden State Warriors. He was also a failed bookstore owner, coached basketball everywhere from Portland to Africa, and spent 24 years teaching high school English.

His eclectic path is made more fascinating in that at age 85 he refuses to become idle and bask in the accomplishment of a life well lived. He says he is "obsessed" with being productive, which for him means writing. He has authored five books of poetry. Written two memoirs. Six novels. He maintains a semi-regular blog. The majority of his literary work has come after he turned 70. He tries to explain the "why" behind his obsession but ultimately concedes that perhaps poet Alfred Lord Tennyson put it best in *Ulysses*:

> *How dull it is to pause, to make an end*
> *To rust unburnished, not to shine in use!*
> *As though to breathe were life*

It's that last line that particularly resonates with the poet, Tom Meschery. *Just because you are breathing doesn't mean you are living.*

In 2005, he was diagnosed with multiple myeloma, a blood cancer that has no cure. Doctors guessed he had five years to live.

"I developed a sense of I better get moving and doing the things I wanted to do," he says. "So I became more dedicated to writing poetry. Because I wasn't sure how much time I had left."

Now 19 years later, he is as prolific as ever, even as he sacrifices an afternoon to break from his computer and regale a visitor with stories. He credits medical science, and in particular the drug Revlimid, for keeping his cancer in remission. But he also feels something deeper, something more powerful, has been behind his late-life renaissance: a love story. His love story.

He is not big on sentimentality, lest it come across as maudlin. However, he is a romantic, and therefore acknowledges that his love story is more than just a poet falling for an artist. Like his poetry, which he says "seems to come out of nowhere," she came from an online dating site and changed his life. Not only changed it, but played a role in saving it.

"I think love acted as a barrier to the cancer," Meschery says. "It was like the door was closed. Maybe it wasn't locked, but the love was holding onto the door and not letting the cancer in. And that kind of love changed my attitude toward living. I started spending all my time thinking about living, rather than dying."

When Tom Meschery received his cancer diagnosis in 2005, he was already in a bit of a spiral. He was newly divorced and had just retired from a teaching job he loved. Living in Truckee, Calif., a ski town on the outskirts of Lake Tahoe, he had become engulfed with loneliness. He was 68 and wrestling with his purpose in life. Now, faced with a diagnosis that sounded like a death sentence, he slipped into what he called a suicidal depression.

His spiral was palpable. After separate visits following his diagnosis, his three children — daughters Janai and Megan and son Matthew — all left concerned.

"We were all really worried about him," Matthew said. "Not just because of the cancer, but also the circumstances of him being alone up on the mountain, just going through that mostly by himself."

The siblings remember comparing notes after visits. They all remarked how the house they grew up in — one filled with activity, laughter, lively discussion — had become so quiet.

"It was a house that was always filled with people, a very social place, and dad was always the one holding court," Janai said. "And the contrast ... was hard on all of us."

By 2008, Meschery could no longer suppress his depression. With Matthew visiting, Meschery remembers halting the ironing of a shirt and blurting out to his son: I'm lonely.

Matthew made a suggestion.

Go online, dad. Everybody does it.

So he put himself out there. The poet went on his first date.

"I wasn't particularly impressed," he sniffed.

His second foray on the dating site seemed improbable from the get go. Her name was Melanie Marchant, and her profile picture was stunning. There is no way, he reasoned, that she is in her 60s; she looks 30. And it seemed too perfect that like he, she was creative, an accomplished painter located two hours away in Sacramento. For a month, they chatted online and on the phone. They would talk about literature, cooking, their children.

On Valentine's Day 2008 a first date was arranged at a Turkish restaurant in downtown Sacramento. He was late. As he hurried into the restaurant, she was waiting with the maître d, toe-tapping in mock disgust. She playfully stuck her tongue out at him.

They exchanged cards. His card to her featured the poem *Wild Geese* by Mary Oliver. The poem represented his vulnerability, his willingness to be open.

> *You do not have to be good.*
> *You do not have to walk on your knees*
> *for a hundred miles through the desert repenting.*
> *You only have to let the soft animal of your body*
> *love what it loves.*
> *Tell me about despair, yours, and I will tell you mine.*
> *Meanwhile, the world goes on.*

Her card for him? A Valentine left over from one of her grandchildren, featuring the Superhero Batman. Almost two decades later, it still humors him.

After dinner, they went to her place. She said she had a surprise for him. As they went up the stairs, he became enraptured. Lining the walls of the staircase were religious icons. He was taken back to his youth, and his Russian Orthodox roots. Then, the surprise: she had rented "Ratatouille" — the animated movie about a rat who has a nose for cooking — which played off their frequent conversations about recipes and cuisine.

"And that was it, babe. I was in love," he says, throwing his hands in the air. "As I drove back to the mountains that night, I knew this was going to be a lifetime relationship. I just knew that she and I were going to be together for the rest of our lives."

One year after their first date, on Valentine's Day 2009, they were married.

She had been divorced for 30 years and simply says "if you go 30 years, you know when you find something." They connected over their creative curiosities and their love of literature — she estimates in their first year dating they spent between $2,000-$3,000 on books. And soon, she became his trusted editor. He figures she has edited 53,000 pages of his writing.

"I would go through his manuscripts and write "Boooooooooring!" Melanie says chuckling. "But I think his writing is wonderful. I do worry when I ask him how he slept, and he says 'Not well …' because that means he has written another book in his head. He's got three or four of them up there now."

He says she has become his muse, but more accurately she has become somewhat of a life coach. She calls him Thomas and he calls her Mel, and they are constantly engaged in playful banter, trying to get the other to chuckle. One of her favorite pastimes is charting what she considers the most handsome players in the NBA (De'Aaron Fox, Steph Curry and Harrison Barnes top the current list). However, she turns stern and blunt when it comes to his cancer. She is adamant that our bodies are not separate from our minds, and from the onset of their relationship, she has conditioned his mind to revel in the now rather than dread what could be ahead.

"When he told me he had cancer, I said, 'Yeah? I know a lot of people who have cancer. When you are 70, people get cancer,'" Melanie said. "I don't do drama. I don't do sobbing. What I'm good at is, if there is a problem, it's not a challenge. You just take it and solve it. And the man I met was so healthy and happy … he has cancer? Not today. That's just how I felt."

His whole mindset changed. He stopped thinking so much about the future, and instead embraced what was in front of him. There was poetry to write, grandchildren to enjoy, dinners to be had, and basketball games to watch.

"When I met Mel, I knew that I had found the love of my life," Meschery said. "And from that point on, I became more positive about myself, and about my cancer, and about how long I would live. I just couldn't whine about it with her, she wouldn't stand it. She inspired me to just let it go, and trust my instincts."

He is on a maintenance dose of Revlimid — 28 days on the drug, 10 days off — and every three months he has blood drawn to chart his cell count and presence of proteins. Every test since he has met Melanie has shown the cancer to be in remission.

"And we laugh about it: Another three months of putting up with me," Meschery says. "It has become a much more casual conversation, almost like it's not life-threatening anymore. And I think that was all her doing, which became my doing. It was like she passed on this belief system to me, and gave it to me as a gift."

NBA players from the 1960s would likely chuckle at the idea of Meschery as a poet, trumpeting the powers of love. To them, he was the *Mad Manchurian* — a 6-foot-7 bear of a man who was known for his intensity and physicality, which sometimes morphed into rage. He played power forward, and after 778 career games — six seasons with the Warriors and four with the Seattle SuperSonics — Meschery posted averages of 12.7 points and 8.6 rebounds. But as his nickname suggests - he was as known for his temperament as he was for his skill.

He once grabbed a chair during a game and chased Lakers center Darrall Imhoff into the stands. And he remembers fighting Philadelphia's Chet Walker, and after both were ejected, charging at him in the back hallway.

He has yet to reconcile with the dichotomy between how he played and how he views himself. He addressed his unease in his last book of poetry, "Clear Path," with the poem *Rumors*.

He writes of his wife on an airplane, and a passenger remarking to her that Meschery "was the meanest son-of-a-bitch I'd ever seen play basketball."

> *there was my epitaph being written*
> *at ten thousand feet above the earth*

by a stranger who might have seen me play
or maybe not at all, and just heard from someone
else that I was mean. How rumors start. How unjust
a life can be, viewed through someone else's eyes.

"It always shocked me that I often reacted so violently on the court," Meschery says today. "I know in my heart I was not a violent man. But if you experience violence once in yourself, I think you are forever going to second guess the possibility that it is a part of your personality. And it can hang there for a lifetime. I can't look in the mirror and see myself as a mean son-of-a-bitch. But I know there was a part of me … and that poem was part of that reflection that I sensed, and regrettably so, that there is something in me that would allow anger to enter. And it's not a good feeling."

He also never bridged the barrier between him and his father, whom he loved but with whom he struggled to connect. His father wanted him to go into the military, and never watched him play basketball, deeming it unworthy as a profession. It was his father who first opened Meschery's eyes to poetry, as he would recite poems in Russian at the dinner table, unafraid to weep. Meschery says one of the great regrets in his life is not arriving in time to say goodbye to his father before he died. In his first collection of poetry, "Nothing We Lose Can Be Replaced," his piece entitled *Tom Meschery* is essentially a letter to his father who once asked 'What kind of work is this for a man?'

> "*Old immigrant, I admit all this*
> *too late. You died before I could explain*
> *newspapers call me a journeyman.*
> *They write I roll up my sleeves*
> *and go to work. They use words*
> *like hammer and muscle to describe me*
> *…father, you would have been proud of me:*
> *I labored in the company of large men.*"

Meschery also recounted the night Wilt Chamberlain scored 100 points against the Knicks in 1962. Meschery started beside Chamberlain and played 40 minutes, amassing 16 points and seven rebounds. In the poem *Wilt,* he captured a viewpoint from the team bus: the contrast between a historic night of work on the hardwood and the ordinary, every-day life in the Pennsylvania countryside.

> *"As a rookie I watched*
> *Wilt score a century in one game*
> *in Hershey, Pa., with the smell*
> *of chocolate floating through the arena*
> *…but mostly, what I remember about that game*
> *is this: …on the bus driving through the dark Amish countryside,*
> *outside a farmer in a horse and buggy,*
> *hurrying home in the all*
> *too brief light of his lantern*

He has more than 100 poems published about sports, and quips that he is subconsciously trying to match the 2,841 personal fouls for which he was whistled during his NBA career. When asked if he ever reflects on the breadth and depth of his life's work, he pauses then equates measuring his life accomplishments to evaluating his poetry.

"I think I've done the best I could," Meschery said. "If I look at life like a whole series of poetry … I can only pick out 15 or 20 poems out of the entire collection that I think are truly inspired poetry. I am just a poet. But I recognize I've written some really, really good poems. But I also recognize that a lot of my poetry is … meh. Not bad. Not awful. And that's okay. I'm not unhappy about it. That's a little bit the way life is. Can you look at your life and honestly say that most of your life has been inspired? Probably not. But you do pick out those moments when you did really good. And I think I've been able to do that. But at the same time, I'm not so egotistical to believe that every moment of my life has been a Kareem Abdul-Jabbar sky hook."

There was another force that helped pull Meschery out of his malaise following his cancer diagnosis. It was a friend from long ago, one with which he hadn't kept in touch: basketball.

In 2006, Matthew, concerned about his father's well being, bought him NBA League Pass, a satellite subscription that provided coverage for every NBA game. By then, basketball had become an afterthought for Meschery. He had not been involved in the NBA since 1976, when he finished a two-year stint as an assistant under Lenny Wilkens in Portland. And he hadn't been involved in basketball period since 1985, when he went to West Africa to coach teams in Mali, Côte d'Ivoire, Gabor and the Republic of the Congo.

When he tuned in, his interest in the NBA was rekindled. He was drawn to his former team, the Warriors, and that 2006 team — an uptempo, free-wheeling and stylistic squad coached by Don Nelson and led by Baron Davis, Monte Ellis, Stephen Jackson and Jason Richardson — stirred him. He was once again inspired by the game he once played.

"I hadn't kept up with the NBA, but once I started watching this new version of basketball, I went crazy. I just loved it," Meschery said. "The ball was moving ... they were flying through the air ... and I was just astounded these guys could do this stuff."

Then, in 2010, under the new ownership of Joe Lacob, the Warriors reached out to Meschery. The organization wanted to reconnect with its past. Meschery, the first NBA All-Star not born in America, and the first Warrior to have his number retired, was brought back into the fold. He was invited to games. Introduced to players. He rode in all four championship parades, including 2022, when Warriors star Klay Thompson spotted from the team bus Meschery riding on the parade route on Market Street. Thompson got off the bus, and while holding the Larry O'Brien trophy, beelined for Meschery, wrapping him in a bear hug.

"There was a time when we were worried about my dad losing a sense of himself," Matthew said. "Basketball was a big part of his life experience and who he is, and the Warriors helped bring that back."

Before this season, the Warriors asked Meschery to write a poem to commemorate Golden State's new City Edition uniforms, which paid homage to the San Francisco cable cars. Meschery recited *Mason Street Line* at the unveiling.

"When I think back on my cancer, love saved me and helped cure me," Meschery said. "But I think the Warriors had a little something to do with it, too."

There is nothing poetic about how the poet handles the moments when the inevitable thoughts come, the thoughts of dying, of the cancer eventually winning.

"I'd be lying if I told you I don't think about it from time to time," Meschery said. "I think anybody who reaches the age of 85 knows they don't have much time left. But I don't dwell on it."

When those moments arrive, he finds he is usually in bed, and the shortness of time overcomes him.

"Then I have a little mantra I say to myself: Tom, you are not going to die tomorrow. And Tom, you are not going to die in the next week. And probably not for the next six months. More likely, not for another year. So f--- it, get on with your life."

Then, he says, he goes back to sleep, intent on seeing his grandchildren, seeing his latest works published, including his memoir "*The Mad Manchurian*" in August, and in October the publication of «*The Case of the VW Hippie Bus*," the third installment in his Brovelli Brothers mystery novels.

In the meantime, he spends most of his nights watching the Warriors, or the Kings. Melanie is often nearby, flipping pages of the latest book she is reading, pausing briefly to make a quip or note the handsomeness of an opposing player.

"I call her my basketball buddy," Meschery said. "And she says 'That's exactly what every woman wants to hear.'"

The point is no longer how long he will live, he says, but rather doing what is enjoyable and productive. That he has found love with Melanie, and in turn found his muse and purpose, gives him a bittersweet vantage on his sunset.

"I think it makes you fear death more," he says. "I'm really going to miss living. The idea of not seeing my grandchildren, the idea of not being able to write a poem, to enjoy a meal ... that can be quite terrifying. But you can't live your life worrying about death."

And so he continues to appreciate living. And laughing. And loving. And ever the poet, he continues writing.

It was three years ago when Meschery wrote the poem *2,841 Personal Fouls*. It has little to do with his basketball career, and more to do with his love story. In the poem, he laments that the "thought of dying still pisses me off" and he equates his anger to the unfairness he felt with many of the 2,841 fouls for which he was whistled. But he counters with the outlook Melanie has so ingrained in him.

"*This morning, didn't I wake up to sunlight
and a warm breeze? Didn't my wife
poke her head into the office
to tell me she loved me? I flavor
my coffee with honey that is sweet as life.
I should live a little longer.*

About the Author

Tom Meschery, born Tomislav Nikolaevich Mescheriakov in Harbin, Manchuria, (China) is an ex-NBA player for the Golden State Warriors and Seattle Sonics, and a retired high school and college English teacher. A graduate of the University of Iowa's Writers Workshop, he has published six collections of poetry. His Brovelli Brothers Mystery Series, beginning with *The Case of the '61 Chevy Impala* and *The Case of the '66 Ford Mustang*, are now available at bookstores and on line at  Amazon. His memoir, The Mad Manchurian is forthcoming. Meschery has coached in the NBA, and traveled to West Africa where he helped coach national teams. He was inducted into the California Bay Area Sports Hall of Fame and the State of Nevada Writers' Hall of Fame. Meschery has been described as the NBA's Poet Laureate. His jersey, number 14, was retired by the Golden State Warriors and hangs in the rafters of Chase Center Arena along with his team mates' Wilt Chamberlain's number 13, and Rick Barry's number 24. Tom Meschery lives in Sacramento, CA with his wife, painter and art historian, Melanie Marchant.

Grand Relative Nikolai Alexandrovich. artist and architect 1753 – 1803 Tretyakov Galleria, Moscow, Russia.

Russian Leaning Tower. The architect is Nikolai Alexandrovich.

Maternal Grendmother, Lvov, nee Tolstoy, Harbin, Manchuria, 1930.

Grandma Tolstoy as young girl.

Lvov family, Harbin, Manchuria. L – R Standing wife of my mom's brother Gregori; Gregori; my mothr, Vanya (Johny) youngest brother; Nathaniel. Seated Maria Tolsova, my grandmother.

My father Nokolai Mescherikov's Cadet School Class. Samara, Russia 1913.

My father, Nikolai Mescheriakov, Lieutenant in White Russian Army during
Bolshevik Revolution.

Nikolai Tostoy, My mothere's favorite cousin Russia, 1918.

Lvov extended family, Russia, 1914. Grandfather Vladimir Nikolaevich Lvov 2nd from left

From L – R My mom, her mother, V.N. Lvov. Oldest brother, Nikolai.

L to R: American consulate, Harbin, Manchuria 1936. My mother top row, sixth from the left.

My uncle, Bishop Nathaniel.

Below: L to R: Nikolaii, my mom's oldest brother and my mom. Tolstoy cousins,
Bagorouslan, Russia.

Senator VN Lvov, Russian
Duma 1914.

Ann & Tom toddlers, Harbin,
Manchuria.

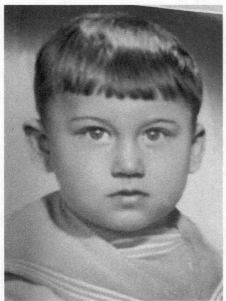

Tom's childhood photograph.

My sister Melitsa Ann and Me.
Harbin, Manchuria, 1940.

Ann and Mischka,
Harbin, Manchuria
1938.

Miss Laura Mauk, Japan 1940.
Missionary, who taught my sister
and I English.

Stamdomg center front: Mr. Katagawa our inernment camp director in U.S. to visit.

Ann and I with nun taken
as we arrived in the United
States after World War II.
San Franciso Chronicle,
August 1946.

Aunt Marousia's father Prince
Krapotkin, Fallon, CA.

Aunt Marousia. Prindess Krapotkin with her son Alex,

Ann, Tom with Dad at Clay
Street, 1951.

Proof of me on my naturalization document.

Grant Elemntary 8th grade class. Standing in the back row, L to R I'm the 4th from the left.

1956 Tom Meschery, Lowell High School.

1958 Saint Mary's Gaels WCC championship season.

My mother, me, my sister Ann, and Dad at graduation from Saint Mary's College, CA 1961.

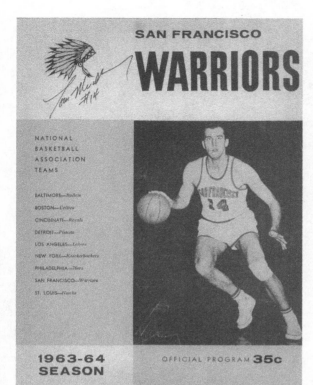

1964 Meschery coverr of program.

Meschery dancing with Enid, Monrovia, Liberia summer of 1964.

Basketball Rules book in
French used on my first trip
to West Africa. Senegal 1964.

Tom coaching basketball players in Mali, West Africa 1964.

Tom coaching Algerian basketball Team. Algiers, 1965.

1965 NBA All Star Tour
in Lebanon.

San Francisco Airport, back after upsetting 76ers in game 5 of the 1967 NBA Finals. L- R me holding daughter Janai; Rick Barry holding son, Scooter; Nate "The Great" Thurmond behind us.

Warriors retire my my jersey, number 14 before my first game back in Bay Area as a Sonic. L to R. My Saint Mary's College coach Jim Weaver; my sister, Ann, my mother. Warrior GM, Bob Ferrick, Me, Warriors' broadcaster Hank Greenwald.

Retiring from Sonics & NBA ceremony, May 1971 L to R: Sonics' Owner, Sam Schulman, presenter, Sonics' GM Dick Vertlieb, me, holding daughter Megan.

1976 My bookstore, Truckee Book and Tea in Triuckee, CA.

My children with my mom L to R: Kneeling, Janai, Matthew standing behind my mother, Megan kneeling.

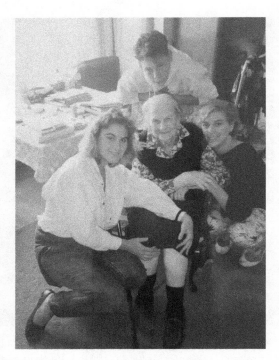

L to R: My induction into Bay Area Sports Hall of Fame with Rick Barry, me, Bill King, broadcaster for the Warriors, Raiders and Oakland A's, Tennis legend Rosie Cassls and Bill Shoemaker.

Teaching British
Literature at Reno High
School, Reno, NV 1998

Anniversary of 1963 Western Division Champs # 45 Add L to R: Announcer,
Coach Alex Hannum, Gary Phillips, Wayne Hightower, me, Nate Thurmond, Wilt
Chamberlain.

Spring 2005 Meschery with students on the last day after teaching High School English for 24 years.

Me and Yeats

Russian sports newspaper #48 Summer, Saint Petersburg, 2007. Seated 3nd from the left, Jerry Lucas, I'm 4th from the left. Standing Wilt Chamberlain on far right

БАСКЕТБОЛ

«БЕШЕНЫЙ РУССКИЙ» НА ИСТОРИЧЕСКОЙ РОДИНЕ

Первый россиянин, принявший участие в «Матче Звезд» НБА, рассказывает о своей судьбе, сегодняшних звездах лиги и оптимальной методике изучения русского языка

В предыдущем номере «Спорт уик-энда» мы опубликовали первую часть интервью с уникальным баскетболистом Томом Мешери, первым русским, удостоившимся чести сыграть в «Матче Звезд» НБА. Впрочем, его биография сама по себе уникальна. Родился Томислав Мещеряков в Харбине. Ветры Гражданской войны занесли в этот китайский город его родителей: отец, будущий звезды НБА воевал на стороне белых, а мать происходила из известной петербургской семьи, давшей России многих выдающихся деятелей науки и культуры.

В годы Второй мировой войны русский парень вместе с сестрой и матерью попал в японский концентрационный лагерь. Только в 1945-м вся семья Мещеряковых воссоединилась в Сан-Франциско.

Чемберлен - крайний справа вверху, Мещеряков - третий слева внизу.

– Русский квартал Сан-Франциско, куда вы попали после Второй мировой войны, жил своей жизнью?

– Там была достаточно большая община, насчитывавшая около 25 - 30 тысяч человек. Действовали церкви, при которых работали воскресные русские школы, выходила газета. Те, кто хотел, вполне могли сохранить свои корни. Могу только пожалеть, что в ту пору моим страстным желанием было стать стопроцентным американцем.

– С этой целью и в баскетбол пошли?

– Мне для этого не пришлось прикладывать никаких усилий. В США очень развит школьный баскетбол. В любом учебном заведении есть своя команда.

– У меня нет чувства зависти к этим ребятам. Мы тоже в 60-е годы были не самыми бедными, по американским меркам, людьми, но работать после завершения карьеры приходилось. Сейчас, глядя на платежные ведомости клубов НБА, хочется воскликнуть: «Люди, которые платят такие деньги, просто крейзи!» Если бы я играл сейчас, то мог бы подумать о покупке крупного издательства для выпуска своих творений.

– Для вас баскетбол тоже был бизнесом?

– Нет, он всегда был игрой. Выходя на площадку, я предавался настоящему азарту. По-настоящему заводился не площадке, не давал спуску ни-

– Согласен, это очень эффективный метод. Только нужно, чтобы эта женщина была красивой.

– Почему вы выбрали языковые курсы в Санкт-Петербурге, а не в Москве?

– Поэт Гавриил Державин, в доме которого я сейчас учусь, был другом моего прапрадедушки, архитектора Александра Львова. Когда жена Львова умерла в молодом возрасте, Державин даже взял их сына на воспитание в свой дом. Да и сам был построен по проекту моего родственника. Я знал эту историю и хотел приехать именно в Санкт-Петербург.

* * *

Soviet national basketball team that beat USA in the 1972 Olympics. At grave site of their Coach Vladmir Kondrashin and the grave of their star player Alexander Belov, Saint Petersburg, Summer 2007. I'm wearing sunglasses, standing in back row, 2nd from right.

L to R, Nikolai, me and Lev, at Lev's home near the city of Torchok, Russia, Summer 2007.

Melanie and Tom at a game at Oracle Arena, 2016.

IF YOU CAN'T BE A
LEGEND,

BE A
WARRIOR!

JOHN CLARK EPPLER (16)
DEC. 1, 2016 - FLOOR, ORACLE ARENA
HONORING NBA LEGEND TOM MESCHERY #14

HAPPY NEW YEAR!

Tom on Jombothon, turned into a birthday card, for my wife's grandson, John Clark. Designed by Grant Eppler, John Clark's dad.

At Warrior 2018 Championship Celebration with granddaughter Carson Guite. At Warriors' headquarters, 2018 Championship Parade.

Above: Back row, standing: my daughter Janai, my son Mattew, and daughter Megan. Front, seated: grandson moses, granddaughter Carson, me with grandson, Van. Granddaughter Ruth, holding my grandson Leo.

Right: L - R: Granddaughter Grace McCormack, me, and Granddaughter Ruth McCormack.

Tom and Melanie Marchant Meschery, July 10, 2024.